This book is respectfully dedicated to
Edward T. Packard of Cleveland Model and Supply
Company—aviation's greatest friend since 1919!

FLYING MODEL WARPLANES:
An International Guide to Plans and Kits

Compiled by
JOHN C. FREDRIKSEN

LC: 89-082636
ISBN: 0-911295-12-7
Printed in USA

AIR AGE PUBLISHING   251 DANBURY RD.   WILTON, CT.   06897
(203) 834-2900   FAX (203) 762-9803

TABLE OF CONTENTS

INTRODUCTION

Part of my job as a librarian is to notice glaring gaps in reference collections and to make appropriate purchases to fill them. In the context of model airplanes, however, this proved an impossibility. Despite a 70-year history and slavish international following, our hobby has remained neglected in terms of even the most rudimentary reference books. Largely for this reason, I could never locate the exact type of warplane plan or kit that I wanted. Time and time again I pondered, "What is out there, anyway?" The book you hold is an outgrowth of all of these concerns.

Flying Model Warplanes is specifically designed to answer almost any modeling question as quickly and painlessly as latent talents would allow. It will inform the reader of what is available, where it is located and the price one can expect to pay for it. This is a compact yet comprehensive reference book whose 8,656 entries will reveal to users a world of model airplanes previously hidden from them. I espouse the usual pretensions toward public service that are inherent in my profession, but this book is actually a labor of love. It was challenging to assemble and an ordeal to type, but I offer it gleefully to my fellow modelers around the world. My sincere hope is that it ushers in a global awareness of model airplane products and stimulates interest in a thoroughly captivating hobby.

The role of the bibliographer is not merely to assemble information, but also to sort it, organize it and present it to readers in some rational order. Confronted with such a mountain of data, I resorted to a scheme that imposed at least four levels of bibliographic control on each type of warplane. In descending order, these are: 1) alphabetical by nationality; 2) alphabetical by manufacturer;

3) alphabetical by name or designation; and 4) physical, smallest to largest, by wingspan. Furthermore, all entries are uniform and attempt to convey the following specifications: wingspan, length, motor, flight mode, company, price, designer [accessories from parent company] [accessories from other sources].

For interpreting the various symbols used throughout the text, please consult the abbreviations list. Having completed a catalog of modeling goods, I wanted to expand its utility to other facets of the hobby. Hence, appendixes on documentation, magazines and organizations have been affixed, along with an international directory and an index of manufacturers. Thus situated, this book should guide the reader to his or her coveted plan or kit. If it fosters an exchange of information and good will to modelers of different countries— for ours is truly an international hobby—this book will have exceeded the author's highest expectations.

One additional note: The model airplane business is thriving, and it would be pretentious of me to assume I have listed every product or located every company around the world. And because I intend to upgrade this catalog every three years or so, I call upon the global modeling community for help. Please send me catalogs, magazines, advertisements, or anything you feel would be useful to our hobby. All contributions will be gratefully received and publicly acknowledged. Your comments and observations are also quite welcome, so feel free to contact me anytime, from any country. Truly, it has been my pleasure to serve you.

John C. Fredriksen
69 Flamingo Dr.
Warwick, RI 02886 USA
(401) 737-7983

ABBREVIATIONS

* = kit	¥ = Japanese yen	NA=price not available
** = semi-kit	3-7 = channels needed	SA=see also
¶ = template available from POND	F= ducted fan/French franc	RC=remote control
[ ] = estimated wingspan	L= Italian lire	CAT=catalog
+ = part of multi-item set	P= Spanish peseta	KCS=Czech korunas
/ = 2-stroke/4-stroke motor	R=rubber-powered	SCH=Austrian schillings
" = inches (1" = 25mm)	V=variable wingspan	Dyna=dynajet-powered
mm = millimeters (25 mm =1")	CL–control line	Elec=electric-powered
S = dollars (US, CAN, AUS, NZ)	DM=German deutschemarks	Bean Rock=contact WILLAIRCO
£ = English pounds sterling	FF=free flight/Belgian francs	

INTRODUCTION

Une partie de mon travail à titre de bibliothécaire consiste à remarquer tous écarts flagrants dans la collection de référence et à faire les achats appropriés pour les combler. Cette tâche s'est, toutefois, avérée impossible dans le contexte des avions-modèles. Bien qu'il existe depuis soixante-dix ans et possède de fervents adeptes dans le monde entier, notre passe-temps n'en demeure pas moins négligé sur le plan des livres de référence, fût-ce les plus élémentaires. C'est essentiellement la raison pour laquelle je n'ai jamais pu repérer le kit ou le plan précis d'avion de guerre désiré. Je me suis souvent demandé: "Qu'y-a-t-il sur le marché de toute manière?" Le livre que vous avez en main est l'aboutissement de toutes ces préoccupations. *Flying Model Warplanes* est conçu spécifiquement de manière à répondre, aussi rapidement et facilement que possible, à la plupart des questions sur les modèles. Le lecteur y trouvera des informations sur les modèles offerts ainsi que les endroits et les prix auxquels il peut se les procurer. Il s'agit d'un livre de référence complet mais compact dont les 8.656 inscriptions révéleront aux utilisateurs un monde d'avions-modèles qui leur était auparavant dissimulé. Je partage les prétentions habituelles à l'égard du service public qui sont inhérentes à ma profession, mais ce livre est effectivement une oeuvre d'amour. Il fut difficile à assembler et taper, mais je l'offre avec joie à tous les autres amateurs du monde entier. J'espère sincèrement que ce livre favorisera une sensibilisation mondiale aux avions-modèles et stimulera un plus grand intérêt pour ce passe-temps passionnant.

Le rôle du bibliographe ne se limite pas à recueillir les informations, mais aussi à les trier, les organiser et les présenter aux lecteurs dans un certain ordre rationnel. Confronté à une telle avalanche de données, j'ai imposé au moins quatre niveaux de contrôle bibliographique à chaque type d'avion de guerre. Les voici en ordre décroissant: 1) alphabétique par nationalité; 2) alphabétique par fabricant; 3) alphabétique par nom ou désignation; et 4) physique, de petite à grande, par envergure. En outre, toutes les inscriptions sont uniformes et tentent de communiquer les spécifications suivantes: envergure, longueur, moteur, mode de vol, fabricant, prix (concepteur) [accessoires de société mère] [accessoires provenant d'autres sources].

Pour interpréter les différents symboles utilisés partout à travers le texte, veuillez consulter la liste d'abréviations. Ayant terminé un catalogue de modèles, je désirais accroître son utilité en ajoutant d'autres aspects du passe-temps. On trouvera donc des appendices sur la documentation, les magazines et les associations, ainsi qu'un répertoire international et un répertoire de fabricants. Ce livre devrait ainsi aider le lecteur à trouver le plan ou le kit qu'il convoite. S'il favorise un échange d'informations et une assistance des amateurs de différents pays—car il s'agit véritablement d'un passe-temps international—ce livre aura dépassé les plus grandes attentes de l'auteur.

L'industrie des avions-modèles est en pleine croissance. Je ne prétends point avoir mentionné chaque produit et chaque fabricant au monde. Comme je compte réviser ce catalogue tous les trois ans environ, je demande aux amateurs du monde entier de m'aider dans cette tâche. Veuillez m'envoyer les catalogues, magazines, annonces ou quoi que ce soit d'utile à notre passe-temps. Nous ferons publiquement état de votre contribution. Vos commentaires sont aussi les bienvenus. N'hésitez pas à vous mettre en contact avec moi où que vous soyez. Ce fut véritablement un plaisir de vous servir.

John C. Fredriksen
69 Flamingo Dr.
Warwick, RI 02886, Etats-Unis
(401) 737-7983

ABRÉVIATIONS

* = Kit	¥ = Yen Japonais	NA = Prix non disponible
** = Demi-kit	3-7 = Voies necessaires	SA = Se reporter egalement a
¶ = Gabarit disponible aupres de Pond	F = Soufflante carenee/Francs Francais	RC = Radiotelecommande
[ ] = Envergure estimative	L = Lires Italiennes	CAT = Catalogue
+ = Partie d'un ensemble a plusieurs pieces	P = Pesetas Espagnoles	KCS = Couronnes Tcheques
/ = Moteur 2 temps/4 temps	R = Mu par bande de caoutchouc	SCH = Schillings Autrichiens
" = Pouces (1" = 25mm)	V = Envergure variable	Dyna = Pulsoreacteur
mm = Millimetres (25mm = 1")	CL = Ligne de controle	Elec = Mu par electricite
S = Dollars	DM = Deutsche mark Allemands	Bean Rock = Se mettre en contact
£ = Livres Sterling	FF = Vol libre/Francs Belges	avec Willairco

EINLEITUNG

Als Bibliothekar ist es meine Aufgabe, alle größeren Fehlbestände im Referenzbestand festzustellen und sie durch entsprechende Käufe aufzufüllen. Bei den Modellflugzeugen stellte sich dies jedoch als Unmöglichkeit heraus. Trotz seiner 70-jährigen Geschichte und der fast sklavischen internationalen Anhängerschaft ist unser Hobby bis heute selbst in den rudimentärsten Nachschlagewerken vernachlässigt geblieben. Dies ist der Hauptgrund, weshalb ich nie eine genaue Skizze oder Bausatz von einem Kriegsflugzeugtyp finden konnte. Immer wieder habe ich mich gefragt: "Was ist eigentlich überhaupt darüber geschrieben worden?" Das Buch, das Sie in Händen halten, ist das Resultat meines besorgten Fragens. *Flying Model Warplanes* ist speziell darauf ausgerichtet, die am häufigsten gestellten Fragen zum Modellbau so schnell und einfach wie möglich zu beantworten. Es informiert den Benutzer darüber, was vorhanden ist und wo man es finden kann und gibt ferner den zu veranschlagenden Preis an. Das vorliegende Nachschlagewerk ist ein kurzgefaßtes, aber dennoch umfangreiches Buch mit 8.656 Eintragungen, die dem Benutzer zum ersten Mal die Gelegenheit geben, die ihm bisher verborgen gebliebene Welt der Modellflugzeuge kennenzulernen. Ich stimme mit den berechtigten Ansprüchen, die an meinen Beruf im Dienste der Öffentlichkeit gestellt werden, überein, doch versichere ich Ihnen, daß das Buch darüber hinaus geht und ein wirklich mit Liebe geschriebenes Werk darstellt. Es war schwierig zusammenzustellen und eine Qual zu tippen, doch ich stelle es meinen ModellbauKollegen rund um die Welt mit Freude zur Verfügung. Ich hoffe sehr, daß es dazu beiträgt, Modellflugzeug-Produkte auf der ganzen Welt bekannter zu machen und das Interesse an diesem fesselnden Hobby zu wecken.

Die Rolle des Bibliographen besteht nicht nur darin, Informationen zu sammeln, sondern diese auch zu sortieren, zu organisieren und dem Leser auf logische Weise zu präsentieren. Angesichts der riesigen Menge von Daten, der ich mich gegenübersah, habe ich bei allen Kriegsflugzeugtypen auf ein Vierstufen-Schema zurückgegriffen, um ein gewisses Maß bibliographischer Kontrolle gewinnen zu können. In umgekehrter Reihenfolge sind die Stufen 1) alphabetisch nach Nationalität, 2) alphabetisch nach Hersteller, 3) alphabetisch nach Namen oder Bestimmung und 4) größenmäßig nach Flügelspannweite—von der kleinsten bis zur größten— geordnet. Alle Eintragungen sind einheitlich gehalten und geben folgende Spezifikationen an: Flügelspannweite— Länge—Motor—Flugart—Firma—Preis—(Hersteller) [Zubehörteile der Muttergesellschaft] [Zubehörteile aus anderen Quellen].

Zum Verständnis der verschiedenen im Text verwandten Symbole verweise ich auf die Liste mit Abkürzungen. Nach Fertigstellung des Katalogs mit Modellbau-Produkten wollte ich diesen auch für andere Aspekte des Hobbys interessant machen. So entstanden die Anhänge mit Dokumentations-, Zeitschriften- und Organisationsregistern, einem internationalen Verzeichnis sowie einem Hersteller-Index. Dadurch gibt das Buch dem Leser die Möglichkeit, die von ihm so begehrte Skizze oder Bausatz zu finden. Wenn es zudem zu einem Informationsaustausch und gegenseitiger Hilfe zwischen Modellbauern in verschiedenen Ländern kommen würde— denn unser Hobby ist wirklich ein internationales-, hätte das Buch die höchsten Erwartungen des Autors übertroffen.

Und noch ein Hinweis. Das Modellflugzeug-Geschäft ist ein blühendes, schnell wachsendes Geschäft. Es wäre daher vermessen anzunehmen, daß ich alle existierenden Produkte oder Firmen weltweit aufgeführt hätte. Da ich beabsichtige, diesen Katalog etwa alle drei Jahre auf den neuesten Stand zu bringen, appelliere ich an die Modellbauer aller Länder, mir bei dieser Aufgabe zu helfen. Bitte schicken Sie mir Kataloge, Zeitschriften, Anzeigen oder sonstiges Material, das Sie für unser Hobby für wichtig erachten. Alle Beiträge werden mit Dank entgegengenommen und öffentlich bekanntgegeben. Auch Ihre Kommentare und Beobachtungen sind willkommen. Setzen Sie sich jederzeit mit mir—gleich aus welchem Land—in Verbindung. Es war mir eine Freude, Ihnen behilflich sein zu können.

John C. Fredriksen
69 Flamingo Dr.
Warwick, RI 02886, USA
(401) 737-7983

ABKÜRZUNGEN

*=Bausatz	¥=Japanische yen	NA=Preis nicht erhältlich
**=Teilbausatz	3-7=Erforderliche kanäle	SA=Siehe auch
¶=Schablone von Ponds erhältlich	F=Impeller	RC=Fernsteuerung
[ ]=Geschätzte spannweite	L=Italienische lire	CAT=Katalog
+=Teil eines vielteil-satzes	P=Spanische peseten	KCS=Tschechische kronen
/=Zweitakt/Viertakt-motor	R=Mit Gummibandantrieb	SCH=Österreichische schillinge
"=Zoll (1" = 25mm)	V=Variable Flügellänge	DYNA=Pulsostrahltriebwerk
MM=Millimeter (25mm = 1")	CL=Halteleine	ELEC=Batteriebetrieben
S=Dollar	DM=Deutsch mark	BEAN ROCK=Kontaktieren sie Willairco
£=Englische pfund	FF=Freiflug/Belgische francs	

INTRODUZIONE

Come bibliotecaio, parte del mio lavoro consiste nel notare qualsiasi evidente mancanza nella collezione di consultazioni ed eseguire acquisti per eliminare questa mancanza. Nel caso del modellismo d'aereoplani però questo è apparso impossibile. Nonostante un passato di 75 anni ed un accanito seguito internazionale, il nostro passatempo e rimasto trascurato, anche per quanto riguarda i più rudimentali libri di consultazione. Principalmente per questa ragione non ho mai potuto localizzare il tipo esatto di progetto o kit per l'aereo da guerra di mia scelta. Parecchie volte ho riflettuto e detto "Che cosa c'è intorno al mondo?" Il libro che avete in mano è il prodotto di tutte queste considerazioni. *Flying Model Warplanes* (fare volare modellini d'areoplano) è specificamente progettato per rispondere alla maggior parte delle domande riguardanti il modellismo in modo veloce e semplice. Informerà il lettore su cosa è disponibile, dove trovarlo, e il prezzo che ci si può aspettare di pagare. Questo è un libro di consultazione compatto ma allo stesso tempo completo, i cui 8656 articoli riveleranno al lettore un mondo di modellini d'aereoplani precedentemente a lui sconosciuto. Io adotto le solite pretese nei confronti del servizio pubblico inerente nella mia professione, ma questo libro è invece il frutto della mia passione. La sua creazione è stata una sfida, e batterlo a macchina un vero sacrificio, ma lo voglio offrire con gioia ai miei amici modellisti di tutto il mondo. La mia più sincera speranza è che introduca una conoscenza globale di prodotti per modellini d'aerei, e stimoli altri verso nuovo interesse per un passatempo veramente coinvolgente.

Il ruolo del bibliografo non è solo quello di raggruppare informazioni, ma inoltre quello di scegliere, organizzare e presentare queste informazioni al lettore sotto una certa razionale forma e ordine. Davanti ad una montagna d'informazioni, ho deciso di basarmi su uno schema il quale dedica quattro livelli di descrizione bibliografica per ogni tipo d'aereo da guerra. In ordine decrescente questi sono: 1) alfabetico per nazionalità;

2) alfabetico per ditta costruttrice; 3) alfabetico per nome o designazione; e 4) fisicamente dal più piccolo al più grande, per larghezza alare. Inoltre, tutte le descrizioni sono uniformi e tendono ad esprimere le seguenti specificazioni: Larghezza alare, Lunghezza, Motore, Tipo di volo, Ditta, Prezzo (disegnatore) [accessori dalla compagnia costruttrice] [accessori da altre fonti].

Per interpretare i vari simboli utilizzati nel libro, consultate la lista d'abbreviazioni. Avendo completato un catalogo di articoli da modellismo, ho avuto il desiderio di espandere la sua utilità verso altri aspetti del passatempo. Quindi, appendici su documentazioni, riviste e organizzazioni sono state allegate assieme ad un elenco internazionale, e una lista di costruttori. In questo modo il libro aiuterà il lettore ad ottenere il progetto o kit che tanto desidera. Se incoraggerà uno scambio d'informazioni e benevolenza tra i modellisti di vari paesi—dal momento che il nostro è veramente un passatempo internazionale—questo libro supererà le più alte aspirazioni dell'autore.

Ancora un commento. Il mondo del modellismo d'aereoplani è prosperoso ed in continua espansione. Sarebbe presuntuoso pretendere di avere elencato tutti i prodotti, o avere menzionato tutte le ditte costruttrici del mondo. Dal momento che ho intenzione di fare aggiunzioni e migliorare questo catalogo ogni tre anni circa, mi rivolgo ai modellisti di tutto il mondo in cerca del vostro aiuto. Vi sarei obbligato se ricevessi cataloghi, riviste, pubblicità o qualsiasi cosa che pensate possa essere d'aiuto al nostro passatempo. Tutti i contributi verranno ricevuti gratamente e menzionati pubblicamente. I vostri commenti e osservazioni sono inoltre ben accettati; non esitate a contattarmi da qualsiasi nazione. Per me è stato un grande piacere servirvi.

John C. Fredriksen
69 Flamingo Dr.
Warwick, RI 02886 USA
(401) 737-7983

ABBREVIAZIONI

* = Kit	¥ = Yen Giapponese	NA = Prezzo non disponibile
** = Semi-kit	3-7 = Necesita di canali	SA = Vedi anche
¶ = Sagoma ottenibile da Pond	F = Ventola intubata/Franco Francese	RC = Radiocomando
[ ] = Stima della larghezza alare	L = Lire Italiane	CAT = Catalogo
+ = Parte di una collezione a piu articoli	P = Peseta Spagnola	KCS = Koruna Cecoslovacca
/ = Motore a 2 tempi/4 tempi	R = Potenziato da gomma	SCH = Schilling Austriaci
" = Pollici (1" = 25mm)	V = Larghezza alare variabile	Dyna = Pulsoreattore
mm = Millimetri (25mm = 1")	CL = Linea di controllo	Elec = Potenziamento elettrico
S = Dollari	DM = Deutschmarks Tedeschi	Bean Rock = Contattare Willairco
£ = Sterline Inglesi	FF = Volo libero/Franco Belga	

INTRODUCCION

En mi oficio de bibilotecario, una de las cosas que debo hacer es percatarme de cualquier falla evidente que haya en la colección de libros de consulta y hacer las compras necesarias para solventarla. Sin embargo, en el contexto de los aviones a escala esto resultó imposible. A pesar de tener setenta años de existencia y una afición internacional muy difundida, nuestro hobby ha permanecido olvidado en lo que se refiere a libros de consulta, hasta los más rudimentarios. En gran parte por esa razón nunca me era posible encontrar el kit o los planos correspondientes al avión de guerra que me interesaba especialmente. Una y otra vez me preguntaba, "¿Qué puede conseguirse?" El presente tomo ha nacido de esa inquietud. *Flying Model Airplanes* fue escrito especialmente para que puedan encontrarse las respuestas a un gran número de preguntas sobre los aviones a escala lo más simple y rápidamente posible. En él, el lector encontrará lo que existe en el mercado, dónde se encuentra, y el precio que puede pagarse por ello. Este es un libro de consulta compacto a la vez que exhaustivo, cuyos 8.656 artículos revelarán al usuario un mundo de aviones a escala previamente oculto. Aunque pretenda esgrimir la consabida motivación del servicio al público inherente a mi profesión, este libro fue hecho por amor. Me resultó difícil de recabar, odioso de pasar a máquina, pero se lo ofrezco encantado a todos los que, como yo, son aficionados a los aviones a escala en cualquier parte del mundo. Mi deseo sincero es que conduzca a un mejor conocimiento de los productos relacionados con los aviones a escala y que estimule el interés de otros en este interesantísimo hobby.

El papel del bibliógrafo no es solamente recabar información, sino también desglosarla, organizarla y presentársela al lector de alguna manera ordenada. Debido a la gran cantidad de datos que recabé, decidí utilizar un sistema que utilizaba al menos cuatro niveles de control bibliográfico para cada avión de guerra. En orden descendiente estos son: 1) alfabéticamente por nacionalidad, 2) alfabéticamente por fabricante, 3) alfabéticamente por nombre o designación y 4) físicamente, del más pequeño al más grande, de acuerdo a su envergadura. Además, todos los items se presentan de manera uniforme intentándose presentar la siguiente información: Envergadura Largo Motor Modo de Vuelo Compañía Precio (Diseñador) [accesorios del fabricante] [accesorios de terceros].

Para le mejor comprensión de los símbolos utilizados a lo largo del texto, consúltese la lista de abreviaturas. Una vez hecho un catálogo de productos del modelaje de aviones, quise aumentar su utilidad incluyendo otras facetas del hobby. Por lo tanto, he anexado apéndices sobre documentación, revistas y organizaciones junto con un directorio internacional y un índice de fabricantes. De esta forma, este libro debe guiar al lector hasta el kit o los planos que tanto desea. Si estimulare un intercambio de información y buena voluntad entre los aficionados de distintos países—ya que el nuestro es un hobby verdaderamente internacional—este libro habría sobrepasado las expectativas más ambiciosas de su autor.

Una palabra más. La industria de los aviones a escala es pujante y siempre creciente. Me sería equivocado pretender que haya enumerado todos los productos y que haya localizado a todas las compañías existentes en el mundo. Además, como pienso poner al día este libro aproximadamente cada tres años, le pido a la comunidad internacional del ramo de los aviones a escala que me ayude en esta tarea. Por favor, envíenme catálogos, revistas, anuncios o cualquier cosa que consideren de utilidad. Recibiré todas las contribuciones con mucho agradecimiento y reconoceré públicamente a quienes las envíen. Tembíen agradeceré cualquier comentario u observación: no duden de comunicarse conmigo en cualquier momento desde cualquier país. Ha sido verdaderamente un placer servirles.

John C. Fredriksen
69 Flamingo Dr.
Warwick, RI 02886, Etats-Unis
(401) 737-7983

ABREVIATURAS

*=Kit	¥=Yen	NA=Precio no conocido
**=Semi-kit	3-7=Canales requeridos	SA=Ver tambien
¶=Molde suministrado por Pond	F=Turbinas/Francos franceses	RC=Radio control
[ ]=Envergadura estimada	L=Liras italianas	CAT=Catálogo
+=Parte de juego multiple	P=Pesetas	KCS=Koruna checoslovaca
/=Motor de 2 tiempos/4 tiempos	R=Impulsado por gomas	SCH=Chelín austríaco
"=Pulgadas (1" = 25mm)	V=Envergadura variable	Dyna=Jet de pulso
mm=Milímetros (25mm – 1")	Cl.=Vuelo circular	Elec=Eléctrico
S=Dólares	DM=Marcos alemanes	Bean Rock=Llamar a Willairco
£=Libras Esterlinas	FF=Vuelo libre/francos belgas	

御 挨 拶

　司書を生業とする筆者は日頃参考文献の整理と収集を行なっております。しかし、残念ながら模型飛行機の分野においては、７０数年の歴史と世界中の献身的な愛好家の努力にもかかわらず、最も基本的な参考文献さえも存在していません。そのため他の愛好家諸兄と同じく筆者も特定の戦闘機に関する設計図やキットの入手には苦心を重ねて来ました。本書は、そのような筆者の「どのような資料や製品が存在するのか」という好奇心に基づいて編集されました。本書「Flying Model Warplanes（飛行する模型戦闘機）」は、何がどこからどの程度の値段で入手可能であるか、など模型飛行機に関する読者のあらゆるの疑問にお答えします。本書は小冊子ではありますが、見出しに８６５６項目を含む堂々とした参考資料で、これまで隠されていた模型飛行機の世界を読者に御紹介いたします。公共の利益を図るのは私の職業上の責務でありますが、本書はむしろ私個人の熱意の産物です。本書の編集に必要な資料を集めるには大変な手間と時間がかかり、また集めた資料をタイプする仕事にも膨大な時間を費やしました。しかし、世界中の模型飛行機愛好家諸兄の利益を念頭に、自ら進んでこの試練に立ち向かった次第です。本書が世界各国の読者の模型飛行機に対する認識を高め、この魅力的なホビーをより多くの人々に理解していただけることを願います。

　本書のようなカタログの編集作業には、情報を収集し、整理し、合理的な順序で読者に提供するという過程が必要とされます。山積するデータを整理するため、私は各型式の戦闘機に関する情報を以下の特長に基づいて分類しました。

　１）国籍（アルファベット順）　　　３）名前または愛称（アルファベット順）
　２）製造メーカー（アルファベット順）　４）翼幅の大きさ（短いものから）。

　また、各項目は以下の仕様に基づき、一定の形式で記述されています。
　　翼幅、全長、エンジン、飛行モード、会社、値段、（設計者）、
　　［メーカー供給の附属品］、　［他社供給の附属品］

　本文中で使われている各種記号の意味については、略語表（abbreviations list）をご参照下さい。本書は模型用品のカタログとしてばかりではなく、模型飛行機全般に関する参考文献としての機能を持ちます。そのため、巻末には付録として関連文書、雑誌、組織の一覧および国際的名簿と製造メーカー別の索引が付け加えてあります。本書編集の意図は読者に必要な設計図やキットに関する情報のすべてを提供することです。模型は世界的なホビーですが、本書が世界中の模型ファンの間で情報の交換と友好の促進に役立つことを祈ります。

　模型飛行機ビジネスは常に成長を続けており、そのため本書に掲載されていない会社や製品が存在することもあり得ます。このカタログは約３年毎に更新する予定ですので、内容のより一層の充実を図るため、世界中の模型ファンの皆様を御協力をお願いいたします。どうか私あてにカタログ、雑誌、広告、その他模型飛行機に関係すると思われる資料をお送りください。お送りいただいた資料は慎んでお受けし、提供者の御氏名は公表させていただきます。また、本書に関する御意見、御希望などもお寄せください。いつでも、どの国からでもお気軽に御連絡ください。みなさまの御協力に心より感謝いたします。

→

　　　　　　　　　敬具
　　　　　　　　　ジョン・フレドリクセン

　　　　　　　　　John C. Fredriksen　　Warwick, RI 02886 U.S.A.
　　　　　　　　　69 Flamingo Dr.　　　電話：US (401)737-7983

ACKNOWLEDGMENTS

I would like to thank the following people for their help in compiling this book. Without them, it could not have been possible.

AUSTRIA: John Scrivener; Modellsport Schweighofer; AUSTRALIA: Frank Lynch, Russell Weir of Aerofan, Jane Earl of the Plan Shop; BELGIUM: Paul Janssens, Fernand Van Hauwaert; CZECHOSLO-VAKIA: Petr Kresja, Tonda Alfery, Lubomir Koutny; CUBA: Pedro Carral Daniel; ENGLAND: Dr. David M. Turner, George Wallbridge of SAMS, Gary Davis of PROKIT, Richard Spreadbury, Ron Sweeney, Alex J. Cornish-Trestrail; FRANCE: Georges (Jo Jo) Chaulet, R. Le Guennou; GERMANY: Tillman Mahkorn, Dr. Horst M. Birkhoff, Manfred Pick, Rainer Heinz, Frank Schwartz of VTH; INDIA: Manjul Prabhat; ITALY: Giorgio Gazza, Franco Tavolato; JAPAN: Nathan P. Sturman, Titus S. Kikuchi, Mark Davies; LUX-EMBOURG: Rodesch Pascal; NEW ZEALAND: Guy Clapshaw, Warren P. Russell of New Zealand Aero Products; POLAND: Grzegorz Ciechanowski, Andrzej Krol; ROMANIA: Tiberiu Buica; UNITED STATES: Henry Sakaida, Diane Petges of Futaba, Josh Harel, Claude D. Meyers, Earl Van Gorder, Bill Hannan, Dick Kidd of RCM, Roger L. Wathen of "PSSSssst-off Sheet" fame and, finally, two accomplished builders from my own state, Fred Menna and Charles Kourmphtes. Thank you all!

略語

* = キット	R = ゴム動力
** = セミキット	V = 可変翼幅
¶ = 雛型はボンドより提供。	CL = 制御線
[] = 推定翼幅	DM = ドイツマルク（ドイツ通貨）
+ = 複数部品を含むセットの一部	FF = 自由飛行／フラン（ベルギー通貨）
/ = 2気筒／4気筒エンジン	NA = 価格は入手不能
" = インチ (1" = 25mm)	SA = 参考
mm = ミリメーター(25mm = 1")	RC = ラジコン
S = ドル	CAT = カタログ
£ = ボンド（英国通貨）	KCS = コルナ（チェコスロバキア通貨）
¥ = 日本円	SCH = シリング（オーストリア通貨）
3-7 = 必要なチャンネル	Dyna = パルスジェット
F = ダクト付ファン／フラン（フランス通貨）	Elec = 電動式
L = リラ（イタリー通貨）	Bean Rock = ウイルエアコに連絡してください。
P = ペセタ（スペイン通貨）	

ARGENTINA
FMA

IA-58 Pucara

56"	-	.15-.19x2	RC	ARGUS RM281	£5.25	(Toyer)
[canopy £6.00; cowls, £4.50]						
1600mm	-	.25x2	RC	AIRBORNE	$21.00AUS	(Heck)
2100mm	-	6.6-7.5x2	RC	MRA 694	150F	

AUSTRALIA
COMMONWEALTH

Wirraway

18"	-	R	FF	POND 49A2	$3.75	(K-Dee)
72½"	-	.61	4-6	ARGUS RM238	£11.00	(Vaughan)

AUSTRIA
AVIATIK

C-1 (SA: 210)

13"	-	R	FF	HANNAN	$2.50	(Alvarez)
19"	-	R	FF	FLY T FTMC-20	$5.00	
*[$20.00]						
36"	-	Elec	4	AIRDROME	$26.00	

D-1 (SA:210)

13"	-	R	FF	POND 41A6	$3.25	(Howard)
15"	-	R	FF	COLE	$5.00	
26"	-	R	FF	MB 1794	$6.50	(Noonan)
26"	-	R	FF	PALADINE 22	$8.00	
40"	-	-	RC	FM CF441	$8.00	(Hines)
52½"	-	-	RC	PALADINE 22	$14.00	
71"	-	-	RC	PROKIT	FORTHCOMING	
72"	-	.60	RC	B&D	$14.95	

HANSA-BRANDENBURG

C-1
52"	–	–	RC	PROKIT	FORTHCOMING

D-1
*13"	–	R	FF	LEE	$6.00
28"	–	R	FF	PALADINE 15	$8.00
56"	–	–	RC	PALADINE 15	$18.00
72"	–	.60	RC	B&D	$14.95

W-29
16½"	–	R	FF	CLEVE CD229	$11.00
22"	–	R	FF	CLEVE CD229	$14.00
35"	–	R	FF	GULF	$5.00 (Midkiff)
37"	–	R	FF	CLEVE CD229	$18.00
66"	–	–	RC	CLEVE CD229	$32.00

LOHNER

Dr 1
21½"	–	R	FF	HOLMAN	$2.50
28½"	–	R	FF	HOLMAN	$2.50

PHONIX

DIII
64"	–	–	RC	PALADINE 19	$18.00
72"	–	.90	RC	B&D	$14.95
96"	–	–	RC	PALADINE 19	$32.00

BRAZIL

EMBRAER

T-27 Tucano (SA:210)
*55"	48"	.40-.50	4	LEICESTER	£70.85
*57"	–	.40-.45	4	CHAMP	$289.00
*78"	57"	15-20cc	4	LEICESTER	£135.61
**55"	–	.30/.46	3-5	CHILTERN	£32.00
*55"	43¼"	.40	4	MODELHOB	NA

CANADA
<u>AVRO</u>

CF-105 Arrow
*50"	60"	.61-.91F	4-5	PARKINSON	$199.00CDN

<u>DEHAVILAND</u>

DHC-1 Chipmunk (SA: 210)
9"	-	R	FF	POND 42A5	$3.25	(Air Trails)
17"	-	R	FF	COLE	$5.00	
*17"	-	R	FF	GUILLOW 903	$4.29	
*20"	-	R	FF	VERON VO407	£3.49	
21"	-	R	FF	SAMS 816	£1.75	(Aerographics)
37"	-	-	CL	POND 27B6	$4.75	(Stafford)
40"	-	2.5-5cc	CL	ARGUS MA247	£3.76	(Buckland)
51½"	-	1cc	FF	ARGUS FSP290	£5.25	(Greenland)
**54"	-	.25/.46	3-5	CHILTERN	£29.00	

[cowl, £3.50; canopy, £3.00]

54"	-	-	CL	POND 36A4	$7.25	(Vanloo)
59"	-	-	RC	GLEASON	$7.00	(Stafford)
59"	-	-	RC	PROKIT	£6.20	(Stafford)
*60"	42"	.60	4	GAGER	$50.00	
68"	-	10cc	RC	BYRANT 5	£6.00	

[cowl, £6.00]

1730mm	-	.45-.61	4	AIRBORNE	$22.00AUS	
*74"	56"	.90/1.20	4	GAGER	$140.00	
82"	-	.60/.90	4-5	ARGUS RM276	£13.50	(Pegg, Kidd)

[cowl; canopy, £21.00]

82½"	61"	.90-1.20	RC	PHOTO	$27.95

[FMG: cowl, $19.00]

102"	-	Q40	5	SMART P4	£13.00

[cowl, £12.75; canopy, £11.50]

103"	76½"	Q2.2	RC	PHOTO	$29.95

[FMG: cowl, $23.00]

DHC-2 Beaver (SA:210)
?	-	-	RC	BEAULIEU 17B	$27.95
?	-	-	-	ARGUS MA93x	£3.75

36"	–	–	CL	POND 27B5	$4.75	(Struhl)
1134mm	640mm	.8cc	3	VTH MT826	DM7,50	(Heil)
48"	–	–	FF	POND 16C6	$4.75	(Sheppard)
48"	–	–	FF	POND 50B1	$5.75	(Berkeley)
*61"	–	.20/.40	4	AIR SAIL	$199.00NZ	
*72"	–	.40	4	FLAIR CAPR15	NA	
72"	–	.40	4	TRAP MW2115	£8.00	
[cowl, £5.50]						
*72"	–	.25/.50	4	UNIONVILLE	$87.95 CDN	
*96"	–	/.90-1.2	4	IKON	$197.50	
*96	–	.60/1.2	4-5	UNIONVILLE	$184.95 CDN	

DHC-3 Otter

*72"	–	.30/.60	4	UNIONVILLE	$94.95 CDN
*96"	–	.70/1.2	4-6	UNIONVILLE	$269.95 CDN

DHC-4 Caribou (SA:211)

97"	74"	.60x2	4-6	BEAULIEU 10B	$27.95 (Smith)

FLEET

Finch

?	–	–	–	ARGUS MA201x	£3.75
*28"	–	R/.020	FF	RN UA41	$22.95
*51½"	–	.40/.90	4	UNIONVILLE	$109.95 CDN
84"	65"	Q35	4	BOSMAN	$25.00

NOORDUYN

Norseman

30"	–	R	FF	POND 55A1	$3.75 (Luck)
60"	–	–	CL	POND 49A6	$7.75 (Luck)
*63"	–	.30/.55	4	UNIONVILLE	$94.95 CDN
*84"	–	.40/.90	4-5	UNIONVILLE	$169.95 CDN
84¼	–	.71-.80	RC	MORGAN 110RC	$19.95
[cowl, $8.50]					

CZECHOSLOVAKIA

AERO

A-42
*34"   –   R   FF   PROKIT   £28.95

A-102
?   –   –   –   CODDING FSI292 $1.00

L-39 Albatros (SA: 211)
*53"   63"   .65F   5   FANJET   £90.00
1200mm   –   6.5cc   4   BOSAK   20 Kcs
58"   –   .60   4   ARGUS RC1424   £8.75   (Bosak)
58"   –   .60   4   RCM 712 $12.50   (Bosak)
1490mm   –   10ccF   RC   BOSAK   40 Kcs
[canopy, 60 Kcs]

AVIA

B-534 (SA: 211)
12"   –   R   FF   POND 26B5 $3.75   (Modernistic)
20"   –   R   FF   HUNT K003 $3.50   (Modelcraft)
20"   –   R   FF   POND 56D4 $3.25   (Bedrich)
38"   –   –   CL   POND 49B7 $6.25   (Bedrich)

BH-3
40"   –   –   CL   POND 49B6 $4.75   (Cizak)
80"   –   /.90   RC   RCM 1008 $14.00   (Mikulasko)

BH-11
19"   –   R   FF   POND 13D2 $3.75   (Koutny)

LETOV

S-239
13"   –   R   FF   POND 42G6 $3.25   (Wieczorek)

EUROPEAN CONSORTIA

DASSAULT/DORNIER

Alpha Jet (SA: 211)
1400mm   1770mm 10ccF   5   VTH MT806   DM29,50   (Voss)

PANAVIA

Tornado (SA: 211)
52"	47½"	GLIDER	2	GREEN	£5.00
1620mm	1750mm	.60-.80F	RC	BERTELLA	L50.000

[canopy, L15.000]

TRANSPORTER ALLIANZ

C160 Transall
*2100mm	1620mm	.40/.60x2	RC	SKYRAIDER	$395.00AUS

FRANCE

ARSENAL

VG-39
22"	–	R		FF	KOUTNY	$5.00
22"	–	R		FF	WOODHOUSE	£2.50	(Koutny)

BERNARD

Bernard 75
740mm	–	R	FF	MRA 305	40F

BLOCH

MB-152
*13"	–	R	FF	DIELS K-6	$26.00
17½"	–	R	FF	DIELS 34	$2.75
18"	–	R	FF	COLE	$5.00
840mm	–	R	FF	MRA 307	40F
1140mm	–	6.5cc	RC	BOSAK	20 Kcs

[canopy, 15 Kcs]

BREGUET

Breguet 14
*13"	–	R	FF	LEE	$6.00

Breguet 27
850mm	–	R	FF	MRA 332	16F

Breguet 691

30"	–	R	FF	POND 14C2	$4.75	(Guillemend)

Breguet 693

42"	–	R	FF	SAMS 935	£9.35	(Newman)

Breguet 790 Nautilus (SA:251)

1400mm	–	6.5cc	RC	BOSAK	20 Kcs	
55½"	–	.40	RC	RCM 1052	$5.75	(Bosak)

Breguet 820

30"	–	R	FF	KOUTNY	$10.00	

Breguet 1150 Atlantic

1400mm	–	–	CL	MRA A367	16F	
56"	–	–	CL	POND 31E2	$5.75	(Le Guennon)

Breguet 1432

37"	–	R	FF	PLANS	$7.00	(Andrus)

CAUDRON

C-714 Cyclon (SA:212)

*17½"	–	R	FF	PROKIT	£23.00	
18"	–	R	FF	KOUTNY	$5.00	
570mm	–	R	FF	AIRBORNE	$5.00 AUS	
30"	–	R	FF	POND 14E1	$4.75	(Paris)

GIII (SA: 212)

16½"	–	R	FF	CLEVE CD206	$9.00	
22"	–	R	FF	CLEVE CD206	$12.00	
33"	–	R	FF	CLEVE CD206	$16.00	
66"	–	–	RC	CLEVE CD206	$30.00	
1840mm	–	6.5-8.5cc	RC	MRA 133	84F	

DASSAULT

Mirage III (SA: 212)

20"	–	R	FF	POND 27B5	$3.25	(Simon)
*27"	29½"	Glider	2	GLASCRAFT	$65.00	
830mm	1340mm	6.5-10cc	3	VTH MT589	DM29,50	(Simon)
1040mm	1410mm	10cc	RC	BOSAK	20 Kcs	
1040mm	1410mm	10cc.	RC	MODELL	DM28,	(Bosak)

42"	55"	.61	RC	RCM 994	$6.00	(Bosak)
*45"	61¼"	7.5 F	5	JHH	$230.00	

Mirage IV
20"	–	Glider	FF	WALLACE	$6.50

Mirage 2000 (SA: 212)
*42"	57"	.40-.60	4	LEICESTER	£68.27
1060mm [canopy, L15.000]	1760mm	.60-.80F	RC	BERTELLA	L50.000
1100mm	–	7.5F	RC	MRA 600.553	112F

Mirage F1 (SA: 212)
860mm [canopy, 15Kcs]	–	6.5cc	4	BOSAK	20 Kcs
34" [canopy, £3.50]	–	.40	4	TRAP MW2186	£6.50	(Bosak)
44" [canopy, £4.50] [DALESMAN: foam wings, £19.75]	64"	4.5F	RC	THORJET	£18.50

DEWOTINE

D-27
13"	–	R	FF	POND 41D1	$3.25	(Smith)
800mm	–	R	FF	MRA 323	40F

D-33
20"	–	R	FF	POND 27B2	$3.75	(Madison Models)
26"	–	R	FF	OLD 264	$3.00	(Faynor)
27"	–	R	FF	PLANS	$6.00	(Andrus)
35½"	–	R	FF	OLD 222	$3.50	(Sturiale)
46"	–	R	FF	PLANS	$8.00	(Andrus)
60"	–	–	RC	POND 16D4	$4.75	(Guillow)

D-500
16"	–	R	FF	POND 16D2	$3.25	(Dubiner)
30"	–	R	FF	GLEASON	$2.05	(Limber)

D-510 (SA: 251)
13"	–	R	FF	FILLON	16F 80
20"	–	R	FF	POND 31C2	$3.25	(Coldrick)
29"	–	R	FF	GLEASON	$4.85	(Mowrer)

30"	–	–	CL	POND 28E5	$4.75	(Mowrer)
960mm	–	R	FF	MRA 324	46F	
1500mm	–	–	RC	AIRBORNE	$15.00 AUS	
69"	–	.40-.60	RC	FM CF396	$7.00	(Spiewack)
2180mm	–	10cc	RC	MRA 510	132F	

D-520 (SA: 212, 251)

810mm	–	R	FF	MRA 325	40F	
31"	–	R	FF	POND 16D1	$4.75	(C/B France)
62"	–	.60	RC	FM CF425	$8.00	(Reiss)
1620mm	–	7.5-10cc	RC	MRA 447.513	112F	
1750mm	–	10cc	RC	MRA 770	119F	
2250mm	–	–	RC	MRA 485	245F	
*2300mm	–	35.60cc	RC	COOP 9600109	2800F	

D-535

18"	–	R	FF	COLE	$5.00	
24"	–	R	FF	HUNT WW19	$3.25	(Stahl)
24½"	–	R	FF	OLD 249	$3.50	(Winter)

FOUGA

CM-170 Magister

*72"	51"	Glider	2	DRAGON	£74.95

GOURDOU-LESSEURE

LGL-341

*13"	–	R	FF	LEE	$6.00	
750mm	–	R	FF	MRA A415	16F	
30"	–	R	FF	POND 19A1	$3.75	(Fillon)

HANRIOT-DUPONT

HD-1 (SA: 212)

13"	–	R	FF	PASMCO	$4.00	
19"	–	R	FF	SAMS 605	£2.95	(Crown)
20"	–	CO2	FF	ALFERY	$5.00	
21½"	–	R	FF	CLEVE CD164	$18.00	
*24"	–	R	FF	SIERRA	$13.95	
28½"	–	R	FF	PALADINE 72	$8.00	

30"	–	–	CL	POND 46B5	$5.25	(Kochman)
56"	–	.25-.40	2-4	ARGUS RC1605	£5.25	(Wright)
56"	–	.40-.60	RC	FM CF341	$8.00	(Eck)
57"	–	–	RC	PALADINE 72	$18.00	
72"	–	.61	4	ARGUS RM95	£8.75	(Neate)
72"	–	.61	4	RCM 494	$10.75	(Neate)

LATECOERE

Late 298

1830mm	–	10cc	RC	MRA 639	126F

LEO ET OLIVER

LeO 451

44"	–	–	CL	POND 51A2	$6.25	(Guillemand)

LOIRE

Loire 46

20"	–	R	FF	HUNT AH180	$3.00	(Kukuvich)

LOIRE-NIEUPORT

Loire-Nieuport 250

17"	–	R	FF	POND 19B6	$4.75	(Wright)

MAX-HOLST

MH-152 Broussard (SA: 213)

?	–	–	–	ARGUS MA233x	£4.50	
?	–	–	–	ARGUS PET593x	£3.00	
54"	–	–	CL	POND 19D1	$5.75	(Aerospeed)
54"	–	–	RC	POND 19D1	$3.75	(Woolls)
64"	–	–	RC	POND 28A7	$5.75	(Fearnley)
*1960mm	–	10-22cc	RC	COOP 9600017	926F	
2200 mm	–	8.5-10cc	RC	MRA 768	126F	

MORANE-SAULNIER

MS-221

22"	–	R	FF	POND 19F3	$3.75	(Rioux)

MS-223

36"	–	R	FF	POND 42C3	$4.75	(Pond)

MS-225 (SA: 213)

840mm	–	R	FF	MRA 350	40F	

MS-325

13"	–	R	FF	OLD 425	$2.00	(Dallaire)
26"	–	R	FF	GLEASON	$2.25	(Lindberg)
29"	–	R	FF	COLE	$5.00	

MS-406

13"	–	R	FF	COLE	$5.00	
16"	–	R	FF	POND 19F4	$3.25	(Hare)
21"	–	R	FF	POND 19F4	$4.75	(Guillemand)
34"	–	–	RC	POND 29C7	$4.75	(Dulaitis)
34½"	–	–	CL	GLEASON AT1261	NA	
1890mm	–	10cc	RC	MRA 764	126F	
2160mm	–	15cc	RC	MRA 539.539	132F	

A-1 Parasol

10½"	–	R	FF	CLEVE CD152	$11.00	
12"	–	R	FF	POND 29C3	$3.25	(Shirley)
13"	–	R	FF	ALFERY	$5.00	
13"	–	R	FF	DIELS 28	$2.00	
13"	–	R	FF	POND 29D2	$3.25	(Norman)
14½"	–	R	FF	CLEVE CD152	$14.00	
19"	–	R	FF	HUNT AH131	$2.75	(Winter)
20"	–	R/CO2	FF	ALFERY	$5.00	
21"	–	CO2	FF	FM CF485	$4.00	(Kruse)
21½"	–	R	FF	CLEVE CD152	$18.00	
22"	–	R/CO2	FF	LIDBERG	$6.00	
27"	–	R	FF	DIELS 63	$3.50	
27"	–	–	CL	GLEASON AT1149	$5.85	
28"	–	R	FF	FSI M-3	$6.00	
28½"	–	R	FF	PALADINE 81	$8.00	
34"	–	8cc	FF	ARGUS FSP924	£2.50	(Rattle)
57"	–	.49	RC	FM CF188	$6.00	(Ziroli)
57"	–	–	RC	PALADINE 81	$18.00	
85"	–	–	RC	PALADINE 81	$32.00	
1900mm	–	10cc	RC	MODELE 3451	100F	
2950mm	1970mm	ZG38	4	MAHKORN	NA	

D-380

2160mm	-	15cc	RC	MODELL	DM60,	

H Monoplane

15"	-	R	FF	COLE	$5.00	
16"	-	R	FF	POND 55D5	$3.25	(Le Modele Reduit)
36"	-	.049-.10	3	FM CF621	$7.00	(Martin)

L Parasol

13"	-	R	FF	HANNAN	$2.50	(Alvarez)
33"	-	R	FF	PALADINE 49	$11.00	
44"	-	-	RC	CLEVE CD152	$30.00	
47¼"	-	.19-.25	RC	RCM 684	$3.50	(Hollison)
66"	-	-	RC	PALADINE 49	$18.00	

M-50

13"	-	R	FF	COLE	$5.00

N Bullet (SA: 213)

12"	-	R	FF	POND 29C2	$3.25	(Guillow)
13"	-	R	FF	OLD 182	$2.00	
15"	-	R	FF	COLE	$5.00	
18"	-	R	FF	POND 38G1	$3.25	(Ward)
20"	-	R	FF	CODDING	$.50	
27"	-	R	FF	POND 29D6	$4.75	(Plecan)
32"	-	R	FF	POND 19F3	$5.75	(Pallanca)
55"	-	.35	RC	FM CF97	$7.00	(Ziroli)
55"	-	-	RC	GLEASON	$7.25	(Moore)
55"	-	-	RC	PROKIT	£6.50	(Moore)
56"	-	.29-.40	3	ARGUS RM101	£5.25	(Searl)

MUREAUX

Mureaux 180

20"	-	R	FF	POND 19F5	$3.75	(Scientific)
23"	-	-	FF	COLE	$5.00	
24"	-	R	FF	POND 19F5	$3.75	(Smith)
25"	-	R	FF	POND 51C3	$3.75	(Berkeley)
56"	-	.19-.40	2-3	WE RC-8S-1	$12.95	

NIEUPORT

Nieuport 11 Bebe

[57]	-	-	4	MB 12831	$14.00	(Hoffer)
13"	-	R	FF	NFFS	$6.00	
*13"	-	R	FF	NOWLEN	$10.95	
13"	-	R	FF	POND 46B4	$3.25	(Comet)
20"	-	R	FF	ALFERY	$5.00	
22"	-	R	FF	HUNT 2155	$4.50	(Ott)
*24"	-	R/.020	CL	GUILLOW 203	$12.50	
*24"	18¼"	R	FF	MODELHOB 110123	NA	
25"	-	R	FF	PALADINE 82	$8.00	
31"	-	-	RC	POND 29F4	$5.25	(Palanek)
37"	-	.75-1.5cc	CL	VELVOLI J6	$6.00	
42"	-	.19	RC	RCM 415	$6.75	(Petersen)
50"	-	-	RC	PALADINE 82	$14.00	
61"	-	.56	3-4	PROCTOR 1004	$35.00	
*[$229.95]						
1770mm	-	.10cc	RC	MRA 778	144F	
75"	-	-	RC	PALADINE 82	$32.00	

Nieuport 12

22"	-	R	FF	FSI N-3	$6.00
29½"	-	-	FF	PALADINE 64	$8.00
59"	-	-	RC	PALADINE 64	$18.00

Nieuport 17 (SA: 213, 252)

?	-	-	-	ARGUS MA274x	£3.00	
10"	-	R	FF	CLEVE CD12B	$8.00	
12"	-	R	FF	POND 19G1	$3.25	(Comet)
12"	-	R	FF	POND 19G1	$3.25	(Dallaire)
12"	-	R	FF	POND 19G1	$3.25	(Peerless)
12"	-	R	FF	POND 58C3	$3.25	(Smith)
13"	-	R	FF	CLEVE CD12B	$10.00	
13"	-	R	FF	FOAM	$2.25	
13"	-	R	FF	OLD 193	$2.00	
13"	-	R	FF	OLD 424	$2.00	(Dallaire)
13"	-	R	FF	POND 19G1	$3.25	(Wherry)
13"	-	R	FF	OLD 432	$2.00	(Megow)

13"	–	R	FF	POND 51C4	$3.25	(Merton)
13½"	–	R	FF	OLD 76	$3.00	(Diel)
14"	–	R	FF	POND 29E5	$3.25	(Delgatto)
14"	–	R	FF	POND 58F3	$3.25	(Smith)
15"	–	R	FF	HUNT PE037	$2.50	(Peerless)
15"	–	R	FF	POND 51C4	$3.25	(Lindberg)
15"	–	R	FF	POND 47B1	$3.25	(Ott)
*15½"	–	R	FF	KEIL KK0037	£3.99	
¶18"	–	R	FF	HUNT C-4	$2.75	(Megow)
18"	–	R	FF	POND 19G2	$3.25	(Supreme)
19½"	–	R	FF	CLEVE CD12B	$14.00	
*19½"	–	R	FF	RN CG503	$19.95+	
19"	–	R	FF	YEST 40	$5.00	(Western)
20"	–	R	FF	FSI N-4	$6.00	
20"	–	R	FF	HUNT AH135	$3.25	(Wherry)
20"	–	R	FF	POND 51C5	$4.25	(Scientific)
20"	–	R	FF	POND 19G2	$3.25	(California)
20"	–	R	FF	CLEVE CB4	$16.00	
20¼"	–	R	FF	HOLMAN	$2.50	
22"	–	R	FF	POND 51C5	$5.75	(Whitman)
23"	–	R	FF	POND 51C5	$4.25	(Megow)
24"	–	–	CL	POND 29G4	$4.75	(Lewis)
*24"	–	R	FF	STERLING A-5	$11.95	
25"	–	R	FF	HUNT C-4	$3.25	(Megow)
25"	–	R	FF	POND 19G3	$4.75	(Palanek)
26"	–	R	FF	POND 29G1	$3.75	(Construct)
27"	–	R	FF	HOLMAN	$2.50	
27"	–	–	CL	POND 19G3	$4.75	(Modern Hobbycraft)
27½"	–	.8cc	FF	ARGUS FSP951	£3.00	(Collins)
27½"	–	–	FF	PALADINE 56	$8.00	
28"	–	–	CL	POND 38C7	$4.75	(Smith)
30"	–	R	FF	POND 19G3	$4.25	(Megow)
39"	–	–	CL	CLEVE CD12B	$24.00	
40½"	–	–	CL	HOLMAN	$4.00	
41½"	–	1-1.5cc	FF	ARGUS FSP285	£4.50	(Bagley)

45½"	-	-	RC	GLEASON	$5.55	(Lindberg)
45½"	-	-	RC	PROKIT	£4.90	(Lindberg)
48½"	-	.35-.40	4	ARGUS RM149	£6.00	(Robinson)
54"	-	-	RC	HOLMAN	$6.95	
54"	-	-	RC	POND 19G4	$6.75	(Lindberg)
55"	-	-	RC	PALADINE 56	$14.00	
1600mm	-	10cc	RC	MRA 594.552	112F	
69"	59"	.90	4	AEROTEK	$35.00	
*[$325.00]						
**80"	-	-	RC	KLARICH	$140.00	
82"	-	-	RC	PALADINE 56	$32.00	

Nieuport 22

24"	-	R	FF	PLANS	$6.00	(Andrus)
27"	-	-	CL	POND 29F7	$5.75	(Musciano)

Nieuport 24

41½"	-	.20	RC	ARGUS RC1384	£4.50	(Boddington)
*92"	-	Q35	RC	DB	£95.00	

Nieuport 27

17"	-	R	FF	COLE	$5.00	
18"	-	R	FF	POND 28G4	$4.75	(Guillow)
27"	-	R	FF	PALADINE 7	$8.00	
*52"	-	.25/.50	4	FLAIR FL1022	£45.07	
54"	-	-	RC	PALADINE 7	$14.80	
60"	-	.35	RC	MAN 21A	$10.25	
60"	-	-	RC	POND 38D4	$8.75	(Leitner)
60"	-	.35	RC	PLANS	$9.00	(Andrus)
81"	-	-	RC	PALADINE 7	$32.00	

Nieuport 28 (SA: 213)

10½"	-	R	FF	CLEVE CD30	$12.00	
14"	-	R	FF	CLEVE CD30	$14.00	
17½"	-	R	FF	HUNT AH186	$3.00	(McEntee)
18"	-	R	FF	POND 28F7	$4.75	(Guillow)
20½"	-	R	FF	HUNT SF-30	$4.50	(Cleveland)
21"	-	R	FF	HUNT AH-136	$3.25	(Hunt)
21"	-	R	FF	CLEVE CD30	$18.00	
27"	-	-	CL	PALADINE 29	$8.00	

30"	–	R	FF	HUNT AH137	$4.25	(Hunt)
33"	–	R	FF	POND 29G2	$6.75	(Gable)
*33"	–	.19-.35	CL	STERLING C-10	$34.95	
34"	–	R	FF	POND 62E2	$5.25	(Davies A/C)
44"	–	–	RC	CLEVE CD30	$32.00	
*1270mm	790mm	.19-.25	3-4	IKUTA	¥16,000	

*[assembled, ¥75,000]

52"	–	8-10cc	RC	ARGUS RC1094	£ 8.75	(Antione)
*1320mm	1080mm	.45	4	IKUTA	¥24,000	

*[assembled, ¥128,000]

51"	40"	.40-.60	4	MAN 3801	$11.50	(Ziroli)
53"	–	–	RC	POND 22D6	$8.25	(Antione)
54"	–	–	RC	PALADINE 29	$14.00	
56"	–	–	RC	POND 41E3	$10.75	(RCM&E)
*56¼"	43"	.40-.60	4	SHACK 100446	$165.00	
1470mm	–	7.5-10cc	RC	MRA 355	100F	
72"	–	.60	RC	B&D	$14.95	
80"	–	–	RC	PALADINE 29	$32.00	
80"	–	.90-1.60	4	PROCTOR 1006	$35.00	

*[$298.95; Super kit, $414.95]

Nieuport 161

11"	–	R	FF	POND 19G5	$3.25	(Weiss)
28"	–	R	FF	HUNT 2973	$5.50	(Whitman)

Nieuport Monoplane

17½"	–	CO2	FF	MA 140	$1.50	(Hannan)
20"	–	R	FF	POND 29G4	$3.75	(Parkhill)
36"	–	R	FF	CODDING FSI-3	$1.00	

Nieuport Triplane

7"	–	R	FF	POND 29F4	$3.25	(Wherry)
10½"	–	R	FF	CLEVE CD171	$10.00	
13"	–	R	FF	GLEASON	$.50	(Grimes)
13"	–	R	FF	DIELS 39	$2.50	
14"	–	R	FF	CLEVE CD171	$13.00	
20¼"	–	R	FF	GLEASON	$1.00	(Grimes)
21½"	–	R	FF	CLEVE CD171	$18.00	
42½"	–	–	CL	CLEVE CD171	$30.00	

NIEUPORT-DELAGE

Nieuport-Delage 29

40"	–	–	RC	PALADINE 83	$11.00	
80"	–	–	RC	PALADINE 83	$32.00	

Nieuport-Delage 580

16"	–	R	FF	COLE	$5.00	
1270mm	–	–	RC	MRA 358	16F	

NORD

Nord 3400

50"	–	–	RC	POND 19G7	$4.75	(Pottin)

POTEZ

Potez 39

50"	–	–	RC	POND 31F6	$4.75	(Trendel)

Potez 63

28"	–	R	FF	POND 51E3	$3.75	(Smith)
32"	–	R	FF	POND 51E3	$4.75	(Guillemand)

Potez 75

21"	–	R	FF	POND 30A4	$3.74	(Duberry)

Potez 542

1870mm	–	6.5ccx2	RC	MRA 763	112F	

RENARD

R-31

20"	–	R	FF	COLE	$5.00	

R-33

34"	–	R	FF	POND 30C3	$3.75	(Fillon)

SALMSON

SAL 2A2

14½"	–	R	FF	CLEVE CD240	$10.00	
19½"	–	R	FF	CLEVE CD240	$12.00	
29"	–	R	FF	CLEVE CD240	$16.00	
820mm	–	R	FF	MRA A360	16F	
32"	–	R	FF	POND 31E4	$4.74	(Trendel)
58"	–	–	RC	CLEVE CD240	$34.00	

SPAD

Spad 7

38"	–	R	FF	POND 21D4	$6.25	(Bagley)
51"	–	–	RC	PALADINE 71	$14.00	
90"	–	.80-.90	RC	HORN MPS-180	$12.00	

Spad 13 (SA: 214)

9½"	–	R	FF	CLEVE CD13B	$9.00	
12" *[FIKE: $6.95]	–	R	FF	POND 21D5	$3.25	
*12"	–	R	FF	COMET 3105	$4.00	
12"	–	R	FF	POND 21D5	$3.25	(Dallaire)
12"	–	R	FF	POND 55B3	$3.25	(Construct)
12"	–	R	FF	POND 30F1	$3.25	(Tropical)
12"	–	R	FF	REPRO 203	$1.50	(Schmadig)
13"	–	R	FF	CLEVE CD13B	$12.00	
13"	–	R	FF	GLEASON	$2.15	(Struck)
13"	–	CO2	FF	ALFERY	$5.00	
13"	–	R	FF	NFFS	$6.00	
13"	–	R	FF	OLD 192	$2.00	
13"	–	R	FF	POND 21D5	$3.25	(Wherry)
13"	–	R	FF	POND 21D5	$3.25	(Davies A/C)
13½"	–	R	FF	OLD 80	$3.00	(Diel)
14"	–	R	FF	POND 30G7	$3.25	(Wentzel)
15"	–	R	FF	COLE	$5.00	
15"	–	R	FF	POND 21D7	$3.75	(Ideal)
15"	–	R	FF	POND 47A5	$3,25	(Ott)
¶16" *[FIKE: $7.95]	–	R	FF	POND 21D7	$3.25	(Comet)
16"	–	R	FF	POND 21D5	$3.25	(Burd)
17"	–	R	FF	POND 55E4	$4.75	(Wading Mfg.)
18"	–	R	FF	HUNT AH153	$3.00	(Wherry)
18"	–	R	FF	POND 28F1	$4.75	(Guillow)
*18½"	–	R	FF	RN CG502	$21.95+	
18½"	–	R	FF	YEST 37	$5.00	(Western)
19"	–	R	FF	CLEVE CD 13B	$15.00	
19"	–	CO2	FF	BLAIR	$5.00	

19"	–	R	FF	POND 21D6	$3.75	(Imperial)
19"	–	R	FF	POND 21D7	$3.25	(California)
20"	–	CO2	FF	ALFERY	$5.00	
20"	–	R	FF	POND 21D6	$3.75	(Ott)
22"	–	R	FF	HUNT C-02	$3.25	(Megow)
24"	–	R	FF	GLEASON	$6.65	(Struck)
24"	–	R	FF	POND 21D6	$4.75	(Modelcraft)
24"	–	R	FF	POND 37C3	$4.75	(Construct)
*24"	–	R	FF	STERLING A-21	$14.95	
26½"	–	–	CL	GLEASON AT860	$5.80	
27"	–	R	FF	PALADINE 4	$8.00	
27"	–	–	CL	POND 52A2	$4.75	(Modern Hobbycraft)
27"	–	–	CL	POND 52A2	$5.75	(Musciano)
33"	–	–	CL	POND 52A1	$5.75	(Delahaye)
36"	–	R	FF	POND 30G1	$3.75	(Modern)
38"	–	R	FF	CLEVE CD13B	$28.00	
54"	42"	.60	4	AEROTEK	$19.95	

*[$195.00]

54"	–	–	RC	PALADINE 4	$14.00	
1500mm	–	10cc	RC	MRA 775	119F	
72"	–	.90	RC	B&D	$14.95	
79"	63"	ST2000	4	AEROTEK	$35.00	

*[$350.00]

79¼"	–	2.3-3.1	3-5	WE RCQS-8	$27.95

[FGM: cowl, $26.00]
**[KLARICH: $150.00]

Spad 20

42"	–	–	RC	POND 21E4	$4.25	(Le Modele Reduit)

Spad 22

13"	–	R	FF	FOAM	$2.25

Spad 510 (SA: 251)

710mm	–	R	FF	MRA 369	40F

Spad SV-2

43"	–	.09	4	FM CF57	$10.00

GERMANY

AEG

G-IV

23"	-	R	FF	CLEVE CD215	$16.00	
30½"	-	R	FF	CLEVE CD215	$20.00	
46"	-	R	FF	CLEVE CD215	$25.00	
61½"	-	-	RC	CLEVE CD215	$38.00	

ALBATROS

B-I

21"	-	R	FF	POND 13B6	$3.75	(Tissiman)
*21"	-	R	FF	PROKIT	£19.50	

B-II (SA: 214)

15"	-	R	FF	VELIVOLI R1	$3.00	
21"	-	R	FF	VELIVOLI T-19	$5.00	

*[FLY T: FTMC-19, $20.00]

C-III

14½"	-	R	FF	CLEVE CD233	$9.00	
21"	-	R	FF	PLANS	$6.00	(Andrus)
23"	-	R	FF	POND 13B6	$3.75	(U.S. Model)
42"	-	-	RC	HOLMAN	$4.00	

D-I

44"	-	/.40	RC	ARGUS RC1489	£6.00	(Hawkins)

D-II

8"	-	R	FF	ALFERY	$5.00	
13"	-	R	FF	ALFERY	$5.00	
*13"	-	R	FF	LEE	$6.00	
19½"	-	R	FF	HOLMAN	$2.50	
20"	-	R	FF	ALFERY	$5.00	
22"	-	R	FF	POND 55A4	$3.75	(R/C Sportsma
26"	-	R	FF	HOLMAN	$2.50	

27"	-	Elec	3	AIRDROME	$12.00	
*28"	-	R	FF	STERLING E9	$19.95	
50"	-	-	RC	GLEASON	$8.65	(Swift)
54"	-	Elec	4	AIRDROME	$36.00	
55"	-	-	RC	PALADINE 61	$14.00	

D-III (SA: 214)

11"	-	R	FF	CLEVE CD16B	$9.00	
12"	-	R	FF	POND 37G5	$3.75	(Guillow)
14½"	-	R	FF	CLEVE CD16B	$12.00	
15"	-	R	FF	POND 37G2	$3.75	(Ott)
17"	-	R	FF	GLEASON	$.50	(Ehling)
17"	-	R	FF	PROKIT	£.75	(Ehling)
19¼"	-	R	FF	CLEVE CD233	$12.00	
21"	-	R	FF	POND 37C3	$3.75	(Norman)
22"	-	R	FF	CLEVE CD16B	$16.00	
22"	-	R	FF	FSI A-1	$6.00	
23"	-	R	FF	PLANS	$6.00	(Andrus)
29"	-	Elec	3	AIRDROME	$12.00	
29"	-	R	FF	CLEVE CD233	$18.00	
44"	-	R	FF	CLEVE CD16B	$35.00	
46"	-	-	RC	PLANS	$6.00	(Andrus)
60"	-	.60	RC	CODDING FS-2	$4.00	
87"	-	Q35	4	PASMCO	$45.00	

D-V (SA: 214)

?	-	-	-	ARGUS MA224x	£3.00	
11"	-	R	FF	CLEVE CD160	$10.00	
11"	-	R	FF	POND 55B3	$3.75	(Construct)
13"	-	R	FF	DATA	$1.60	(McCombs)
13"	-	R	FF	FILLON	10F 40	
14"	-	R	FF	POND 55A5	$3.75	(Musciano)
14½"	-	R	FF	CLEVE CD160	$13.00	
15"	-	R	FF	POND 55A3	$3.75	(Bayet)
17½"	-	R	FF	GLEASON	$1.35	(Stahl)
450mm	-	R	FF	AIRBORNE	$5.00 AUS	

18"	–	R	FF	POND 28F6	$4.75	(Guillow)
18"	–	R	FF	POND 26B6	$3.00	(Ehling)
22"	–	R	FF	CLEVE CD160	$18.00	
*23"	–	R	FF	REPRO R-12	$8.50	
24"	–	R	FF	HUNT K002	$3.50	(Construct)
24"	–	R	FF	PLANS	$6.00	(Andrus)
25"	–	R	FF	HUNT E501	$3.00	(Stahl)
*25"	–	R	FF	PROKIT	£30.00	
*28"	–	R	FF	COMET 2602	$15.50	
30"	–	–	CL	GLEASON AT161	$6.35	(Musciano)
30"	–	–	CL	PALADINE 10	$8.00	
30"	–	–	CL	HOLMAN	$2.50	
32"	–	R	FF	HUNT E501E	$3.00	(Stahl)
34"	–	R	FF	POND 13B5	$4.75	(Bayet)
40"	–	–	RC	HOLMAN	$4.00	(Petrevan)
44"	–	1-1.5cc	FF	ARGUS 646	£6.00	(McHard)
44"	–	–	RC	CLEVE CD160	$30.00	
59"	48"	.60	4	AEROTEK	$19.95	

*[$195.00]

59½"	–	.40-.60	3-4	HOLMAN	$9.95	(Petrevan)

**[KLARICH: $125.00]

60"	–	–	RC	PALADINE 10	$18.00	
71"	57"	/1.20	RC	PHOTO	$27.00	

**[KLARICH: $125.00]

72"	–	.60	RC	B&D	$14.95	
84"	–	ST2000	RC	HOLMAN	$35.00	(Huttons)
*89"	73"	Enya 240	4	PROCTOR	$695.00	
90"	–	–	RC	PALADINE 10	$32.00	

D-IX (SA: 214)

18"	–	R	FF	HUNT AH53	$3.00	(Wherry)

W-4

13"	–	R	FF	KOUTNY	$4.00	

ARADO

Ar-68

13"	–	R	FF	AIME	20F	
19"	–	R	FF	HUNT AH57	$2.50	(Plecan)

26"	–	–	CL	POND 55B2	$3.75	(Lanzo)
27½"	–	R	FF	HUNT AH58	$3.50	(Plecan)
58"	–	–	RC	POND 26B7	$7.25	(Lanzo)

Ar-76

19"	–	R	FF	POND 13C4	$4.25	(Semrad)
20"	–	R	FF	OLD 162	$3.50	(Plecan)
32"	–	R	FF	OLD 331	$3.50	(Sykora)
32"	–	R	FF	POND 57D6	$4.25	(Plecan)
860mm	–	R	FF	MRA A279	16F	
34"	–	R	RR	POND 13C3	$4.25	(Fillon)

Ar-96

16"	–	R	FF	FRANK 13	$2.00	(Comet)
*⌈FIKE: $6.95)						
18"	–	R	FF	MB 3833	$5.00	(Houle)
36"	–	.75-1cc	FF	VELIVOLI J5	$6.00	
990mm	–	–	CL	VTH MT694-K	DM7,50	(Kriz)
1660mm	1350mm	6.5-10cc	5	VTH MT694-G	DM24,	(Kriz)

Ar 196

1650mm	1350mm	10cc	4	VTH MT341	DM29,50	(Kriz)
2261mm	1850mm	70cc	4	VTH MT/K 388	DM39,	(Kriz)

Ar-198

13"	–	R	FF	KOUTNY	$4.00	
21"	–	R	FF	POND 55A5	$3.75	(Fillon)
47"	–	R	FF	POND 14A1	$5.75	(Fillon)
1180mm	–	R	FF	MRA 301	40F	

Ar-240

30"	–	R	FF	KOUTNY	$10.00	

Ar-396

1500mm	1290mm	6.5-10cc	4	VTH MT745	DM29,50	(Nietzer)

BLOHM UND VOSS

BV-40

?	–	–	–	ARGUS RC1078x	£2.00	
50"	–	–	RC	POND 31E5	$5.25	(Headley)
1270mm	860mm	Glider	2	VTH MT548	DM7,50	

BV-141 (SA: 214)

28¼"	–	R	FF	GLEASON	$4.00	(Aldrich)
28¼	–	R	FF	LIDBERG	$6.00	
810mm	–	R	FF	VTH MT777K	DM7,50	
54"	–	.40	4	MAN 6237	$11.00	(Ziroli)
1380mm	–	–	RC	MRA 308	67F	
54"	–	–	RC	POND 13G6	$6.75	(Le Modele Reduit)
1780mm	1200mm	10cc	4	VTH MT777-G	DM24,	(Hepperle)

BV-P170

30"	–	R	FF	HUNT AH72	$4.00	(Hunt)

BRANDENBERG

C-I

110"	–	ST2000	4	PASMCO	$40.00

BUCKER

Bu-131 Jungmann (SA: 215, 252)

12"	–	R	FF	POND 26C2	$3.25	(Wentzel)
13"	–	R	FF	FOAM	$2.25	
13"	–	R	FF	MOONEY	$1.00	
21"	–	R	FF	POND 26D5	$3.75	(Beck)
24"	–	R	FF	COLE	$5.00	
*33"	–	.049	2-4	FLYLINE 116	$31.95	
38"	–	.8-1cc	FF	ARGUS FSP661	£4.50	(Coates)
39"	–	–	RC	POND 37D3	$7.25	(Staub)
990mm	–	–	RC	VTH MT752K	DM12,	(Staub)
58"	–	.51-.61	RC	RCM 218	$16.50	(Leake)
67"	–	–	RC	POND 47B3	$10.75	(Staub)
1710mm	1490mm	15cc	4	VTH MT752-G	DM36,	(Staub)
*72"	–	.60/.90	4	FLAIR CAPR23	NA	
72"	–	.60/.90	4	TRAP MW2123	£9.00	(CAP)
*2110mm	1860mm	.60	4	OK APBS002	¥52,000	
2470mm	2220mm	50-70cc	4	VTH MT/K378	DM39,	(Kriz)

Bu-133 Jungmeister (SA: 215, 252)

[72]	–	Q35	RC	MB 5821	$21.50	(Pond)

[TDF: cowl, $26.50; fenders, $9.95]

?	–	–	–	ARGUS FSP1135x	£3.00

8¼"	–	R	FF	CLEVE CD333	$10.00	
11"	–	R	FF	CLEVE CD333	$12.00	
13"	–	R	FF	AIME	20F	
13"	–	R	FF	PECK BHP434	$1.75	(Callaghan)
13"	–	R	FF	POND 26C4	$3.25	(Mouton)
13"	–	R	FF	POND 26C4	$3.25	(Vasek)
16½"	–	R	FF	CLEVE CD333	$16.00	
18¼"	–	R	FF	OLD 100	$3.50	(McRae)
19"	–	R	FF	POND 14D2	$3.72	(Abe)
22"	–	R	FF	FM CF202	$7.00	(Blankenship)
24"	–	R	FF	HUNT AH73	$3.00	(McRae)
25¼"	–	–	CL	GLEASON	$3.45	(Hall)
27"	–	R	FF	POND 29A3	$4.75	(Lister)
29"	–	R	FF	POND 26D6	$6.25	(Shier)
31½"	–	2.5-3.5cc	CL	ARGUS CL1020	£3.00	(Hall)
32"	–	–	CL	POND 14D2	$3.75	(Kau)
32¼"	–	.049	2-3	MAN 5791	$10.25	(Kau, Peterka)
33"	–	R	FF	CLEVE CD333	$26.00	
36"	–	–	CL	GLEASON	$6.80	(Hall)
38"	–	–	RC	POND 26D2	$4.25	(Ledertheil)
960mm	–	–	RC	VTH 477-K	DM7,50	(Ledertheil)
40"	–	–	CL	GLEASON	$8.60	(Hall)
40½"	–	.20-.25	4	ARGUS RM217	$6.00	(Whitehead)
40½	–	.20-.25	4	RCM 856	$4.25	(Whitehead)
*1070mm	920mm	.19-.25	3-4	OK APQX011	¥15,600	
43"	–	.35.-.40	4	ARGUS RC1392	£6.00	(Curd)
46"	–	–	CL	POND 26D6	$5.25	(Hasek)
¶ 54"	–	–	RC	POND 47E7	$7.25	(Mini Flite)
54"	–	–	RC	POND 57A6	$7.75	(Pilot)
54"	–	–	RC	POND 14D3	$6.25	(Ulrey)
55"	–	–	4	POND 26D3	$7.25	(Ledertheil)
1400mm	100mm	5-10cc	4	VTH MT477-G	DM19,50	(Ledertheil)
*58"	–	.60	4	FLAIR CAPR03	NA	
58"	–	.61	4	TRAP MW2103	£8.50	(CAP)

[cowl, £9.20]
*[KLARICH: $55.00]

*60"	51"	.61/1.2	4-5	PICA	$154.95

[cockpit, $12.95]

65"	-	.60-.90	RC	RCM 738	$15.25	(Platt)

[TDF: cowl, $24.95; SHATTLEROE: landing gear, $23.50; cabane, $22.50;
 GAGER: fiberglass fuselage, $125.00; JD: cockpit, $40.00]
**[KLARICH, $95.00]
*[PLATT: $179.00]

1640mm	-	10cc	RC	MRA 777	150F
66"	-	-	RC	CLEVE CD333	$45.00
*1650mm	1473mm	.60-.90	RC	SVENSON	NA
77"	69"	2-5hp	4-5	HOSTETLER	$29.50

[TDF: cowl, $31.95; fenders, $9.95; SHATTLEROE: landing gear, $30.00
  cabane, $21.50]
**[R&M: $185.00]

*2000mm	1750mm	35cc	4-6	RODEL 01 1550	DM720,	
86½"	-	3.7-.4.2	4	DRY	$60.00	
2300mm	2030mm	20-40cc	4	FANTINI	L45.000	
95"	-	2-3.6	4-5	ARGUS RM252	£11.00	(Greenfield)

Bu-134 Bestmann

16"	-	R	FF	ARONSTEIN	$1.50	
17"	-	R	FF	POND 14D2	$3.25	(Truedsson)
*69½"	51½"	5hp	4-5	KRICK 10180	DM289,	

DFS

DFS 230

27"	-	Glider	FF	POND 38A3	$3.25	(Wherry)
32"	-	Glider	RC	POND 56D2	$7.25	(Nietzer)
1020mm	630mm	Glider	FF	VTH MT4	DM7,50	(Frauenhofer)
70"	-	Glider	RC	POND 37ED	$7.25	(Nietzer)
1960mm	-	Glider	RC	VTH MT602K	DM7,50	
2700mm	1550mm	Glider	4	VTH MT602G	DM29,50	

DORNIER

Do-18

66"	-	.29x2	RC	FM CF75	$14.50	(Swanston)

Do-27 (SA: 215, 252)

33"	-	-	RC	POND 27C6	$4.75	(R/C Techniqu
50"	-	-	RC	POND 16D7	$7.25	(Robbe)

Do-212

13"	-	R	FF	SWAMP	$1.50	(Brown)

Do-215

44"	–	2.5-3.5cc	CL	ARGUS CL627	£6.00	(Milani)
1120mm	1010mm	2.5ccx2	CL	VTH MT202	DM19,50	(Milani)
66"	–	.35x2	4	ARGUS 2040	£7.50	(Humber)
[canopy, £3.20]						

Do-335 Pfeil (SA: 215, 252)

[60]	–	.60	4	FM CF725	$8.00	(Reiss)
13"	–	R	FF	SWAMP	$1.50	(Brown)
15"	–	R	FF	COLE	$5.00	
18"	–	R	FF	MA 312	$1.25	
18"	–	R	FF	GLEASON	$2.60	(Srull)
22½"	–	R	FF	DIELS 54	$4.25	
36"	–	R	FF	KOUTNY	$10.00	
36"	–	R	FF	WOODHOUSE	£3.00	(Koutny)
42"	–	–	CL	POND 27A4	$7.25	(Swanston)
70"	–	.60x2	4	AIR MASTERS	$25.00	
1840mm	1846mm	10, 6.5	5	VTH MT/R351	DM29,80	(Rommler)

D-I

*13"	–	R	FF	LEE	$6.00
26"	–	R	FF	PALADINE 63	$8.00
39"	–	.19	1	PASMCO	$20.00
45"	–	Elec	4	AIRDROME	$33.00
52"	–	–	RC	PALADINE 63	$14.00

ETRICH

Taube (SA: 215)

22"	–	R	FF	COLE	$5.00
*80"	–	/.30-.40	3	FLAIR FL1024	£59.20

EULER

D-2

8"	–	R	FF	MOONEY	$1.00
13"	–	R	FF	MOONEY	$1.00

Dr-1

18"	–	R	FF	HOLMAN	$2.50
24"	–	R	FF	HOLMAN	$2.50

FIESELER

F1-156 Storch (SA: 215, 252)

13"	–	R	FF	POND 41C1	$3.25	(Nikitenko)
20"	–	R	FF	POND 17C1	$3.75	(Czech)
22"	–	R	FF	POND 27E6	$3.75	(Wentzel)
23"	–	R	FF	HUNT AH120	$3.00	(Delgatto)
23"	–	R	FF	POND 38A2	$3.25	(Marlow)
24"	–	R	FF	POND 27G3	$4.75	(Guillow)
25"	–	R	FF	OLD 89	$3.50	(Delgatto)
30"	–	R	FF	HUNT AH95	$3.00	(Marlow)
32"	–	R	FF	SAMS 607	£2.95	(Crown)
1030mm	690mm	1cc	FF	VTH MT25	DM7,50	(Ledertheil)
43"	–	–	RC	POND 17C1	$4.75	(Le Modele Reduit)
45"	–	R	FF	GLEASON	$3.85	(Ahremak)
45"	–	.049-.51	CL	HORN S-2	$8.00	(Osborne)
46½"	–	–	FF	ARGUS FSP669	£4.50	(Whittaker)
58½"	40"	.049	FF	WESTERN 05	$6.00	
*60"	42½"	Elec	3	GUILLOW 3002	$84.95	
1584mm	–	–	RC	ENGEL 1723	DM14.80	
68"	–	.23-.45	5	MA 136	$4.00	(Bowers)
70"	–	.40	RC	BRYANT 8	£6.00	
[cowl, £1.50]						
70"	–	.40	RC	HORN S-3	$12.00	(Osborne)
1870mm	–	3.5-5cc	RC	MRA 434	106F	
92"	–	.71-.80	4-5	MORGAN 106RC	$18.95	
2360mm	1640mm	10-15cc	5	VTH MT/R350	DM45,	(Lang)
*2375mm	1560mm	10-20cc	RC	SVENSON	NA	
3500mm	2417mm	50cc	4	VTH MT/K385	DM39,	(Kriz)
*144"	–	3.6	6	HANGAR	FORTH COMING	
3600mm	–	35-80cc	RC	MRA PB5301	150F	

Fi-167

30"	–	R	FF	FM CF635	$6.00	(Bowers)

FOCKE-WULF

Fw-44 Stiglitz (SA: 215, 252)

21¼"	–	R	FF	OLD 295	$3.00	(Delgatto)

32"	-	R	FF	HUNT AH102	$3.25	(Apelergsgatan)
35"	-	R	FF	POND 50C7	$5.25	(Wentzel)
42"	-	.8-1cc	FF	ARGUS FSP617	£3.75	(Barton)
1640mm	1320mm	6.5-10cc	4	VTH MT680	DM24,	(Kriz)
89½"	-	-	RC	HOLMAN	$24.00	(Morse)

Fw-56 Stosser (SA: 216, 253)

13"	-	R	FF	DIELS 1	$2.00	
13"	-	R	FF	POND 53A5	$3.25	(Thompson)
18"	-	R	FF	HUNT AH97	$2.50	
21"	-	R	FF	HUNT AH98	$3.00	(Delgatto)
24"	-	R	FF	HUNT AH99	$3.25	(Plecan)
24"	-	R	FF	POND 17D1	$3.75	(Kreslil)
26"	-	R	FF	HUNT AH100	$3.00	(Limber)
30"	-	R	FF	HUNT AH101	$3.75	(Plecan)
34½"	-	R	FF	GLEASON	$3.50	(Barton)
41"	-	R	FF	POND 50C7	$5.25	(Mittelstaedt)
43"	-	-	RC	GLEASON	$5.15	(Barton)
43"	-	-	RC	PROKIT	£4.55	(Barton)
1080mm	800mm	.3-1cc	1	VTH MT290	DM7,50	(Barton)
50"	-	-	FF	POND 50D2	$5.25	(Limber)
56"	-	Elec	4	AIRDROME	$30.00	
103½"	75"	-	RC	HOLMAN	$24.00	(Morse)
2630mm	1900mm	50cc	3	VTH MT/K340	DM32,	(Kriz)

Fw-58 Weihe

2160mm	1440mm	6.5ccx2	4	VTH MT363	DM36,	(Tanzler)

Fw-189 Uhu

32"	-	R	FF	HUNT AH96	$3.00	(Feblason)
1460mm	-	R	FF	MRA 332	40F	
2270mm	-	3.5-6ccx2	RC	MODELL	DM28,80	(Schrufer)

Fw-190 (SA: 216, 253)

?	-	-	-	ARGUS MA271x	£3.00	
*10"	-	Glider	FF	PAPER	$3.95	
16"	-	R	FF	COLE	$5.00	(Whitman)
*16½"	-	R	FF	GUILLOW 502	$5.00	

*17½"	–	R	FF	KEIL KK0044	£3.99	
21"	–	R	FF	POND 57C6	$3.75	(Comet)
*24"	–	R	FF	STERLING A-20	$14.95	
25"	–	–	CL	GLEASON AT953	$3.05	(Musciano)
25"	–	–	CL	POND 27D2	$3.75	(Hawkins)
25"	–	R	FF	POND 17D3	$3.75	(Ott)
26"	–	–	CL	POND 50D1	$5.25	(Berkeley)
*26½"	22"	R	FF	MODELHOB 110125	NA	
*27"	–	R/.020	FF	GUILLOW 406	$16.00	
28"	–	1cc	FF	ARGUS FSP935	£3.75	(Palmer)
28"	–	R	FF	CLEVE CD82	$18.00	
31"	–	R	FF	PALADINE 34	$8.00	
34"	–	–	CL	POND 17D4	$4.75	(Modern Hobbycraft)
35"	–	.049	RC	VELIVOLI S-3	$6.00	
36"	–	R	FF	ORIGINAL	£4.50	(Martin)
940mm	–	–	FF	MRA 333	40F	
*960mm	–	2.5cc	CL	AMZ 303	DM150,	
45" [canopy, £4.50]	–	.25-.40	3-4	ARGUS RSQ1551	£3.75	(Booth)
45" [canopy, $5.00]	–	–	RC	HOLMAN	$5.95	(Nicely)
45"	–	–	FF	POND 50D2	$5.25	(Hodgson)
*1228mm	964mm	.19--35	3-5	OK APQX020	¥14,800	
*50"	–	.29-.40	4	DYNA 4002	$115.95	
*51"	–	.40-.60	4-6	DAVEY	$99.95	
51" [canopy, $5.00]	–	–	RC	HOLMAN	$5.00	(Dalton)
54"	–	.45-.56	RC	FM CF163	$7.00	(Ziroli)
*54"	–	.29-.45	4	WING 702	$37.50	
56"	–	.60	RC	RCM 411	$12.00	(Mitchell)
*1470mm	1147mm	.40/.90	4-5	OK 11033	¥43,500	
58"	–	.35-.45	RC	MA 591	$13.50	(Brown)
*60" [retracts, $240.00; spinner, $30.00AUS]	–	–	RC	MODEL 029	$169.00AUS	
1520mm	–	10cc	RC	MRA BT4	119F	(Taylor)
60¼" [cowl, £5.50; canopy, £3.00; spinner, £4.50; balsa pack, £26.00]	–	,60	4	TAYLOR	£6.00	
*61"	–	.60	4-6	HOLMAN	$149.95	

*1530mm	1310mm	.50/.90	4-6	MARUTAKA 20	¥30,000	
62"	-	-	RC	PALADINE 34	$18.00	
1580mm	1220mm	8-10cc	5	VTH MT724	DM24,	(Kriz)
*65"	42"	-	RC	SAIL	NA	
*1650mm	-	10cc	RC	COOP 9600019	1725F	
68"	-	-	RC	HOLMAN	$10.95	(Nicely)

[canopy, $6.00]

*1700mm	1260mm	10-15cc	RC	SKYRAIDER	$265.00AUS

[prop, $30.00AUS: spinner, $25.00AUS: retracts, $285.00AUS]

69"	59"	.90-1.08	4-5	INNOVATIVE	$25.00

*[$229.95]

70"	-	.60	RC	MA 384	$16.50
*1880mm	1625mm	20-35cc	RC	SKYRAIDER	$695.00AUS

[retracts, $295.00AUS]

79¼"	-	ST2500	5	RCM 965	$17.50	(Platt)

[cockpit: JD, $40.00; AVCO, $22.95; PLATT: retracts, $219.00]
**[Platt RC-1, $319.00]

80"	-	-	RC	HOLMAN	$19.95	(Taylor)

[canopy, $10.00]

**80"	-	-	RC	HOLMAN	$230.00
85½"	70½"	.90-1.5	4-6	INNOVATIVE	$30.00
**103"	-	-	RC	R&M	$145.00	(Morse)
2760mm	2350mm	50-70cc	4	VTH MT/K375	DM32,	(Kriz)

Fw-190D (SA: 216, 253)

17½"	-	R	FF	FM CF298	$3.00	(Bruning)
22"	-	R	FF	KOUTNY	$5.00
*43"	-	1.5-2.5	2-3	LEICESTER 26	£37.83
50"	-	.29-.40	RC	HORN S-15	$14.00	(Osborne)
*50"	-	.29-.50	4	VORTECK	$114.94
*54"	-	.40/.90	4-5	INDY	$169.95
1570mm	-	10cc	RC	BOSAK	20 Kcs

[canopy, 20 Kcs]

62½"	_	.60	RC	FM CF375	$11.00	(Eck)
63½"	-	.60	RC	RCM 599	$13.50	(Platt)
*65"	59"	.61/.90	4-5	PICA	$149.95

[cockpit, $12.95]

68"	-	.60-.80	4-6	MAN 12712	$21.50	(Smith)
*68"	-	40-90cc	RC	REEVES 2080	£102.50
69"	67"	.90-1.08	4-5	INNOVATIVE	$25.00

*[$249.95]

**80"	–	–	RC	HOLMAN	$245.00	
85½"	80¼"	.90–1.5	4–6	INNOVATIVE	$30.00	

Fw-198

15"	–	R	FF	POND 37B5	$3.25	(Megow)
28"	–	R	FF	HUNT 2942	$5.50	(Whitman)
30"	–	R	FF	POND 17D4	$3.75	(Megow)

Fw-200 Kurier

2000mm	–	5ccx4	RC	VTH MT980K	DM16,	(Schmalzgruber
3000mm	2100mm	5ccx4	6	VTH MT980G	DM36,	(Schmalzgruber

Fw TA-152 (SA: 216)

24"	–	R	FF	GLEASON	$2.10	(Cover)
29"	–	R	FF	KOUTNY	$5.00	
29"	–	R	FF	WOODHOUSE	£3.00	(Koutny)
34"	–	R	FF	HUNT AH100	$4.50	(Hunt)
36"	–	R	FF	POND 22F5	$6.75	(Graupner)
47" [canopy, $5.00]	–	–	RC	HOLMAN	$5.50	(Dalton)
*51"	37"	.9–.15	2	METCALFE	£39.95	
62"	–	–	RC	POND 58C6	$4.75	(RC Modelle)
65"	–	–	RC	POND 61B7	$10.25	(Osborne)
1800mm	–	6.5–7.5cc	RC	MRA 570.546	100F	
72"	–	–	RC	ENT	$9.95	(Dalton)
95¼"	71"	.90–1.08	4–6	INNOVATIVE	$25.00	
113½"	85"	.90–1.5	4–6	INNOVATIVE	$30.00	
*144"	–	3.6	6	HANGAR	FORTHCOMING	

Fw TA-154 Moskito (SA: 253)

32"	–	R	FF	KOUTNY	$10.00	
38"	–	–	CL	POND 15C7	$4.75	(Wheldon)
1760mm	–	6.5x2	RC	MRA 147	132F	(Meier)
1760mm	–	6.5x2	RC	MODELL	DM29,80	(Meier)
70"	–	.40x2	RC	RCM 642	$15.75	(Meier)
80"	–	.60x2	RC	HORN S-2	$10.00	(Osborne)
*100"	79"	2.2x2	6	GLASCO	$350.00	

FOKKER

B-II (SA: 216)

25"	-	R	FF	PALADINE 73	$8.00	
50"	-	-	RC	PALADINE 73	$14.00	

D-II

*24"	-	R	FF	SIERRA	$13.95	
44½"	-	-	RC	PALADINE 68	$14.00	
89"	-	-	RC	PALADINE 68	$32.00	

D-III

?	-	-	-	ARGUS CL623x	£3.75	
30"	-	-	CL	POND 43B2	$4.75	(Beatty)

D-VI

[51]	-	.40	RC	MB 8731	$10.00	(Foster)
12½"	-	R	FF	PECK BH118	$1.25	(Mooney)
25"	-	R	FF	PALADINE 78	$8.00	
36"	-	.60	4	ARGUS RM313	£7.50	(Cousins)
50"	-	-	RC	PALADINE 78	$14.00	
75"	-	-	RC	PALADINE 78	$32.00	

D-VII (SA: 216, 253)

10½"	-	R	FF	CLEVE CD15B	$9.00	
*12"	-	R	FF	COMET 3104	$4.00	
13"	-	R	FF	DATA	$1.60	(McCombs)
13"	-	R	FF	NFFS	$6.00	
13"	-	R	FF	OLD 417	$2.50	(Dallaire)
13"	-	R	FF	OLD 431	$2.00	(Megow)
13"	-	R	FF	OLD 475	$2.75	(Scientific)
13"	-	R	FF	OLD 457	$2.00	(Peerless)
13"	-	R	FF	POND C2C6	$3.25	(Takeuchi)
13"	-	R	FF	POND 17D6	$3.25	(Guillow)
13"	-	R	FF	POND 27E7	$3.25	(Wentzel)
*13"	-	R	FF	SIERRA	$11.95	
14"	-	R	FF	CLEVE CD15B	$12.00	
14"	-	R	FF	POND 17D6	$3.25	(Struck)
14"	-	R	FF	POND 50D3	$3.25	(Sturdi-Built)
15"	-	R	FF	POND 50D5	$3.25	(Universal)
15"	-	R	FF	POND 63A6	$7.00	(Springfield)

15"	–	R	FF	POND 50D3	$3.25	(Megow)
15"	–	R	FF	POND 17D7	$3.25	(Modelcraft)
15"	–	R	FF	POND 17D7	$3.25	(Lindberg)
16"	–	R	FF	FRANK 39	$2.00	(Comet)

*[FIKE, $6.95]

16"	–	R	FF	POND 17D6	$3.25	(Super Models)
*18"	–	R	FF	EASY FF26	$6.00CDN	
18"	–	R	FF	HUNT C1	$2.75	(Megow)

*[SEAGLEN: $8.00]
*[FIKE: $9.95]

18"	–	R	FF	HUNT PE018	$2.50	(Peerless)
18"	–	R	FF	KOUTNY	$5.00	
18"	–	R	FF	POND 17D7	$3.25	(Modelcraft)
18"	–	R	FF	POND 28E7	$4.75	(Guillow)
19"	–	R	FF	POND 17D7	$3.75	(Bunch)
19"	–	R	FF	POND 24E3	$3.75	(Cleveland)
19"	–	R	FF	POND 50D5	$3.25	(Megow)
19"	–	R	FF	FM 783	$8.00	(Kruse)
*19½"	–	R	FF	SWALLOW	$8.95	
20"	–	R/CO2	FF	ALFERY	$5.00	
20"	–	R	FF	POND 27D1	$3.75	(Scientific)

*[REPRO: $7.50]

20"	–	R	FF	POND 17E1	$3.75	(Ott)
20"	–	R	FF	POND 16D6	$3.75	(Barrett)
20½"	–	R	FF	YEST 54	$4.00	(Continental)
21"	–	R	FF	ARGUS FSR297	£2.50	(Hughes)
21"	–	R	FF	CLEVE CD15B	$16.00	
21"	–	R	FF	POND 50D4	$3.25	(Continental)
21"	–	R	FF	POND 50D4	$3.75	(Hughes)
21¼"	–	R	FF	OLD 69	$3.00	(Markwiese)
*21½"	–	R	FF	RN CG502	$21.95+	
21½"	–	R	FF	YEST 39	$5.00	(Western)
22"	–	R	FF	POND 41A1	$5.25	(Davies A/C)
22"	–	R	FF	POND 50D5	$3.75	(Toledo)
22"	–	R	FF	POND 50D5	$3.25	(California)
22"	–	R	FF	POND 24E3	$4.25	(Cleveland)
23"	–	R	FF	POND 50D4	$3.75	(Megow)
23½"	–	R	FF	NFFS	$3.50	(Koopman)

24"	-	R	FF	GLEASON	$5.10	(Struck)
*24"	-	R	FF	STERLING A1	$15.95	
24¼"	-	R	FF	OLD 84	$3.00	(Diel)
25½"	-	R	FF	HUNT PE019	$3.50	(Peerless)
27"	-	R	FF	POND 27D3	$3.75	(Miller)
27"	-	-	CL	POND 27D7	$4.25	(Modern Hobbycraft)
28"	-	-	RC	POND 62C2	$5.25	(Modelcraft)
29"	-	3.5	CL	ARGUS CL403	£3.75	(Ward)
29"	-	.5-1cc	FF	ARGUS FSP916	£2.50	(McHard)
29"	-	-	RC	HOLMAN	$2.50	
29"	-	-	RC	PALADINE 66	$8.00	
29"	-	-	CL	POND 38G5	$4.75	(Ward)
30"	-	-	CL	POND 50D4	$5.25	(Beacon)
31½"	-	-	FF	HUNT PE020	$4.00	(Peerless)
*32½	-	.19-.35	CL	STERLING C8	$34.95	
33"	-	.049-.09	CL	FM CF10	$10.00	(Delgatto)
33"	-	R	FF	POND 27E5	$5.75	(Davies A/C)
35"	-	-	RC	POND 27D7	$5.75	(Friedrich)
37"	-	.15	CL	RCM 537	$3.50	(Cunningham)
37"	-	-	CL	POND 50D6	$6.25	(Wright)
890mm	-	-	RC	VTH MT541-K	DM12,	(Friedrich)
42"	-	-	RC	CLEVE CD15B	$30.00	
42"	-	-	RC	GLEASON	$6.80	(Suellentrop)
*1070mm	790mm	.19-.25	3-4	IKUTA	¥15,000	
*[assembled, ¥75,000]						
43"	-	-	RC	HOLMAN	$4.00	
*1230mm	1040mm	.40-.45	3-4	IKUTA	¥27,000	
*[assembled, ¥128,000]						
50"	-	.40/.60	4	MAN 4852	$12.50	(Uravich)
51½"	-	/.40-.45	4	TRAP MW2031	£8.00	(Whitehead)
51½"	-	/.40-.46	4	RCM 996	$11.00	(Whitehead)
52"	-	-	RC	POND 27E3	$6.75	(Meixell)
1310mm	1040mm	5-10cc	3	VTH MT 541-G	DM29,50	(Friedrich)
57"	-	.049	FF	GLEASON	$16.75	(Stahl)
58"	-	-	RC	HOLMAN	$7.95	
*58½"	-	/.65-.90	4	AERODROME	$169.00	
58"	-	-	RC	PALADINE 66	$18.00	

59"	47"	.60	4	AEROTEK	$35.00	
*[$175.00]						
59½"	–	.49–.61	4	ARGUS RM23	£7.50	(Butcher)
59½"	–	.40–.61	4	RCM 368	$12.00	(Butcher)
60"	–	.61	RC	FM CF81	$10.00	(Ziroli)
1600mm	–	15cc	RC	MODELL	DM60,	(Preisler)
72"	–	.60	RC	B&D	$14.95	
80"	–	Q35	4	JACKSON	$35.00	
1970mm	–	10cc	RC	MRA 781	138F	
84"	–	–	RC	CLEVE CD15B	$49.00	
85"	72"	ST2000	4	AEROTEK	$35.00	
*[$350.00]						
87"	–	–	RC	PALADINE 66	$32.00	
88"	67"	Q35	4	BEAULIEU 15B	$27.95	
[TDF: cowl, $24.95]						
88"	71"	Q40	4	BEHRENS	$30.00	
[formed wire set, $12.95][FGM: cowl, $16.00]						
**100"	–	–	RC	KLARICH	$125.00	

D-VIII (SA: 217, 253)

?	—	—	—	ARGUS MA260x	£3.00	
?	–	–	–	ARGUS RC996x	£5.25	
8"	–	R	FF	AERO ERA	$.65	
8"	–	R	FF	MACE	$1.25	(Mace)
10"	–	R	FF	CLEVE CD34B	$9.00	
*12"	–	R	FF	FIKE	$6.95	(Megow)
12"	–	R	FF	POND 17E2	$3.25	(Comet)
12"	–	R	FF	POND 17E2	$3.25	(Dallaire)
13"	–	R	FF	AERO ERA	$1.25	
13"	–	R	FF	FOAM	$2.25	
13"	–	R	FF	POND 62B5	$3.25	(Suzuki)
*13"	–	R	FF	STERLING P-1	$7.95+	
13½"	–	R	FF	CLEVE CD34B	$12.00	
14"	–	R	FF	OLD 74	$3.00	(Diel)
13"	–	R	FF	OLD 189	$2.00	
14"	–	R	FF	POND 27D3	$3.25	(Davies A/C)
14"	–	R	FF	POND 24F7	$3.25	(Cleveland)
15"	–	R	FF	HUNT PE017	$2.50	(Peerless)
*[FIKE: $6.95]						

15"	–	R	FF	POND 42F2	$3.25	(Ott)
15"	–	R	FF	POND 27E5	$3.25	(Wentzel)
15"	–	R	FF	POND 17E2	$3.25	(Comet)
*16"	–	R	FF	KEIL KK0039	£3.99	
16"	–	R	FF	POND 50E1	$4.75	(Keil Kraft)
17"	–	R	FF	KOUTNY	$5.00	
18"	–	R	FF	POND 28F3	$4.75	(Guillow)
18"	–	R	FF	POND 50D7	$3.25	(Hobby Supreme)
19"	–	R	FF	HUNT 87	$3.00	(Stahl)
20"	–	R	FF	COLE	$5.00	
*20"	–	R	FF	VERON VO414	£3.49	
20½"	–	R	FF	CLEVE CD34B	$15.00	
21"	–	R	FF	FSI F-4	$6.00	
21"	–	R	FF	OLD 292	$3.00	(Schaffer)
21"	–	R	FF	POND 50D7	$3.75	(Toledo)
*21"	–	R/.020	FF	RN CG504	$19.95+	
*21"	–	R	FF	STERLING A-16	$11.95	
22"	–	R	FF	POND 17E3	$3.50	(Moulton)
25"	–	R	FF	POND 50D7	$3.35	(Burd)
26½"	–	R	FF	NFFS	$3.50	(Koopman)
27"	–	.5cc	FF	ARGUS MA353	£3.00	(Hawkins)
27"	–	–	CL	POND 50D7	$4.75	(Modern Hobbycraft)
27½"	–	R	FF	HOLMAN	$2.50	
28"	–	–	FF	PALADINE 24	$8.00	
28"	–	R	FF	POND 50E1	$3.75	(Grezesczak)
30"	–	R	FF	CLEVE IT-34	$10.00	
30"	–	R	FF	POND 46F2	$4.72	(Ott)
34"	–	–	CL	POND 27E3	$3.75	(Girard Models)
34½"	–	–	CL	HOLMAN	$4.00	
35½"	18"	.020	FF	LAMBERT	$5.00	
35"	–	–	CL	POND 27C1	$4.75	(Stevenson)
35"	–	R	FF	POND 46B5	$3.75	(Day)
38"	–	Elec	3	AIRDROME	$15.00	
¶39"	–	–	FF	POND 27E1	$6.75	(Miniature A/C)
41"	–	–	RC	CLEVE CD34B	$32.00	
42"	–	.19	1	PASMCO	$20.00	
42"	–	–	RC	GLEASON	$6.80	(Suellentrop)

*1050mm	740mm	1.7-2.5cc	6	GRAUPNER 4669	NA	
42"	-	-	RC	PROKIT	£6.00	(Suellentrop)
47"	-	2.5	1	ARGUS RL996	£5.25	(Tranfield)
52"	-	-	RC	POND 41A2	$8.75	(Hegi)
*53½"	-	/.40-.50	4	FLAIR FL1033	NA	
55"	-	-	RC	GLEASON AT358	$11.65	(Smith)
55"	-	-	RC	HOLMAN	$6.95	
55"	-	.19-.36	4	MAN 6852	$15.50	(Musciano)
55"	-	-	RC	PALADINE 24	$14.00	
55"	-	-	RC	POND 17E3	$6.25	(Musciano)
55"	-	-	RC	PROKIT	£10.25	(Smith)
57"	-	.10/.20	3	ARGUS BB203	£5.25	(Buckle)
*57"	-	.10/.20	3	BUCKLE	£39.95	
57"	-	.23	RC	MB 1180 OT	$9.50	(Stahl)
70"	-	.45-.60	RC	MA 203	$9.00	(Owens)
72"	-	.60	RC	B&D	$14.95	
81"	-	-	RC	CLEVE CD34B	$52.00	
82"	-	-	RC	PALADINE 24	$32.00	
**82"	-	-	RC	R&M	$130.00	(Scratch)
83½"	-	/.90	RC	MA 500	$16.00	
*82½"	-	.15-.20cc	RC	LEICESTER 34	£116.96	
100"	69¼"	2.4	RC	MAN GS12811	$25.00	
[TDF: cowl, $26.50]						
100"	69¼"	Q35	4	MESSER	$25.00	(S.T.A.R.S.)

Dr-I (SA: 217, 253)

?	-	-	-	ARGUS CL307x	£3.00	
9"	-	R	FF	CLEVE CD14B	$8.00	
11½"	-	R	FF	CLEVE CD14	$10.00	
12"	-	R	FF	CODDING	$.35	(National)
12"	-	R	FF	POND 37B2	$3.25	(Megow)
*[FIKE: $7.95]						
12"	-	R	FF	POND 17E4	$3.25	(Rainey)
12"	-	R	FF	POND 24E5	$3.25	(Cleveland)
12"	-	R	FF	POND 17E4	$3.25	(Cartercraft)
12"	-	R	FF	POND 17E4	$3.25	(Dallaire)
12"	-	R	FF	POND 17E4	$3.25	(Ideal)

12¼"	−	.020	CL	MA 548	$2.25	
12½"	−	R	FF	OLD 73	$3.00	(Diel)
13"	−	R	FF	AERO ERA	$1.25	
*13"	−	R	FF	DUBOIS PS-8	$8.75	
13"	−	R	FF	GLEASON	$.75	(Howell)
*13"	−	R	FF	LEE	$6.00	
13"	−	R	FF	NFFS	$6.00	
13"	−	R	FF	OLD 418	$2.50	(Dallaire)
13"	−	R	FF	OLD 187	$2.00	
13"	−	R	FF	HUNT PL125	$1.25	(Lindberg)
13"	−	R	FF	POND 17E4	$3.25	(Comet)
14"	−	R	FF	POND 31A6	$3.75	(Howard)
15"	−	R	FF	POND 17E5	$3.25	(Rainey)
17½"	−	R	FF	CLEVE CB6	$16.00	
18"	−	R	FF	CLEVE CD14B	$14.00	
18½"	−	R	FF	GLEASON	$1.80	(Howell)
18¼"	−	R	FF	YEST 57	$4.00	(Peerless)
19"	−	R	FF	CLEVE P1753	$14.00	
19"	−	R	FF	POND 17E5	$3.25	(Wherry)
20"	−	R/CO2	FF	ALFERY	$5.00	
*20"	−	R/.020	FF	GUILLOW 204	$12.50	
20"	−	R	FF	POND 17E5	$3.25	(Berkeley)
23½"	−	R	FF	AUTHENTIC	£1.35	(Towner)
23½"	−	−	CL	GLEASON	$4.10	(Musciano)
23½"	−	R	FF	PALADINE 1	$8.00	
23½"	−	−	CL	PROKIT	£3.60	(Musciano)
*23½"	−	R/.020	CL	STERLING E2	$19.95	
24"	−	−	CL	POND 42E7	$6.75	(Sterling)
25"	−	R	FF	COLE	$5.00	
26½"	−	R	FF	HUNT PE022	$3.50	(Peerless)
*27"	−	R	FF	COMET 3648	$19.50	
30"	−	R	FF	PLANS	$6.00	
33"	−	−	CL	POND 41D2	$5.75	(Fencharek)
35"	−	R	FF	CLEVE CD14B	$26.00	
35"	−	.19-.29	RC	HOLMAN	$5.95	
40½"	−	1.5-2.5	FF	ARGUS FSP453	£4.50	(Norman)

41"	–	–	FF	POND 27E2	$5.75	(Meerman)
47"	38"	.60	4	AEROTEK	$17.95	
*[$125.00]						
47"	–	–	RC	PALADINE 1	$14.00	
47"	–	.40/.45	4	TRAP MW2187	£7.50	(Hurrell)
48"	–	.50-.61	4	FM CF93	$8.00	(Peterson)
*49"	–	.25/.50	4	FLAIR FL1021	£47.20	
54"	–	10cc	RC	ARGUS RC1213	£10.00	(Lunt)
1440mm	1150mm	5.6-10cc	4	VTH MT562	DM29,50	(Meerman)
1550mm	–	10cc	RC	MRA 334.483	106F	
63"	52"	Q35	RC	ZIROLI	$27.00	
[TDF: cowl, $24.95; SHATTLEROE: landing gear, $35.50, cabane, $21.50]						
**[KLARICH: $80.00]						
*[HANGAR: $220.00]						
71"	59"	.90-1.20	4	AEROTEK	$29.95	
*[$295.00]						
72"	–	.78-2.3	3-5	WE RCQS-6	$24.95	
[FGM: cowl, $19.00]						
*73"	–	.60/1.20	4	FLAIR FL1031	£91.44	
1828mm	–	20- 40cc	4	VTH MT/VS0283	DM57,	(Kriz)
76"	56"	Q50	4	BEAULIEU 9B	$27.95	
[TDF: cowl, $26.50]						
**[KLARICH: $85.00]						
**108"	–	–	RC	KLARICH	$165.00	(Perett)
2870mm	2300mm	70-100cc	4	VTH MT/K381	DM48,	(Kriz)

E-I

13"	–	R	FF	AERO ERA	$1.25	
13"	–	R	FF	POND 27D3	$3.75	(Hall)
19"	–	–	CL	POND 27F2	$3.75	(Musciano)

E-III (SA: 217)

[70]	–	.60	RC	MB 2722	$10.00	(Huber)
12½"	–	R	FF	CLEVE CD144	$9.00	
16"	–	R	FF	GLEASON	$.95	(Wherry)
16½"	–	R	FF	CLEVE CD144	$12.00	
20"	–	R/CO2	FF	ALFERY	$5.00	
21½"	–	R	FF	PECK BHP448	$2.00	(Thomas)
22"	–	–	CL	POND 27D3	$3.25	(Simmerance)
23¼"	–	.020	CL	MA 501	$2.00	(Jay)
24½"	–	R	FF	CLEVE CD144	$16.00	

*25"	–	R	FF	STERLING A-23	$15.95	
760mm	–	R	FF	VTH MT430-K	DM7,50	(Carkhuff)
31½"	–	–	CL	GLEASON AT652	NA	(Musciano)
33"	–	–	RC	HOLMAN	$2.50	
36"	–	.5-.8cc	FF	ARGUS FSP551	£3.00	(Edwards)
40"	–	.035	2	VELIVOLI J2	$6.00	
41"	–	–	FF	POND 50D6	$5.25	(Deitchman)
44"	–	–	RC	HOLMAN	$6.95	
*1150mm	730mm	3.5-5cc	3	ENGEL 1395	DM200,	
49"	–	–	RC	CLEVE CD144	$30.00	
49"	–	.15	RC	RCM 193	$6.75	(Srull)
49½"	–	–	RC	HOLMAN	$2.50	
52"	–	–	CL	GLEASON	$10.95	(Carkhuff)
1300mm	900mm	2.5-5cc	CL	VTH MT430-G	DM19,50	(Carkhuff)
52"	–	–	CL	PROKIT	£8.75	(Carkhuff)
55"	–	.35	3-4	FM CF114	$7.00	(Ziroli)
58"	–	.25-.35	3	TRAP MW2218	£6.50	(Tattam)
62"	–	.35-.40	3	ARGUS RM158	£5.25	(Searl)
62"	–	–	RC	POND 46C3	$5.25	(Carter)
1600mm	–	6.5-8cc	RC	MRA 115	95F	
66"	47"	.60	4	AEROTEK	$19.95	
*[$135.00]						
66"	–	–	RC	HOLMAN	$6.95	
66½"	–	.45-.60	4	GLEASON	$8.20	(Carter)
67"	–	.60	RC	HORN S-34	$9.00	
68"	–	6-10cc	RC	ARGUS RC1124	£8.75	(Huber)
68"	–	.35-.40	4	MORGAN 104RC	$6.95	
99½"	71½"	.91	3-4	HOLMAN	$18.95	(Lockwood)

E-IV

36"	–	R	FF	POND 17E1	$4.75	(Edwards)
45"	–	–	FF	POND 27D7	$5.25	(Cole)

E-V

27"	–	R	FF	POND 36D3	$4.25	(Hawkins)
42"	–	–	RC	POND 55G7	$5.75	(Suellentrop)

V-29

49½"	–	–	RC	HOLMAN	$4.00	

FRIEDRICHSHAVEN

G-II
23"	-	R	FF	COLE	$5.00

GOTHA

Go-145
13"	-	R	FF	AIME	20F
13"	-	R	FF	FILLON	16F 80

G-IV
29¼"	-	R	FF	CLEVE CD245	$18.00
43¾"	-	R	FF	CLEVE CD245	$24.00
58½"	-	-	RC	CLEVE CD245	$32.00
117"	-	-	RC	CLEVE CD245	$40.00

Taube
45"	-	Elec	RC	MB 6763	$9.50	(Stroman)
84"	-	-	RC	FM CF321	$14.50	(Ziroli)

RML-I
2000mm	-	-	4	VTH MT733K	DM19,50	(Nietzer)
3000mm	1550mm	10ccx2	4	VTH MT733G	DM39,	(Nietzer)

Ursinus
15½"	-	R	FF	VELIVOLI T16	$8.00
39"	-	R/CO2	FF	FLY T FTMC16	$7.50
*[$25.00]

HALBERSTADT

CL-II
18"	-	R	FF	POND 28G3	$4.50	(Guillow)
20"	-	R	FF	COLE	$5.00	
35"	-	R	FF	PALADINE 50	$11.00	
70"	-	-	RC	PALADINE 50	$18.00	
70½"	-	.60	RC	GLEASON	$22.75	(Theiss)

D-I (SA: 217)
20"	-	R	FF	POND 38C4	$4.75	(Danielson)
29"	-	-	CL	POND 41F7	$5.75	(Musciano)

D-II
*13"	-	R	FF	LEE	$6.00

21½"	-	R	FF	HOLMAN	$2.50	
29"	-	R	FF	HOLMAN	$2.50	
29"	-	-	CL	GLEASON AM168	NA	(Musciano)
58"	-	.60	4	ARGUS RM233	£6.00	(Bolam)
58"	-	/.40	4	TRAP MW2044	£7.50	(Hurrell)

HANNOVER

CL-III

14½"	-	R	FF	CLEVE CD163	$10.00	
19½"	-	R	FF	CLEVE CD163	$13.00	
29"	-	R	FF	CLEVE CD163	$18.00	
49"	-	.20	4	ARGUS RM248	£4.50	(Woodward)
57½"	-	-	RC	CLEVE CD163	$30.00	
57½"	-	-	RC	CLEVE CD163	$30.00	
60"	-	-	RC	HOLMAN	$4.50	

HEINKEL

He-5

| 38" | - | .8-1cc | FF | ARGUS FSP608 | £3.75 | (Aeromodeler) |

He-42

17"	-	R	FF	POND 55B5	$4.75	(Friedrich)
28"	-	R	FF	POND 28B6	$4.75	(Friedrich)
38"	-	-	RC	POND 37E1	$7.25	(Budin)
1460mm	1045mm	5.6-10cc	4	VTH MT618G	DM29,50	(Budin)

He-45

| 38½" | _ | R | FF | GLEASON | $9.25 | (McClure) |

He-46

| 13" | - | R | FF | GREGA 228 | $1.00 | |
| 17" | - | R | FF | POND 28B1 | $3.25 | (McHard) |

He-51 (SA: 218)

?	-	-	-	ARGUS FSR141X	£3.00	
24"	-	R	FF	GLEASON	$2.65	(Davidson)
*24"	-	R	FF	SIERRA	$13.95	
27¼"	-	R	FF	GLEASON	$3.30	(Davidson)
30"	-	R	FF	POND 50G2	$5.75	(Woolett)
36"	-	-	CL	GLEASON	$6.35	(Musciano)

44¼"	–	–	CL	GLEASON	$8.75	(Musciano)
48"	–	–	CL	GLEASON	$10.50	(Musciano)
72½"	–	.90/1.20	RC	RCM 943	$17.50	(Murray)

[TDF: cowl, $25.50; wheel pants, $22.45; gas tank, $14.00]

90"	66"	1.8-2	6	SMITH	$34.00

He-72 Kadett (SA: 218)

1620mm	1350mm	10cc	4	VTH MT732	DM36,	(Staub)

He-100 (SA: 218, 254)

13"	–	R	FF	ARONSTEIN	$1.00	
13"	–	R	FF	GLEASON	$.50	(Katagiri)
13"	–	R	FF	POND 41B4	$3.25	(Clutton)
16"	–	R	FF	GLEASON	$1.35	(Katagiri)
18½"	–	R	FF	WOODHOUSE	£2.00	(Koutny)
20"	–	R	FF	GLEASON	$1.95	(Katagiri)
*24"	–	R	FF	FLYLINE 110	$15.95	
*40"	35"	.50	3-4	GAGER	$60.00	
54"	–	.40-.60	RC	RCM 568	$6.00	(Ziroli)
61½"	–	.40	CL	MA 582	$12.50	
62"	–	.60	RC	HORN S-50	$14.00	(Osborne)
77"	–	–	RC	HOLMAN	$9.95	

He-111

74¼"	–	.25x2	5	ARGUS RM260	£13.50	(Maund)
2250mm	–	10ccx2	RC	MODELL	DM28,80	(Boog)

He-112

13"	–	R	FF	POND 28A5	$3.25	(Roden)
13"	–	R	FF	POND 62C6	$3.25	(Yamamori)
18"	–	R	FF	POND 18C6	$3.75	(Plecan)
¶ 21"	–	R	FF	POND 18C6	$3.25	(Comet)

*[REPRO: $8.50]

22"	–	R	FF	HUNT 2215	$4.50	(Whitman)
*24"	–	R	FF	EASY FF29	$7.00CDN	
32"	–	–	CL	POND 42E2	$7.25	(Musciano)
35"	–	R	FF	GLEASON	$9.95	(Musciano)

He-114

13"	–	R	FF	KOUTNY	$4.00	
31"	–	R	FF	POND 18C6	$4.25	(Becker)
800mm	600mm	.3-1cc	RC	VTH MT410	DM7,50	

He-162 Salamander (SA: 218, 254)

28"	-	-	FF	POND 28B7	$4.75	(Ledertheil)
710mm	790mm	.8-1.5cc	FF	VTH MT269	DM7,50	(Ledertheil)
1000mm	-	-	RC	VTH MT771-K	DM12,	(Gallena)
*1380mm	1500mm	6.5ccF	RC	BAUER 790001	DM579,	
55"	-	.40F	RC	FM CF389	$10.00	(Ziroli)
1515mm	1175mm	6.5F	3	VTH MT771-G	DM29,50	(Gallena)

He-177 Grief (SA: 218)

32"	-	-	RC	POND 55B4	$3.75	(Nietzer)
1830mm	-	-	RC	VTH MT627-K	DM19,50	(Nietzer)
2700mm	1800mm	5.6x2	4	VTH MT627-G	DM39,	(Nietzer)
3140mm	2200mm	15ccx2	5	AERONAUTICA	DM120,	

He-177B

3140mm	2200mm	15ccx4	5	AERONAUTICA	DM120,

He-219 Uhu (SA: 218)

37"	-	R	FF	KOUTNY	$15.00	
61"	-	-	CL	GLEASON AM1164	NA	(Musciano)
1848mm	1554mm	10ccx2	4	AERONAUTICA	DM80,	

HENSCHEL

Hs-123 (SA: 218)

18"	-	R	FF	POND 18C7	$3.75	(Marsh)
34"	-	R	FF	POND 28A2	$4.75	(Jones)
1150mm	-	-	RC	VTH MT952-K	DM7,50	(Angermeier)
1720mm	1410mm	15-20cc	4	VTH MT952-G	DM29,50	(Angermeier)
82"	63"	Q35	4-5	CORK	$35.00CDN	
103"	-	3.7-4.2	4	PASMCO	$40.00	

Hs-126 (SA: 218)

15"	-	R	FF	POND 37A7	$3.25	(Megow)
18"	-	R	FF	COLE	$5.00	
30"	-	R	FF	HUNT J28	$3.50	(Megow)
48"	-	R	FF	POND 46A2	$6.25	(Walker)
77"	-	10cc	RC	BRYANT 17	£9.00	

[canopy, £5.50]

Hs-129 (SA: 218)

36"	-	1-1.5cc	CL	ARGUS MA330	£3.75	(Wheldon)
67"	-	.29x2	4-5	MAN 4711	$10.50	(Reusch)

HORTEN

Horten IX 229 (SA: 218)

| 80" | – | Fx2 | 3-6 | YOUNG | $15.00 | |

JEANNIN-STAHL

Taube

| 23" | – | CO2 | FF | FM CF461 | $4.00 | (Stroman) |

JUNKERS

Ju-52 (SA: 218)

26"	–	R	FF	POND 47D5	$3.75	(Cervtti)
1810mm	–	6.5cc	RC	BOSAK	20 Kcs	
1810mm	–	6.5cc	RC	MODELL	DM22,80	(Bosak)
71"	–	.40	4	TRAP MW2070	$6.50	(Bosak)
95½"	–	.61, .49	RC	RCM 479	$14.75	(Pyner)
2400mm	1530mm	6.5ccx2	5	VTH MT/R364	DM32,80	(Glockner)

Ju-87 Stuka (SA: 218, 254)

?	–	–	–	ARGUS RC884x	£4.50	
15"	–	R	FF	POND 18F4	$3.25	(Megow)
*16½"	–	R	FF	GUILLOW 508	$5.00	
17"	–	R	FF	CLEVE CD84U	$12.00	
17"	–	R	FF	POND 41G5	$3.75	(Guillow)
17"	–	R	FF	POND 28E1	$3.25	(McHard)
19"	–	R	FF	HUNT AH119	$3.00	(Delgatto)
20"	–	R	FF	HUNT 3874	$4.50	(Whitman)
*20"	–	R	FF	KEIL KKOO43	£3.99	
*20"	–	R	FF	STERLING A-6	$11.95	
¶22"	–	R	FF	POND 2205	$4.50	(Ott)
22"	–	R	FF	POND 28D1	$3.71	(Wentzel)
23"	–	R	FF	CLEVE CD84U	$14.00	
¶25"	–	R	FF	POND 52F4	$3.25	(Comet)
28"	–	R	FF	HUNT 2948	$5.50	(Whitman)
*30"	–	R	FF	EASY FF75	$11.00 CDN	
¶30"	–	R	FF	HUNT L17	$3.50	(Megow)
32"	–	R	FF	POND 18F4	$3.75	(Ott)
34"	–	5cc	FF	ARGUS FSP675	£3.75	(Aeromodeller)

34"	–	R	FF	CLEVE CD84U	$20.00	
*34½"	–	.049-.09	CL	GUILLOW 1002	$29.00	
40"	–	R	FF	POND 50G6	$4.75	(H & F Models)
1100mm	–	R	FF	MRA 373	46F	
45"	–	–	RC	CLEVE CD84U	$34.00	
50"	–	–	RC	OLD G5	$4.00	(Megow)
*1380mm	1110mm	.29-.45	3-4	IKUTA	¥24,000	
*[assembled, ¥98,000]						
59"	–	–	CL	POND 28D5	$6.25	(MAN)
*60"	–	.40-.61	4	FLAIR CAPR10	NA	
60"	–	.40-.61	4	TRAP MW2110	£8.00	(CAP)
[cowl, £9.50; canopy, £4.50; spinner, £3.00; spats, £5.00]						
62½"	–	.60	RC	RCM 488	$7.50	(Byrne)
64"	–	.60	RC	FM CF357	$7.00	(Eck)
*1630mm	1360mm	.60	3-4	IKUTA	¥35,000	
*1663mm	1365mm	.60/.90	4-5	MARUTAKA 6	¥30,000	
66½"	–	.60	5	MAN 9704	$13.00	(Pickup)
*66½"	51"	15cc	4	SKYRAIDER	$450.00AUS	
*67½"	54"	.60	4	DIVELY	$200.00	
68"	–	.60	4-5	MORGAN 303RC	$16.95	
1720mm	1300mm	6-10cc	4	VTH MT/R640	DM29,80	(Schmalzgruber)
1810mm	–	10cc	RC	MRA	119F	
100"	77"	3-4.2	4-5	ZIROLI	$30.00	
[cowl, $38.00; wheel pants, $14.00; canopy, $16.00]						
2760mm	2220mm	/1.20	RC	MODULO	FORTHCOMING	
*114"	–	Q50	5-6	CONSOLIDATED	$265.00	

Ju-88

[66]	–	–	–	MB 2802	$12.50	(Baltes)
24"	–	R	FF	POND 56D3	$3.25	(Nietzer)
25½"	–	R	FF	CLEVE CD225	$16.00	
34"	–	R	FF	CLEVE CD225	$22.00	
51"	–	–	RC	CLEVE CD225	$30.00	
1460mm	–	–	RC	VTH MT703-K	DM19,50	(Nietzer)
68"	–	–	RC	CLEVE CD225	$44.00	
72"	–	.30x2	4-5	ARGUS RM166	£3.75	(Scott)
72"	–	.30x2	4-5	HOLMAN	$16.25	(Scott)
2001mm	1455mm	10ccx2	4	AERONAUTICA	DM80,	
2185mm	1550mm	6.5x2	4	VTH MT703-G	DM36,	(Nietzer)

Ju-188

2200mm	1491mm	10ccx2	4	AERONAUTICA	DM80,	

Ju-290

2950mm	–	3.5ccx4	4	VTH MT681-G	DM39,00	(Nietzer)

CL-I

56"	–	.45	RC	FM CF159	$8.00	(Burgholzer)
56"	–	.45	RC	HORN MSP-170	$3.50	

D-I (SA: 254)

8"	–	R	FF	AERO ERA	$.65	
13"	–	R	FF	AERO ERA	$1.25	
13"	–	R	FF	PECK BHP439	$1.50	(Frugoli)
15"	–	R	FF	CODDING	$.50	(Madison Models)
28"	–	–	CL	POND 28E6	$4.75	(C/L Technique)
54"	–	–	RC	POND 47G7	$5.75	(Air Trails)
60"	–	–	RC	PALADINE 75	$18.00	
90"	–	–	RC	PALADINE 75	$32.00	

J-I

18"	–	R	FF	COLE	$5.00	
20"	–	R	FF	POND 55A4	$3.25	(Nietzer)
1060mm	–	–	RC	VTH MT698-K	DM7,50	(Nietzer)
1600mm	1105mm	5.8cc	4	VTH MT698-G	DM29,50	(Nietzer)

J-II

58"	–	Elec	4	AIRDROME	$29.00

J-VII

47½"	–	.020x2	CL	MA 567	$3.75

J-X

[60]	–	–	–	MB 6801	$10.00	(Allen)
13"	–	R	FF	ARONSTEIN	$1.00	

W-33 Bremen

28"	–	R	FF	POND 18F3	$4.25	(Popular Science)
33"	–	R	FF	POND 28D3	$4.25	(Friedrich)
36"	–	R	FF	POND 18F3	$3.75	(MAN)

KLEMM

L-25 (SA: 219)

44"	-	-		RC	POND 28F5	$4.50	(Friedrich)
64"	-	-		RC	POND 51B2	$7.25	(Denzin)
*1860mm	1500mm	3.5/6.5cc	4		KRICK 10170	DM199,90	

MESSERSCHMITT

Me-108 Taifun

30"	-	R	FF	FSI M-1	$6.00	
37"	-	R	FF	POND 29C7	$4.25	(Friedrich)
1060mm	-	-	RC	VTH MT689-K	DM7,50	(Kriz)
1140mm	800mm	2.5cc	CL	VTH MT204	DM7,50	(Friedrich)
1710mm	1220mm	6.5-10cc	5	VTH MT689-G	DM24,	(Kriz)

Me-109E (SA: 219, 254)

?	-	-	-	ARGUS MA27x	£3.00	
?	-	-	-	ARGUS MA399x	£3.75	
*10"	-	Glider	FF	PAPER FP505	$3.95	
12"	-	R	FF	CLEVE CD74B	$12.00	
13"	-	R	FF	FOAM	$2.25	
13"	-	R	FF	POND 46G7	$3.25	(Norman)
13"	-	R	FF	POND 19D3	$3.25	(Weiss)
14"	-	R	FF	POND 51B2	$3.25	(Model A/C)
15"	-	R	FF	POND 29D5	$3.25	(Wentzel)
16"	-	R	FF	CLEVE CD74B	$15.00	
16"	-	R	FF	GLEASON	$1.05	(Schienz)
¶16"	-	R	FF	HUNT A37	$2.50	(Comet)
*[FIKE: $7.95]						
*16½"	-	R	FF	GUILLOW 505	$5.00	
16¼"	-	R	FF	GLEASON	$2.10	(McHard)
*16½"	-	R	FF	KEIL KK0026	£4.99	
17"	-	R	FF	HUNT 3892	$4.50	(Whitman)
*17"	-	R	FF	KEIL KK0046	£3.99	
*18"	-	R	FF	BENTOM	$9.95	
*19"	-	R	FF	IHC 527	$12.98	
20"	-	R	FF	KOUTNY	$5.00	
20"	-	R	FF	POND 51B2	$4.25	(Pollitt)
20"	-	R	FF	POND 56D5	$4.25	(Nietzer)

20"	–	R	FF	WOODHOUSE	£2.50	(Koutny)
20½"	–	R	FF	HUNT MAC-14	$2.50	(Model A/C)
530mm	–	R	FF	AIRBORNE	$5.00AUS	
21"	–	R	FF	HUNT ES22	$3.00	(Stahl)
22"	–	–	CL	POND 29C2	$4.25	(Lewis)
¶22"	–	R	FF	POND 56F5	$3.75	(Ott)
24"	–	1.5cc	CL	ARGUS CL709	£3.00	(Kingswood)
*24"	–	R	FF	EASY FF28	$7.00CDN	
24"	–	R	FF	CLEVE CD74B	$20.00	
24"	–	R	FF	POND 51B2	$3.75	(Continental)
24"	–	R	FF	POND 46G6	$3.75	(Norman)
24¼"	–	–	CL	GLEASON AT1252	$3.45	(Musciano)
25"	–	R	FF	POND 19D3	$3.75	(Struhl)
26"	–	R	CL	CODDING	$1.00	
*28"	–	R/.020	CL	GUILLOW 401	$16.00	
28"	–	R	FF	HUNT 2971	$5.50	(Whitman)
29"	–	R	FF	HUNT ES22E	$3.50	(Stahl)
*30"	–	R	FF	EASY FF76	$11.00CDN	
30"	–	R	FF	POND 19D2	$3.75	(Modelcraft)
780mm	–	R	FF	MRA 348	40F	
31"	–	–	RC	PALADINE 44	$8.00	
32"	–	–	CL	GLEASON AT861	NA	(Musciano)
32"	–	–	CL	POND 19D2	$4.75	(Modern Hobbycraft)
32"	–	R	FF	POND 29C5	$5.75	(Cole)
33"	–	–	CL	POND 44E1	$6.75	(Musciano)
36"	–	R	FF	CLEVE T74	$12.00	
36"	–	R	FF	HUNT E572E	$4.00	(Stahl)
*900mm	750mm	.051-.10	2-3	MARUTAKA 43	¥7,800	
36"	–	–	CL	POND 52E2	$5.25	(Japan)
40"	–	1.5cc	FF	ARGUS MA335	£4.50	(Cole)
41¼"	–	–	RC	OLD D56	$5.00	(Stahl)
*42"	36"	.15	3-4	GAGER	$60.00	
*42"	–	.15-25	2-3	LEICESTER 23	£37.83	
*1050mm	830mm	1.5-2.5cc	3ch	RODEL 011395	DM123,	
42½"	–	.20	2-4	ARGUS RC1326	£3.75+	(Peacock)
43"	–	–	RC	POND 37E5	$6.75	(Nietzer)
*46"	–	Glider	2	SLOPE	$99.95	

1100mm	–	6.5	RC	BOSAK	20 Kcs	

[canopy, 15 Kcs]

47½"	–	.40	3-4	TRAP MW2159	£5.50	(Bosak)

[canopy, £4.00]

48"	–	–	RC	CLEVE CD74B	$38.00	
*1206mm	970mm	.19-.35	3-5	OK APQX015	¥13,800	
*1225mm	1086mm	.19-.25	4-6	TETTORA ME25SR	¥13,500	
*49½"	–	.29-.40	RC	SKYWAY	£40.00	
*50"	36"	.29-.45	3-4	FARNS A1016	$84.95	
*51"	–	.29-.46	4	DYNA 4001	$104.95	
54"	–	.40-.50	RC	RCM 590	$10.75	(Longfellow)
61"	–	.61	4	ARGUS RM73	£8.75	(Taylor)

[cowl, £7.50; canopy, £5.25]

*61"	–	.45/.90	4-5	GAL/NOR	£64.95	
*1541mm	1366mm	.60/1.20	4-6	MARUTAKA 37	¥30,000	
61"	–	–	RC	PALADINE 44	$18.00	
61"	–	.60	4	TAYLOR	£7.00	

[cowl,£3.00; canopy, £3.00; balsa pack, £27.50][UNITRACTS: retracts, £34.50]

1550mm	–	7.7-10cc	4	MRA BT10	132F	(Taylor)
*1550mm	1280mm	20cc	4	ROGA	DM368,	
63"	56"	.40-.60	RC	PHOTO	$9.95	
*64"	–	–	RC	MODEL 028	$169.00AUS	

[spinner, $30.00AUS; retracts, $240.00AUS]

65"	–	.60	4-5	ARGUS RC1421	£8.75	(Mapua)
*65"	48"	–	RC	SAIL	NA	
*66"	56"	.60-.90	4-5	AERODROME	$165.00	
68"	–	.60	RC	TAYLOR	NA	
*1790	–	10-22cc	RC	COOP 9600020	2034F	
*2200mm	–	25-40cc	4	BRABEC	4200Sch	
*2200mm	–	50cc	RC	COOP 9600040	2450F	

Me-109F   (SA: 219, 254)

*13"	–	R	FF	ALFERY	$12.00	
13"	–	R	FF	POND 44F7	$3.25	(Crosswinds)
20"	–	R	FF	KOUTNY	$5.00	
32½"	–	R	FF	TOKO	$4.00	(Wilson)
34"	–	5-8cc	FF	ARGUS FSP1017	£2.50	(Cole)
44"	–	–	RC	POND 52E1	$4.75	(Steinkuhl)
1210mm	–	4cc	RC	MRA 579.551	73F	
44¼"	–	.40	4	MARTIN MW110	£7.00	

[canopy, £1.40; template, £6.00]

| 61" | – | .60 | 6 | TAYLOR | £6.00 | |

[cowl, £5.50; canopy, £3.00; spinner, £5.50; balsa pack, £27.00]
**[HOLMAN: $139.95]

1600mm	–	10cc	RC	MRA BT11	119F	(Taylor)
65½"	59½"	.60-.90	4	INNOVATIVE	$25.00	
80"	–	–	RC	HOLMAN	$25.00	(Taylor)
*97"	85"	100cc	6-8	AIRSCREW	$3000CDN	

Me-109G (SA: 219, 254)

13"	–	R	FF	ALFERY	$5.00	
13"	–	R	FF	GLEASON	$1.60	(Schanzle)
16½"	–	R	FF	GLEASON	$2.75	(Schanzle)
16"	–	R	FF	POND 29C5	$3.25	(Hawkins)
*17"	–	R	FF	STERLING A-8	$9.95	
23½"	–	R	FF	GLEASON	$4.65	(Schanzle)
24¼"	–	–	CL	GLEASON	$3.45	(Musciano)
32"	–	–	CL	HOLMAN	$4.00	
*65¼"	59¼"	.60-.90	4-6	INNOVATIVE	$229.95	
*1660mm	–	10cc	RC	WEGA 163	DM465,	
1810mm	1640mm	10-12cc	5	VTH MT/R359	DM34,80	(Muller)
**79"	–	.90	5	PLATT RC3	$149.00	

[retracts, $219][cockpits: JD, $40.00; AVCO, $22.95]
*[$289.00]

*101½"	84½"	60cc	5	SKYRAIDER	$850.00AUS	
2610mm	2340mm	50cc	4	VTH MT/K376	DM32,	(Kriz)
*3000mm	–	100cc	3	COOP 9600067	2500F	

Me-109H

24"	–	R	FF	KOUTNY	$5.00	
*650mm	–	2.5cc	CL	AMZ 302	DM175,	

Me-109K

24"	–	R	FF	KOUTNY	$5.00	

Me-110 (SA: 220, 254)

39½"	–	–	CL	MA 301	$4.25	(Musciano)
39½"	–	–	CL	GLEASON AT458	NA	(Musciano)
40"	–	–	CL	POND 52E1	$6.25	(Graupner)
43"	–	–	RC	POND 29C5	$5.25	(Meerman)
1100mm	–	–	RC	VTH MT596-K	DM7,50	(Meerman)

53½"	-	-	CL	GLEASON AM566	NA	(Musciano)
1624mm	1170mm	5.6ccx2	5	VTH MT596-G	DM19,50	(Meerman)
71"	-	.30x2	4	TAYLOR	£6.00	

[cowl, £5.50; canopy, £3.00; balsa pack, £29.00]

1800mm	-	6-7ccx2	4	MRA BT12	119F	
1850mm	-	5ccx2	RC	MODELL	DM24,80	(Wolf)
81"	-	.60x2	RC	HOLMAN	$9.95	(Fingler)

[canopy, $10.00; nacelle, $25.00; wing cores, $45.00]

Me-163 Komet   (SA: 220, 254)

?	-	-	-	ARGUS G917x	£2.00	
[61]	-	-	-	MAN 11761	$14.50	(Moss)
17½"	-	-	-	HUNT J170	$3.50	
31"	-	-	FF	POND 29C7	$5.25	(Rattle)
33"	-	.049	RC	FM CF574	$7.00	(Adamsin)
36"	-	-	FF	POND 29C1	$4.75	(Becker)
1040mm	670mm	.3-8cc	FF	VTH MT273	DM7,50	(Becker)
44"	-	.19-.25	2-3	TRAP MW2021	£5.50	(Humber)

[canopy, £3.20]

49½"	-	.30	4	TAYLOR	£4.50	

[cowl, £2.00; canopy, £2.50; balsa pack, £20.]

1270mm	-	3.5-5cc	RC	MRA BT21	95F	(Taylor)
1300mm	-	10cc	RC	MODELL	DM22,80	(Boder)
*1350mm	-	6.6-10cc	RC	WEGA 154	DM179,	
61"	-	10cc	RC	BRYANT 15	£6.00	

[cowl, £3.00; canopy, £5.50][HOLMAN: fuselage, $159.95]

*1550mm	990mm	6.5-10cc	RC	WEGA 153	DM339,	
1600mm	-	.8-1.6cc	2	VTH MT/R	DM42,	(Glockner)
*1860mm	1170mm	10-18cc	RC	WEGA 162	DM434,	
3100mm	1890mm	70-100cc	4	VTH MT/K389	DM43,	(Kriz)

Me-209

19¼"	-	R	FF	BELL 011	$5.00	

Me-210 Hornisse   (SA: 220)

44"	-	-	CL	ARGUS MA395	£3.75	(Mackie)

Me-262 Schwalbe   (SA: 220, 254)

20½"	-	-	-	HUNT J171	$4.00	(Hunt)
25½"	-	Jetex	FF	BELL 021	$9.50	
26"	-	-	FF	HUNT J172	$5.00	(Hunt)

31"	–	Glider	FF	WALLACE	$6.50	
51"	–	40.	4	ARGUS RSQ1525	£7.50	(Booth)
*1900mm	1500mm	6.5x2F	RC	KRANZ	DM360,	
1950mm	1700mm	1.4-2.6cc	5	VTH MT/R358	DM,39	(Glockner)
2000mm	–	7.5x2	RC	MRA 664.585	132F	
*2085mm	1767	10ccx2F	RC	BAUER 90001	DM995,	
*84"	69"	7.5x2F	4	AIR FLAIR	$295.00	
*96"	–	.82x2F	6	HOBBY BARN	$600.00	
*2600mm	2200mm	15ccx2F	RC	KRANZ	DM670,	

Me-264

| 2360mm | – | – | RC | VTH MT833-K | DM19,50 | (Nietzer) |
| 3580mm | 1930mm | 3.2ccx4 | 4 | VTH MT833-G | DM36, | (Nietzer) |

Me-323 Gigant (SA: 220)

| 46" | – | – | RC | POND 52E4 | $9.25 | (Nietzer) |

Me-410 Hornisse (SA: 220)

| 70" | – | .40x2 | RC | ARGUS RC1443 | $7.50 | (Golds) |

Me-609

| 30" | – | R | FF | KOUTNY | $10.00 | |
| 30" | – | R | FF | WOODHOUSE | £3.00 | (Koutny) |

PFALZ

D-I

| 13" | – | R | FF | POND 37A5 | $3.25 | (M & L) |
| 15" | – | R | FF | POND 37G3 | $3.25 | (Ott) |

D-III (SA: 220)

[62]	–	.60	RC	FM CF223	$23.00	(Spievak)
11½"	–	R	FF	CLEVE CD161	$10.00	
13"	–	R	FF	POND 41F2	$3.25	(Norman)
15½"	–	R	FF	CLEVE CD161	$13.00	
18"	–	R	FF	POND 30C6	$4.75	(Guillow)
20"	–	R	FF	ALFERY	$5.00	
20"	–	R	FF	POND 19F6	$5.00	(McCorrison)
23"	–	R	FF	CLEVE CD161	$18.00	
23½"	–	R	FF	GLEASON	$2.05	(Layton)
23½"	–	R	FF	GLEASON	$1.90	(Smith)

23½"	–	R	FF	PROKIT	£2.25	(Smith)
24"	–	R	FF	POND 37G2	$4.25	(Great Lakes)
31"	–	R	FF	PALADINE 36	$8.00	
46"	–	–	RC	CLEVE CD161	$30.00	
46½"	–	1.5-2.5cc	FF	ARGUS FSP 775	£5.25	(Palmer)
61"	–	–	RC	PALADINE 36	$18.00	

D-VII

13"	–	R	FF	OLD 190	$2.00	

D-XII

13"	–	R	FF	POND 41D2	$3.25	(Balunek)
15"	–	R	FF	COLE	$5.00	
21"	–	R	FF	HUNT AH144	$3.25	(Norman)
*24"	–	R	FF	SIERRA	$13.95	
24½"	–	R	FF	PALADINE 11	$8.00	
30"	–	–	CL	POND 41E6	$4.25	(Musciano)
49"	–	–	RC	PALADINE 11	$14.00	
59"	–	10cc	RC	BRYANT 18	£6.00	
73½"	–	–	RC	PALADINE 11	$32.00	

D-XIII

11"	–	R	FF	CLEVE CD162	$10.00	
15"	–	R	FF	OLD 77	$3.00	(Diel)
15"	–	R	FF	CLEVE CD162	$13.00	
44"	–	–	RC	CLEVE CD162	$30.00	

Dr-I

13"	–	R	FF	POND 41G1	$3.75	(Balunek)
21"	–	R	FF	HUNT KO27	$3.50	(Great Lakes)
24"	–	R	FF	COLES	$5.00	
28"	–	R	FF	PALADINE 20	$8.00	
56"	–	–	RC	PALADINE 20	$18.00	
74"	–	–	RC	PALADINE 20	$32.00	

E-I

33"	–	R	FF	PALADINE 35	$11.00	
66"	–	–	RC	PALADINE 35	$18.00	

ROLAND (LFG)

C-II Wahlfisch
26"	–	R	FF	COLE	$5.00	
34"	–	R	FF	GLEASON	$5.55	(Musciano)

C-VI
19"	–	R	FF	KOUTNY	$5.00

D-II
26"	–	–	CL	POND 51F4	$3.75	(Newell)
27"	–	R	FF	FM CF677	$8.00	(Rees)
29½"	–	R	FF	PALADINE 43	$8.00	
40"	–	.75-1cc	FF	ARGUS FSP1321	£6.00	(Dennis)
59"	–	–	RC	PALADINE 43	$18.00	

D-XVI
21½"	–	R	FF	HOLMAN	$2.50
26½"	–	R	FF	HOLMAN	$2.50

RUMPLER

C-IV
32"	–	R	FF	CLEVE CD154	$28.00	
48"	–	–	RC	POND 30D2	$6.75	(Ledertheil)
1200mm	–	–	RC	VTH MT526-K	DM12,	(Ledertheil)
72"	–	–	RC	POND 41D4	$9.75	(Ledertheil)
1830mm	1140mm	5cc	4	VTH MT526-G	DM29,50	(Redaktion, FMT)
82"	–	.60-.90	4	ARGUS RM324	£13.50	(Cousins)

C-V
?	–	–	–	ARGUS MA402x	£3.00	
14"	–	R	FF	POND 31C2	$3.25	(Norman)
22"	–	R	FF	COLE	$5.00	
22½"	–	R	FF	GLEASON	$1.50	(Musciano)
24"	–	R	FF	POND 28D6	$4.75	(Guillow)
25"	–	R	FF	POND 31C4	$3.75	(Norman)
32"	–	R	FF	GLEASON	$2.90	(Musciano)
32"	–	R	FF	PROKIT	£2.25	(Musciano)
40"	–	–	FF	POND 36D2	$4.75	(Rattle)

D-I

20"	-	R	FF	COLE	$5.00	

Taube (SA: 220)

17"	-	R	FF	CLEVE CD234	$9.00	
19"	-	R	FF	HUNT AH189	$3.00	(Struck)
22"	-	R	FF	POND 20G1	$3.75	(Struck)
*22"	-	R	FF	RN CG503	$19.95+	
23½"	-	R	FF	CLEVE CD234	$12.00	
24"	-	R	FF	GLEASON	$2.65	(Musciano)
24"	-	R	FF	PLANS	$6.00	(Andrus)
30"	-	.5-.9cc	FF	ARGUS MA186	£3.00	(Lewis)
32"	-	R	FF	POND 30C5	$4.75	(Enticknap)
33"	-	R	FF	GLEASON AT1051	$3.75	(McHard)
34"	-	R	FF	CLEVE CD234	$16.00	
36"	-	R	FF	POND 20G1	$4.75	(Ideal)
48"	-	R	FF	PLANS	$7.00	(Andrus)
56"	-	.19-.45	3	MAN 1711	$10.50	(Ziroli)
*62"	-	.35-.50	3	BALSA 439	$29.99	

SIEMENS-SCHUCKERT

D-I

20"	-	R	FF	FSI S-1	$6.00
27"	-	R	FF	PALADINE 13	$8.00
52"	-	-	RC	PALADINE 13	$14.00

D-III

27½"	-	R	FF	PALADINE 21	$8.00
55"	-	-	RC	PALADINE 21	$14.00
84"	47"	.90	4	AEROTEK	$35.00

*[$375.00]

D-IV

10½"	-	R	FF	CLEVE CD244	$8.00
14"	-	R	FF	CLEVE CD244	$10.00
21"	-	R	FF	CLEVE CD244	$14.00
42"	-	-	RC	CLEVE CD244	$28.00
72"	-	.90	RC	B&D	$14.95
84"	-	-	RC	CLEVE CD244	$46.00

D-VI
23¼"	–	R	FF	HOLMAN	$2.50	
31"	–	R	FF	HOLMAN	$2.50	

E-I
13"	–	R	FF	MOONEY	$1.00	
16"	–	R	FF	COLE	$5.00	

GREAT BRITAIN
AIRSPEED

Horsa
22"	–	Glider	FF	POND 26A5	$3.75	(Base)
1080mm	–	Glider	FF	MRA 298	40F	

Oxford
34"	–	.020x2	FF	AUTHENTIC	£2.10	(Towner)

ARMSTRONG-WHITWORTH

FK-3
38"	–	R	FF	POND 13C5	$4.25	(Elsegood)

FK-10
15"	–	R	FF	COLE	$5.00	

FK-12
21"	–	R	FF	POND 13C2	$3.00	(Modernistic)

Siskin (SA: 221)
15"	–	R	FF	POND 55A7	$3.75	(Williams)
17"	–	R	FF	POND 28D3	$3.75	(Coldrick)
22½"	–	1-1.5cc	CL	ARGUS CL742	£3.00	(Hall)
33"	–	–	FF	POND 13C6	$5.75	(Williams)

Quad
11"	–	R	FF	CLEVE CD11B	$8.00	
14"	–	R	FF	CLEVE CD11B	$10.00	
21"	–	R	FF	CLEVE CD11B	$14.00	

AUSTER

A.O.P. 6
18"	–	R	FF	POND 13D2	$3.75	(Nikitendo)

*20"	-	R	FF	VERON VO402	£3.42	

A.O.P. 9

18"	-	R	FF	HUNT MAC-01	$2.50	(Model A/C)
36"	-	.5-.8cc	FF	ARGUS FSP580	£3.75	(Moulton)
81"	-	.40-61	4	TRAP MW2037	£8.00	(Humber)
[canopy, £8.20]						

J-4

*72"	-	/.40	4	FLAIR CAPRO9	NA	
72"	-	?.40	4	TRAP MW2109	£8.00	(CAP)
[canopy, £8.00]						

AUSTIN-BALL

A.F.B.-1

*13"	-	R	FF	LEE	$6.00
46½"	-	-	RC	PALADINE 26	$14.00

AVRO

Avro 504 (SA: 221)

?	-	-	-	PROKIT	NA	
*13"	-	R	FF	LEE	$6.00	
15"	-	R	FF	POND 55A6	$3.75	(Booth)
18"	-	R	FF	POND 31E5	$3.75	(Malmstrom)
22"	-	CO2	FF	SAMS 696	£2.95	(Crown)
*24"	18½"	R	FF	PAI 272	$18.00	
27"	-	R	FF	CLEVE CD167	$18.00	
36"	-	.8-1cc	FF	ARGUS FSP343	£5.25	(Booth)
48"	-	.19-.20	3-4	ARGUS RM199	£7.50	(Whitehead)
48"	-	.20-.30	3-4	RCM 826	$6.00	(Whitehead)
*56"	-	.23-.36	3	VERON VO719	£72.99	
72"	-	.60	4	ARGUS RC1420	£7.50	(Boddington)

Anson

36"	-	.020x2	FF	AUTHENTIC	£2.10	(Towner)
84"	-	.30x2	4-6	HUTSON 12	£14.75	
[cowls, £18.25; canopy, £7.75; turret, £5.50; balsa pack, £18.50]						

Athena

?	-	-	-	ARGUS MA312x	£3.75	
9"	-	R	FF	POND 55B3	$3.75	(Bennett)

Avro 707 Delta

?	–	–	–	ARGUS RC649x	£4.50	
13"	–	–	FF	POND 55B3	$3.75	(Ledertheil)
14"	–	Jetex	FF	HUNT J103	$3.25	(Keil Kraft)
700mm	630mm	.5-1cc	FF	VTH MT94	DM7,50	(FMT)
46"	–	–	CL	POND 44A2	$6.25	(Pond)
60"	–	–	RC	POND 57A4	$9.25	(CAP)

Lancaster (SA: 221, 255)

11"	–	R	FF	POND 55B1	$3.75	(Easy Built)
23"	–	R	FF	POND 56C7	$3.25	(Towner)
25"	–	R	FF	POND 13B7	$4.75	(Easy Built)
51"	–	–	FF	MA 556	$6.50	(Norman)
52"	–	.09x4	CL	ARGUS CL1081	£8.75	(Towner)
74"	–	Elec	3	ARGUS RM333	£6.00	(Holland)
90"	–	.20x4	7	ARGUS RC1457	£11.00	(Golds)

[cowls, canopy, turrets, £23.50]

| *102" | 68" | .30x4 | 6-8 | POWERMAX LS1 | £260.00 | |

Shackelton

| 61" | – | 5-6ccx4 | CL | ARGUS CL746 | £5.25 | (Bodley) |

Spider (SA: 221)

| 8" | – | R | FF | MOONEY | $1.00 | |

Tutor

| 68" | – | 10cc | RC | BRYANT 2 | £6.00 | |

[cowl, £4.00]

Vulcan

*15"	–	Jetex	FF	EASY JX01	$10.00CDN	
20"	–	Jetex	FF	POND52F2	$4.75	(Skyleada)
20"	–	–	FF	POND 55A1	$3.75	(Pond)
35"	–	Glider	FF	WALLACE	$6.50	
46"	–	.40	RC	MAN 187	$8.50	
50"	–	Glider	3	ARGUS 1528	£5.25	(Benson)
*60"	–	.60	4	FLAIR CAPR16	NA	
60"	–	.60	4	TRAP MW2116	£8.00	

[cowl, £6.50; canopy, £3.50]

| 65" | 56" | Glider | 2 | GREEN | FORTHCOMING | |
| 180" | 172" | .90x4F | 10 | GAZZA 018 | FORTHCOMING | |

BAC

Jet Provost (SA: 221)

| 47" | - | .19-.25 | 4-5 | TRAP MW2183 | £6.50 | (Howell) |

TSR-2 (SA: 221)

| 30" | - | .25 | 4 | ARGUS RC1552 | £5.25 | (Collins) |

BAe

Harrier (SA: 221)

| 18" | - | Glider | FF | WALLACE | $6.50 | |
| 910mm | - | 6.5cc | RC | BOSAK | 40 Kcs | |

[canopy, 15 Kcs]

36"	-	6.5cc	RC	ARGUS RC1462	£8.75	(Bosak)
36"	-	.40	RC	RCM 907	$8.50	(Bosak)
48½"	44"	Glider	2	GREEN	£3.75	
*56"	-	.60-.90	RC	LEICESTER	£131.53	

Hawk (SA: 221)

| 46" | 52" | .40-.45F | 4 | ARGUS RC1450 | £8.75 | (Gray) |

[canopy, foam wings, £8.75]

*48"	52"	.40-.45	4-5	LEICESTER	£70.87	
*52"	61½"	.65F	5	FANJET	£85.00	
*54"	54"	.40F	4	DIVELY	$199.95	
*59"	51"	.77-.81F	4-6	CENTURY	$189.95	
57"	-	.40	4	ARGUS RC1358	£6.00	(Crawford)
*62"	71¼"	.77F	4	RJ	$420.00AUS	
1620mm	-	10cc	RC	MODELL	DM38,40	(Steffen)

Hawk 200

| 46" | 52" | .40-.45F | RC | AEROFAN | $23.00AUS | |
| 47½" | 46" | Glider | 2 | GREEN | £4.75 | |

BEARDMORE

W.B. II

| 20" | - | R | FF | POND 13D4 | $4.25 | (Gough) |

BLACKBURN

Baby

| 13" | - | R | FF | POND 31F5 | $3.25 | (Stott) |

Firebrand

?	-	-	CL	ARGUS CL380x	£3.00	
?	-	-	CL	ARGUS CL1189x	£4.50	
13"	-	R	FF	DIELS 13	$1.75	

Roc

21"	-	R	FF	POND 26D4	$3.75	(Jones)
23"	-	R	FF	POND 13G2	$3.75	(Booton)

Shark

28"	-	R	FF	POND 26C6	$4.75	(Moore)
35"	-	R	FF	POND 13G1	$4.25	(Comet)

Skua

15"	-	R	FF	POND 13G2	$3.25	(Aer-O-Kits)
16"	-	R	FF	HUNT MACO2	$2.50	(Model A/C)
19"	-	R	FF	HUNT 3876	$4.50	(Whitman)
590mm	-	R	FF	AIRBORNE	$5.00AUS	
25"	-	R	FF	GLEASON	$1.80	(Stahl)
¶25"	-	R	FF	POND 13G1	$3.75	(Comet)
*25"	-	R	FF	PROKIT	£23.50	
30"	-	R	FF	POND 28C3	$4.75	(Megow)
35"	-	R	FF	HUNT ES04	$3.50	(Stahl)

YA-5

24"	-	R	FF	HUNT 5365	$5.50	(Whitman)

BOULTON-PAUL

Defiant (SA: 255)

13"	-	R	FF	POND 44F4	$3.25	(Norman)
¶16"	-	R	FF	POND 14C2	$3.25	(Burd)
18"	-	R	FF	POND 37C1	$3.25	(K-Dee)
19"	-	R	FF	POND 52F3	$3.75	(Guillow)
19"	-	R	FF	HUNT MACO2	$2.50	(Model A/C)
20"	-	R	FF	POND 44F5	$3.75	(Norman)
22"	-	R	FF	POND 14C2	$3.75	(Continental)
24"	-	R	FF	HUNT ES06	$3.00	(Stahl)
¶25"	-	R	FF	POND 14C2	$3.75	(Comet)
*[REPRO: $9.50]						
27"	-	R	FF	POND 26D7	$3.75	(Astral)
27¼"	_	R	FF	AUTHENTIC	£1.45	(Towner)
*30"	-	R	FF	EASY FF74	$11.00CDN	

32"	–	R	FF	POND 14C1	$6.25	(Ott)
36"	–	R	FF	HUNT 5377	$5.50	(Whitman)
36"	–	R	FF	ORIGINAL	£4.50	(Martin)
37"	–	R	FF	GLEASON	$4.35	(Stahl)
950mm	–	R	FF	MRA 310	40F	
40"	–	–	CL	POND 57A2	$4.75	(CAP)
50"	–	–	CL	POND 41B1	$5.75	(Price)
60"	–	.60	RC	FM CF406	$7.00	(Makovich)

P.111

?	–	–	–	ARGUS J548x	£3.00	
16"	–	Jetex	FF	POND 26C3	$3.25	(Dautin)
24"	–	Jetex	FF	POND 36A7	$4.75	(Golding)

BRISTOL

Beaufighter

?	–	–	–	ARGUS MA275x	$3.75	
13"	–	R	FF	AUTHENTIC	£.75	(Towner)
20"	–	R	FF	POND 55C3	$3.75	(Jones)
39"	–	2.5ccx2	CL	ARGUS MA275	£3.75	(Fry)
39"	–	.049x2	CL	ORIGINAL	£4.50	(Martin)

Blenheim (SA: 255)

| 26" | – | R | FF | AUTHENTIC | £1.45 | (Towner) |

Bulldog

13"	–	R	FF	CLEVE CD194	$12.00	
17½"	–	R	FF	CLEVE CD194	$16.00	
26¼"	–	R	FF	CLEVE CD194	$20.00	
28"	–	.75-1cc	FF	AUTHENTIC	£1.45	(Towner)
34"	–	1-1.5cc	FF	ARGUS FSP762	£4.50	(Allnut)
52"	–	–	RC	CLEVE CD194	$32.00	
63"	–	.60	RC	BRYANT 16	£6.00	
[cowl, £5.00]						
68"	–	–	RC	CLEVE CD194	$44.00	

F2B Fighter (SA: 221)

| ? | – | – | – | ARGUS FSP1021x | £2.00 | |
| 13" | – | R | FF | AERO ERA | $1.25 | |

13"	–	R	FF	OLD 194	$2.00	
14½"	–	R	FF	CLEVE CD68BU	$9.00	
15"	–	R	FF	FRANK 46	$2.00	(Comet)
16"	–	R	FF	POND 14C6	$3.25	(McCready)
19"	–	R	FF	GLEASON	$2.25	(Lindberg)
19½"	–	R	FF	CLEVE CD68BU	$11.00	
20"	–	R	FF	OLD 72	$3.00	(Diel)
20"	–	R/CO2	FF	ALFERY	$5.00	
20½"	–	R	FF	YEST 10	$3.00	(Air King)
*24"	–	R	FF	SIERRA	$13.95	
27"	–	R	FF	POND 14C6	$3.75	(Roberts)
29"	–	R	FF	CLEVE CD68BU	$14.00	
29"	–	R	FF	FSI B-6	$6.00	
39"	–	R	FF	CLEVE CD68BU	$20.00	
40"	–	–	RC	PALADINE 67	$11.00	
40"	–	–	RC	POND 26D7	$4.75	(Model A/C)
59"	–	–	RC	CLEVE CD68BU	$32.00	
72"	–	–	RC	ARGUS RM347	£8.75	(Kidd)
78"	–	–	RC	CLEVE CD68BU	$44.00	
80"	–	–	RC	PALADINE 67	$32.00	
118"	–	–	RC	CLEVE CD68BU	$58.00	

M 1 Bullet

11½"	–	R	FF	CLEVE CD236	$8.00	
12"	–	R	FF	POND 26C6	$3.25	(Castti)
13"	–	R	FF	AERO ERA	$1.25	
13"	–	R/.02	FF	MA 180	$2.00	(Headley)
13"	–	R	FF	MOONEY	$1.00	
13"	–	R	FF	COLE	$5.00	
16"	–	R	FF	COLE	$5.00	
16¼"	–	R	FF	CLEVE CD236	$11.00	
18"	–	R	FF	POND 28G2	$4.75	(Guillow)
18"	–	R	FF	POND 14C6	$3.75	(Schroder)
19"	–	R	FF	KOUTNY	$5.00	
20"	–	CO2	FF	ALFERY	$5.00	
23"	–	R	FF	CLEVE CD236	$16.00	
*28"	–	CO2	FF	PROKIT	£34.50	

30"	-	-	RC	POND 43A3	$4.75	(Headley)
33"	-	R	FF	POND 14C6	$3.75	(Le Modele Reduit)
34"	-	.049	FF	GULF	$5.00	(Midkiff)
900mm	-	1cc	FF	AIRBORNE	$10.00AUS	
37"	-	R	FF	ARGUS FSR226	£3.75	(Riding)
940mm	-	R	FF	MRA A353/192	25F	
46"	-	1-1.5cc	FF	ARGUS FSP759	£4.50	(Barton)
46"	-	-	RC	CLEVE CD236	$30.00	
48"	-	-	RC	POND 26D2	$6.75	(Wallace)
52"	-	.40	RC	FM CF326	$7.00	(Eck)
*62"	-	.40/.60	3	BALSA 436	$35.99	
**72"	-	-	RC	KLARICH	$55.00	(MAN)
92½"	-	.90-1.20	3	SWEITZER 2003	$36.00	

[spinner, $35.00]

Scout A

*13"	-	R	FF	NOWLEN	$13.95	
24½"	-	.3-.5cc	FF	ARGUS FSP1267	£2.00	(Whitehead)
49"	-	.40-.45	4	TRAP MW2020	£7.50	(Hurrell)

Scout C

18"	-	R	FF	COLE	$5.00	
49"	-	-	CL	PROKIT	£6.00	(Stinson)
49"	-	-	CL	GLEASON	$6.80	(Stinson)

Scout D (SA: 222, 255)

6½"	-	R	FF	ARONSTEIN	$.75	
*13"	-	R	FF	LEE	$6.00	
13	-	R	FF	MICRO X	$2.25	(Masters)
18"	-	R	FF	COLE	$5.00	
18"	-	R/CO2	FF	PECK BH195	$2.50	(Hamlen)
18½"	-	R	FF	CLEVE CD168	$16.00	
20"	-	CO2	FF	ALFERY	$5.00	
24½"	-	R	FF	PALADINE 74	$8.00	
31"	-	.049-.51	CL	HORN S-6	$6.00	(Osborne)
42½"	-	3.5cc	3	ARGUS RC1201	£6.00	(Fardell)
49"	-	-	RC	PALADINE 74	$14.00	
54"	-	.61	4	ARGUS RM161	£7.50	(Wormersley)
*60"	-	.30/.60	4	FLAIR FL1001	£50.37	

73½"	–	–	RC	PALADINE 74	$32.00	
74"	–	.91-1.50	RC	MA 328	$16.50	(Iltzsch)

[TDF: cowl, $26.50]

DEHAVILAND

DH-1

24"	–	R	FF	POND 38A2	$4.25	(Danielson)
39"	–	R	FF	POND 27B1	$4.50	(Winter)

DH-2 (SA: 222)

10½"	–	R	FF	CLEVE CD156	$11.00	
13"	–	R	FF	PASMCO	$4.00	
14"	–	R	FF	CLEVE CD156	$14.00	
21"	–	R	FF	CLEVE CD156	$18.00	
28"	–	R	FF	PALADINE 3	$8.00	
42"	–	–	RC	CLEVE CD156	$30.00	
42½"	–	–	RC	PAMSCO	$22.00	
56"	–	.35-.45	4	MAN 17501	$12.00	(Zundel)
57"	–	–	RC	PALADINE 3	$18.00	
60"	–	1.5-2.5cc	FF	ARGUS FSP388	£5.25	(Moore)
60"	–	–	RC	RCM 572	$13.50	(Meek)

[templates, $4.95]

63"	–	.60	4	MAN 5762	$16.75	(Neate)
63½"	–	.61	4	ARGUS RC1245	£10.00	(Neate)
85"	–	–	RC	PALADINE 3	$32.00	

DH-4

12"	–	R	FF	POND 16B3	$3.25	(Universal)
13"	–	R	FF	POND 42A1	$3.50	(M&L Models)
16"	–	R	FF	CLEVE CD3	$8.00	
21"	–	R	FF	CLEVE CD3	$10.00	
21"	–	R	FF	POND 38D5	$3.25	(Comet)
24"	–	R	FF	AERO ERA	$1.75	
27"	–	R	FF	POND 28D7	$4.75	(Guillow)
32"	–	R	FF	CLEVE CD3	$14.00	
36"	–	R	FF	POND 16B4	$5.25	(Ideal)
42"	–	–	RC	POND 16B4	$4.75	(Meixell)
42½"	–	–	CL	GLEASON	$4.10	(Musciano)

42"	–	–	CL	PROKIT	£3.60	(Musciano)
50"	–	R	FF	PLANS	$8.00	(Andrus)
53"	–	–	RC	CLEVE CD3	$20.00	
62½"	–	.40-.60	RC	MAN 8821	$24.50	(Fearnley)

DH-5 (SA: 222)

?	–	–	–	ARGUS FSP879x	£3.00	
10"	–	R	FF	POND 27C5	$3.25	(McCorrison)
14"	–	R	FF	HUNT AH86	$2.75	(Knoble)
18"	–	R	FF	POND 61G3	$3.75	(Powell)
19½"	–	R	FF	CLEVE CD148	$18.00	
25½"	–	R	FF	PALADINE 69	$8.00	
30"	–	R	FF	HUNT AH87	$3.75	(Knoble)
51"	–	–	RC	PALADINE 69	$14.00	
77"	–	–	RC	MB 12851	$30.00	(Iltzsch)

[TDF: cowl, $26.50]

DH-6 (SA: 222)

8"	–	R	FF	MOONEY	$1.00	
13"	–	R	FF	FOAM	$2.25	
13"	–	R	FF	MOONEY	$1.00	
18"	–	R	FF	FLY T FTMC9	$5.00	

*[$20.00]

18"	–	CO2	FF	FM CF427	$4.00	(Stroman)
18"	–	R/CO2	FF	VELIVOLI T9	$5.00	

DH-9

?	–	–	–	ARGUS MA174x	£3.00	
32"	–	R	FF	GULF	$5.00	(Midkiff)
32"	–	R	FF	COLE	$5.00	
35"	–	–	CL	POND 27A1	$4.25	(Fearnley)
49½"	–	1-1.5cc	FF	ARGUS 1243	£5.25	(Coates)
84"	–	.40/.60	RC	ARGUS RC1468	£10.00	(Fardell)

DH-10

49½"	–	.020	RC	FM CF402	$5.00	(Stroman)

DH-82 Tiger Moth (SA: 222, 255)

?	–	–	–	ARGUS MA26x	£3.00	
13"	–	R	FF	AIRBORNE	$3.00AUS	
13"	–	R	FF	CLEVE CD190	$10.00	

13"	–	R	FF	POND 44A7	$3.25	(Jones)
15"	–	R	FF	POND 16B5	$3.75	(Ott)
16"	–	R	FF	POND 16B6	$3.25	(Comet)
17"	–	R	FF	POND 16B6	$3.75	(Model A/C)
18"	–	R	FF	POND 53A4	$3.75	(Tern Aero)
18"	–	R	FF	POND 27B1	$3.75	(Veron)
*19"	–	R	FF	MODELAIR	$9.20NZ	
*20"	–	R	FF	EASY FF61	$8.00CDN	
20"	–	–	CL	GLEASON AT1150	NA	
20"	–	R	FF	SAMS 536	£1.75	(Aerographics)
*20"	15"	R	FF	SWALLOW	$8.95	
*20"	–	R	FF	VERON VO408	£3.49	
23"	–	R	FF	POND 27B5	$3.75	(Codding)
24"	–	.049	FF	AUTHENTIC	£1.35	(Towner)
26"	–	–	CL	POND 14D1	$4.75	(Buckland)
26"	–	R	FF	POND 52F1	$4.74	(Keil Kraft)
30"	–	R	FF	POND 41C2	$4.75	(Ott, Pond)
*33"	–	1cc	FF	KEIL MO210	£14.99	
¶33"	–	R	FF	POND 15C3	$5.75	(Mercury)
*33"	–	R/.020	CL	STERLING E13	$24.95	
37"	–	R	FF	PLANS	$7.00	(Andrus)
43"	–	.23	RC	FM245	$4.00	(Foster)
44"	–	1.1.5cc	FF	ARGUS FSP555	£5.25	(Aeromodeller)
44"	–	–	RC	ARGUS FSR197	£4.50	(Moore)
44"	–	–	FF	POND 50A7	$6.25	(Coasby)
*45"	–	.25/.60	4	GEE BEE	$67.25	
47½"	–	.20	4	ARGUS RM213	£6.00	(Whitehead)
*1190mm	938mm	.19-.35	3-4	OK APQX017	¥16,000	
47½"	–	.20-.25	4	RCM 793	$6.75	(Whitehead)
1270mm	–	.40	4	AIRBORNE	$22.00AUS	
*50"	–	.20-.35	3	VERON VO720	£57.95	
*51½"	–	.30/.60	4	UNIONVILLE	$99.95 CDN	
1350mm	–	.61	4	AIRBORNE	$25.00AUS	
*1448mm	1155mm	.40/.90	4	OK AP4X006	¥25,000	
*57"	–	.40/.60	4	FLAIR CAPRO2	NA	
57"	–	.40-.61	4	TRAP MW2102	£8.50	(CAP)
[canopy, £43.00; cowl, £46.50]						
1490mm	–	5cc	RC	DIMUZIO	L55.000	

*58"	-	/.40-.50	RC	DB	£47.80	
60"	-	.45-.61	RC	RCM 392	$6.75	(Prentice)
*60"	-	.40-.60	RC	SKYWAY	£39.50	
66"	-	10cc	RC	BRYANT 21	£7.50	
[cowl, £3.00]						
*66"	-	.40-.91	4	PREMIER	£89.95	
*70½"	-	/.60-.90	4	FLAIR CAPR 19	NA	
70½"	-	/.60-.90	4	TRAP MW2119	£8.00	(CAP)
[cowl, £9.50; canopy, £3.00]						
*1860mm	1530mm	10-20cc	4	CLARK MI:4,8	DM438,	
*88"	72"	Q35	4-5	NORTHCRAFT	$455.00CDN	
88"	-	Q35	4	SMART P3	£13.00	
[cowl, £12.75; wingtank, £8.75]						
*2235mm	1770mm	.60-.90	4	OK APBS003	¥52,000	
*2700mm	2190mm	Titan G38	4	CLARK	DM698,	

DH-94 Moth Minor

15"	-	R	FF	POND 16B5	$3.25	(Aer-o-Kits)
15"	-	R	FF	POND 46D7	$3.25	(Modelair)
36"	-	R	FF	POND 16B5	$5.25	(Day)
*1796mm	1175mm	.40-.45	4	OK AP4X007	¥24,000	
*82"	-	.60	RC	SKYWAY	£49.50	

DH-98 Mosquito (SA: 222)

20"	-	R	FF	POND 16C5	$3.25	(Model Craft)
24"	-	R	FF	POND 27A6	$3.25	(Norman)
25"	-	R	FF	POND 27A4	$4.25	(Easy Built)
26"	-	R	FF	POND 42F5	$6.75	(Guillow)
27½"	-	R	FF	CLEVE CD145	$18.00	
28"	-	.020x2	FF	AUTHENTIC	£1.75	(Towner)
37½"	-	R	FF	CLEVE CD145	$24.00	
38"	-	.15x2	CL	HORN MPS236	$4.00	(Palanek)
40"	-	4cc	CL	ARGUS CL570	£6.00	(Aeromodeller)
40½"	-	R	FF	HUNT 4802	$6.50	(Ott)
41"	-	-	RC	CLEVE CD145	$35.00	
52"	-	.19-.23x2	CL	HORN MPS233	$5.00	(Palanek)
54"	-	.10x2	4	MA 412	$8.25	(Baker)
*63"	-	/.25x2	4	FLAIR CAPR05	NA	
63"	-	.25x2	4	TRAP MW2105	£8.50	(CAP)
[canopy, £4.50; spinners, £3.00]						

66½"   –   .40x2   RC   RCM 744 $11.50   (Metlen)

71"   –   .25-.40x2 4-6   TAYLOR   £9.00
[cowls, £9.00; canopy, £2.50; spinners, £9.50; balsa pack, £30.25]
**[KLARICH: $125.00]

1800mm   –   4-5cc   RC   MRA BT14.520   162F   (Taylor)

*1870mm   1330mm   .40-.45x2 4-5   IKUTA   ¥48,000
*[assembled, ¥248,000]

75"   47"   .40x2   RC   PHOTO $19.95

76"   –   .40x2   RC   ARGUS RC1543   £8.75   (Major)

81"   –   –   RC   CLEVE CD145 $50.00

81"   –   /.40x2   6-7   TAYLOR   £13.50
[cowls, canopy, spinners, £42.00]
**[HOLMAN: $200.00]

*95"   72"   10-15cc   6-8   POWERMAX MS-1   £375.00

108"   –   –   RC   CLEVE CD145 $65.00

*128"   –   .90x2   6-8   KRAFTERS $425.00

*161"   –   ZG23x2   6-8   KRAFTERS $495.00

DH-100 Vampire (SA: 222)

1500mm   –   10ccF   RC   MODELL   DM28,80   (Fry)

36"   –   Elec   RC   POND 27C6 $5.75   (Aeromodeller

DH-103 Hornet (SA: 223)

28"   –   R   FF   KOUTNY $10.00

33½"   27½"   .15x2   CL   JVS $8.00

45"   –   .10x2   4   ARGUS RM275   £5.25   (Whitehead)

45"   –   .10x2   4   RCM 933 $6.00   (Whitehead)

DH-108   Swallow

?   –   –   –   ARGUS J479x   £2.50

20"   –   Jetex   FF   POND 58E7 $3.75   (Golding)

DH-110 Sea Vixen (SA: 223)

?   –   –   –   ARGUS MA231x   £3.75

*20"   –   Jetex   FF   EASY JX06 $11.00CDN

56"   –   .35   RC   FM CF33 $5.00   (Sheeks)

DH-112 Venom

16"   –   Jetex   FF   HUNT J123 $3.25   (Keil Kraft)

*18"   –   Jetex   FF   EASY JX05 $11.00CDN

ENGLISH ELECTRIC

Canberra

?	-	x2F	RC	CENTURY	FORTHCOMING	
57"	-	.21x2	RC	ARGUS RSQ1495	£10.00	(Boddington)

[nacelle, canopy, £11.00]

Lightning

21"	-	Glider	FF	WALLACE	$6.50	
37½"	37"	Glider	2	GREEN	£2.75	
*40"	-	Glider	2-3	FLAIR FL1028	£51.60	
46½"	50"	Glider	2	GREEN	FORTHCOMING	

P.1

14"	-	Jetex	FF	POND 27C1	$3.75	(Bassett)
14"	-	Jetex	FF	POND 16G1	$3.75	(Mansour)

FAIREY

Albacore

?	-	-	-	ARGUS RC1136x	£5.25	
25½"	-	.09-.15	CL	MORGAN 200UC	$3.95	$3.95
43"	-	R	FF	AUTHENTIC	£2.30	(Towner)
75"	-	10-15cc	5	TRAP MW2198	£8.50	(Saunders)

Barracuda (SA: 223, 255)

360mm	-	R	FF	AIRBORNE	$5.00AUS	
15"	-	R	FF	GLEASON	$.90	(Stahl)
15"	-	R	FF	POND 50C5	$4.25	(Whitman)
20"	-	R	FF	COLE	$5.00	
24½"	-	R	FF	CODDING	$.50	
26½"	-	.049	FF	AUTHENTIC	£1.35	(Towner)
830mm	-	R	FF	MRA A294	16F	
36"	-	R	FF	POND 42E3	$4.75	(Headley)

Battle

*14"	-	R	FF	PAI 292	$6.00	
15"	-	R	FF	POND 17B6	$3.25	(Aer-o-Kits)
16"	-	R	FF	HUNT 3881	$4.50	(Whitman)
20"	-	R	FF	POND 24D7	$3.75	(Cleveland)
24"	-	R	FF	GLEASON	$1.40	(Smith)
24"	-	R	FF	POND 50C4	$4.25	(Ledvina)
30"	-	R	FF	HUNT J6	$3.50	(Megow)

30"	–	R	FF	MB 1180CP	$5.00	(Megow)

*[SEAGLEN: $12.00]

33"	–	.049	FF	AUTHENTIC	£2.10	(Towner)
72"	–	.90	RC	B&D	$14.95	

Firefly (SA: 223)

?	–	-	–	ARGUS MA371x	£6.00	
15"	–	R	FF	HUNT MAC09	$2.50	(Model A/C)
50"	–	-	CL	POND 27E5	$6.75	(Swanston)
*61½"	–	.61	4	FLAIR CAPR18	NA	
61½"	–	.61	4	TRAP MW 2118	£8.00	(CAP)
77"	–	-	RC	HOLMAN	$25.00	

Flycatcher

29"	–	R	FF	POND 27D1	$5.75	(Perry)
30"	–	R	FF	POND 17B6	$3.75	(Fillon)
58"	–	.61	RC	ARGUS RM26	£8.75	(Taylor)

Fox

*20"	–	R	FF	EASY FF33	$8.00CDN	
61"	–	.60-.75	4	ARGUS RC1597	£7.50	(Rogers)

Fulmar

?	–	-	–	ARGUS MA363x	£3.00	
13"	–	R	FF	ALFERY	$5.00	
13"	–	R	FF	DIELS 19	$1.75	
22"	–	R	FF	HUNT 2214	$4.25	(Whitman)
23½"	–	R	FF	DIELS 48	$3.25	
24"	–	R	FF	POND 27E7	$3.75	(Jones)
30"	–	R	FF	POND 50C4	$4.75	(Hawkins)
31¼"	–	R	FF	GULF	$5.00	(Midkiff)
60"	–	.61	RC	RCM 771	$12.50	(Williams)

FD-2

39"	–	1ccF	FF	VINTAGE	£2.50

Gannet

¶19"	–	Jetex	FF	POND 28C2	$3.75	(Keil Kraft)
*20"	–	R	FF	KEIL KK0047	£3.99	
21½"	–	R	FF	FM CF622	$5.00	(Srull)

| 38" | – | 3.5 | CL | ARGUS CL631 | £3.75 | (Bodey) |
| 40" | – | – | CL | POND 44D2 | $5.25 | (Randle) |

Sea Fox

| 34" | – | 1-1.5cc | FF | AUTHENTIC | £2.10 | (Towner) |

Spearfish

13"	–	R	FF	DIELS 7	$2.00	
20"	–	R	FF	HUNT MAC10	$2.50	(Model A/C)
*22"	–	R	FF	VERON VO311	£3.49	

Swordfish

?	–	–	–	ARGUS FSP535x	£3.00	
?	–	–	–	ARGUS MA178x	£3.00	
*20"	–	R	FF	VERON VO421	£3.49	
31"	–	R	FF	POND 48B3	$4.75	(Moore)
34"	–	R	FF	FSI F-5	$6.00	
*60½"	–	.60/.60	4	FLAIR CAPR13	NA	
60½"	–	.60/.60	4	TRAP MW2113	£8.00	(Cap)
[cowl, £6.50]						

FOLLAND

Gnat

10"	–	Jetex	FF	POND 17F3	$3.75	(Sebel)
*48"	–	.40-.45F	4	KRICK 10120	DM349,50	
*52"	65"	.45-.60F	4-5	CARPENTER	£115.00	

Midge

| 11" | – | Jetex | FF | POND 27D5 | $3.25 | (Darnell) |

GENERAL AIRCRAFT

Cygnet

| 77¼" | – | .61 | 4 | TRAP MW2047 | £7.50 | (Burton) |

Hamilcar

| [44] | – | Glider | FF | MAN 118 | $8.75 | |
| 1320mm | – | Glider | FF | MRA 337 | 46F | |

Hotspur

590mm	–	Glider	FF	AIRBORNE	$5.00AUS	
24"	–	Glider	FF	POND 17G2	$3.25	(Wennerstrom)
46"	–	Glider	FF	ARGUS G144	£4.50	(Warring, Dean)

GLOSTER

Gamecock

30"	–	1cc	FF	AUTHENTIC	£1.50	(Towner)
36"	–	1.5-2.5cc	FF	ARGUS FSP410	£5.25	(Norman)
59"	–	.61	4	ARGUS RM145	£8.75	(Whitehead)
59"	–	.61	4	RCM 697	$10.50	(Whitehead)

Gauntlet

21"	–	R	FF	GLEASON	$2.65	(Reder)
21"	–	R	FF	POND 17G4	$4.25	(Comet)

Gladiator (SA: 223)

?	–	–	–	ARGUS MA322x	£5.25	
*15"	–	R	FF	EASY FF51	$5.00CDN	
17¼"	–	R	FF	CLEVE CD210	$14.00	
18"	–	CO2	FF	ARGUS 1452	£2.50	(Cole)
18½"	–	R	FF	GLEASON	$.80	(Towner)
19"	–	R	FF	POND 17G4	$3.75	(Finegold)
20½"	–	R	FF	HUNT MAC11	$2.50	(Model A/C)
21"	–	R	FF	GLEASON	$3.40	(Mills)
21"	–	R	FF	PROKIT	£3.00	(Mills)
22"	–	R	FF	YEST 6	$4.00	(Flying Aces)
23"	–	R	FF	CLEVE CD210	$17.00	
27"	–	R	FF	POND 17G7	$3.74	(Aeromodeller)
30"	–	R	FF	HUNT AH106E	$4.00	(Mills)
32"	–	.8-1cc	FF	ARGUS FSP719	£3.75	(McHard)
42½"	–	.25	4	ARGUS RM306	£7.50	(Royale)

[template, £2.80; canopy, £4.25]

48"	–	–	RC	CLEVE CD210	$30.00	
56"	–	.60-.91	4	TRAP MW2108	£9.00	(CAP)

[cowl, £9.50; canopy, £5.00; spinner, £3.00]

*56"	–	.61-.91	4	FLAIR CAPR08	NA	
56"	–	.60	4-5	TAYLOR	£7.00	

[cowl, £5.00; canopy, £2.50; spinner, £4.50; balsa pack, £24.00]

1420mm	–	10cc	RC	MRA BT20	138F	(Taylor
63"	–	–	RC	PHOTO	$24.95	(Pepino)
75"	–	–	RC	HOLMAN	$25.00	(Taylor)
79"	–	–	RC	PHOTO	$27.95	(Pepino)

[FGM: cowl, $28.00]

Goldfinch

| 23" | – | R | FF | COLE | $5.00 | |

Javelin

| 15" | – | Jetex | FF | POND 52G4 | $3.75 | (Keil Kraft) |

Meteor   (SA: 223)

?	–	–	–	ARGUS J293x	£2.50	
20"	–	Jetex	FF	POND 17G7	$3.75	(Keil Kraft)
20"	–	–	FF	POND 47G4	$4.75	(Crosswinds)
*25"	–	Bean Rock	FF	WILLAIRCO	$26.25	
*37"	–	Bean Rock	FF	WILLAIRCO	$38.40	
1080mm	–	R	FF	MRA 349	40F	
*55"	–	Bean Rock	FF	WILLAIRCO	$69.75	
56"	67"	2xF	RC	PHOTO	$19.95	
58½"	–	.40x2	CL	GLEASON	$13.90	(Nelson)
84"	100½"	2xF	RC	PHOTO	$29.95	

HANDLEY-PAGE

0/400

17"	–	R	FF	POND 18B2	$3.75	(Struck)
20"	–	R	FF	POND 18B2	$3.25	(U.S. Model)
25"	–	R	FF	COLE	$5.00	
30¼"	–	R	FF	GLEASON	$3.25	(Struck)
37½"	–	R	FF	CLEVE CD275	$35.00	
50"	–	R	FF	CLEVE CD275	$45.00	
66"	–	.049x2	RC	MB 3812	$9.00	(Dennis)
66"	–	.75x2	RC	SAMS 727	£4.80	(Dennis)
75"	–	–	RC	CLEVE CD275	$56.00	
100"	–	–	RC	CLEVE CD275	$65.00	

Halifax   (SA: 223)

34"	–	R	FF	AUTHENTIC	£1.60	(Towner)
38"	–	R	FF	POND 50F5	$5.25	(Jones)
49½"	–	–	RC	ARGUS FSP140	£3.75	(Jones)
54"	–	1.5-2.5cc	CL	ARGUS CL919	£6.00	(Bodey)

Hampden

| 27" | – | R | FF | AUTHENTIC | £1.45 | (Towner) |
| 31½" | – | CO2 | FF | SAMS 1089 | £3.50 | (Newman) |

[24 piece molded fitting set, £29.95]

Harrow

*60½"	–	.25x2	4	FLAIR CAPR24	NA	
60½"	–	.25x2	4	TRAP MW2124	£8.50	(CAP)

[canopy, £4.00; cowl, £3.50]

Heyford

25"	–	CO2	FF	POND 44D7	$4.75	(Coldrick)
38"	–	.020x2	FF	AUTHENTIC	£2.30	(Towner)

HAWKER

Demon

?	–	–	–	ARGUS MA42x	£3.75	
28"	–	R	FF	SHOP	£5.00	(Keelbild)
46½"	–	.20	4	ARGUS RM182	£6.00	(Whitehead)
46½"	–	.19-.30	4	RCM 757	$6.25	(Whitehead)

Fury (SA: 223)

?	–	–	–	ARGUS MA40x	£2.50	
11¼"	–	R	FF	CLEVE CD20A	$8.00	
12"	–	R	FF	POND 18B4	$3.25	(National)
15"	–	R	FF	CLEVE CD20A	$10.00	
15"	–	R	FF	SHOP	£1.50	(Keelbild)
15"	–	R	FF	POND 47D1	$3.75	(Aermodeller)
15"	–	R	FF	POND 18B4	$3.25	(Aer-o-Kits)
16"	–	R	FF	POND 52G1	$3.25	(Burd)
17"	–	R	FF	POND 48B3	$3.75	(Veron)
18"	–	R	FF	POND 38E1	$3.75	(Enterprise)
19"	–	R	FF	GLEASON	$2.75	(Chevedden)
19"	–	R	FF	POND 50F6	$3.75	(Comet)
20"	–	R	FF	ARGUS CL745	£2.50	(Hall)
*20"	–	R	FF	VERON VO426	£3.49	
22½"	–	R	FF	CLEVE CD20A	$14.00	
22½"	–	R	FF	SHOP	£3.50	(Keelbild)
24"	–	R	FF	GLEASON	$3.50	(Chevedden)
24"	–	R	FF	HUNT AH177	$3.25	(Ferris)
24"	–	R	FF	POND 38G5	$4.75	(Mates)
27"	–	R	FF	BUCKLE	£3.75	(Chevedden)
29"	–	R	FF	POND 31B2	$3.75	(Aeromodels)
30"	–	R	FF	POND 28B1	$4.75	(Jones)

45"	–	–	RC	CLEVE CD20A	$30.00	
60"	–	10cc	RC	BRYANT 14	£6.00	
[cowl, £5.00]						
60"	–	–	RC	POND 41C6	$8.75	(Elite)
84"	–	Q35	RC	MB 11831	$21.50	(Prentice)

Fury II

11½"	–	R	FF	CLEVE CD20B	$9.00	
12"	–	R	FF	POND 18B5	$3.25	(Rainey)
12"	–	R	FF	POND 18B5	$3.25	(Dallaire)
13"	–	R	FF	FILLON	16F 80	
15"	–	R	FF	CLEVE CD20B	$11.00	
16"	–	R	FF	POND 18B4	$3.25	(Rainey)
18¼"	–	R	FF	GLEASON	$2.25	(Lindberg)
19"	–	R	FF	HUNT PL129	$3.25	(Lindberg)
20"	–	R	FF	PLANS	$6.00	(Andrus)
22"	–	R	FF	POND 37C4	$3.75	(Great Lakes)
22½"	–	R	FF	CLEVE CD20B	$15.00	
25"	–	R	FF	HUNT K020	$3.50	(Berkeley)
45"	–	R	FF	CLEVE CD20B	$32.00	

Hart (SA: 223)

26"	–	R	FF	POND 49A2	$4.65	(Trundel)
40"	–	3.5-6cc	CL	ARGUS MA374	£4.50	(Hall)

Henley

28"	–	R	FF	HUNT 2941	$5.50	(Whitman)

Hind

14"	–	R	FF	CLEVE CD507	$12.00	
14"	–	R	FF	OLD 448	$2.50	(Peerless)
¶17"	–	R	FF	YEST 49	$4.00	(Peerless)
18½"	–	R	FF	CLEVE CD507	$16.00	
18½"	–	R	FF	CLEVE P1751	$15.00	
27½"	–	R	FF	CLEVE CD507	$20.00	
27½"	–	R	FF	CLEVE P1751	$20.00	
25"	–	R	FF	POND 18B6	$3.75	(Marsh)
37"	–	R	FF	POND 50F7	$6.75	(Marsh)
38"	–	.8cc	FF	ARGUS FSP476	£5.25	(Marsh)
55"	–	–	RC	CLEVE CD507	$35.00	

Hunter

8"	–	–	FF	POND 58F5	$3.25	(Model Builder)
10"	–	Jetex	FF	POND 16G1	$3.75	(Sebel)
*13½"	–	Jetex	FF	KEIL KK0060	£3.99	
18"	–	–	FF	POND 58F5	$3.75	(Model Builder)
20"	–	Jetex	FF	HUNT J159	$3.50	
*22½"	–	Bean Rock	FF	WILLAIRCO	$26.25	
*33½"	–	Bean Rock	FF	WILLAIRCO	$38.40	
36"	–	–	FF	POND 58F5	$5.75	(Model Builder)
*970mm	1190mm	Glider	2-3	FLAIR FL1027	£42.75	
*50½"	–	Bean Rock	FF	WILLAIRCO	$69.75	
1460mm	–	10cc	RC	MODELL	DM15,	(Meier)
1460mm	–	10cc	RC	MRA 640	112F	
68"	–	.60	RC	HORN S-38	$8.00	
*2000mm	–	10-15cc	RC	COOP 9390268	2200F	

Hurricane (SA: 223, 255)

?	–	–	–	ARGUS MA166x	£3.00	
?	–	–	–	ARGUS MA207x	£3.75	
[61]	–	Elec	3-4	MA 415	$11.75	(Crowe)
?	–	.30-.40	CL	MB 10881	$17.00	(Felton)
10"	–	R	FF	POND 52G4	$3.25	(Hi-Flier)
*12"	–	R	FF	EASY FF42	$4.00CDN	
13"	–	R	FF	AIRBORNE	$3.00AUS	
13"	–	R	FF	FOAM	$2.25	
13"	–	R	FF	OLD 435	$2.00	(Megow)
13"	–	R	FF	POND 41F7	$3.25	(James)
13"	–	R	FF	SAMS 600	£1.65	(Aerographics)
*16"	–	R	FF	FIKE	$7.95	(Comet)
16"	–	R	FF	CODDING	$.35	(Hi Flier)
16"	–	R	FF	HUNT MAC12	$2.50	(Model A/C)
*16½"	–	R	FF	GUILLOW 506	$5.00	
*17½"	–	R	FF	KEIL KK0023	£4.99	
18"	–	R	FF	HUNT 3871	$.50	(Whitman)
18"	–	R	FF	POND 37B7	$3.25	(Ideal)
*19½"	–	R	FF	KEIL KK0041	£3.99	
20"	–	R	FF	ALFERY	$5.00	
20"	–	CO2	FF	STAN	£3.20	

*20"	–	R	FF	EASY FF19	$6.00CDN	
20"	–	R	FF	POND 29A3	$4.75	(Guillow)
20"	–	R	FF	POND 18B6	$3.25	(Peerless)
20"	–	R	FF	POND 28B1	$3.25	(Easy Built)
20"	–	R	FF	POND 24F6	$3.75	(Cleveland)
20"	–	R	FF	SHOP	£2.00	(Keelbild)
21"	–	R	FF	POND 18B6	£3.75	(Modelcraft)
*21"	–	R	FF	VERON VO410	£3.49	
560mm	–	R	FF	AIRBORNE	$5.00AUS	
¶22"	–	R	FF	HUNT 2204	$4.25	(Ott)
23"	–	R	FF	HUNT C23	$3.25	(Megow)
25"	–	R	FF	KOUTNY	$5.00	
26"	–	R	FF	GLEASON	$1.80	(Stahl)
26"	–	R	FF	HUNT WW03	$3.25	(Winter)
27"	–	R	FF	GLEASON	$2.70	(Lindberg)
28"	–	R	FF	POND 28A4	$3.75	(Winter)
30"	–	R	FF	CLEVE CD78	$18.00	
30"	–	–	CL	GLEASON AT953	$3.05	(Musciano)
30"	–	R	FF	POND 28C3	$4.75	(Fearnley)
30"	–	R	FF	POND 42G7	$4.75	(Practical)
¶30"	–	R	FF	POND 28C5	$4.75	(Berkeley)
33"	–	R	FF	MB 1277OT	$5.00	(Stahl)
*36"	–	R	FF	EASY FF79	$12.00CDN	
36"	–	R	FF	CLEVE T78	$12.00	
36"	–	R	FF	HUNT ES19E	$3.50	(Stahl)
37"	–	–	CL	GLEASON AM64	NA	(Musciano)
40"	–	.8-1.5cc	FF	ARGUS FSP862	£6.00	(Meixell)
40"	–	–	RC	POND 28B6	$5.25	(Mansfield)
41"	–	–	RC	PALADINE 57	$11.00	
50"	–	.09-.15	2	ARGUS RM102	£5.25	(Cole)
*50"	–	.35-.40	4	BOWMAN	£49.95	
*50"	–	R	FF	EASY FF57	$28.00CDN	
*51"	37"	.19-.35	4-5	OK APQX021	NA	
43"	–	R	FF	OLD D55	$5.00	(Stahl)
53¼"	–	.45	4	MARTIN MW108	£8.00	

[canopy, £2.70; template, £10.50]

56"	–	–	CL	GLEASON	$9.95	(Warden)
*60"	–	.60	RC	WILLAIRCO	$60.00	(Berkeley)

*60"   -   .61   4   FLAIR CAPR14   NA

60"   -   .61   4   TRAP MW2114   £8.00   (CAP)
[cowl, £6.10; spinner, £3.00; canopy, £3.50]

61"   -   .61   RC   FM CF400 $10.00   (Eck)

61"   -   -   RC   PALADINE 57 $18.00

62"   49"   .61-.90   5   AERODROME $22.95
[plan pack, $62.00; retracts, $71.00]
*[$225.00]

*63"   44½"   -   RC   SAIL   NA

*1620mm   1215mm   .60/1.20   4-6   IKUTA   ¥39,000

65"   -   .60   4   TAYLOR   £7.00
[cowl, £3.00; canopy, £2.00; spinner, £5.00; balsa pack, £29.00]

68"   -   .61   4   ARGUS RM87   £8.75   (Taylor)
[cowl, £6.75; canopy, £5.25]

70"   -   .60   RC   RCM 141 $9.75   (Dwight)

70"   -   .60/.80   6   TAYLOR   £9.00
[cowl, £7.00; canopy, £2.50; spinner, £5.00; wheels, £3.50;
 balsa pack, £29.00][UNITRACTS: retracts, £22.25]

1780mm   -   10cc   RC   MRA BT23   150F   (Taylor)

1850mm   -   10cc   RC   MRA 771   119F

80"   -   -   RC   HOLMAN $19.95   (Taylor)
[canopy, $6.00; spinner, $15.00]

*80"   62"   .90-1.08   6   INNOVATIVE $249.00

*80"   -   .60-.90   RC   REEVES 2040RK   £129.95

90"   72"   ST200   RC   PHOTO $29.95   (Pepino)

92"   74"   Q35   4-5   VAILLY $27.00
[cowl, $28.00; canopy, $12.50; scoop, $14.50; spinner, $29.00]

*120"   95¼"   100cc   6-8   AIRSCREW $3200CDN

Sea Fury (SA: 224, 255)

33½"   -   .60   RC   MAN 253 $8.00

48"   -   .40   4   TRAP 2136   £7.50   (Smit)

51"   -   .45-.60   RC   HOLMAN $6.95   (Williams)

56"   -   10cc   4   ARGUS RC1204   £8.75   (Dodwell)

*70"   62"   .90-1.08   6   JM $375.00AUS
[retracts, $295.00AUS]

**77"   69½"   ST2500   7-9   TOMEO $78.00
*[$275.00]

86"   70"   2.5-3.7   6   SMITH $42.00

*86"   74"   .30-.69   6-8   JM $1100.00AUS
[retracts, $385.00AUS]

*86"	-	2-3.7	5	RC		$239.00	
90"	81"	3.4-4.2	4-6	VAILLY		$32.00	

[cowl, $30.00; canopy, $16.00; spinner, $36.00][LIKES: retracts, $300]
**[HANGAR: $175.00]

Tempest (SA: 224, 256)

*14"	-	R		FF	MODELAIR	$7.70NZ	
15"	-	-		CL	POND 18C1	$3.75	(Milford)
21"	-	R		FF	POND 41B6	$3.25	(Brown)
25¾"	-	R		FF	KOUTNY	$5.00	
25¾"	-	R		FF	WOODHOUSE	£3.00	(Koutny)
26"	-	R		FF	POND 38A6	$4.75	(Veri-Tru)
31"	-	-		CL	POND 42F4	$4.75	(Pridmore)
41"	-	-		CL	POND 50F7	$4.75	(Modern Hobbycraft)
41"	-	-		CL	POND 38A6	$4.75	(Musciano)
61½"	-	.61		RC	RCM 351	$6.75	(McTaggart)
61½"	-	.60	4		TAYLOR	£6.00	

[cowl, £5.00; canopy, £3.00; spinner, £5.50; balsa pack, £29.00]

1560mm	-	10cc		RC	MRA BT17	119F	(Taylor)
75"	-	.90	4-5		HOLMAN	$19.95	(Taylor)

[cowl, $25.00; canopy, $6.00; spinner, $25.00]

75½"	-	1.2	6		ARGUS RM308	£13.50	(Keeley)

[cowl, £18.50; spinner,£46.00][UNITRACTS: retracts, £36.80]

1950mm	-	15-20cc		RC	MRA 697	132F	
*80"	67"	ST2500	7-9		TOMEO	$275.00	
88"	63½"	2.4-3.7	5-6		GARMHAUSEN	$27.50	

[FGM: cowl, $31.00]

Tomtit

*52"	-	.23-.40	3		VERON VO708	£79.99	

Typhoon (SA: 224, 256)

?	-	.29-.40		CL	FM CF226	$7.00	(Palanek)
12"	-	R		FF	COLE	$5.00	
12"	-	R		FF	POND 55C5	$3.75	(Coleman)
15¾"	-	R		FF	CLEVE CD99A	$10.00	
*18"	-	R		FF	GUILLOW 906	$4.29	
21"	-	R		FF	CLEVE CD99A	$14.00	
21"	-	R		FF	DIELS 32	$3.00	
25"	-	R		FF	GLEASON	$2.95	(Boys)
*28"	-	R		FF	EASY FF67	$10.00CDN	

28"	–	R	FF	GLEASON	$2.95	(Towner)
28"	–	.09	FF	AUTHENTIC	£1.35	(Towner)
30"	–	R	FF	HUNT 503	$5.50	(Ott)
31"	–	–	CL	PROKIT	£3.20	(Delgatto)
31¼"	–	–	CL	GLEASON	$3.65	(Musciano)
32"	–	R	FF	CLEVE CD99A	$18.00	
32"	–	R	FF	POND 28A2	$4.75	(Arca)
36"	–	R	FF	CLEVE T99	$12.00	
1010mm	–	–	RC	MRA 378	40F	
42"	–	–	CL	POND 50F7	$5.25	(Modern Hobbycraft)
45"	–	–	CL	POND 44E4	$6.75	(Salisbury)
62"	–	10cc	RC	BRYANT 12	£6.00	

[cowl, £6.00; canopy, £3.50][UNITRACTS: retracts, £35.88]

HAWKER-SIDDELEY

Buccaneer

| 15" | – | Jetex | FF | HUNT J160 | $3.00 | |

HUNTING

Provost

| 17½" | – | .5-.8cc | CL | ARGUS CL720 | £2.50 | (Hall) |

MARTIN-BAKER

MB-2

| 21" | – | – | CL | POND 19D1 | $4.75 | (Revel) |
| 23" | – | – | CL | POND 29C6 | ^3.75 | (Arnould) |

MB-3

| 540mm | – | 1.5-2.5cc | CL | MRA A349 | 16F | |

MB-5 (SA: 224)

| 55" | – | .60 | RC | HOLMAN | $14.95 | (Parson) |

[canopy, $8.00]

| 1440mm | – | 6.5-10cc | RC | MRA 347 | 100F | |

MARTINSYDE

F.4 Buzzard

| ? | – | – | – | ARGUS 327x | £3.00 | |
| 20" | – | R | FF | KOUTNY | $5.00 | |

33"	–	R	FF	PALADINE 77	$11.00	
48"	–	–	RC	POND 29B5	$5.75	(RC Technique)
66"	–	–	RC	PALADINE 77	$18.00	
72"	–	.60	RC	B&D	$14.95	

G100 Elephant

20"	–	R	FF	KOUTNY	$5.00	
22"	–	R	FF	HUNT AH129	$3.00	(Stott)
24"	–	R	FF	KOUTNY	$5.00	
38"	–	R	FF	PALADINE 23	$11.00	
72"	–	.60	RC	B&D	$14.95	
76"	–	–	RC	PALADINE 23	$32.00	

S.1

27½"	–	R	FF	PALADINE 25	$8.00
55"	–	–	RC	PALADINE 25	$14.00

MILES

M. 14 Magister (SA: 225)

*12"	–	R	FF	PECK PP002	$8.95	
15"	–	R	FF	POND 62B4	$5.25	(Matsuo)
18"	–	R	FF	SHOP	£2.00	(Keelbild)
21"	–	R	FF	GLEASON	$1.80	(Stahl)
28"	–	R	FF	HUNT ES35	$3.00	(Stahl)
700mm	–	R	FF	AIRBORNE	$5.00AUS	
*28"	–	R	FF	PROKIT	£23.50	
34"	–	R	FF	POND 29D6	$3.75	(Denny)
54"	–	R	FF	OLD DS11	$5.00	(Stahl)
55"	–	.40/.40	4-5	HUTSON 11	£7.00	

[cowl, £9.50; canopy, £4.85; wheel pants, £10.75; balsa pack, £19.20]

68"	–	10cc	RC	BRYANT 7	£6.00	

[cowl, £2.50]

67½"	51½"	.45-.60	RC	PHOTO	$19.95	(Pepino)
68"	–	.60	RC	RCM 219	$11.75	(Platt)
77"	68"	.90-1.20	RC	PHOTO	$24.95	(Pepino)
*83"	–	.60-.90	4	BOWMAN	£95.99	
96"	85½"	Q35	RC	PHOTO	$27.95	(Pepino)
2570mm	–	–	RC	MODULO	L40.000	
2600mm	1950mm	30-50cc	4	VTH MT869-G	DM39,	(Boersch)

M.19 Master

15"	–	R	FF	POND 19E1	$3.25	(Aer-o-Kits)
16"	–	R	FF	HUNT 3895	$4.50	(Whitman)
20"	–	R	FF	POND 29C1	$3.75	(Jones)
580mm	–	R	FF	AIRBORNE	$5.00AUS	
23"	–	R	FF	HUNT SR513	$3.00	(Struhl)

M.20

13¼"	–	R	FF	SAMS 877	£1.75	(Frugoli)
26"	–	–	CL	POND 29C4	$4.75	(Smith)

M.38 Messenger

36"	–	R	FF	POND 19E2	$5.75	(Pridmore)

NIEUPORT

Nighthawk

21"	–	CO2	FF	ARGUS FSP1447	£3.00	(Palfrey)
28"	–	R	FF	PALADINE 60	$8.00	
56"	–	–	RC	PALADINE 60	$18.00	
84"	–	–	RC	PALADINE 60	$32.00	

PERCIVAL

Jet Provost

*52"	–	.35/.48	4	GAL/NOR	£39.95

Provost

*19"	–	R	FF	KEIL KK0048S	£3.99	
** 54"	–	.30/.46	3-5	CHILTERN	£29.00	
[canopy, £3.00]						
60"	–	.61	4-5	ARGUS RM38	£7.50	(Yates)

ROYAL AIRCRAFT FACTORY

BE-2c (SA: 225)

?	–	–	–	ARGUS FSR215x	£3.00	
14½"	–	R	FF	CLEVE CD209	$9.00	
19½"	–	R	FF	CLEVE CD209	$12.00	
26½"	–	R	FF	FLY T	$5.00	
*[$20.00]						
29"	–	R	FF	CLEVE CD209	$16.00	
35"	–	R	FF	POND 23G7	$4.75	(Le Model Reduit)

41"	–	.8-1cc	FF	ARGUS FSP721	£5.25	(McDonough)
41"	–	.75-1cc	FF	SAMS 729	£3.00	(Dennis)
52"	–	–	FF	POND 49D1	$6.91	(Codding)
58"	–	–	RC	CLEVE CD209	$28.00	
*2020mm	1590mm	10cc	4	CLARK M1;5	DM418,	
80"	–	.40-.60	5	RCM 467	$16.75	(Scott)
84"	–	10-15cc	RC	BRYANT	£10.00	

BE-12b

45"	–	1.-1.5cc	FF	ARGUS FSP1183	£5.25	(Coates)
47"	–	–	RC	PALADINE 45	$14.00	
70½"	–	–	RC	PALADINE 45	$18.00	

FE-8

31½"	–	R	FF	PALADINE 14	$8.00	
39"	–	.8-1cc	FF	ARGUS FSP495	£4.50	(King)
63"	–	–	RC	PALADINE 14	$18.00	
90"	–	–	RC	PALADINE 14	$32.00	

RE-8 (SA: 225)

32"	–	R	FF	CLEVE CD166	$18.00	
42½"	–	–	CL	GLEASON	$7.10	(Beatty)
43"	–	.8-1cc	FF	ARGUS FSP418	£3.75	(Hughes)
96"	–	–	RC	HOLMAN	$35.00	

SE-2a

27½"	–	R	FF	PALADINE 5	$8.00	
55"	–	–	RC	PALADINE 5	$14.00	

SE-5a (SA: 225, 257)

?	–	–	–	ARGUS FSR274K	£3.00	
?	–	–	–	ARGUS MA18x	£3.75	
?	–	–	–	ARGUS MA261x	£3.00	
[37]	–	.15	CL	MAN 222	$8.50	(Lanzo)
8"	–	R	FF	AERO ERA	$.65	
8"	–	R	FF	MOONEY	$1.00	
10½"	–	R	FF	CLEVE CD9C	$8.00	
12"	–	R	FF	POND 30E1	$3.25	(National)
12"	–	R	FF	POND 51G2	$3.25	(Megow)

12"	–	R	FF	POND 21B2	$3.25	(Comet)
12"	–	R	FF	POND 21B2	$3.25	(Universal)
13"	–	R	FF	AERO ERA	$1.25	
13"	–	R	FF	FOAM	$2.25	
13"	–	R	FF	DATA	$1.60	(McCombs)
13"	–	R	FF	HANNAN	$3.00	(Alvarez)
13"	–	R	FF	MOONEY	$1.00	
13"	–	R	FF	OLD 419	$2.50	(Dallaire)
13"	–	R	FF	POND 37G5	$3.25	(Moore)
*13"	–	R	FF	STERLING P-1	$7.95+	
13¼"	–	R	FF	HOLMAN	$2.50	
13¼"	–	R	FF	HUNT PE044	$2.50	(Peerless)
13½"	–	R	FF	CLEVE CD9C	$10.00	
13½"	–	R	FF	OLD 78	$3.00	(Diel)
14"	–	R	FF	CLEVE P752	$8.00	
14"	–	R	FF	POND 30E7	$3.25	(Cartercraft)
14"	–	R	FF	POND 21B2	$3.25	(Sturdi-Built)
15"	–	R	FF	POND 46C1	$3.25	(Keil Kraft)
15"	–	R	FF	POND 51G2	$3.75	(Modelcraft)
15"	–	R	FF	POND 46F6	$3.25	(Model Aviati
15"	–	R	FF	POND 30E4	$3.25	(Fly-A-Way)
15"	–	R	FF	POND 51G1	$3.25	(Ott)
*16"	–	R	FF	KEIL KK0036	£3.99	
16"	–	R	FF	POND 30E3	$3.75	(McEntee)
16"	–	R	FF	POND 21B1	$3.25	(Wherry)
*16"	–	R	FF	PROKIT	£20.00	
*16"	14"	R	FF	SWALLOW	$8.95	
17"	–	R	FF	POND 51G2	$3.75	(Booth)
17"	–	R	FF	POND 21B3	$3.75	(Supreme)
*18"	–	R	FF	EASY FF63	$16.00 CDN	
18"	–	R	FF	POND 28E6	$4.75	(Guillow)
18"	–	R	FF	POND 21B3	$3.25	(Megow)
*20"	–	R	FF	RN CG504	$19.95+	
20"	–	R	FF	YEST 50	$4.50	(Tomasco)
20"	–	R	FF	ALFERY	$5.00	
20"	–	R	FF	CLEVE CD9C	$14.00	
20"	–	CO2	FF	BLAIR	$5.00	

20"	–	R	FF	FSI S-6	$6.00	
20"	–	R	FF	POND 21B4	$3.25	(California)
¶ 20"	–	R	FF	POND 51G4	$4.75	(Scalemaster)
20"	–	R	FF	POND 21B3	$3.25	(Guillow)
20"	–	R	FF	POND 51G3	$4.25	(Ott)
21"	–	R	FF	POND 21B4	$3.75	(Western)
*22"	–	R	FF	STERLING A-17	$11.95	
22"	–	R	FF	POND 51G4	$5.75	(Whitman)
22"	–	R	FF	HUNT 2154	$4.25	(Ott)
23"	–	R	FF	POND 21B3	$4.25	(Megow)
*24"	–	R/.020	FF	GUILLOW 202	$12.50	
24"	–	R	FF	POND 30G6	$3.75	(Lambert)
24"	–	R	FF	POND 28D3	$4.75	(Hearn)
*26"	20¼"	R	FF	MODELHOB 110124	NA	
26"	–	–	CL	POND 46B6	$5.75	(Blake)
*26¼"	–	R	FF	COMET 2601	$15.50	
26½"	–	R	FF	HOLMAN	$2.50	
26½"	–	R	FF	LAMBERT	$5.00	
26½"	–	R	FF	NFFS	$3.50	(Koopman)
27"	–	R	FF	PALADINE 18	$8.00	
27"	–	–	CL	POND 51G3	$4.75	(Palanek)
28"	–	–	CL	GLEASON AT160	NA	(McCudden)
28"	–	R	FF	POND 51G3	$4.75	(Spittle)
28"	–	–	CL	POND 51F7	$6.25	(Musciano)
28½"	–	.5-.8	FF	ARGUS FSP682	£3.75	(McHard)
29"	–	R	FF	POND 30E7	$3.75	(Jones)
30"	–	R	FF	POND 30F3	$3.75	(Megow)
30"	–	–	CL	POND 38G2	$5.75	(Ealy)
30"	–	R	FF	POND 46C1	$4.75	(Ott, Pond)
30"	–	R	FF	POND 51G1	$5.75	(Phipps)
32"	–	–	CL	POND 46E5	$5.75	(Casburn)
*32"	–	.19-.35	CL	STERLING C-6	$34.95	
32"	–	.09	3	ARGUS RC1415	£3.75	(Boddington)
39"	–	R	FF	POND 21B1	$6.25	(Deitchmann)
40"	–	R	FF	HOLMAN	$4.00	
40"	–	–	RC	CLEVE CD9C	$28.00	

40"	–	–	RC	POND 35F5	$5.25	(Miniature A
40"	–	–	RC	POND 30F6	$5.75	(Garry)
46"	–	–	RC	POND 21B1	$5.75	(Lanzo)
*47"	–	.25	4	FLAIR CAPR22	NA	
47"	–	.30	4	TRAP MW2122	£6.50	(CAP)
48"	–	/.35	4	ARGUS RM263	£6.00	(Healey)
48"	–	–	RC	POND 21C7	$5.75	(Kronfelt)
50"	–	/.60	4	MAN 3852	$13.00	(Uravitch)
*50"	–	R	FF	EASY FF59	$30.00CDN	
*51"	–	.35/.60	4	FLAIR FL1032	£48.12	
52½"	–	.61	RC	FM CF104	$8.00	(Ziroli)
53"	–	10cc	RC	BRYANT 3	£6.00	
53"	–	–	RC	HOLMAN	$6.95	
1370mm	–	.61	4	AIRBORNE	$25.00AUS	
54"	–	–	RC	PALADINE 18	$14.00	
*56"	–	/.60	RC	DB	£47.80	
72"	–	.90	RC	B&D	$14.95	
*73"	–	.90/.120	4	HUTSON	£199.00	
79½"	62"	Q40	4	SCHWEISS	$25.00	
*80"	–	ST2000	RC	DB	£89.50	
80"	–	.90-1.20	RC	BRYANT 23	£18.00	
80¼"	–	1.9-2.4	3-5	WE RCQS7	$24.95	
81"	–	–	RC	PALADINE 18	$32.00	

SAUNDERS-ROE

A-1
22"	–	Jetex	FF	HUNT J201	$4.00	(Wilmont)

SCOTTISH AVIATION

Bulldog
**54"	–	.25/.60	3-5	CHILTERN	£30.00	

[cowl, £3.50; canopy, £3.20]

65"	–	.49-.61	RC	ARGUS RC1241	£7.50	(Evans)

[cowl, canopy, £17.50]

SHORT

Seamew (SA: 225)
?	–	–	–	ARGUS MA218x	£3.00	
*20"	–	R	FF	VERON VO406	£3.49	
36"	–	R	FF	POND 30E1	$4.75	(Fearnley)
46"	–	–	RC	POND 42G2	$5.75	(Cole)

Stirling

37"	–	R	FF	AUTHENTIC	£2.10	(Towner)
74"	–	–	RC	MA 613	$20.50	(Baker)

SOPWITH

Baby (SA: 225)

13"	–	R	FF	COLE	$5.00	
19½"	–	R	FF	CLEVE CD138	$16.00	
*24"	–	R	FF	SIERRA	$13.95	
64"	–	.81	4	ARGUS RM174	£8.75	(Downham)

Camel (SA: 225, 256)

10½"	–	R	FF	CLEVE CD10B	$8.00	
12"	–	R	FF	POND 47D3	$4.25	(Ideal)
*12"	–	R	FF	FIKE	$6.95	(Megow)
14"	–	R	FF	POND 21C5	$3.25	(Model A/C)
14"	–	R	FF	POND 21C5	$3.25	(Cartercraft)
14"	–	R	FF	POND 37G5	$3.25	(Davies A/C)
14¼"	–	R	FF	OLD 79	$3.00	(Diel)
15"	–	R	FF	POND 46C4	$3.25	(Ott)
*16"	–	R	FF	KEIL KK0038	£3.99	
18"	–	R	FF	POND 30F2	$3.25	(Veron)
18"	–	R	FF	POND 28F2	$4.75	(Guillow)
*19"	12½"	R	FF	SWALLOW	$8.95	
20"	–	R	FF	ALFERY	$5.00	
20"	–	R	FF	HUNT AH152	$3.00	(Wherry)
20"	–	R	FF	HUNT PL145	$3.25	(Lindberg)
20"	–	R	FF	POND 21C5	$3.75	(Peerless)
*20"	–	R	FF	VERON VO419	£3.49	
21"	–	R	FF	CLEVE P1752	$14.00	
21"	–	R	FF	CLEVE CD10B	$14.00	
22"	–	R	FF	POND 21C5	$3.75	(Wherry)
24"	–	R	FF	PLANS	$7.00	(Andrus)
*24"	–	R	FF	STERLING A-26	$15.95	
27"	–	–	CL	POND 21C6	$4.75	(Modern Hobbycraft)
27"	–	–	CL	POND 36E2	$4.75	(Musciano)
28"	–	.5-.8cc	FF	ARGUS FSP1143	£2.50	(Collins)
28"	18½"	.049	FF	MAN 8761	$8.00	(Mathews)

*28"	–	.09	CL	GUILLOW 801	$21.00	
28"	–	R	FF	PALADINE 2	$8.00	
29"	–	R	FF	POND 30E7	$4.75	(Collin)
29"	–	R	FF	POND 21C6	$3.75	(Jones)
30"	–	R	FF	HUNT PE046	$4.00	(Peerless)
*32"	–	R	FF	COMET 3647	$19.50	
820mm	–	R	FF	MRA A324	16F	
41"	–	–	RC	CLEVE CD10B	$28.00	
42"	–	–	FF	ARGUS FSP441	$4.50	(Saunders)
42"	–	–	FF	POND 30G4	$5.25	(Norman)
48"	36"	.40-.50	4	AEROTEK	$19.95	
1200mm	815mm	6.5	4	VTH MT894-G	DM19,50	(Brockmann)
56"	–	8-10cc	4	ARGUS RC1099	£7.50	(Meier)
56"	–	.60	RC	HORN S-35	$10.00	
56"	–	–	RC	PALADINE 2	$18.00	
56"	–	.61	4	TRAP MW2036	£8.00	(Hodson)
1440mm	–	10cc	RC	MODELL	DM24,80	(Meier)
66½"	–	/.90	4	TRAP MW2042	£8.50	(Tattam)
72"	–	.60	RC	B&D	$14.95	
84"	–	–	RC	PALADINE 2	$32.00	
84"	–	15-30cc	RC	REEVES	£20.00	
84"	–	.78-2.2	3-5	WE RCQS-11	$24.95	
[FGM: cowl, $19.00]						
112"	–	40-100cc	RC	REEVES	£25.00	

Dolphin

9"	–	R	FF	POND 53G6	$3.25	(Wherry)
12¼"	–	R	FF	CLEVE CD173	$10.00	
16¼"	–	R	FF	CLEVE CD173	$13.00	
24"	–	R	FF	MA 335	$1.75	(Noonan)
24"	–	R	FF	POND 21D1	$3.75	(Smith)
*24"	–	R	FF	SIERRA	$13.95	
24¼"	–	R	FF	CLEVE CD173	$18.00	
32"	–	–	CL	GLEASON AT151	NA	
38"	–	–	CL	GLEASON	$3.25	(Manfredi)
49"	–	–	RC	CLEVE CD173	$28.00	
51½"	–	.45	4	ARGUS RM322	£5.25	(Sapcote)
65"	–	–	RC	CLEVE CD173	$40.00	

Pup (SA: 225)

[49]	-	.45-.60	4	MAN 4773	$12.75	(Roane)
10"	-	R	FF	CLEVE CD139U	$9.00	
13½"	-	R	FF	CLEVE CD139U	$12.00	
17"	-	R	FF	SAMS 608	£2.95	(Crown)
*18"	-	R	FF	PROKIT	£20.00	
20"	-	CO2	FF	ALFERY	$5.00	
20"	-	R	FF	CLEVE CD139U	$16.00	
*23½"	-	R	FF	PROKIT	£25.00	
26½"	-	.5-.8cc	FF	ARGUS FSP750	£3.75	(McDonough)
26½"	-	-	RC	PALADINE 17	$8.00	
30"	-	.049	1	GULF	$5.00	(Midkiff)
36"	-	.75-1.5cc	4	VELIVOLI J3	$6.00	
*39½"	29¼"	.15-.25	2-3	CHART A-DB-9	£49.00	
39½"	-	-	RC	CLEVE CD139U	$28.00	
40"	-	1-1.5cc	FF	SAMS 730	£3.00	(Dennis)
40½"	-	-	FF	ARGUS FSP305	£4.50	(Fisher)
41"	-	R	FF	POND 21D2	$3.75	(Peguilhan)
51"	-	-	RC	GLEASON AM1262	$9.95	(Smith)
53"	-	.45-.60	3-4	ARGUS RC990	£7.50	(Boddington)
53"	-	-	RC	PALADINE 17	$14.00	
58"	-	-	RC	GLEASON	$11.35	(Smith)
59"	-	.60	RC	FM CF391	$10.00	(Puleo)
*77"	-	/.91-1.2	RC	DB	£79.50	
78½"	-	-	RC	CLEVE CD139U	$45.00	
79"	-	-	RC	PALADINE 17	$32.00	
79"	-	20cc	4	TRAP MW2011	£11.00	(Griffiths)
80"	58"	Q35	4	BEHRENS	$30.00	

[formed wire set, $17.95][FGM: cowl, $20.00]

90"	75"	-	RC	RCM 844	$25.00	(Bukovchik)

**[KLARICH, $125.00]

90"	76"	40cc	4	REEVES	£22.50	

[cowl, £22.50]

*2450mm	1840mm	30cc	4	CLARK	DM998,	
**102"	-	-	RC	KLARICH	$140.00	
*108"	-	2.2-3.7	4	BALSA 461	$149.99	

Salamander

30"	–	R	FF	PALADINE 6	$8.00	
60"	–	–	RC	PALADINE 6	$18.00	
75"	–	–	RC	PALADINE 6	$32.00	

Snipe

11½"	–	R	FF	CLEVE CD153	$10.00	
15"	–	R	FF	CLEVE CD153	$14.00	
18"	–	R	FF	POND 31A3	$4.75	(Guillow)
20"	–	R	FF	HUNT AH153	$3.00	(Wherry)
23½"	–	R	FF	CLEVE CD153	$18.00	
25"	–	R	FF	POND 21D3	$4.25	(Ealy)
31"	–	R	FF	PALADINE 9	$8.00	
45"	–	–	CL	HOLMAN	$4.00	
46½"	–	–	RC	CLEVE CD153	$30.00	
47½"	–	1.5-2.5cc	FF	ARGUS MA339	£4.50	(Simmance)
62"	–	–	RC	PALADINE 9	$18.00	
93"	–	–	RC	PALADINE 9	$32.00	

1½ Strutter (SA: 256)

?	–	–	–	ARGUS FSP907x	£4.50	
25"	–	R	FF	CLEVE CD147	$18.00	
26"	–	R	FF	FSI S-2	$6.00	
29"	–	R	FF	COLE	$5.00	
29"	–	R	FF	GULF	$5.00	(Midkiff)
34"	–	R	FF	PALADINE 80	$32.00	
48"	–	–	CL	POND 21D4	$6.75	(Sichi)
*48"	–	.15-.19	2	VERON VO712	£72.99	
68"	–	–	RC	PALADINE 80	$18.00	
72"	–	.60-1.34	RC	WEST	$28.00	

Swallow (SA: 256)

22"	–	CO2	FF	FM CF590	$5.00	(Walker)
41"	–	–	FF	ARGUS FSP625	£4.50	(Darrell)
48"	–	–	CL	POND 21D4	$6.25	(Darrell)

Tabloid (SA: 256)

9½"	–	R	FF	CLEVE CD143	$9.00
13"	–	R	FF	AERO ERA	$1.25
13"	–	R	FF	CLEVE CD143	$12.00

15"	–	R	FF	POND 30F7	$3.25	(Dean)
17"	–	CO2	FF	PECK BHP430	$2.25	(Callaghan)
19½"	–	R	FF	CLEVE CD143	$16.00	
20"	–	R	FF	COLE	$5.00	
21"	–	R	FF	PECK BH154	$1.50	(Kau)
26"	–	R	FF	PALADINE 65	$8.00	
26"	–	R	FF	POND 21D2	$5.75	(McDonough)
39"	–	R	FF	CLEVE CD143	$30.00	
42"	–	.19	3	MB 8751	$10.00	(Moes)
1100mm	–	3.5	RC	MRA A414	16F	
50"	–	6-10cc	3	ARGUS RC1144	£6.00	(Boddington)
51"	–	/.40	3-4	TRAP MW2149	£7.00	(Hurrell)
[cowl, £6.50]						
52"	–	–	RC	PALADINE 65	$14.00	
63¼"	55"	.60-.90	4	BEAULIEU 14B	$24.95	(Polapink)
[TDF: cowl, $18.95]						
72"	–	.60	RC	B&D	$14.95	

Triplane (SA: 256)

?	–	–	–	ARGUS CL361x	£2.50	
?	–	–	–	ARGUS FSP545x	£5.25	
10"	–	R	FF	CLEVE CD140	$9.00	
13"	–	R	FF	CLEVE CD140	$12.00	
13"	–	R	FF	MICRO X	$2.50	(Masters)
13½"	–	R	FF	GLEASON	$1.15	(Kukuich)
18"	–	R	FF	POND 30E2	$3.75	(Le Modele Reduit)
20"	–	R	FF	CLEVE CD140	$15.00	
20"	–	R	FF	FSI S-5	$6.00	
20"	–	R	FF	HUNT AH154	$3.00	
*20"	–	R	FF	VERON VO420	£3.49	
24"	–	R	FF	POND 52F6	$7.75	(Monroe)
26¼"	–	.3-.5cc	FF	ARGUS FSP1320	£2.00	(Whitehead)
26½"	–	R	FF	NFFS	$3.50	(McCracken)
26½"	–	R	FF	PALADINE 76	$8.00	
35"	–	R	FF	POND 51G7	$5.75	(King)
40"	–	–	RC	HOLMAN	$4.50	
40"	–	R	FF	CLEVE CD140	$28.00	
42"	–	.45-.60	RC	HOLMAN	$9.95	

52"	–	.45-.60	3-4	HOLMAN	$13.50	
53"	–	–	RC	PALADINE 76	$14.00	
72"	–	.60	RC	B&D	$14.95	
80"	–	Q35	4	BEHRENS	$30.00	

[formed wire set, $12.95][FGM: cowl, $20.00]

SUPERMARINE

Attacker

16"	–	Jetex	FF	POND 52G3	$3.25	(Keil Kraft)
17½"	–	Jetex	FF	HUNT J203	$3.25	(Buragas)
*17½"	–	Jetex	FF	EASY JX07	$10.00 CDN	
18"	–	Jetex	FF	POND 22A6	$3.25	(Veron)
22½"	–	Jetex	FF	HUNT J204	$4.50	(Buragas)
30"	–	Jetex	FF	POND 22A6	$3.75	(Dean)

Sea Otter

?	–	–	–	ARGUS MA153x	£3.75	
30"	–	R	FF	POND 31D7	$5.25	(Moore)
46"	–	.30	4	ARGUS RC1281	£8.75	(Fearnley)

Spiteful (SA: 257)

22"	–	R	FF	BELL 005	$5.00	
22"	–	R	FF	KOUTNY	$5.00	
22"	–	R	FF	WOODHOUSE	£2.50	(Koutny)
26¼"	–	.40	CL	BELL 022	$5.00	
27"	–	1.5-2.5cc	CL	ARGUS MA183	£3.00	(Bishop)
35½"	–	.10-.15	CL	RCM 987	$6.75	(Smalley)
52"	–	.40	5	TRAP MW2052	£7.50	(Nicholson)

[spinner, £2.50; canopy, £3.00]

Spitfire (SA: 226, 257)

?	–	–	–	ARGUS MA235x	£3.00	
**8"	–	R	FF	ALFERY	$10.00	
*10"	–	Glider	FF	PAPER	$3.95	
**13"	–	R	FF	ALFERY	$12.00	
13"	–	R	FF	FILLON	16F 80	
13"	–	R	FF	POND 62C6	$3.25	(Takekuchi)
13"	–	R	FF	POND 62E4	$3.25	(Roberts)
13"	–	R	FF	SAMS 614	£1.75	(Preston)
13½"	–	R	FF	CLEVE CD73	$12.00	

*13½"	–	R	FF	MRC	$8.95	
15"	–	R	FF	POND 37B5	$3.25	(Guillow)
15"	–	R	FF	POND 30G3	$3.25	(Comet)
*[FIKE: $8.95]						
16"	–	R	FF	HUNT 3891	$4.50	(Whitman)
*16"	–	R	FF	KEIL KK0022	£4.99	
16"	–	R	FF	POND 52A7	$3.25	(Modelcraft)
*16½"	–	R	FF	GUILLOW 504	$5.00	
440mm	–	R	FF	AIRBORNE	$5.00AUS	
*17"	–	R	FF	EASY FF49	$5.00CDN	
*17"	–	R	FF	MODELAIR	$7.70NZ	
17"	–	R	FF	POND 52A7	$3.25	(Model A/C)
17¼"	–	R	FF	GLEASON	$1.80	(Stahl)
*18"	–	R	FF	BENTOM	$9.95	
18"	–	R	FF	CLEVE CD73	$15.00	
18"	–	R	FF	GLEASON	$2.10	(McHard)
18"	–	R	FF	HUNT AB11	$2.75	(Booton)
*18"	–	R	FF	KEIL KK0040	£3.99	
19"	–	R	FF	SHOP	£2.00	(Keelbild)
*19"	–	R	FF	IHC 526	$12.98	
*19½"	–	R	FF	COMET 1620	$12.00	
*20"	–	R	FF	COMET 3402	$7.50	
21"	–	R	FF	POND 42E5	$3.75	(Cleave)
22"	–	R	FF	POND 30G3	$3.75	(Koutny)
¶22"	–	R	FF	POND 22A2	$3.75	(Ott)
*22"	–	R	FF	VERON VO409	£3.49	
23"	–	R	FF	BELL 001	$5.00	
23"	–	R	FF	KOUTNY	$5.00	
¶23"	–	R	FF	POND 52A6	$3.75	(Megow)
24"	–	R	FF	HUNT WW01	$3.25	(Winter)
*24"	18"	R	FF	MODELHOB 110126	NA	
*24"	–	R	FF	EASY FF25	$7.00CDN	
24"	–	R	FF	POND 52A6	$3.75	(Modelcraft)
24"	–	R	FF	POND 52A6	$3.75	(Guillow)
*24"	–	R	FF	STERLING A-19	$14.95	
24½"	–	R	FF	SHOP	£2.00	(Keelbild)

25"	–	–	CL	POND 30F2	$3.75	(Bruce)
25"	–	R	FF	HUNT ES28E	$3.00	(Stahl)
26"	–	–	CL	POND 22A5	$5.25	(Struhl)
26"	–	R	FF	SHOP	£3.00	(Keelbild)
27"	–	R	FF	ARGUS FSP607	£3.75	(Whittaker)
690mm	–	R	FF	AIRBORNE	$5.00AUS	
¶ 27"	–	R	FF	POND 22G7	$3.75	(Ott)
27¼"	–	R	FF	CLEVE CD73	$20.00	
27¼"	–	R	FF	PROKIT	£4.50	(Cleveland)
27¼"	–	R	FF	GLEASON AT1252	$3.45	(Musciano)
*28"	–	R	FF	GUILLOW 403	$16.00	
28"	–	R	FF	POND 22A4	$5.25	(Whitman)
28"	–	–	CL	POND 22A5	$5.25	(Berkeley)
¶ 30"	–	R	FF	POND 22A4	$4.75	(Capitol)
30"	–	R	FF	POND 52A6	$3.75	(Megow)
31"	–	.5cc	FF	ARGUS MA376	£3.75	(Cole)
¶ 32"	–	R	FF	HUNT 3212	$4.50	(Ott)
32"	–	R	FF	PALADINE 37	$11.00	
34"	–	R	FF	HUNT 105	$5.50	(Ott)
*35"	–	R	FF	EASY FF7	$14.00CDN	
36"	–	R	FF	CLEVE T73	$12.00	
*900mm	730mm	.051-.10	2-3	MARUTAKA 42	¥7,800	
900mm	–	R	FF	MRA 370	46F	
36½"	–	R	CL	GLEASON AM766	$5.85	(Musciano)
37"	–	–	CL	POND 22G7	$4.75	(Modern Hobbycraft)
40"	–	Elec	3-4	ARGUS RC1564	£3.75	(Peacock)
¶40"	–	R	FF	POND 30F4	$5.25	(Capitol)
40½"	–	.20	2-4	ARGUS RC1326	£3.75	(Peacock)
*42"	36"	.15	3-4	GAGER	$60.00	
*42"	–	.15-.25	2-3	LEICESTER 22	£37.83	
42"	–	–	CL	POND 30F7	$5.75	(Peuker)
42½"	–	.29	3	ARGUS RM184	£5.25+	(Kinnear)
*44"	40"	.19-.25	3-4	CHART AFW1B	£59.95	
45"	–	–	CL	POND 41D2	$4.75	(Baker)
46"	–	–	CL	GLEASON AT559	NA	(Musciano)
1160mm	–	2.5-3.5	RC	MRA 695.589	40F	
47½"	–	.40	4	MARTIN DM114	£7.50	

[canopy, £1.40; template, £7.50]

1180mm	–	6.5	RC	BOSAK	20 Kcs	
[canopy, 15 Kcs]						
*1200mm	980mm	.19-.25	3-4	IKUTA	¥15,000	
*48"	–	.25-.40	RC	SKYWAY	£45.00	
*1208mm	981mm	.19-25	4-5	TETTORA SF25SR	¥12,000	
49½"	42"	Glider	2	WESTERN 012	$5.00	
*50"	–	R	FF	EASY FF55	$28.00CDN	
50"	–	–	RC	MB 786-CP	$9.50	(Megow)
*1240mm	945mm	.19-.35	3-5	OK APQX016	¥14,800	
*50"	–	.35-.40	3-4	SURE FLITE	$63.95	
*[K-BEE: assembled, $149.95]						
*53½"	43¾"	.40-.45	RC	ROYAL 79-280	$144.95	
54"	–	R	FF	OLD DS15	$5.00	(Stahl)
54½"	–	–	RC	CLEVE CD73	$38.00	
56"	–	.40	4	ARGUS RC1342	£6.00	(Ingroville)
*56 "	–	.40-.61	4	FLAIR CAPR07	NA	
56"	–	.40-.61	4	TRAP MW2107	£8.00	(CAP)
[cowl, £3.50; canopy, £3.50; spinner, £3.00]						
56"	–	.45-.61	6	RCM 1036	$11.00	(Whitehead)
56"	–	/.40	4-6	TRAP MW2053	£8.00	(Whitehead)
1400mm	–	6-10cc	RC	MODELL	DM15,	(Schmalzgruber)
*1460mm	1050mm	.40-.45	3-4	IKUTA	¥26,000	
*1500mm	1210mm	6.5	RC	BAUER 301	DM560,	
61"	–	10cc	RC	BRYANT 16	£6.00	
[cowl, £4.00; canopy, £3.00][UNITRACTS: retracts, £36.80]						
63"	–	–	RC	ARGUS RC1513	£8.75	(Millinship)
[cowl, canopy, £11.00; spinner, £3.00]						
*63"	–	.40-.60	RC	REEVES BRK2020	£79.95	
64"	–	–	RC	PALADINE 37	$18.00	
64"	–	–	RC	POND 35F7	$8.75	(Harris)
*64"	–	.45/.80	RC	STERLING FS14	$129.95	
64½"	–	.61	4	ARGUS RM64	£8.75	(Taylor)
[cowl, £7.50; canopy, £5.25][UNITRACTS: retracts, £36.80]						
64½"	–	–	RC	GLEASON AM262	NA	
1640mm	–	10cc	RC	MRA BT15	119F	(Taylor)
*1637mm	1350mm	.60/.90	4-6	MARUTAKA 21	¥28,000	
*65"	52"	.61/.90	4-5	PICA	$139.95	
*66"	–	10-15cc	RC	MODEL 019	$169.00AUS	
[spinner, $30.00AUS; retracts, $240.00AUS]						
1660mm	–	10cc	RC	MODELE 3171	95F	

```
 *1660mm   1230mm   .60        4-6   IKUTA        ¥35,000
 *67"      47½"      -          RC    SAIL         NA
  69"       -        .60/.80    6     TAYLOR       £8.00      (Mk. 1)
 [cowl, £9.00; canopy, £2.50; spinner, £5.00; balsa pack, £26.00;
  retracts, £35.00][UNITRACTS: retracts, £22.25]
  1750mm    -        10cc       RC    MRA BT22     150F       (Taylor)
  69"       -        .60        6     TAYLOR       £8.00      (Mk. 14)
 [cowl, £9.00; canopy, £2.50; spinner, £5.50; balsa pack, £32.00;
  retracts, £35.00][UNITRACTS: retracts, £22.25]
**[KLARICH: $100.00]
  1750mm    -        10cc       RC    MRA BT16     150F       (Taylor)
  1830mm    -        10cc       RC    MRA 761      119F
  72"       -        .60.90     5     HOLMAN       $19.95     (Taylor)
**[$149.95]
  74"       65½"     .90-1.08   6     INNOVATIVE   $30.00
  74"       -        .60/1.20   RC    REEVES       £7.50
**[£75.00][UNITRACTS: retracts, £36.80]
 *81"       -        ST2000     RC    DB           £120.75
 [UNITRACTS: retracts, £24.84]
**85"       -        .60-.90    RC    HOMEWOOD     $175.00NZ
  2130mm    -        20-25cc    RC    MRA 677.583  187F
 *88"       77"      .90-1.2    4-6   PICA         $239.95
 [cockpit, $14.95] [retracts: IMPACT, $125.00; ROBINAIRE, $245.00]
 *88"       78"      ST2500     4-6   YELLOW       $315.00
 [IMPACT: retracts, $125.00]
**88½"      -        .90        5     PLATT        $149.00
 [retracts, $219.00][cockpits: JD, $40.00; AVCO, $22.95]
 *[$329.00]
 *95"       72"      30-50cc    6-8   POWERMAX Sp-4 £290.00
 *96"       -        30-50cc    RC    MODEL  020   $299.00AUS
 [spinner, $45.00AUS; retracts, $240.00AUS]
 *2450mm    -        50cc       RC    COOP 9600039  2850F
 *108"      -        3-5.2      5     RC           $295.00
 *112"      98"      100cc      5-8   AIRSCREW     $2800CDN

  Swift
  14"        -       Jetex      FF    POND 30G6    $3.25      (Keil Kraft)
 *14½"       -       Jetex      FF    EASY JX04    $10.00CDN
  20"        -       Jetex      FF    POND 22A6    $4.75      (Mansour)
 *21½        -       Bean Rock  FF    WILLAIRCO    $26.25
 *32½"       -       Bean Rock  FF    WILLAIRCO    $38.40
 *48½"       -       Bean Rock  FF    WILLAIRCO    $69.75
```

Walrus (SA: 226)

38"	-	R	FF	POND 47B7	$5.25	(Wright)
38"	-	.8-1cc	FF	ARGUS FSP661	£4.50	(Aeromodeller)
69"	-	.61	4	ARGUS RM164	£8.75	(Gray)

VICKERS

FB-5

14"	-	R	FF	CLEVE CD208	$9.00	
18½"	-	R	FF	CLEVE CD208	$12.00	
20"	-	R	FF	HUNT AH195	$3.00	(Struck)
24"	-	R	FF	GLEASON	$2.90	(Struck)
27½"	-	R	FF	CLEVE CD208	$16.00	
55"	-	-	RC	CLEVE CD208	$32.00	
110"	-	-	RC	CLEVE CD208	$52.00	

FB-12

11¼"	-	R	FF	CLEVE CD207	$9.00
15"	-	R	FF	CLEVE CD207	$12.00
22½"	-	R	FF	CLEVE CD207	$16.00
30"	-	R	FF	PALADINE 84	$8.00
45"	-	R	FF	CLEVE CD207	$30.00
59"	-	-	RC	PALADINE 84	$32.00

FB-19

24"	-	R	FF	PALADINE 8	$8.00
48"	-	R	FF	PALADINE 8	$14.00

Jockey

13"	-	R	FF	OLD 472	$2.00	(Scientific)
20"	-	R	FF	PLANS	$6.00	(Andrus)
20"	-	R	FF	HUNT SC128	$3.25	(Scientific)
760mm	-	R	FF	MRA A398	16F	
78"	-	1.2	4	GOLDEN ERA	$29.00	

[engine cooling plate, wheel pants, $40.00]

Vildebeast

15"	-	R	FF	POND 22E4	$3.25	(Aer-o-Kits)
17"	-	R	FF	POND 46E4	$3.25	(Jones)
37½"	-	R	FF	ARGUS FSG1401	£3.75	(Newman)

Wellesley

15"	–	R	FF	POND 22E4	$3.25	(Aer-o-Kits)
37"	–	.051	2-3	MAN 12822	$9.00	(Musciano)
52"	–	–	CL	POND 44G1	$5.75	(Musciano)
89"	–	/.40	RC	MA 589	$12.50	(Pelly-Fry)

Wellington

36"	–	.020x2	FF	AUTHENTIC	£2.10	(Towner)
66"	–	.10x2	RC	MA 320	$4.50	(Baker)
86"	–	5ccx2	4-6	ARGUS RC1308	£10.00	(Evans)

[canopy, cowls, turrets, £35.50]

WESTLAND

Dreadnought

24"	–	R	FF	POND 30C3	$3.25	(Stott)

Lysander (SA: 226)

*15"	–	R	FF	EASY FF50	$5.00CDN	
15"	–	R	FF	POND 23C4	$3.25	(Megow)
17½"	–	R	FF	HUNT MAC23	$2.50	(Model A/C)
*18"	–	R	FF	KEIL KK0042	£3.99	
19"	–	R	FF	ARGUS FSR1179	£2.00	(Kennedy)
19"	–	R	FF	CLEVE CD231	$14.00	
19"	–	R	FF	POND 23C4	$3.25	(Comet)
19"	–	R	FF	POND 31G6	$4.75	(Keelbild)
20"	–	R	FF	HUNT MAC24	$2.40	(Model A/C)
20"	–	R	FF	POND 23C2	$3.25	(Model Craft)
20"	–	R	FF	POND 49A2	$3.25	(Easy Built)
23"	–	R	FF	POND 23E5	$3.75	(Wentzel)
24"	–	R	FF	POND 23C4	$4.75	(Leovina)
25"	–	R	FF	CLEVE CD231	$18.00	
25"	–	R	FF	HUNT AB14	$3.25	(Booton)
25"	–	R	FF	GLEASON	$2.25	(Lindberg)
25"	–	R	FF	POND 23E6	$3.25	(Jones)
28"	–	R	FF	POND 23C5	$5.75	(Whitman)
30"	–	R	FF	POND 23C5	$3.75	(Megow)
33"	–	R	FF	HUNT PL159	$4.00	(Lindberg)
*36"	–	R	FF	EASY FF78	$12.00CDN	
37"	–	R	FF	HUNT AH166	$3.75	(Plecan)

37½"	–	R	FF	CLEVE CD231	$24.00	
38"	–	R	FF	POND 23C5	$3.75	(Aircraft Plan)
1200mm	–	R	FF	MRA 344	40F	
50"	–	R	FF	ARGUS FSR161	£5.25	(Boyes)
50"	–	R	FF	EASY FF58	$28.00 CDN	
50"	–	R	FF	POND 23G5	$7.25	(Cueva)
1400mm	1160mm	10-15cc	5	VTH MT336	DM29,50	(Kriz)
60"	–	2.5cc	RC	ARGUS FSP160	£5.25	
60"	–	–	CL	POND 23C6	$7.75	(Weisberg)
70"	–	/.40-.48	4-5	HUTSON 14	£18.50	

[cowl, £9.75; canopy, £9.25; spats, £9.25; balsa pack, £26.95]

75"	–	–	RC	CLEVE CD231	$38.00	
76"	–	10cc		MRA 773	112F	
81"	–	10cc	RC	BRYANT 9	£9.00	
85"	49"	/.60-.90	4-6	FLITECRAFT	£101.50	
86"	52"	.60/.90	5	BOSMAN	$30.00	
100"	–	–	RC	CLEVE CD231	$52.00	
128"	73"	Q35	5	BOSMAN	$35.00	

Wallace

| 18" | – | R | FF | POND 44E2 | $3.25 | (Comet) |
| 28" | – | R | FF | GLEASON | $4.25 | (Horback) |

Whirlwind (SA: 227)

17"	–	R	FF	CLEVE CD105	$14.00	
23"	–	R	FF	CLEVE CD105	$18.00	
27"	–	R/CO2x2	FF	DIELS 30	$4.00	
28"	–	R	FF	HUNT 2943	$5.50	(Whitman)
34"	–	R	FF	CLEVE CD105	$24.00	
36"	–	R	FF	CLEVE T105	$12.00	
54"	–	–	CL	POND 36B6	$6.25	(Plecan)
55"	–	.10x2	RC	MA 515	$11.50	(Baker)
65"	–	.30x2	4	ARGUS RM111	£8.75	(Cronin)
68"	–	–	RC	CLEVE CD105	$40.00	
74"	–	.40x2	RC	HORN S-47	$20.00	(Osborne)

Wyvern

| ? | – | – | – | ARGUS MA106x | £3.75 | |
| 20" | – | R | FF | POND 46E3 | $3.75 | (Pishnery) |

34"	–	.60	CL	MAN 5711	$8.25	(Martinez)
67"	–	–	RC	POND 58C2	$9.25	(Burgess)

ISRAEL
IAI

Kfir
14½"	–	Glider	FF	WALLACE	$6.50	
*44½"	82½"	.77F	5	BYRON 6130121	$340.45	

[retracts, $84.95; nose wheel, $87,95; power package, $367.95]

ITALY
AERMACCHI

MB-339 (SA: 228, 257)
*66"	54"	Glider	2	DRAGON	£79.95

ANSALDO

A-1 Balilla
20"	–	R/CO2	FF	ALFERY	$5.00	
26½"	–	R	FF	PALADINE 12	$8.00	
53"	–	–	RC	PALADINE 12	$14.00	

SVA-5 Primo (SA: 227)
?	–	–	–	ARGUS MA359x	£3.00	
13"	–	R	FF	HANNAN	$3.00	(Alvarez)
14"	–	R	FF	POND 55A7	$3.25	(Wherry)
15"	–	R	FF	POND 13C2	$3.75	(Ott)
15"	–	R/CO2	FF	VELIVOLI T6	$5.00	
*[Fly T: $20.00]						
*19"	–	R	FF	STERLING A-18	$11.95	
23"	–	R	FF	CLEVE CD169	$18.00	
23"	–	R	FF	HUNT AH56	$3.35	(Daily)
30"	–	–	CL	POND 49B5	$4.75	(Bedrich)
30"	–	R	FF	POND 44D6	$5.75	(Wherry)
30"	–	R	FF	POND 46F3	$4.75	(Ott, Pond)
31"	–	R	FF	PALADINE 70	$8.00	
44"	–	–	CL	POND 44C3	$6.75	(Milani)

45¼"	-	.60	RC	RCM 453	$10.75	(Morfis)
62"	-	-	RC	PALADINE 70	$18.00	

SVA-9

13"	-	R	FF	POND 26B4	$3.75	(McCorrison)

CAPRONI

AP-1 Bergamasca

1850mm	-	15cc	4	MODULO	L30.000

CA-3

39"	-	R	FF	VELIVOLI T15	$8.00

CA-5

17"	-	R	FF	POND 14D7	$3.25	(U.S. Models)

CA-134 (SA: 227)

13"	-	R	FF	POND 62D6	$3.25	(Rees)

CA-355 Tuffo

910mm	-	R	FF	VTH MT781-K	DM7,50	(Stengele)
1833mm	1430mm	10cc	4	VTH MT781-G	DM24,	(Stengele)

CH-1

13"	-	R	FF	POND 55D3	$3.25	(Bruning)
22"	-	R	FF	POND 55D1	$4.24	(Bruning)
25"	-	R	FF	COLE	$5.00	

300 HP

39"	-	R/CO2x2	FF	FLY T FTMC-15	$7.50

*[$20.00]

FIAT

CR-30

15"	-	R	FF	POND 50C6	$3.75	(Semrad)
1610mm	1170mm	.61	RC	MODULO	L50.000	

CR-32 (SA: 257)

[65]	-	1.2	4	MB 687	$10.00	(Swift)
14"	-	R	FF	POND 27D3	$3.25	(Bruning)

CR-42 Falco (SA: 227)

63"	-	.60	RC	HORN S-7	$10.00
1640mm	-	10cc	RC	DIMUZIO	L95.000
79"	64"	.90	5	GAZZA 017	L90.000

G-46

24"	–	R	FF	HUNT 5366	$5.50	(Whitman)
2008mm	–	–	RC	MODULO	L40.000	

G-50 Freccia (SA: 227)

680mm	–	R	FF	AIRBORNE	$5.00AUS	
27"	–	R	FF	GLEASON	$2.15	(Daily)
27"	–	R	FF	HUNT WW06	$3.25	(Winter)
27"	–	R	FF	PROKIT	£2.00	(Winter)

*[£26.50]

72"	–	–	RC	PROKIT	NA
2200mm	1630mm	30-45cc	5	FANTINI	L45.000

[cowl, L40.000]

G-55 Centauro (SA: 227)

23"	–	R	FF	KOUTNY	$5.00
1800mm	–	10cc	RC	MRA 769	119F

G-91 (SA: 228)

980mm	–	6.5ccF	RC	MRA 165	95F
*1550mm	1360mm	10-13cc	3	BETTINI ART0009	NA

IMAM

RO-58

30"	–	R	FF	KOUTNY	$10.00

MACCHI

Macchi 406

880mm	–	R	FF	MRA 352	40F

M. 5

14½"	–	R	FF	CLEVE CD213	$10.00
19½"	–	R	FF	CLEVE CD213	$13.00
29"	–	R	FF	CLEVE CD213	$18.00
58"	–	–	RC	PALADINE 79	$18.00
58"	–	–	RC	CLEVE CD213	$30.00

MC-200 Saetta (SA: 228)

26"	–	–	CL	POND 19C3	$4.65	(Musciano)

MC-202 Folgore (SA: 228)

13"	–	R	FF	DIELS 29	$2.00
17"	–	R	FF	COLE	$5.00

17½"	–	R	FF	DIELS 24	$3.00	
18"	–	R	FF	POND 56E4	$3.25	(Bruning)
22"	–	R	FF	KOUTNY	$5.00	
26"	–	–	CL	GLEASON AT954	NA	
29"	–	R	FF	FM CF716	$5.00	(Midkiff)
*54"	–	.29-.45	4	WING 703	$37.50	
1505mm	–	–	RC	MODULO	L50.000	
61"	–	10cc	RC	BRYANT 11	£6.00	
61"	–	.45-.61	RC	RCM 221	$12.50	(Bryant)
83½"	70"	.90-1.5	4-6	INNOVATIVE	$30.00	

MC-205 Veltro (SA: 228)

21"	–	–	CL	POND 29E5	$4.25	(Ziffer)
2500mm	2050mm	30-60cc	6	FANTINI	L48.000	

[cowl, L45.000; spinner, L46.000]

MARCHETTI

S-50

13"	–	R/CO2	FF	VELIVOLI P2	$3.00

REGGIANE

Re-2005 Sagittario (SA: 228)

13"	–	R	FF	POND 42C5	$3.25	(Bennett)
18"	–	R	FF	POND 42C3	$3.25	(Bennett)
22"	–	R	FF	KOUTNY	$5.00	
63"	–	.60	4-6	MAN 7811	$28.50	(Grassi)

SAVOIA-MARCHETTI

SM-79 Sparviero (SA: 229)

35"	–	Rx3	FF	DIELS 52	$5.50	
48½"	–	1.5cc	FF	ARGUS FSP1077	£5.25	(Potest)

SM-81 Pipistrello

49"	–	R	FF	POND 36C7	$5.75	(Potest)

SM-92

36"	–	Rx2	FF	KOUTNY	$10.00

S.I.A.

S.I.A. 71

13"	–	R	FF	VELIVOLI P9	$3.00

22"	–	R		FF	FLY T FTMC-4	$5.00	

*[$20.00]

SIAI-MARCHETTI

SF-260

990mm	–	R		FF	VTH MT696-K	DM7,50	(Kriz)
1700mm	1400mm	10cc	5		VTH MT696-G	DM24,	(Kriz)

JAPAN

AICHI

D3A ("VAL")

18"	–	R		FF	POND 55A5	$3.75	(Wheldon)
880mm	–	R		FF	MRA 379	40F	
39"	–	2.5cc		CL	ARGUS MA349	£3.75	(Wheldon)

B7A Ryusei ("GRACE")

33"	–	R		FF	FM CF702	$7.00	(Midkiff)

M6A Seiran

**13"	–	R		FF	ALFERY	$15.00	

KAWANISHI

H6K ("MAVIS")

87"	–	–		RC	POND 28F6	$7.25	(RC Technique

H8K ("EMILY")

*1800mm	1250mm	Elec	3-4		KYOTO	¥9,500	
*3800mm	2780mm	.60x4	4-6		IKUTA	¥160,000	

N1K Shiden-kai ("GEORGE") (SA: 229, 258)

*1300mm	880mm	.19-.25	3-4		IKUTA	¥15,000	

*[assembled, ¥75,000]

*1460mm	1065mm	.29-.45	4-5		IKUTA	¥24,000	

*[assembled, ¥98,000]

64"	–	.60	4		TAYLOR	£6.00	

[cowl, £5.50; canopy, £2.50; spinner, £4.50; balsa pack, £28.00]

1630mm	–	10cc	RC		MRA BT8.576	119F	(Taylor)
*1765mm	1175mm	.60	4-6		IKUTA	¥32,000	

KAWASAKI

<u>Ki-10</u> ("PERRY") (SA: 229)

12"	–	R	FF	POND 28G2	$3.75	(Tropical)
12"	–	R	FF	POND 28F2	$3.25	(Codding)
13"	–	R	FF	OLD 423	$2.00	(Dallarie)
22"	–	R	FF	HUNT EZ03	$3.00	(Pilzer)
27"	–	R	FF	POND 28F4	$3.25	(Iida)

<u>Ki-61 Hien</u> ("TONY") (SA: 229)

[1800]	–	.60	4-5	AIRBORNE	$20.00AUS	
*10"	–	Glider	FF	PAPER	$3.95	
13"	–	R	FF	POND 37A1	$3.25	(Norman)
19"	–	R	FF	POND 37A2	$3.25	(Norman)
20"	–	R	FF	ALFERY	$5.00	
24"	–	R	FF	KOUTNY	$5.00	
24"	–	R	FF	WOODHOUSE	£2.50	(Koutny)
26"	–	R	FF	HUNT AN121	$3.25	(Prisel)
29"	–	–	CL	POND 28G1	$4.50	(Musciano)
32"	–	R	FF	GULF	$5.00	(Midkiff)
40"	–	–	RC	POND 47A3	$6.25	(Arigiya)
40"	–	.049	2-4	VELIVOLI J1	$6.00	
1230mm [canopy, 15Kcs]	–	6.5cc	RC	BOSAK	20 Kcs	
*1270mm *[assembled, ¥65,000]	950mm	.19-.25	3-4	IKUTA	¥12,000	
*1300mm	992mm	.19.-25	3-5	TETTORA HN20	¥10,800	
*1390mm	971mm	.20/.40	4-5	MARUTAKA 54	¥15,000	
*1440mm *[assembled, ¥98,000]	1057mm	.29-.45	3-4	IKUTA	¥22,000	
1600mm	–	7.5-10cc	RC	MRA 139	67F	
*1626mm	1167mm	.60	4-6	IKUTA	¥32,000	
*66" [retracts, $240.00AUS; spinner, $30.00AUS]	–	10cc	RC	MODEL 023	$169.00AUS	
68"	–	8-10cc	4	ARGUS RC931	£6.00	(Bando)
68"	–	.61	RC	RCM 203	$8.25	(Albrecht)
*68½"	49"	.45-.80	RC	ROYAL 79-275	$214.95	
88"	–	–	RC	POND 57A4	$8.25	(Bando)
89"	65½"	.90-1.08	5	INNOVATIVE	$30.00	

Ki-100 Goshiki ("TONY") (SA: 258)

89"	65½"	.90-1.5	4-5	INNOVATIVE	$30.00	

Ki-102 ("RANDY")

*1200mm	850mm	Elec	2-3	KYOTO	¥9,500	

KYUSHU

J7W Shinden (SA: 229, 258)

[62]	–	.61	RC	MB 8841	$15.00	(Thacker)
13"	–	R	FF	POND 55D5	$3.25	(Smith)
18¼"	–	R	FF	DIELS 55	$ 4.50	
*[$15.50]						
24"	–	R	FF	FM CF577	$5.00	(Srull)

K11 W2 Shiragiku

?	–	–	–	ARGUS MA383x	£3.75	
13"	–	R	FF	POND 62C2	$3.25	(Yamamori)
37"	–	–	CL	POND 41G3	$5.75	(Hawkins)
86½"	58½"	.90-1.5	4-6	AERO PLANS	$25.00	

MITSUBISHI

1MT1

19"	–	R	FF	POND 19E3	$3.75	(Stott)

Type 10

?	–	–	–	ARGUS RTP942x	£3.00	

A5M ("CLAUDE")

32"	–	R	FF	GULF	$5.00	(Midkiff)
36"	–	–	CL	GLEASON AM162	$6.05	(Musciano)
58"	–	.35-.46	RM	FM CF515	$7.00	(Sheeks)
*1536mm	1152mm	.40-.45	4-6	IKUTA	¥49,000	
*1920mm	1440mm	.45-.60	4-6	IKUTA	¥68,000	
*2400mm	1800mm	.90	4-6	IKUTA	¥89,000	

A6M Reisen ("ZERO") (SA: 229, 258)

*13"	–	R	FF	PECK PP9	$6.95	
*13"	–	R	FF	STERLING P4	$7.95+	
*13½"	–	R	FF	MRC	$8.95	
16"	–	R	FF	HUNT 3885	$4.50	(Whitman)
*18"	–	R	FF	BENTOM	$9.95	

¶18"	-	R	FF	POND 29C3	$3.25	(Comet)
18"	-	R	FF	POND 19E3	$3.75	(Modelcraft)
*19"	-	R	FF	IHC 525	$12.98	
20"	-	R	FF	ALFERY	$5.00	
21"	-	R	FF	POND 31D1	$4.75	(Comet)
*24"	-	R	FF	STERLING A-15	$15.95	
*27"	-	R/.020	FF	GUILLOW 404	$16.00	
27"	-	-	CL	POND 29D3	$3.75	(Hawkins)
28"	-	-	CL	POND 52D6	$4.25	(Musciano)
30"	-	R	FF	CLEVE CD86	$18.00	
34"	-	-	CL	POND 29B2	$5.75	(TMHK)
36"	-	.75-1cc	FF	ARGUS RC1165	£4.50	(Fleming)
*916mm	760mm	.051-.10	2-3	MARUTAKA 39	¥7,800	
36"	-	R	FF	ORIGINAL	£4.50	(Martin)
38"	-	.29-.60	CL	HORN MPS263	$3.00	
39½"	-	R	FF	FM CF660	$7.00	(Houle)
*40"	-	Elec	4	KYOSHO	¥14,800	
40"	-	-	CL	POND 51B5	$4.75	(Modern Hobbycraft)
42"	-	-	RC	PALADINE 41	$11.00	
*44"	28"	Glider	2	CLIFF	$89.95	
*1100mm	912mm	.20-.24	4-6	IKUTA	¥16,000	
*[assembled, ¥75,000]						
*1200mm	850mm	Elec	2-3	KYOTO	¥9,500	
*1200mm	910mm	.25/.40	4-5	MARUTAKA 45	¥33,000	
*1240mm	984mm	.20/.40	3-5	MARUTAKA 26	¥14,000	
1270mm	-	.65cc	RC	BOSAK	20Kcs	
[canopy, 15 Kcs]						
50"	-	6.5cc	4-5	TRAP MW2161	£5.50	(Bosak)
50"	-	-	RC	POND 51B5	$5.75	(Kato)
*1280mm	977mm	.40-.45	4-6	IKUTA	¥24,000	
*[assembled, ¥98,000]						
*1290mm	974mm	.19-.25	3-5	TETTORA 0-20	¥12,000	
*1320mm	940mm	.19-.35	3-5	OK APQX013	¥14,800	
*54"	-	.35-.46	4	VORTECK	$109.95	
*54"	-	.29-.45	4	WING 700	$37.50	
*1480mm	1160mm	.40/.60	3-5	MARUTAKA 2	¥23,000	
*1480mm	1160mm	.40-.50	4-5	MARUTAKA 35	¥60,000	

60"   42"   .40-.60   4-5   BEAULIEU 4B $19.95   (Parenti)
*[HOLMAN: $129.95]

*1510mm 1154mm   .40-.45   4-5   OK 11038   ¥43,500

60"   -   .40-.60   4   WING 220 $9.95
[cowl, $12.95; canopy, $6.00]

*61"   50"   .60-.75   4-6   TOP RC-25 $145.95

*62"   -   .40-.60   4-5   FLAIR CAPR17   NA

62"   -   .40-.60   4   TRAP MW2117   £7.50   (CAP)

*1592mm 1318mm   .60/1.20   4-6   MARUTAKA 1   ¥30,000

63¼"   -   .50-.60   4-5   MORGAN 116RC $15.95

*1680mm 1160mm   .40/.60   4-5   MARUTAKA 48   ¥60,000

*1720mm 1270mm   /.60-.90   4-6   IKUTA   ¥32,000

68½"   57¼"   .90-1.08   4-5   INNOVATIVE $25.00

79"   -   .90-1.5   5   RCM 912 $18.50   (Platt)

*80"   69"   1.2   RC   YELLOW $325.00
[AVCO: cockpit, $25.95]

**80"   -   .90-1.08   5   PLATT RC-4 $159.00
[drop tank, $19.00; retracts, $219.00; tail wheel, $33.00]
[cockpits: JD, $40.00; AVCO, $25.95; AVCO: exterior panels, $10.95]
*[$319.00]

*88"   75"   Q50   5-6   BYRON 613028 $385.00
[retracts, $241.60; tail wheel, $34.65; prop system, $642.45]

91"   73"   2-4   4-5   ZIROLI $30.00
**[KLARICH: $140.00; R&M: $135.00]
*[HANGAR: $220.00]

Ki-15 ("BABS")(SA: 230)

13"   -   R   FF   POND 62C1 $3.25   (Matsuo)

22"   -   R   FF   HUNT 2216 $4.50   (Whitman)

30"   -   R   FF   FSI M-2 $6.00

44"   -   -   RC   POND 28C1 $4.75   (RC Technique

66"   -   -   RC   POND 18F2 $5.75   (RC Technique

F1M ("PETE")

*1920mm 1425mm   .60-.90   4   IKUTA   ¥89,000

T-2

*980mm   1038mm   .25   3-4   MARUTAKA 61   ¥17,000

*1140mm 1460mm   .40-.50   5-6   MARUTAKA 62   ¥65,000

J2M Raiden ("JACK")(SA: 230)

13"	–	R	FF	DIELS 22	$2.00	
13"	–	R	FF	POND 38F7	$3.25	(Bruning)
18"	–	R	FF	DIELS 45	$3.25	
18"	–	R	FF	COLE	$5.00	
27"	–	R	FF	GULF	$5.00	(Midkiff)
*920mm	825mm	.10/.40	3-4	MARUTAKA 44	¥10,800	
*1270mm	1140mm	.25/.60	4-5	MARUTAKA 49	¥23,000	
68"	–	.60-.61	4	FM CF784	$8.00	(Reiss)
*1543mm	1385mm	.60/1.20	6	MARUTAKA 50	¥63,000	

Ki-46 ("DINAH")

*1450mm	1150mm	.19x2	4-5	IKUTA	¥26,000
*[assembled, ¥148,000]					
*1750mm	1275mm	.45x2	4-5	IKUTA	¥39,800
*[assembled, ¥248,000]					

Ki-83 (SA: 230)

26¼"	–	R	FF	FM CF811	$7.50	(Howard)

G4M ("BETTY")

*1460mm	1050mm	.25x2	4-5	IKUTA	¥26,000
*[assembled, ¥148,000]					
*1700mm	1220mm	Elec	3-4	KYOTO	¥16,500
*1756mm	1220mm	.40x2	4-5	IKUTA	¥39,000
*[assembled, ¥198,000]					
*3000mm	2450mm	.60x2	4-5	IKUTA	¥130,000
*[assembled, ¥498,000]					

NAKAJIMA

Type 90

38"	–	R	FF	POND 29F2	$6.75	(JNMC)

Type 96

18"	–	R	FF	POND 19F6	$3.25	(Bligh)

A6M2 ("RUFE")

–	–	–	–	MAN 9872	$8.00	
[conversion plan for any .60-size ZERO]						
*16½"	–	R	FF	GUILLOW 507	$5.00	
18"	–	R	FF	POND 19E3	$3.75	(Wherry)
24"	–	R	FF	KOUTNY	$5.00	
*1480mm	1160mm	.60/1.20	4-5	MARUTAKA 4	¥33,000	

| 60" | 42" | .40-.60 | 4-5 | BEAULIEU 11B | $19.95 | (Parenti) |

B5N ("KATE")

?	-	-	-	ARGUS MA372x	£5.25	
37"	-	-	CL	POND 29F5	$5.75	(Hawkins)
*1600mm	1015mm	.40-.45	4-5	IKUTA	¥24,500	
*[assembled, ¥98,000]						
*1885mm	1200mm	.60	4-6	IKUTA	¥32,000	
*[assembled, ¥148,000]						

B6N Tenzan ("JILL")

15"	-	R	FF	COLE	$5.00	
30"	-	R	FF	FM CF711	$5.00	(Rees)
36"	-	2.5-3.5cc	CL	ARGUS MA268	£3.75	(Hawkins)

C6N Saiun ("MYRT")

[76]	-	.60	CL	MA 145	$2.45	(Baltes)
16"	-	R	FF	GLEASON	$1.20	(Midkiff)
20"	-	R	FF	GLEASON	$2.40	(Midkiff)
24"	-	R	FF	MB 4872	$5.00	(Schreyer)
29"	-	R	FF	FM CF742	$8.00	(Midkiff)

J1N Gekko ("IRVING")

*1730mm	1200mm	.20x2	4-6	IKUTA	¥26,000	
*[assembled, ¥148,000]						
*2160mm	1420mm	.40x2	4-6	IKUTA	¥39,000	
*[assembled, ¥198,000]						

Ki-27 ("NATE") (SA: 230)

13"	-	R	FF	MOONEY	$1.00	
18"	-	R	FF	HUNT AH132	$3.00	(Kirschbaum)
25"	-	R	FF	HUNT AH133	$3.50	(Kirschbaum)
38"	-	R	FF	ORIGINAL	£3.65	(Martin)
*1920mm	-	15cc	3	COOP 9600068	2100F	
93"	-	2.0	4-5	HANGAR	$30.00	
[cowl, $20.00; canopy, $14.00; wheel pants, $20.00]						
*[$290.00]						

Ki-43 Hayabusa ("OSCAR")

*1170mm	905mm	.19-.25	4-5	IKUTA	¥13,500	
*[assembled, ¥75,000]						
*1500mm	1115mm	.29-.45	4-5	IKUTA	¥24,000	
*[assembled, ¥98,000]						
*1500mm	1250mm	.50/.90	4-6	MARUTAKA 5	¥28,000	

Ki-44 Shoki ("TOJO")

| 13" | - | R | | FF | OLD 218 | $2.00 | |

Ki-84 Hayate ("FRANK")(SA: 230, 258)

13"	-	R		FF	ALFERY	$5.00	
18"	-	R		FF	COLE	$5.00	
22"	-	R		FF	KOUTNY	$5.00	
22"	-	R		FF	WOODHOUSE	£3.00	(Koutny)
54"	-	.60		RC	FM CF434	$8.00	(Hines)
88"	73"	2.5-3.7	6		SMITH	$42.00	

[cowl, $30.00; canopy, $27.00]

SHIN MEIWA

PS-1

| *3800mm | 2780mm | .60x4 | 4-6 | IKUTA | ¥180,000 |

TACHIKAWA

Ki-9 ("SPRUCE")

| 13" | - | R | FF | POND 42G6 | $3.25 | (Bruning) |

Ki-55 ("IDA")

| 29" | - | R | FF | FSI T-1 | $6.00 | |

YOKOSUKA

D4Y Suisei ("JUDY")(SA: 258)

18"	-	R		FF	POND 60D1	$3.75	(Smith)
30"	-	R		FF	GULF	$5.00	(Midkiff)
*1200mm	950mm	.20-.25	3-4		IKUTA	¥24,000	

*[assembled, ¥98,000]

| *1440mm | 1270mm | .40-.45 | 4-6 | IKUTA | ¥32,000 |

*[assembled, ¥140,000]

| *1900mm | 1560mm | .60-.90 | 4-6 | IKUTA | ¥68,000 |

*[assembled, ¥220,000]

K5Y ("WILLOW")

*1460mm	1070mm	.40	4	IKUTA	¥35,000
*1830mm	1340mm	.60	4-6	IKUTA	¥65,000
*1840mm	1350mm	.90/1.20	5	MORI	¥75,000

NETHERLANDS
FOKKER

C. XIV
13"	–	R	FF	MOONEY	$1.00	
22"	–	R	FF	POND 17E7	$3.25	(Struck)

D. XVII
?	–	–	–	ARGUS CL712x	£3.00	
13"	–	R	FF	OLD 421	$2.00	(Dallaire)
24"	–	R	FF	POND 17E6	$3.75	(Berkeley)
30"	–	–	CL	GLEASON	$3.95	(Hempen)

D.XXI
17"	–	R	FF	POND 17E6	$4.25	(Wright)
17"	–	R	FF	HUNT 1702	$3.50	(Ott)
20"	–	R	FF	HUNT W102	$3.00	(Weiss)
24"	–	R	FF	POND 17E6	$3.75	(Weiss)
36"	–	.048-.49	RC	RCM 829	$3.50	(Miller)
43½"	–	.15-.21	RC	FM CF651	$7.00	(Sundquist)
86"	59"	ST2000	4-5	BEAULIEU 13B	$24.95	(Farrell)

[TDF: cowl, $26.95]

D. XXIII (SA: 230)
22"	–	R	FF	KOUTNY	$5.00	
36"	–	R	FF	POND 17E6	$5.25	(Le Modele Reduit)

G. 1
26"	–	R	FF	HUNT AB08	$3.25	(Booton)

KOOLHOVEN

FK-55
21"	–	R	FF	POND 18G3	$3.25	(Smith)

FK-58
24"	–	R	FF	HUNT AB09	$3.00	(Booton)

POLAND

LUBIN

R-XIV

24"	–	R	FF	COLE	$5.00	
43"	–	R	FF	MAN 9821	$10.50	(Noonan)

PZL

P-1 (SA: 230)

13"	–	R	FF	POND HSDT	$3.25	(McEntee)
15"	–	R	FF	POND 20C4	$3.25	(Modelcraft)
18"	–	R	FF	POND 20C4	$3.75	(McEntee)
24"	–	R	FF	GREGA 111	$2.00	(McEntee)
36"	–	–	CL	POND 30A3	$6.25	(Sterling)

P-6

12½"	–	R	FF	CLEVE CD6U	$8.00	
15"	–	R	FF	POND 20C5	$3.25	(Ott)
16½"	–	R	FF	CLEVE CD6U	$10.00	
25"	–	R	FF	CLEVE CD6U	$14.00	
50"	–	R	FF	CLEVE CD6U	$24.00	

P-7

13"	–	R	FF	FILLON	$16^F 80
23½"	–	R	FF	OLD 297	$3.00	(McEntee)

P-9

26"	–	R	FF	TOKO	$4.00	(Wilson)

P-11 (SA: 231)

12"	–	R	FF	POND 20C4	$3.25	(Megow)
*[FIKE: $6.95]						
13"	–	R	FF	AIRBORNE	$3.00AUS	
20"	–	R	FF	HUNT ME03	$3.00	(Megow)
24"	–	R	FF	PLANS	$6.00	(Andrus)
30"	–	–	CL	POND 20C4	$4.75	(Wiestaw)
35"	–	R	FF	POND 20C4	$5.75	(Bryant)
40"	–	.049	2-3	FM CF617	$6.00	(Nagy)
*70"	–	/.90-.120	4-5	FLITECRAFT	£126.00	

P-23 Karas (SA: 231)

99"	–	Q35	6	GORDON	$42.00

P-24

| 760mm | – | R | FF | MRA A418 | 16F | |
| 35" | – | 1-1.5cc | FF | ARGUS FSP487 | £4.50 | (Bryant) |

P-37 Los

| 47" | – | – | CL | POND 20C6 | $10.75 | (Kocskodat) |

RWD

RWD-8 (SA: 231)

| 55" | – | Elec | RC | AIRDROME | $30.00 | |
| 65" | – | – | RC | POND 21B7 | $8.75 | (Welsburg) |

ROMANIA
INDUSTRIAL AERO ROMANIA

IAR-14

| 24" | – | R | FF | HUNT AH188 | $3.00 | (Weathers) |

SOVIET UNION
ILYUSHIN

IL-2 Sturmovik (SA: 231, 259)

16"	–	R	FF	HUNT 3884	$4.50	(Whitman)
20"	–	R	FF	POND 60G5	$3.25	(Mather)
¶20"	–	R	FF	POND 52F7	$4.75	(Comet)
24"	–	R	FF	HUNT AH30	$3.50	(Wennerstron)
24"	–	R	FF	POND 18E7	$3.25	(Model Craft)
25"	–	R	FF	POND 28E4	$3.75	(Easy Build)
27"	–	R	FF	OLD 263	$3.50	(Wennerstron)
740mm	–	R	FF	AIRBORNE	$5.00AUS	
32"	–	R	FF	GULF	$5.00	(Midkiff)
70"	–	.90/1.20	RC	RCM 1042	$15.75	(Andersen)

LAGG

Lagg-3

| 20" | – | R | FF | KOUTNY | $5.00 | |

LAVOCHKIN

La-5 (SA: 231)

16"	–	R	FF	COLE	$5.00	
16¼"	–	R	FF	DIELS 23	$3.00	
*[$14.00]						
20"	–	R	FF	KOUTNY	$5.00	
1120mm	–	.35	4	AIRBORNE	$9.00AUS	
1140mm	–	6.5cc	RC	BOSAK	20 Kcs	
[canopy, 15 Kcs]						
44½"	–	6.1	4	TRAP MW2086	£6.00	(Bosak)

La-7 (SA: 232)

16"	–	R	FF	COLE	$5.00	
20"	–	R	FF	ALFERY	$5.00	
32"	–	–	CL	POND 41F6	$4.75	(Musciano)
35"	–	–	CL	POND 19A1	$4.25	(Fara)

La-9

20"	–	R	FF	KOUTNY	$5.00	
20"	–	R	FF	WOODHOUSE	£2.50	(Koutny)

La-17

37"	–	Jetex	FF	POND 51A2	$4.75	(Veron)

MIKOYAN-GUREVICH

Mig-3 (SA: 232)

18"	–	R	FF	POND 29C4	$3.75	(Bruning)
21"	–	R	FF	KOUTNY	$5.00	
570mm	–	R	FF	AIRBORNE	$5.00AUS	
22½"	–	R	FF	GLEASON	$1.80	(Stahl)
*22½"	–	R	FF	PROKIT	£20.00	
23"	–	R	FF	FM CF561	$5.00	(Kruse)
28"	–	R	FF	HUNT ES34E	$3.50	(Stahl)
28"	–	–	CL	POND 29D1	$5.75	(Musciano)
*34¼"	24½"	.15-.21	CL	MODELHOB 110136	NA	
36"	–	R	FF	HUNT ES57E	$4.00	(Stahl)
62"	–	.60	4	FM CF715	$7.00	(Reiss)
67"	–	–	RC	PROKIT	FORTHCOMING	
*1760mm	1330mm	12.5/20	RC	BAUER 2301	DM576,	
71"	–	.60	RC	HORN S-14	$14.00	(Osborne)

*82"	–	.68-.80	RC	DIVELY	$225.00	
101"	80"	3.0	5-6	ROAMIN	$30.00	

[TDF: cowl, $37.50; canopy, $10.95; SHATTLEROE: landing gear, $14.50

Mig-8

21"	–	R	FF	POND 19D5	$3.75	(Modernistic)

Mig-15 (SA: 232, 259)

?	–	–	–	ARGUS FSP603x	£3.75	
?	–	–	–	ARGUS MA172x	£2.00	
13"	–	Jetex	FF	HUNT J173	$1.50	
*15"	–	Jetex	FF	KEIL KKO063	£3.99	
15"	–	Jetex	FF	POND 29C7	$3.25	(Hatful)
16"	–	Jetex	FF	POND 42B3	$4.75	(Guillow)
*16½"	–	Jetex	FF	EASY JX02	$11.00CDN	
21"	–	Jetex	FF	POND 25A6	$3.75	(Cleveland)
27"	–	–	FF	POND 29D7	$5.75	(Paxton)
35"	–	–	FF	POND 52D7	$5.75	(Norman)
44"	–	Dynajet	CL	POND 52D5	$5.75	(Yonkers)
46½"	–	.40-.45F	4	ARGUS RM227	£5.25	(Norman)
**53"	54"	.60-.90F	RC	TURBOFAN	£89.00	
1440mm	1420mm	.60-.80F	RC	BERTELLA	L.50.000	

[Canopy, L15.000]

*57"	55"	.77F	4-5	BYRON 6130010	$319.00	

[retracts, $128.00; power package, $365.95]

1510mm	–	13ccF	RC	BOSAK	40 Kcs	

[canopy, 30 Kcs]

Mig-17 (SA: 232)

25"	–	Glider	FF	WALLACE	$6.50	
28"	–	–	FF	POND 29D2	$4.72	(Koch)
33"	–	.19-.20	3	ARGUS RM169	£3.75	(Bosak)
880mm	760mm	.3-1cc	FF	VTH MT296	DM7,50	(Koch)
1205mm	1408mm	.60-.80F	RC	BERTELLA	L50.000	

[canopy, L15.000]

Mig-19

1280mm	2120mm	.60x2F	RC	BERTELLA	L50.000	

[canopy, L15.000]

Mig-21 (SA: 232)

?	–	–	–	ARGUS RC1083x	£3.00	
19½"	–	Glider	FF	WALLACE	$6.50	
37"	65"	.77F	3	BEAULIEU 16B	$24.95	(Farrell)
1250mm	1800mm	.60-.80F	RC	BERTELLA	L50.000	

Mig-25 (SA: 232)

*?	–	Glider	RC	SKYTIME	FORTHCOMING	
20"	–	Glider	FF	WALLACE	$6.50	
34"	–	–	RC	POND 58E7	$3.75	(Weiss)
900mm	–	6.5cc	RC	BOSAK	20 Kcs	
[canopy, 10 Kcs]						
36"	–	.40	4-5	TRAP MW2127	£5.50	(Bosak)
[canopy, £3.20]						
*47"	75"	.81x2F	7	KNIGHTS	$345.00	
*55"	85"	.61x2F	7	TJM	$375.00	

Mig DIS

34"	–	R	FF	KOUTNY	$10.00

PETLYAKOV

PE-2

40"	–	R	FF	GULF	$5.00	(Midkiff)

PE-3

36"	–	R	FF	KOUTNY	$10.00

POLIKARPOV

D-1

24"	–	R	FF	HUNT AH168	$3.25	(Pilzer)
24"	–	R	FF	POND 30A5	$3.75	(GHQ)

I-16 Rata (SA: 233)

11"	–	R	FF	CLEVE CD217	$9.00	
16½"	–	R	FF	CLEVE CD217	$12.00	
17"	–	R	FF	POND 19F5	$3.25	(Halls)
20"	–	R	FF	HUNT AH148	$3.25	
22"	–	R	FF	CLEVE CD217	$18.00	
22"	–	–	CL	POND 23E4	$4.25	(Brittain)
23"	–	R	FF	POND 19F5	$3.25	(Thomas)
26"	–	R	FF	POND 51C3	$4.25	(Le Modele Reduit)

840mm	–	R	FF	MRA 361	40F	
44"	–	–	FF	POND 51C3	$7.25	(Kresil)
1650mm	–	10cc	RC	MRA 541	106F	
2360mm	1610mm	50-70cc	4	VTH MT/K 387	DM32	(Kriz)

I-153 Chaika

72"	–	.60	RC	B&D	$14.95

ITP M-2

20"	–	R	FF	ALFERY	$5.00

Po-2/U-2 (SA: 233)

13"	–	R	FF	FILLON	16^F 80	
20"	–	R	FF	HUNT AH163	$2.75	(Howard)
25"	–	–	CL	POND 20G2	$3.75	(Russia)
32"	–	R	FF	POND 20G2	$4.75	(Bowers)
40"	–	R	FF	GULF	$5.00	(Midkiff)
48"	–	.09-.15	RC	MA 181	$3.00	(Bowers)
1800mm	–	10cc	RC	MODELL	DM24,80	(Meier)
74"	53"	.60	RC	RCM 530	$16.50	(Meier)
1880mm	–	10cc	RC	MRA 150	132F	

SUKHOI

Su-15/20 (SA: 233)

29"	–	Glider	FF	WALLACE	$6.50

TUPOLEV

SB-2

37"	–	R	FF	WOODHOUSE	£3.50	(Koutny)

Tu-2

31"	–	R	FF	DIELS 50	$5.00

YAKOVLEV

Yak-3 (SA: 234, 259)

13"	–	R	FF	POND 37F7	$3.25	(Pishnery)
17"	–	R	FF	COLE	$5.00	
19"	–	R	FF	KOUTNY	$5.00	
22"	–	R	FF	POND 37F7	$3.75	(Brown)
33"	–	–	CL	POND 61A2	$6.25	(Musciano)

56½"	–	.45-.60	5-6	MAN 10721	$10.50	(Reusch)

Yak-4 (SA: 259)

?	–	–	–	ARGUS MA346x	£3.75	
22"	–	–	CL	POND 55A5	$3.75	(Taylor)
50"	–	–	CL	POND 31E4	$5.75	(Taylor)

Yak-9 (SA: 234, 259)

?	–	–	–	ARGUS CL11x	£3.75	
18"	–	–	CL	POND 55A3	$3.75	(Uminski)
18"	–	–	CL	POND 55A2	$3.75	(Fara)
20"	–	–	CL	POND 55B5	$3.75	(Budin)
26"	–	–	CL	PALADINE 48	$8.00	
28"	–	.5-1cc	FF	ORIGINAL	£3.00	(Martin)
800mm	–	R	FF	MRA 382	40F	
36"	–	–	CL	POND 31G6	$4.75	(Fara)
40"	–	–	CL	POND 31G4	$10.75	(Uminski)
45"	–	–	RC	POND 37E3	$7.75	(Budin)
1150mm	–	–	RC	VTH MT669-K	DM12,	(Budin)
52"	–	–	RC	PALADINE 48	$14.00	
61"	–	.60	RC	FM CF377	$7.00	(Reiss)
1700mm	1450mm	10cc	4-5	VTH MT669-G	DM29,50	(Budin)

Yak-15 (SA: 234)

700mm	–	–	FF	MRA A191	16F

Yak-23

1448mm	1360mm	.60-81F	RC	BERTELLA	L50.000

[canopy, L15.000]

Yak-25

19"	–	–	CL	POND 55B3	$3.25	(Kostura)
43"	–	–	CL	POND 31F1	$6.75	(Kostura)

SWEDEN

FFVS

J-22 (SA: 259)

13"	–	R	FF	DIELS 26	$2.00	
16"	–	R	FF	POND 30G5	$3.25	(Wentzel)

16½"	–	R	FF	DIELS 46	$3.00	

SAAB

A-32 Lansen
15"	–	Jetex	FF	POND 30G6	$3.75	(Wentzel)

B-18
?	–	–	–	ARGUS MA300x	£5.25	
27"	–	R	FF	POND 30F2	$3.75	(Wentzel)
40"	–	–	CL	POND 31A2	$5.75	(Chiun)

J-21
10"	–	R	FF	COLE	$5.00	
49"	–	.35-.60	RC	GLEASON	$13.25	(Angel)

J-29 Tunan (SA: 234)
1210mm	–	6.5cc	RC	BOSAK	20 Kcs
[canopy, 20 Kcs]					

J-35 Draken
12"	–	Jetex	FF	POND 42D1	$3.25	(Karlstrom)
17"	–	Glider	FF	WALLACE	$6.50	

J-37 Viggen
530mm	–	.08F	RC	MRA A431	16F	
32"	38"	.40F	RC	ZIROLI	$10.00	
43"	56"	.40-45F	RC	ARGUS RC1970	£10.00	(Ghisleri)
43"	56"	.45F	RC	BARN	$34.00	
*45"	64"	.65-.77F	5	CRESS	$329.00	
[power package, $480.00]						
45"	–	.81F	4	GOLDEN ERA	$19.95	(Thacker)

J-39 Grippen (SA: 235, 259)
*66"	42"	.61F	4	MIKE	$229.00

S-17
22"	–	R	FF	POND 21A7	$3.75	(Wentzel)

THULIN

Type K
35"	–	R	FF	POND 22C5	$3.75	(Wentzel)

UNITED STATES

AERONCA

L-3 Grasshopper
105"	62"	1.0/1.2	4	AERO PLANS	$25.00	

L-3B Grasshopper
105"	62"	1.0/1.2	4	AERO PLANS	$25.00	

L-16 Grasshopper
16"	-	R	FF	FOAM	$2.50	
18"	-	R	FF	POND 56D5	$2.75	(Musciano)
84"	53"	.60/.90	4	AERO PLANS	$25.00	

[FGM:cowl, $19.50]

L-58 Defender (SA: 235)
13"	-	R	FF	MOONEY	$1.00	
25"	-	-	CL	POND 55B1	$3.75	(Fearnley)
28"	-	R	FF	POND 49B1	$4.75	(Mooney)
38"	-	R	FF	POND 13B1	$5.75	(Musciano)

BEECHCRAFT

C-45 (SA: 235, 260)
53½"	-	.15x2	RC	RCM 397	$5.50	(Peterson)

C-78
78½"	-	.60x2	RC	B&D	$14.95	

T-34 Mentor (SA: 235)
16"	-	R	FF	GLEASON	$1.70	(Cole)
20"	-	R	FF	GLEASON	$2.50	(Cole)
22"	-	-	CL	POND 55A1	$3.75	(Musciano)
25"	-	R	FF	GLEASON	$4.10	(Cole)
33"	-	-	CL	POND 31A5	$5.75	(Berkeley)
48"	-	-	CL	POND 31G6	$7.25	(Musciano)
*56"	-	.35-.45	4	ACE 50K222	$69.95	
69½"	-	-	RC	GLEASON AM268A	NA	(Atkinson)

BELL

XP-39
13"	-	R	FF	POND 13D7	$3.75	(Weiss)

P-39 Airacobra (SA: 235, 260)

?	-	-	-	ARGUS FSR100x	£2.50	
13"	-	R	FF	HANNAN	$2.50	(Alvarez)
13"	-	R	FF	OLD 489	$2.00	(Whitman)
¶14"	-	R	FF	POND 53A2	$3.75	(Megow)
*15"	-	R	FF	KEIL KK0025	£4.99	
¶16"	-	R	FF	POND 53A1	$3.75	(Megow)
16"	-	R	FF	POND 53F2	$3.75	(Hi-Flier)
17"	-	R	FF	GLEASON	$2.40	(Mather)
17"	-	R	FF	POND 52F3	$3.75	(Wright)
20"	-	R	FF	POND 26E1	$4.75	(Whitman)

*[REPRO: $10.50]

22"	-	R	FF	GLEASON	$1.80	(Stahl)
23"	-	R	FF	HUNT C-28	$3.25	(Megow)
600mm	-	R	FF	AIRBORNE	$5.00AUS	
*24"	-	R	FF	EASY FF27	$7.00CDN	
¶24"	-	R	FF	POND 13E4	$4.25	(Guillow)
¶25"	-	R	FF	POND 13D7	$3.75	(Comet)
25½"	-	R	FF	CLEVE CD76	$16.00	
26"	-	R	FF	AUTHENTIC	£1.45	(Towner)
26"	-	R	FF	POND 13E1	$3.75	(Hi-Flier)
26"	-	R	FF	POND 58B3	$5.25	(Guillow)
28"	-	R	FF	POND 26D2	$3.75	(Musciano)
30"	-	R	FF	CLEVE IT-76	$10.00	
31"	-	R	FF	HUNT E502E	$3.50	(Stahl)
¶32"	-	R	FF	HUNT 3214	$.50	(Ott)
32"	-	R	FF	POND 53A5	$4.75	(Smalley)
33"	-	.29-.60	CL	HORN MPS-261	$3.00	
¶34"	-	R	FF	POND 13E3	$5.25	(Miniature A/
34"	-	-	CL	POND 13E3	$5.25	(Musciano)
*35"	-	R	FF	EASY FF3	$12.00CDN	
36"	-	R	FF	CLEVE T-76	$12.00	
36"	-	R	FF	POND 46D4	$5.25	(Megow)
*1290mm	1007mm	.19-.25	3-4	IKUTA	¥13,5000	

*[assembled, ¥75,000]

*51"	-	.40	5-6	SURE FLITE	$63.95	

*[K-BEE: assembled, $149.95]

52"	-	-	CL	POND 26D3	$6.25	(Pyron)

53½"	–	.45	CL	MA 367	$12.75	(Stolly)
*55"	–	.24-.45	3	WING 705	$37.50	
*1464mm	1100mm	.40-.45	3-4	IKUTA	¥24,000	
*59½"	–	.61	4	FLAIR CAPR21	NA	
59"	–	.61	4	TRAP MW2121	£8.50	(CAP)
*60"	50"	.60	4-6	TOP RC-18	$126.95	
*1630mm	1185mm	.60	4-5	IKUTA	¥32,000	
68"	60"	ST2000	RC	PHOTO	$24.00	(Pepino)
*1800mm	1500mm	10cc	RC	KRANZ	DM250,	
*2100mm	1800mm	15cc	RC	KRANZ	DM390,	
85½"	75½"	ST3000	RC	PHOTO	$28.00	(Pepino)
*96"	–	Q50	5-6	CONSOLIDATED	$240.00	

P-63 Kingcobra (SA: 236)

15"	–	R	FF	HUNT 3701	$4.50	(Whitman)
25"	–	R	FF	KOUTNY	$5.00	
25"	–	R	FF	WOODHOUSE	£3.00	(Koutny)
26"	–	–	CL	POND 26D7	$5.25	(Musciano)
34"	–	–	CL	POND 13E3	$5.25	(Musciano)
930mm	–	R	FF	MRA 340	40F	
70"	–	–	RC	POND 35A6	$7.75	(Maxey)
*114"	–	Q50	6	CONSOLIDATED	$265.00	

X-1 (SA: 236)

*5½"	6½"	Glider	FF	PAI 245	$3.75
10½"	–	Glider	FF	CLEVE CD189	$10.00
14"	–	Glider	FF	CLEVE 189	$12.00
*18½"	–	Bean Rock	FF	WILLAIRCO	$26.25
21"	–	Glider	FF	CLEVE CD189	$16.00
*28"	–	Bean Rock	FF	WILLAIRCO	$38.40
*42"	–	Bean Rock	FF	WILLAIRCO	$69.75

XFL-1 Airabonita

13"	–	R	FF	MOONEY	$1.00	
18"	–	R	FF	HUNT 3872	$4.50	(Whitman)
¶ 22"	–	R	FF	HUNT 2206	$3.50	(Ott)
25"	–	R	FF	POND 13E4	$3.75	(Modelcraft)
36"	–	R	FF	HUNT 5376	$5.50	(Whitman)

XP-59 Airacomet (SA: 260)

| ¶18" | – | Jetex | FF | POND 52F3 | $3.75 | (Comet) |

XP-77

| 33" | – | – | CL | POND 26D3 | $4.25 | (Everett) |

YFM-1 Airacuda (SA: 236)

| 13¼" | – | R | FF | PROKIT | £2.25 | |

BELLANCA

YO-50

| 24" | – | R | FF | POND 26D1 | $3.75 | (Pond) |

BERLINER-JOYCE

OJ-2 (SA: 260)

19"	–	R	FF	HUNT AH68	$3.00	(Zier)
25"	–	R	FF	FSI B-7	$6.00	
25"	–	R	FF	GLEASON	$2.15	(Zier)
29"	–	R	FF	COLE	$5.00	
102"	77"	3.7	5-6	HOLMAN	$24.00	(Morse)

P-16 (SA: 260)

13"	–	R	FF	CLEVE CD39	$12.00	
17"	–	R	FF	CLEVE CD39	$15.00	
25½"	–	R	FF	CLEVE CD39	$22.00	
34"	28¼"	.049	FF	LAMBERT	$5.00	
51"	–	–	RC	CLEVE CD39	$35.00	
60"	–	–	CL	POND 13F5	$7.75	(Lindberg)
66"	–	–	RC	POND 48F2	$8.75	(Evans)
72"	–	–	RC	MB 2770T	$12.00	(Evans)

[SHATTLEROE: landing gear, $73.00]

| 102½" | 83 | – | 4-6 | HOLMAN | $25.00 | (Morse) |

[SHATTLEROE: landing gear, $73.00]
**[KLARICH: $120.00]

XFJ-1

10½"	–	R	FF	CLEVE CD238	$10.00	
14"	–	R	FF	CLEVE CD238	$14.00	
21"	–	R	FF	CLEVE CD238	$18.00	
27"	–	R	FF	PLANS	$6.00	(Andrus)
42"	–	–	RC	CLEVE CD238	$30.00	

55½"	–	.40-.61	RC	RCM 579	$6.75	(DeVries)
84"	–	–	RC	CLEVE CD238	$52.00	

BOEING

Boeing 100

11"	–	R	FF	CLEVE CB1CU	$10.00
22"	–	R	FF	CLEVE CB1CU	$18.00

B-9

12"	–	R	FF	POND 14A4	$3.35	(Construct)
26"	–	R	FF	GLEASON	$3.15	(McEntee)
29"	–	R	FF	CLEVE CD1005	$18.00	
38½"	–	R	FF	CLEVE CD1005	$24.00	
49"	–	R	FF	PLANS	$8.00	(Andrus)
58"	–	–	RC	CLEVE CD1005	$32.00	

B-17 Flying Fortress (SA: 236)

?	–	.20x4	4	FM CF286	$15.50	(Cook)
26"	–	R	FF	FRANK 41	$2.50	(Modelcraft)
32"	–	R	FF	HUNT 3219	$4.50	(Ott)
37"	–	R	FF	AUTHENTIC	£1.70	(Towner)
38½"	–	R	FF	CLEVE CD100AU	$32.00	
39"	–	.020x4	CL	STERLING E-11	$29.95	
44"	–	–	CL	POND 13D3	$7.75	(Laumer)
45"	–	.049x2	CL	GUILLOW 2002	$44.00	
45"	–	R	FF	POND 14B4	$5.75	(Miniature A/C)
51"	–	–	RC	CLEVE CD100AU	$40.00	
52"	–	–	CL	POND 14B4	$6.25	(Berkeley)
60"	–	–	FF	POND 26C3	$6.25	(Le Guennon)
77"	–	–	RC	CLEVE CD100AU	$52.00	
1980mm	1396mm	.20/.35x4	4-6	MARUTAKA 27	¥42,000	
2110mm	1510mm	.19x4	4-5	IKUTA	¥65,000	
103"	–	–	RC	CLEVE CD100AU	$65.00	
120"	–	.40x4	RC	ARGUS RSQ1550	£18.50	(Henkens)

[cowls, canopy, turrets, £26.00][AEROMARINE: retracts: $275.00]

120"	85"	.60x4	4-5	WESCRAFT	$395.00

[fiberglass fuselage and wings, $879.00][retracts: AEROMARINE,
 $275.00; SCHMALZIGAN, $245.00; WHEELS, $275.00]

3200mm	2050mm	.45x4	4-5	IKUTA	¥130,000

B-29 Superfortress (SA: 236)

27"	–	R	FF	POND 24B3	$4.25	(Cleveland)
35"	–	R	FF	POND 14B1	$8.75	(Guillow)
42"	–	R	FF	HUNT 2001	$6.00	(Ott)
70"	–	.29x4	CL	CODDING	$4.00	(M&O)
**82½"	58"	.15x4	4	MURPHY	$75.00	
**114½"	80½"	.40x4	5-7	MURPHY	$175.00	
*3800mm	2800mm	.60x4	4-6	IKUTA	¥148,000	

*[assembled, ¥498,000]

B-47 Stratojet (SA: 236, 260)

19"	–	Glider	FF	PROKIT	£1.50	(Arnould)
22½"	–	Glider	FF	CLEVE SM185	$6.00	
29"	–	Glider	FF	HUNT J108	$3.00	(V/C Plan)
*38½"	36"	Bean Rock	FF	WILLAIRCO	$36.75	
46"	–	–	CL	POND 26D1	$6.75	(Parks)

B-52 Stratofortress (SA: 236)

24½"	–	Glider	FF	CLEVE SM195	$6.00
*61½"	52"	Bean Rock	FF	WILLAIRCO	$42.50
78"	66"	Glider	2-4	GREEN	£8.25
*106"	70"	Glider	2-4	SKYTIME	£100.00

F2B-1

23"	–	R	FF	FSI B-3	$6.00

F3B-1

17"	–	R	FF	COLE	$5.00
25"	–	R	FF	CFI B-4	$6.00

F4B-1 (SA: 260)

11¼"	–	R	FF	CLEVE CD29B	$14.00	
12"	–	R	FF	FRANK 17	$2.50	(Comet)
13"	–	R	FF	DIELS 52	$2.50	
13"	–	R	FF	OLD 474	$2.00	(Scientific)
13"	–	R	FF	OLD 447	$3.00	(Peerless)
14"	–	R	FF	POND 26C1	$3.25	(Wentzel)
15"	–	R	FF	CLEVE CD29B	$16.00	
15"	–	R	FF	CLEVE P1453	$12.00	
*15"	–	R	FF	DIELS 1	$14.00	
15"	–	R	FF	POND 14B5	$3.25	(Rainey)

15"	–	R	FF	POND 14B5	$3.25	(Comet)
16"	–	R	FF	GLEASON	$2.20	(Chevedden)
16"	–	R	FF	POND 14B5	$3.25	(Burd)
16"	–	R	FF	POND 26B7	$3.75	(Guillow)
18"	–	R	FF	POND 14B5	$3.75	(Modelcraft)
20"	–	1-1.5cc	CL	ARGUS MA290	£3.00	(Barrett)
20"	–	R	FF	REPRO 171	$1.50	(Scientific)
22"	–	R	FF	FSI B-5	$6.00	
22"	–	R	FF	HUNT K007	$3.50	(Miniature A/C)
22"	–	R	FF	HUNT PE008	$4.00	(Peerless)
*22"	–	R	FF	REPRO R-13	$8.50	(AMCO)
22¼"	–	R	FF	GLEASON	$4.40	(Tomasco)
22¼"	–	R	FF	CLEVE CD29B	$20.00	
¶ 22½"	–	R	FF	WISCONSIN	$4.00	(Toledo)
25"	–	R	FF	HUNT WW10	$3.25	(Winter)
30"	–	–	CL	POND 49D5	$4.75	(Aircraft Plan)
30"	–	–	CL	POND 49D5	$4.75	(Scalemaster)
31"	–	R	FF	HUNT WW05	$4.00	(Winter)
44½"	–	R	FF	CLEVE CD29B	$32.00	
45"	–	–	CL	POND 49D6	$7.25	(Galloway)
45¼"	–	.40-.50	CL	ARGUS CL1273	£6.00	(Truelove)
59½"	–	–	RC	CLEVE CD29B	$44.00	
60"	–	.51-.60	4	MORGAN 107RC	$14.95	
60"	–	.60	RC	RCM 382	$8.50	(Bowers)
66"	–	–	FF	POND 14B2	$8.75	(Miniature A/C)

**[KLARICH: $90.00]

1780mm	–	15-20cc	RC	MRA 638	144F
72"	–	.90	RC	B&D	$14.95
72"	51"	Q35	4	BOSMAN	$30.00
89"	–	–	RC	CLEVE CD29B	$58.00
90"	–	2.2	5-6	HOLMAN	$24.00 (Morse)

[SHATTLEROE: landing gear, $37.00; TDF: cowl, $30.95]
**[R&M: $150.00]

FB-5

24"	–	R	FF	FSI B-2	$6.00

XL-15

49"	–	R	FF	POND 26C2	$5.25	(Martin)

L-15 Scout

?	–	–	–	ARGUS FSP395x	£3.00	
940mm	–	R	FF	MRA 309	40F	
31"	–	R	FF	POND 14B1	$3.75	(Struhl)
40"	–	–	CL	GLEASON	$4.10	(Palanek)
40"	–	–	CL	PROKIT	£3.60	(Palanek)
40"	–	–	CL	POND 26C5	$4.25	(Plecan)

MB-3A

10"	–	R	FF	CLEVE CD157	$8.00
13"	–	R	FF	CLEVE CD157	$9.00
19½"	–	R	FF	CLEVE CD157	$15.00
39"	–	R	FF	CLEVE CD157	$28.00

P-12 (SA: 237)

11¼"	–	R	FF	CLEVE CD8B	$14.00	
12"	–	R	FF	POND 14A3	$3.25	(Paul Jones)
12" *[FIKE: $6.95]	–	R	FF	POND 37A4	$3.25	(Megow)
12"	–	R	FF	POND 37A3	$3.75	(Guillow)
12"	–	R	FF	POND 47F7	$3.25	(Ideal)
14"	–	R	FF	POND 14A3	$3.25	(Falcon Models
14"	–	R	FF	POND 14A2	$3.25	(Comet)
14"	–	R	FF	POND 14A2	$3.25	(Sturdi-Built)
15"	–	R	FF	CLEVE CD8B	$16.00	
15"	–	R	FF	POND 47A6	$4.74	(Ott)
19"	–	R	FF	PLANS	$6.00	(Andrus)
20"	–	R	FF	HUNT K008	$3.25	(Construct)
20"	–	R	FF	HUNT PA-15	$4.50	(Ott)
20"	–	R	FF	POND 14A3	$3.75	(Imperial)
22"	–	R	FF	REPRO 118	$2.25	(Tomasco)
22¼"	–	R	FF	CLEVE CD8B	$20.00	
22"	–	R	FF	POND 14A3	$3.75	(Peerless)
23"	–	R	FF	POND 14A2	$3.75	(Bowers)
24"	–	R	FF	POND 55E4	$5.25	(Davies A/C)
24"	–	R	FF	GLEASON	$4.90	(Ott)
24"	–	R	FF	PLANS	$6.00	(Andrus)
30"	–	R	FF	POND 26C4	$4.75	(Ealy)
44½"	–	–	RC	CLEVE CD8B	$32.00	

59½"	-	-	RC	CLEVE CD8B	$44.00	
89"	-	-	RC	CLEVE CD8B	$58.00	

P-26 Peashooter

10¼"	-	R	FF	CLEVE CD23U	$9.00	
14"	-	R	FF	CLEVE CD23U	$11.00	
20½"	-	R	FF	CLEVE CD23U	$15.00	

P-26A Peashooter (SA: 237)

?	-	-	-	ARGUS MA123x	£3.00	
10½"	-	R	FF	CLEVE CD60	$12.00	
12"	-	R	FF	POND 14A4	$3.25	(Comet)
13"	-	R	FF	DIELS 6	$2.00	
13"	-	R	FF	OLD 482	$3.00	(Lindberg)
13"	-	R	FF	POND 14A4	$3.25	(Air-King)
14"	-	R	FF	CLEVE CD60	$15.00	
14¼"	-	R	FF	DIELS 47	$2.25	
16"	-	R	FF	POND 61C2	$3.25	(Modelcraft)
16"	-	R	FF	POND 14A4	$3.25	(Hi-Flier)
16"	-	R	FF	FRANK 27	$2.00	(Comet)
*[FIKE: $6.95]						
16"	-	R	FF	POND 14A5	$3.75	(Duncan)
17"	-	R	FF	POND 14A5	$3.75	(Construct)
17"	-	R	FF	POND 14A5	$3.75	(Rainey)
17½"	-	R	FF	CODDING	$.35	(Lindberg)
19"	-	R	FF	POND 14A6	$4.25	(Sturdi-Built)
20"	-	R	FF	PLANS	$6.00	(Andrus)
20"	-	R	FF	POND 14A6	$3.75	(Ott)
21"	-	R	FF	CLEVE CD60	$20.00	
21"	-	-	CL	POND 14A6	$4.75	(Berkeley)
21"	-	R	FF	POND 14A7	$5.75	(Ideal)
21¼"	-	R	FF	OLD 82	$3.00	(Diel)
23"	-	-	CL	POND 26D2	$4.25	(Lewis)
24"	-	R	FF	HUNT PL110	$3.50	(Lindberg)
25"	-	R	FF	OLD 339	$3.00	(Comet)
27½"	-	.09-.20	CL	AUTHENTIC	£1.75	(Towner)
27"	-	-	CL	POND 41F1	$5.75	(Struhl)
27"	-	-	CL	POND 49D3	$5.73	(Muscinao)

28"	–	R	FF	CLEVE SGP-60A	$16.00	
28"	–	R	FF	CODDING FSI-17	$1.00	(Scale Models
*28"	–	R/.020	CL	STERLING E10	$19.95	
31"	–	.049	FF	GULF	$5.00	(Midkiff)
41½"	–	–	CL	GLEASON	$6.85	(Worth)
41½"	–	–	CL	PROKIT	£6.00	(Worth)
42"	–	–	RC	CLEVE CD60	$32.00	
57"	48"	.60	4	AEROTEK	$21.95	
*1702mm	1438mm	.90/1.20	4-5	MARUTAKA 71	¥48,000	
1500mm	–	15cc	4	MODULO	L20.000	
63"	–	–	RC	CLEVE CD60	$45.00	
72"	–	.60	RC	B&D	$14.95	
80"	68½"	Q50	4	PHOTO	$29.95	
84"	–	–	RC	CLEVE CD60	$58.00	
84"	–	2-2.5	4	MAN 9822	$28.00	(Santich)

[TDF: gear case, $34.50; ring cowl, $26.50; fairings, $26.95; wheel
  pants, $24.50; SHATTLEROE: landing gear, $24.50]
**[KLARICH: $85.00; R&M: $165.00]

PW9-C

24"	–	R	FF	FSI B-1	$6.00	

XF5B-1

19"	–	.020	FF	MA 407	$4.25	(Gable)
20½"	–	R	FF	FRANK 35	$2.25	(Comet)

XF6B-1

20½"	–	R	FF	GLEASON	$2.75	(Bibichkow)
22"	–	R	FF	OLD 336	$3.00	(Scrameggs)

XF7B-1

13"	–	R	FF	DIELS 5	$2.00	
20½"	–	R	FF	OLD 66	$3.00	(Markwiese)

XP-940

17¼"	–	R	FF	GLEASON	$2.25	(Lindberg)
24"	–	R	FF	HUNT PL108	$3.75	(Lindberg)

XFB-1

32"	–	R	FF	GULF	$5.00	(Midkiff)

BREWSTER

F2A Buffalo (SA: 237, 260)

?	–	–	–	ARGUS MA367x	£3.75	
12"	–	R	FF	POND 13E5	$3.75	(Halls)
13"	–	R	FF	POND 14C4	$3.25	(Weiss)
13"	–	R	FF	DIELS 14	$1.75	
17¼"	–	R	FF	DIELS 38	$2.75	
18"	–	R	FF	POND 26C3	$3.75	(Wentzel)
26"	–	R	FF	CLEVE CD87B	$18.00	
26½"	–	R	FF	GLEASON	$3.45	(Mills)
27"	–	R	FF	POND 46C6	$3.75	(Jones)
29"	–	R	FF	HUNT 2967	$5.50	(Whitman)
35"	–	R	FF	POND 26C5	$5.25	(Clements)
37"	–	–	CL	POND 42D1	$5.75	(Wheldon)
44"	–	–	CL	GLEASON	$.60	(Lindberg)
54"	–	.45–.60	RC	HOLMAN	$6.96	(Williams)
2660mm	1950mm	60–100cc	5	VTH MT/K418	DM45,	(Kriz)

SB2A Buccaneer/Bermuda

¶12"	–	R	FF	POND 52F3	$5.25	(Guillow)
13"	–	R	FF	DIELS 12	$1.75	
18"	–	R	FF	HUNT AH71	$2.75	
18"	–	R	FF	DIELS 17	$2.50	
23½"	–	R	FF	DIELS 53	$3.25	
24"	–	R	FF	GLEASON	$2.25	(Hollinger)
36"	–	R	FF	ORIGINAL	£4.50	(Martin)
¶38"	–	R	FF	POND 14D1	$4.75	(Ott)
47"	–	R	FF	POND 14C3	$5.75	(Hollinger)

SBN-1

13"	–	R	FF	DIELS 2	$2.00

XA-32

13"	–	R	FF	DIELS 20	$2.00

XSBA-1

19"	–	R	FF	POND 14C4	$3.25	(Limber)
19"	–	R	FF	MAN 2791	$4.00	(Stark)

CESSNA

L-19 Bird Dog (SA: 237)

*17"	–	R	FF	STERLING A-12	$9.95	
18"	–	R	FF	POND 31A5	$4.75	(Guillow)
18"	–	R	FF	FOAM	$2.75	
18"	–	R	FF	PECK BH130	$1.50	(Kusik)
23"	–	R	FF	POND 14F4	$4.25	(Berkeley)
33"	–	R	FF	POND 26G6	$4.25	(Fearnley)
35"	–	R	FF	POND 26E3	$3.75	(Le Modele Reduit)
¶ 36"	–	–	FF	GLEASON AT1052	$5.50	(Berkeley)
36"	–	R	FF	GLEASON	$4.15	(Kochman)
37"	–	–	–	ARGUS FSP568	£3.75	(Fearnley)
72"	–	.45-.50	4	TRAP MW2067	£8.00	(Ward)
2000mm	1420mm	6.10cc	4	VTH MT/R349	DM36,	(Feifel)
*2240mm	1495mm	.61/1.20	5	MARUTAKA 51	¥45,000	

01-E Bird Dog

*18"	–	R	FF	GUILLOW 902	$4.29	
54"	–	–	RC	GLEASON AM762	$9.50	(Wischer)

CHASE

C-122 Avitruck

36"	–	–	CL	POND 26E4	$4.75	(Musciano)

CONSOLIDATED

A-11 Attack

20"	–	R	FF	POND 24C2	$3.25	(Cleveland)

B-24 Liberator (SA: 237)

15"	–	R	FF	COLE	$5.00	
55"	–	.02x4	RC	GLEASON	$8.40	(Kiracofe)
69"	–	–	CL	GLEASON AT954	$9.40	(Lashek)
**90"	54"	.19x4	5-7	MURPHY	$100.00	
**110"	67"	.25x4	5-7	MURPHY	$150.00	

BT-7

6"	–	R	FF	GLEASON	$.50	(Petrlik)
16"	–	R	FF	FRANK 24	$2.00	(Comet)
*[FIKE: $6.95]						
20"	–	R	FF	HUNT A150	$2.50	(Comet)

31½"	-	R	FF	OLD G1	$4.00	(Comet)
31"	-	R	FF	POND 26F3	$5.25	(Davies A/C)

P-30

12"	-	R	FF	POND 14G5	$3.25	(Megow)
19¼"	-	R	FF	OLD 36	$3.00	(Lindberg)
21"	-	R	FF	POND 14G5	$3.75	(Lindberg)
21"	-	R	FF	POND 26G5	$3.75	(Wentzel)
23"	-	R	FF	POND 14G5	$4.25	(Megow)
24"	-	R	FF	POND 14G5	$4.25	(Guillow)
24"	-	R	FF	POND 62D5	$5.25	(Paul Jones)

PB-2A

22"	-	R	FF	POND 14G6	$3.75	(Weiss)
24"	-	R	FF	GLEASON	$2.25	(Lindberg)
41"	-	-	CL	POND 26F3	$4.75	(Musciano)

PBY Catalina (SA: 237, 260)

¶ 22"	-	R	FF	HUNT 2208	$4.00	(Ott)
26"	-	R	FF	POND 14G2	$4.25	(Modelcraft)
39"	-	R	FF	CLEVE CD285	$38.00	
40"	24"	.40x2	CL	JVS	$8.00	
45"	-	-	CL	POND 49E7	$6.75	(Palanek)
52"	-	-	RC	CLEVE CD285	$48.00	
*54"	-	Elec	3	EASY ERC-17	$60.00CDN	
63"	-	4ccx2	CL	ARGUS CL606	£5.25	(Buckland)
67"	43"	.15x2	3	RCM 649	$11.50	(Chappell)
1800mm	-	3.5x2	RC	MRA 537.537	100F	
72"	-	.35x2	4	MORGAN 105R/RC	$14.94	
78"	-	-	RC	CLEVE CD285	$60.00	
*84"	50"	.40x2	4	G&P	$239.00	
*90"	58"	.40x2	5	GLASCO	$250.00	
*102"	66"	.60x2	5	TIGER	$620.00	
104"	-	-	RC	CLEVE CD285	$74.00	
108"	-	.60x2	4-5	MORGAN 105RC	$18.95	
*156"	84"	Q50x2	5	WESCRAFT	$495.00	

[SCHMALZIGAN: retracts, $450.00; nose wheel, $130.00]

*232"	156"	5.8x2	6-10	CUSTOM	$1700.00	
*240"	144"	G62x2	6	KNIGHTS	$957.00	

[retracts, $937.00]

PT-1

20"	–	R	FF	HUNT AH76	$3.00	(Winter)
36"	–	R	FF	HUNT AH77	$3.50	(Reiners)
*36"	–	.049	FF	RN GF109	$24.95	
69½"	54½"	.56-.60	RC	RCM 216	$12.00	(Etching)

PT-3

17"	–	R	FF	COLE	$5.00	
69"	–	.60	RC	HORN S-55	$16.00	(Osborne)

PT-11

24"	–	R	FF	HUNT AH78	$3.50	(Hamilton)
24"	–	R	FF	POND 14G4	$3.75	(Stiglmeier)
30"	–	R	FF	HUNT AH79	$3.50	

XBY-1

27"	–	R	FF	MB 9882	$7.50	(Fineman)

Fleetster

17"	–	R	FF	POND 24C2	$3.75	(Cleveland)
25"	–	R	FF	POND 14G3	$4.25	(Battaglia)

XP-81

25"	–	–	CL	POND 26E7	$3.75	(Ealy)
28"	–	–	CL	POND 26G5	$4.25	(Metzger)

CONVAIR

Convair 48

600mm	–	R	FF	AIRBORNE	$12.00AUS

B-36 Peacemaker (SA: 237)

28"	–	Jetex	FF	POND 26F7	$3.75	(Le Modele Reduit)
*76½"	54"	Bean Rock	FF	WILLAIRCO	$64.25	
**112"	79"	.25x6	4	MURPHY	$175.00	
**115"	81"	.29x6	5-7	MURPHY	$175.00	
*168"	104"	2.0x6	7	GLASCO	$600.00	

XF-92A

11"	–	Jetex	FF	HUNT J114	$3.50	(Hunt)
14"	–	Jetex	FF	HUNT J115	$3.25	(Hunt)
22"	–	Jetex	FF	HUNT J116	$4.50	(Delgatto)

XFY-1 Pogo (SA: 238)

18½"	–	–	CL	GLEASON	$6.70	(Furlong)
18½"	–	–	CL	PROKIT	£5.90	

CURTIS

Curtis 18-T

24"	–	R	FF	MB 11792	$6.50	(Noonan)
25"	–	R	FF	COLE	$5.00	

A-8 Shrike

15"	–	R	FF	POND 15E4	$3.25	(United Model)
16½"	–	R	FF	CLEVE CD25U	$14.00	
19"	–	R	FF	COLE	$5.00	
22"	–	R	FF	CLEVE CD25U	$18.00	
22" *[$20.00]	–	R	FF	DIELS 57	$5.25	
26"	–	R	FF	POND 26E2	$3.75	(McEntee)
33"	–	R	FF	CLEVE CD25U	$24.00	
66"	–	–	RC	CLEVE CD25U	$35.00	
72"	–	.60	RC	B&D	$14.95	

A-12 Shrike

19"	–	R	FF	COLE	$5.00	
33"	–	–	CL	POND 15E4	$5.25	(Berkeley)
63"	–	–	RC	CHARLIE	$17.00	
63"	–	–	RC	MB 7741	$11.00	(C. Smith)

A-38 Attack Falcon

18"	–	–	CL	POND 26E4	$4.25	(Musciano)

AT-9 Jeep

*104"	–	.90x2	6-8	KRAFTERS	$425.00
*121	–	Zen G23x2	6-8	KRAFTERS	$495.00

B-2 Condor

30"	–	.020x2	FF	POND 26G1	$3.75	(Ehling)
82"	–	.40x2	RC	MORGAN 108	$16.95	

BF2C-1 Hawk

15½"	–	R	FF	DIELS 42	$3.25	
20"	–	CO_2	FF	POND 26G2	$3.75	(Wherry)

22"	–	R	FF	POND 50A2	$3.75	(Booton)
24"	–	R	FF	FSI C-15	$6.00	
32"	–	–	CL	POND 15G2	$4.75	(Mechanics)

C-46 Commando

28"	–	R	FF	DIELS 62	$5.50	
40½"	–	R	FF	DIELS 59	$7.00	
41"	–	R	FF	COLE	$5.00	

Export Falcon

12"	–	R	FF	FRANK 1	$2.00	(Megow)

*[FIKE: $20.00]

13"	–	R	FF	OLD 426	$3.00	(Dallaire)
13"	–	R	FF	POND 24D1	$3.25	(Cleveland)
20"	–	R	FF	POND 15D5	$3.75	(Davidson)

Hawk 75

36"	–	.35	CL	FM CF84	$6.00	(Palanek)
36"	–	–	CL	HORN MPS-82	$3.00	

F6C-1 Hawk

24"	–	R	FF	FSI C-6	$6.00	
63"	–	.60	4	CHARLIE	$17.00	
63"	–	.60	RC	HOLMAN	$10.95	(Martin)

F7C-1 Seahawk

12"	–	R	FF	CLEVE CD249	$15.00	
15½"	–	R	FF	CLEVE CD249	$18.00	
18"	–	R	FF	HUNT AH20	$2.50	(Mueller)
23½"	–	R	FF	CLEVE CD249	$24.00	
24"	–	R	FF	POND 26F2	$3.75	(Continental)
25"	–	R	FF	FSI C-7	$6.00	
26"	–	R	FF	HUNT K010	$3.50	(Brooklyn)
32"	–	–	CL	POND 26G2	$4.25	(Esposito)
47"	–	–	RC	CLEVE CD249	$38.00	
63"	–	–	RC	CLEVE CD249	$50.00	
65"	–	–	RC	HOLMAN	$9.95	
94"	–	–	RC	CLEVE CD249	$65.00	

F8C-1 Helldiver

12"	-	R	FF	POND 15F4	$3.25	(Balsa Products)
12"	-	R	FF	POND 15F4	$3.25	(Megow)
12"	-	R	FF	POND 47C1	$3.25	(Construct)
12"	-	R	FF	POND 46B1	$3.25	(Universal)
13"	-	R	FF	POND 15F4	$3.25	(Comet)
16"	-	R	FF	POND 37A6	$3.25	(Burd)
18"	-	R	FF	POND 15F4	$3.75	(Sturiale)
24"	-	R	FF	POND 24C7	$4.75	(Cleveland)
24"	-	R	FF	FSI C-10	$6.00	

F9C-1 Sparrow Hawk

¶ 9½"	-	R	FF	CLEVE CD22C	$12.00	
11"	-	R	FF	FRANK 28	$1.00	(Universal)
12"	-	R	FF	POND 46E1	$3.25	(Davies A/C)
12"	-	R	FF	POND 15F5	$3.25	(Dallaire)
12"	-	R	FF	POND 41C3	$3.25	(M&L)
12"	-	R	FF	POND 15F5	$3.25	(Ideal)
12½"	-	R	FF	CLEVE CD22C	$15.00	
15"	-	R	FF	POND 15F5	$3.25	(Paul Jones)
19"	-	R	FF	CLEVE CD22C	$22.00	
20"	-	R	FF	HUNT PA12	$4.40	(Ott)
20"	-	R	FF	POND 58G4	$3.25	(Guillow)
20"	-	R	FF	POND 15F6	$3.75	(Imperial)
26"	-	-	CL	POND 15F6	$3.75	(Aircraft Plan)
38"	-	R	FF	CLEVE CD22C	$35.00	
48"	-	.45	CL	CHARLIE	$13.00	
48"	-	.45	CL	MB 3751	$10.00	(C. Smith)
50½"	-	-	RC	CLEVE CD22C	$48.00	
76"	-	-	RC	CLEVE CD22C	$58.00	

F11C-2 Goshawk

12"	-	R	FF	CLEVE CD49	$15.00	
13"	-	R	FF	OLD 416	$2.50	(Dallaire)
13"	-	R	FF	POND HSDT	$3.25	(Megow)
16"	-	R	FF	POND 15G1	$3.25	(Duncan)
16"	-	R	FF	POND 24D1	$3.25	(Cleveland)
18"	-	R	FF	POND 52F2	$4.25	(Sturdi-Built)

19"	–	R	FF	POND 50A2	$4.25	(Comet)
19"	–	R	FF	OLD 38	$3.00	(Lindberg)
19½"	–	R	FF	GLEASON	$2.70	(Bibichkow)
19½"	–	R	FF	PROKIT	£2.36	(Bibichkow)
20"	–	R	FF	GLEASON	$2.25	(Lindberg)
20"	–	R	FF	YEST 61	$6.00	(Modernistic)
20"	–	R	FF	POND 27G1	$3,75	(Scientific)
21"	–	R	FF	GLEASON	$2.75	(Booton)
23"	–	R	FF	POND 50A2	$3.75	(Megow)
23"	–	–	CL	POND 50A2	$3.75	(Michaels)
23"	–	R	FF	POND 15G2	$5.25	(Ideal)
23½"	–	R	FF	CLEVE P2751	$22.00	
23½"	–	R	FF	CLEVE CD49	$24.00	
24"	–	R	FF	FSI C-8	$6.00	
24"	–	–	CL	POND 15G3	$5.25	(Berkeley)
31"	–	–	CL	POND 15G4	$4.25	(Aircraft Pla
¶32"	–	–	CL	MB 879CP	$8.00	(Miniature A/
32"	–	R	FF	POND 23D1	$4.25	(Plecan)
47"	–	R	FF	CLEVE CD49	$36.00	
63"	–	–	RC	BARRON	$23.00	

[TDF: cowl, $19.95; wheel pants, $19.95]
**[KLARICH, $100.00]

63"	–	–	RC	CLEVE CD49	$48.00	
*81"	–	.90	6	KRAFTERS	$315.00	
*93"	–	Zen G23	6	KRAFTERS	$385.00	
94"	–	–	RC	CLEVE CD49	$60.00	
94½"	–	–	RC	BARRON	$36.50	

[TDF: cowl, $26.50; wheel pants, $26.50]
**[KLARICH: $140.00]

Hawk I

24"	–	R	FF	HUNT PE015	$4.00	(Peerless)
30"	–	R	FF	HUNT PE016	$4.50	(Peerless)

JN4D Jenny (SA: 238)

?	–	–	–	ARGUS MA197x	£3.00	
*13"	–	R	FF	STERLING P-6	$7.95	
16¼"	–	R	FF	CLEVE CD4B	$14.00	
18"	–	R	FF	POND 15B7	$3.25	(U.S. Model)

21½"	-	R	FF	CLEVE CD4B	$18.00	
*22"	13½"	R	FF	SWALLOW	$8.95	
*24"	-	R	FF	COMET 3304	$8.00	
24"	-	R	FF	POND 46F1	$4.25	(Price)
24"	-	R	FF	GLEASON	$2.35	(Struck)
29"	-	R	FF	POND 46F1	$3.75	(Lewis)
32"	-	R	FF	CLEVE CD4B	$24.00	
*33"	-	R/.020	FF	STERLING E1	$19.95	
33"	-	R	FF	POND 15B7	$3.75	(Burd)
34"	-	R	FF	POND 15B7	$4.25	(Kelly)
36"	-	R	FF	POND 15B6	$4.25	(Ideal)
42"	-	-	CL	POND 26G4	$4.75	(Musciano)
42"	-	-	1	FM CF52	$4.00	(Ziroli)
43"	-	-	RC	POND 26F6	$4.24	(Magazine Plan)
44"	-	-	RC	GLEASON	$9.45	(Beck)
44"	-	-	RC	POND 15B7	$4.75	(Scalemaster)
46"	-	R	FF	PLANS	$7.00	(Andrus)
52"	-	.15-.20	3	AUTHENTIC	£4..50	(Towner)
65"	-	-	RC	CLEVE CD4B	$38.00	
66"	-	.45	4	AERODROME RC110		$30.00

*[$159.00]

72"	-	.60	RC	B&D	$14.95	
1840mm	-	7.5-10cc	RC	MRA 111	100F	
86½"	-	-	RC	CLEVE CD4B	$52.00	
87"	-	-	RC	PROCTOR 1007	$35.00	

*[$349.95; deluxe kit, $414.95; super deluxe kit, $474.95]

100"	-	-	RC	POND 47C3	$8.75	(Hanson)

N2C-1 Fledgling (SA: 238)

12"	-	R	FF	POND 31F5	$3.25	(Harden)
30"	-	R	FF	HUNT AH81	$3.00	(Harden)
30"	-	.020	FF	PASMCO	$20.00	
41"	-	R	FF	POND 46G3	$4.25	(Osborne)
60"	-	.60	4	PASMCO	$40.00	

NC-4

19"	-	R	FF	POND 38C3	$3.75	(Mazan)
27"	-	R	FF	POND 15B5	$5.75	(Ideal)
36½"	-	R	FF	GLEASON	$2.95	(Struck)

57"	–	–	RC	CLEVE CD400	$55.00	
62½"	–	–	RC	CLEVE CD400	$66.00	
94"	–	–	RC	CLEVE CD400	$89.00	

O-39

28"	–	R	FF	FSI C-13	$6.00

O-52 Owl

?	–	–	–	ARGUS MA159x	£3.00	
20"	–	R	FF	HUNT SRS02	$3.00	(Struhl)
30"	–	R	FF	MB 1085	$8.50	(Albert)
¶ 40"	–	R	FF	HUNT 4002	$6.00	(Ott)
41"	–	–	CL	POND 26G2	$4.25	(Bridgewood)
43"	–	–	FF	POND 15F7	$6.00	(Struhl)

O-1E Falcon

14½"	–	R	FF	CLEVE CD214	$16.00	
15"	–	R	FF	POND 15E2	$3.25	(Ideal)
*16"	–	R	FF	FIKE	$6.95	(Comet)
16"	–	R	FF	POND 47C3	$3.25	(Guillow)
18"	–	R	FF	POND 44E1	$3.25	(Modelcraft)
19"	–	R	FF	CLEVE CD214	$20.00	
23"	–	R	FF	POND 57G3	$4.75	(Aeronautical
23"	–	R	FF	POND 26E1	$3.75	(Bugler)
24"	–	R	FF	POND 50A1	$3.75	(GHQ)
24"	–	R	FF	POND 50A1	$3.75	(Comet)
28"	–	R	FF	CLEVE CD214	$26.00	
28"	–	R	FF	FSI C-11	$6.00	
57"	–	–	RC	CLEVE CD214	$48.00	
114"	83"	2.3-3.5	3-5	WE RCQS-13	$29.95	

[FGM: cowl, $31.00]
**[R&M: $275.00]

O2C-2 Helldiver

15"	–	R	FF	POND 15F4	$3.25	(Ott)
24"	–	–	CL	POND 26G7	$4.25	(Musciano)

OC-2 Falcon

13"	–	R	FF	POND 46C4	$3.25	(Bruning)
24"	–	R/Elec.	FF	MA 648	$3.25	(Srull)
28"	–	R	FF	FSI C-14	$6.00	

Osprey

| 24" | - | R | FF | HUNT WW08 | $3.25 | (Winter) |
| 31" | - | R | FF | POND 16A1 | $3.75 | (Comet) |

P-1 Hawk (SA: 238, 261)

13"	-	R	FF	OLD 491	$2.00	(Markwiese)
23½"	-	R	FF	CLEVE CD132	$22.00	
24"	-	R	FF	CLEVE MP1B	$18.00	
24"	-	R	FF	REPRO 216	$1.50	(Markwiese)
24"	-	R	FF	POND 46A1	$5.25	(Michigan)
24"	-	R	FF	POND 16C6	$4.25	(Red Wing)
*24"	-	R	FF	SIERRA	$13.95	
31"	-	-	CL	POND 42A4	$5.25	(Musciano)
63"	-	.60	4	CHARLIE	$17.00	
94½"	68"	1.3-2.3	4	WE RCQS-14	$24.95	

[FGM: cowl, $30.00]

P-6E Hawk (SA: 261)

?	-	-	-	ARGUS CL539x	£5.25	
6"	-	R	FF	GLEASON	$.80	(Horback)
12"	-	R	FF	CLEVE CD21B	$12.00	
12"	-	R	FF	POND 15D1	$3.24	(Falcon)
12"	-	R	FF	POND 15D1	$3.25	(Comet)
12"	-	R	FF	POND 15D2	$3.25	(Guillow)
15"	-	R	FF	HUNT PE010	$2.50	(Peerless)
15"	-	R	FF	POND 15D1	$3.25	(Modelcraft)
15"	-	R	FF	POND 47A7	$3.25	(Ott)
15"	-	R	FF	POND 15D2	$3.25	(Selley Mfg.)
15¼"	-	R	FF	FRANK 2	$2.00	(Comet)
15½"	-	R	FF	CLEVE CD21B	$15.00	
15½"	-	R	FF	GLEASON	$2.05	(Chevedden)
15½"	-	R	FF	PROKIT	£1.80	(Chevedden)
16"	-	R	FF	CLEVE P1004	$12.00	
16"	-	R	FF	PROKIT	£2.00	(Ferris)
16"	-	R	FF	HUNT CO112	$2.75	(Comet)

*[FIKE: $6.95]

16"	-	R	FF	POND 49F5	$3.25	(Northwest)
16"	-	R	FF	HUNT 011	$3.00	(Peerless)
16"	-	R	FF	POND 15D1	$3.25	(Modelcraft)

16"	–	R	FF	POND 15D1	$3.25	(Burd)
16"	–	R	FF	POND 49F5	$3.25	(Rainey)
*16"	–	R	FF	STERLING A-10	$9.95	
20"	–	R	FF	FOAM	$3.00	
20"	–	R	FF	HUNT SC105	$3.25	(Scientific)
20"	–	–	CL	POND 58E4	$3.25	(Musciano)
22"	–	R	FF	HUNT PE012	$3.50	(Peerless)
22"	–	R	FF	POND 15D2	$3.75	(Modelcraft)
23½"	–	R	FF	CLEVE CD21B	$22.00	
23½"	–	R	FF	WISCONSIN	$4.00	(Toledo)
23½"	–	R	FF	YEST 51	$4.50	(Tomasco)
24"	–	R	FF	GLEASON	$4.20	(Chevedden)
24"	–	R	FF	HUNT PE013	$4.00	(Peerless)
24"	–	R	FF	POND 15D2	$3.75	(Modelcraft)
24"	–	–	CL	POND 49F7	$4.75	(Berkeley)
24"	–	R	FF	POND 49F6	$3.75	(Dallaire)
26"	–	R	FF	PLANS	$6.00	(Andrus)
31"	–	–	CL	POND 49F7	$4.75	(Musciano)
32"	–	–	CL	POND 49F6	$4.25	(Plecan)
33½"	–	R	FF	WISCONSIN	$4.50	(Cleveland)
36"	–	–	CL	POND 44C1	$6.25	(Deely)
36"	–	–	CL	POND 49F5	$5.75	(Falcon)
36"	–	R	FF	POND 26G2	$4.75	(Model Airplane)
47"	–	–	RC	CLEVE CD21B	$44.00	
50½"	–	.35-.45	RC	RCM 836	$12.75	(Rich)
56"	–	.60	4	MAN 4722	$16.00	(Marsh)
60"	–	.60	4	MILLER	$14.95	
62"	–	–	CL	POND 58D7	$9.25	(Musciano)
63"	–	–	RC	BARRON	$23.00	

[TDF: cowl, $25.20; wheel pants, $19.95]
**[KLARICH: $100.00]

63"	–	–	RC	CLEVE CD21B	$56.00	
63"	–	.40-.60	4	PROKIT	£18.00	
63"	–	–	RC	CHARLIE	$17.00	
*1600mm	1105mm	.61/.90	4	MARUTAKA 65	¥40,000	
66"	–	–	RC	POND 25F5	$8.25	(Davies A/C)
72"	–	.60	RC	B&D	$14.95	
*81"	–	.90	6	KRAFTERS	$315.00	
*2140mm	–	40cc	RC	WINTRICH B0004	DM615,	

84"   63½"   2-5hp   4-5   HOSTETLER $29.50
[TDF: cowl, $39.95; wheel pants, $26.50; SHATTLEROE: landing gear,
  $30.00; cabane, $21.50]
**[R&M: $215.00]

*93"   -   Zen G23   6   KRAFTERS $385.00

94"   -   -   RC   CLEVE CD21B $68.00

94½"   -   -   RC   BARRON $36.50
[TDF: Cowl, $33.50; wheel pants, $25.50; AVCO: Cockpit, $21.95]
**[KLARICH: $140.00]

P-12 Hawk

13"   -   R   FF   OLD 451 $2.40   (Peerless)

13"   -   R   FF   OLD 440 $2.00   (Megow)

@P-36 Hawk (SA: 238)

14"   -   R   FF   CLEVE CD277 $12.00

16"   -   R   FF   POND 15D5 $3.25   (Comet)
*[FIKE: $8.95]

18"   -   R   FF   POND 30C2 $3.25   (Wentzel)

18½"   -   R   FF   CLEVE CD277 $15.00

19"   -   R   FF   HUNT PL142 $3.00   (Lindberg)

26"   -   R   FF   POND 26G3 $4.25   (Musciano)

28"   -   R   FF   CLEVE CD277 $20.00

28"   -   R   FF   HUNT 29G2 $5.50   (Whitman)

30"   -   R   FF   POND 49G3 $3.75   (Guillow)

56"   -   -   RC   CLEVE CD277 $34.00

112"   -   -   RC   CLEVE CD277 $56.00

YP-37 Hawk

11"   -   R   FF   POND 37A2 $3.25   (Hi-Flier)

18"   -   R   FF   POND 49G3 $3.25   (Hi-Flier)

21"   -   R   FF   COLE $5.00   (Lindberg)

37"   -   R   FF   HUNT L7 $3.00   (Comet)

XP-40

13"   -   R   FF   POND 49G1 $3.25   (Weiss)

20"   -   R   FF   POND 49G1 $3.25   (Davidson)

26"   -   R   FF   HUNT K012 $3.50   (Berkeley)

28"   -   R   FF   POND 15D7 $3.75   (Burd)

P-40 (SA: 238, 261)

?   -   -   -   ARGUS MA257x   £3.00

13"   -   R   FF   DIELS 60 $3.00
*[$13.50]

13"   -   R   FF   CLOUD $5.00   (Bruning)

14"	–	R	FF	CLEVE CD77U	$14.00	
16"	–	R	FF	HUNT 3894	$4.50	(Whitman)
¶16"	–	R	FF	POND 37A2	$3.75	(Megow)
16"	–	R	FF	POND 51F1	$2.25	(Hi-Flier)
*16½"	–	R	FF	GUILLOW 501	$5.00	
17"	–	R	FF	POND 41G6	$3.75	(Guillow)
*18"	–	R	FF	COMET 3201	$6.50	
¶18"	–	R	FF	POND 42E1	$3.25	(Comet)
*18"	–	R	FF	MODELAIR	$7.70NZ	
18½"	–	R	FF	CLEVE CD77U	$18.00	
19"	–	R	FF	GLEASON	$2.15	(McHard)
19"	–	R	FF	POND 26G4	$3.25	(Halls)
20"	–	R	FF	HUNT 3894	$5.00	(Whitman)
*20¼"	–	.049	CL	COX	$36.25	
21"	–	–	CL	POND 26E5	$3.75	(Taccani)
22"	–	R	FF	HUNT 2203	$3.00	(Ott)
22½"	–	R	FF	WOODHOUSE	£3.00	(Koutny)
23½"	–	R	FF	BELL 004	$5.00	
620mm	–	R	FF	AIRBORNE	$5.00AUS	
*24"	–	R	FF	EASY FF64	$7.00CDN	
24"	–	R	FF	GLEASON	$1.80	(Stahl)
24"	–	R	FF	POND 15D6	$3.75	(Berkeley)
26"	–	R	FF	POND 49G4	$3.75	(Hi-Flier)
¶27"	–	R	FF	HUNT 2704	$4.50	(Ott)
*27"	–	R/.020	FF	STERLING E4	$19.95	
28"	–	R	FF	BELL 020	$5.00	
28"	–	R	FF	BELL 015	$7.50	
28"	–	R	FF	CLEVE CD77U	$22.00	
28"	–	R	FF	HUNT 2203	$3.00	(Ott)
28"	–	R	FF	POND 49G4	$3.75	(Gough)
28"	–	R	FF	POND 49G5	$5.25	(Ideal)
28"	–	R	FF	HUNT 2945	$5.50	(Whitman)
*28"	–	R/.020	CL	GUILLOW 405	$16.00	
28"	–	R	FF	GULF	$5.00	(Midkiff)
30"	–	R	FF	CLEVE IT-77	$10.00	
30"	–	R	FF	POND 15D7	$4.75	(Capitol)

31"	–	.5cc	FF	ARGUS FSP1382	£3.75	(Coker)
*31"	–	R	FF	COMET 3649	$19.50	
32"	–	–	CL	POND 49G5	$4.25	(McCullough)
32"	–	R	FF	POND 49G6	$5.25	(Ott)
33"	–	–	CL	POND 26G3	$4.25	(Model A/C)
33½"	–	.10-.15	RC	RCM 923	$3.75	(Whitehead)
34"	–	R	FF	HUNT ES09E	$3.50	(Stahl)
36"	–	R	FF	CLEVE T77	$12.00	
36"	–	.29-.60	CL	HORN MPS-262	$3.00	
36"	–	–	RC	PALADINE 28	$11.00	
37"	–	–	CL	POND 15D7	$4.75	(Aircraft Plan)
38"	–	R	FF	HUNT ES40	$4.00	(Stahl)
40"	–	–	CL	POND 26G2	$4.75	(Capitol)
*44"	–	Glider	2	CLIFF	$89.95	
46"	–	–	CL	POND 49G2	$5.25	(Berkeley)
¶48"	–	–	CL	POND 52D4	$6.75	(Miniature A/C)
48½"	–	–	RC	OLD DS2	$5.00	(Stahl)
*50"	–	R	FF	EASY FF56	$20.00CDN	

*51"   –   .40   4-5   SURE FLITE $66.95
[ROBART: retracts, $54.95]
*[K-BEE: assembled, $169.95]

54"	–	–	RC	PALADINE 28	$14.00

*55"   –   .29-.45   4   WING 701 $37.50
[ROBART:retracts, $54.95]

56"	–	–	RC	CLEVE CD77U	$36.00

56"   –   .60   RC   FM CF403 $7.00   (Reiss)
[ROBART: retracts, $54.95]

*60"   –   .60   4   DIVELY $160.00
*[deluxe kit, $200.00]

*60"   49"   .60   4-6   TOP RC-17 $124.95
[ROBART: retracts, $54.95]

65¼"   –   .60   4   TAYLOR   £6.00
[cowl, £5.00; canopy, £3.00; spinner, £5.50; balsa pack, £27.00]
[ROBART: retracts: £54.95]

1650mm	–	.60	RC	MRA BT9	119F	(Taylor)

75"   –   –   RC   HOLMAN $19.95   (Taylor)
[canopy, $6.00; spinner, $18.00][LIKES: retracts, $332.00]

80"   –   .90   RC   MB 6811 $18.50   (Johnson)
[LIKES: retracts, $332.00]

82"   –   .90-2.0   5   BATES $40.00
[LIKES: retracts, $332.00]
**[$175.00]

*82"   69"   Q50   7   BYRON 6130209 $439.95
[retracts, $219.95; tailwheel, $38.70; cockpit, $27.45; prop
  system, $701.95]

*94"   -   -   RC   MODEL   030 $299.00AUS
[retracts, $240.00AUS; spinner, $60.00AUS]

94"   77"   -   5   ZIROLI $30.00
[cowl, $42.00; canopy, $10.00; spinner, $29.00][AVCO: cockpit, $21.⬥
**[KLARICH: $140.00; R&M: $150.00]
 *[HANGAR: $230.00]

*96"   79"   Zen 62   7   AHS $260.00

102"   -   3.5   5-6   HOLMAN $33.00   (Morse)
**[R&M: $140.00]

SBC-1 Helldiver (SA: 239)

*12"   -   R   FF   FIKE $6.95   (Megow)

12½"   -   R   FF   CLEVE CD80U $14.00

12½"   -   R   FF   FRANK 48 $1.00   (Comet)

13"   -   R   FF   POND 44A7 $3.25   (Bruning)

16"   -   R   FF   HUNT PA13 $3.50   (Ott)

17"   -   R   FF   CLEVE CD80U $18.00

17"   -   R   FF   DIELS 25 $3.25
*[$16.00]

17"   -   R   FF   POND 50A3 $3.25   (Booton)

18"   -   R   FF   PLANS $6.00   (Andrus)

23"   -   .049   FF   AUTHENTIC   £1.35   (Towner)

24"   -   R   FF   POND 15G7 $3.75   (Berkeley)

25½"   -   R   FF   CLEVE CD80U $24.00

28"   -   R   FF   HUNT 2974 $5.50   (Whitman)

51"   -   R   FF   CLEVE CD80U $44,00

*80"   -   .90   6   KRAFTERS $350.00

85"   67"   2.5-5.0   4-5   DP $30.00

*101"   -   Zen G23   6   KRAFTERS $415.00

SB2C Helldiver (SA: 239)

*?(¼)   -   50cc   RC   DP   FORTHCOMING

13"   -   R   FF   DIELS 9 $1.75

18½"   -   R   FF   CLEVE CD226 $20.00

22"   -   R   FF   HUNT 2236 $4.50   (Whitman)

24"   -   R   FF   POND 50A4 $4.25   (Guillow)

25"   -   R   FF   DIELS $3.25

25"   -   R   FF   CLEVE CD226 $25.00

*28"   -   R   FF   EASY FF72 $10.00CDN

30"	–	R	FF	GULF	$5.00	(Midkiff)
30"	–	.15	CL	PLANS	$7.00	(Andrus)
36"	–	–	CL	POND 15G7	$4.25	(Magazine Plan)
37¼"	–	R	FF	CLEVE CD226	$35.00	
48"	–	.56-.61	RC	RCM 600	$6.00	
61"	–	.60	RC	FM CF706	$7.00	(Reiss)
**73"	–	–	RC	KLARICH	$75.00	
74"	–	–	RC	CLEVE CD226	$60.00	
*86"	64"	ST2000	6-8	YELLOW	$280.00	
97"	75"	Q35	5	SMOLINSKI	$22.00	

[TDF: cowl, $28.95]

SC-2 Seahawk

| 20" | – | R | FF | HUNT AH85 | $3.00 | (Plecan) |

SNC-1

| 22" | – | R | FF | HUNT SRS03 | $3.00 | (Struhl) |

SOC-1 Seagull (SA: 239)

24"	–	R	FF	HUNT WW20	$3.25	(Winter)
30"	–	R	FF	HUNT WW18	$4.00	(Winter)
90"	–	–	RC	MA 607	$24.00	(Byrum)

SO3C-1 Seamew

14"	–	R	FF	CLEVE CD142	$14.00	
16"	–	R	FF	POND 52F1	$4.25	(Megow)
19"	–	R	FF	CLEVE CD142	$18.00	
22"	–	R	FF	GLEASON	$1.80	(Stahl)

*[FLYLINE: $15.95]

24"	–	R	FF	POND 15G6	$3.25	(Hi-Flier)
*24"	–	R	FF	PROKIT	£23.50	
28½"	–	R	FF	CLEVE CD142	$24.00	
31"	–	R	FF	HUNT ES11E	$3.50	(Stahl)
36"	–	R	FF	HUNT 2953	$5.25	(Whitman)
910mm	–	R	FF	MRA 322	40F	
38"	–	–	CL	POND 26F5	$3.75	(Ealy)
38"	–	–	CL	POND 46G4	$4.25	(Moynihan)
57"	–	–	RC	CLEVE CD142	$36.00	

XF-13

| 13" | – | R | FF | POND 13G4 | $3.25 | (Scientific) |

24"	–	R	FF	POND 26F6	$3.75	(Winter)
20"	–	R	FF	HUNT SC106	$3.25	(Scientific)
20"	–	R	FF	POND 15G5	$3.75	(Cross)
24"	–	R	FF	HUNT WW04	$3.00	(Winter)

XF-15

18"	–	R	FF	POND 26G3	$3.25	(Musciano)

XP-23 Hawk

13"	–	R	FF	POND 55D2	$3.25	(Hales)
63"	–	–	RC	CHARLIE	$17.00	
63"	–	–	RC	MB 1771	$12.00	(C. Smith)

XP-31 Swift

12"	–	R	FF	POND 47C3	$3.25	(Paul Jones)
12"	–	R	FF	POND 37A4	$3.25	(M&L)
12"	–	R	FF	POND 37A3	$3.25	(Megow)
13"	–	R	FF	OLD 415	$2.50	(Dallaire)
13"	–	R	FF	OLD 453	$2.00	(Peerless)
13½"	–	R	FF	CLEVE CD504	$12.00	
15"	–	R	FF	POND 15D3	$3.25	(Comet)
18"	–	R	FF	CLEVE CD504	$15.00	
18"	–	R	FF	HUNT KO11	$3.00	(Dallaire)
18"	–	R	FF	POND 15D3	$3.25	(Peerless)
19"	–	R	FF	POND 15D4	$3.75	(Imperial)
20"	–	R	FF	PLANS	$6.00	(Andrus)
20"	–	R	FF	POND 15D4	$3.75	(Ott)
27"	–	R	FF	CLEVE CD504	$20.00	
27"	–	R	FF	HUNT PE014	$3.50	(Peerless)
54"	–	–	RC	CLEVE CD504	$35.00	

XP-42

20"	–	R	FF	POND 15E1	$3.75	(Davidson)
22"	–	R	FF	POND 15E1	$3.75	(Ott)
34"	–	R	FF	POND 49G7	$3.75	(Air King)

XP-55 Ascender

[19]	–	R	FF	MB 2782	$5.00	(Nallen)
?	–	.15-.25	CL	MB 6822	$8.00	

15½"	–	R	FF	GLEASON	$.90	(Stahl)
410mm	–	R	FF	AIRBORNE	$5.00	
26"	–	R	FF	OLD 289	$3.00	(Stahl)
30"	–	R	FF	HUNT ES10	$4.00	(Stahl)
36"	–	R	FF	HUNT ES10E	$4.50	(Stahl)
1000mm	–	R	FF	MRA 321	46F	

XPW-8
32"	–	–	CL	GLEASON AT650	$3.20	(Frake)

Y1A-18
23"	–	R	FF	HUNT W101	$3.25	(Weiss)

YO-40 Raven
18"	–	R	FF	POND 44E4	$3.25	(Comet)

DOUGLAS

8A-5
20"	–	R	FF	POND 16F2	$3.25	(Shaw)
23"	–	R	FF	POND 29F1	$4.25	(Wentzel)
26½"	–	R	FF	HUNT SRS05	$3.00	(Stahl)
30"	–	R	FF	POND 16F2	$3.75	(Megow)

A2D Skyshark
24"	–	R	FF	HUNT 5361	$5.50	(Whitman)
30"	–	–	CL	POND 41F4	$3.75	(Musciano)

A3D Skyknight
15"	–	Jetex	FF	POND 42D5	$3.25	(Comet)
*24¼"	25½"	Bean Rock	FF	WILLAIRCO	$24.50	

A-4 Skyhawk (SA: 239)
*9"	–	Glider	FF	MRC FJ1	$5.98
18"	–	Jetex	FF	BELL 018	$6.50
*18¼"	–	Bean Rock	FF	WILLAIRCO	$26.25
*27"	–	Bean Rock	FF	WILLAIRCO	$38.40
*810mm	910mm	.19-.25	3-4	IKUTA	¥19,000
*[assembled, ¥55,000]					
*840mm	1170mm	.40-.45	4-5	IKUTA	¥25,000
*[assembled, ¥98,000]					
*40"	57"	.60F	5	YELLOW	$215.00
*[kit, engine, fan, $565.00]					
*41¼"	–	Bean Rock	FF	WILLAIRCO	$69.75

*45"	68"	.77F	4-5	BYRON 6130081	$350.00	

[retracts, $128.85; power package, $367.95]

46"	–	10cc	4-5	ARGUS RC1295	£10.00	(Scowan)
*47"	57"	7.5F	5	JHH	$325.00	
*1200mm	1600mm	.60-.90	4-5	IKUTA	¥55,000	

*[assembled, ¥248,000]

*1320mm	1780mm	10-15ccF	RC	BAUER 780001	DM793

A-20 Havoc (SA: 239)

*?(¼)	–	–	RC	KRAFTERS	FORTHCOMING	
23"	–	R	FF	HUNT SRS06	$3.00	(Struhl)
23"	–	R	FF	CLEVE CD115	$25.00	
24"	–	R	FF	POND 16F6	$3.75	(Guillow)
30½"	–	R	FF	CLEVE CD115	$37.00	
38"	–	R	FF	GULF	$5.00	(Midkiff)
46"	–	R	FF	CLEVE CD115	$52.00	
1200mm	–	R	FF	MRA A376/77	40F	
52"	–	–	CL	POND 16F6	$6.25	(Fillon)
72"	–	.60x2	RC	B&D	$14.95	

A-26 Invader (SA: 239)

¶30"	–	R	FF	HUNT 3501	$4.00	(Comet)
46"	–	1.5x2	CL	ARGUS CL520	£5.25	(Deeley)
52"	–	–	CL	POND 27B4	$6.75	(Atkins)
54"	–	.19x2	4	FM CF704	$8.00	(Sarpolus)
*68"	–	.25x2	4	WING 720	$64.95	
87"	–	–	RC	POND 50B4	$6.75	(Berkeley)
91"	64"	.50x2	RC	BEAULIEU 1B	$24.95	(Parcell)

[AVCO: canopy, $15.95; TDF: cowls, $20.95; nose, $12.95; nacelle,$14.95; tip tanks, $23.50]

140"	96"	Q35x2	5-6	SCHWEISS	$45.00

AD/A-1H Skyraider (SA: 239)

13"	–	R	FF	MOONEY	$1.00	
*17"	–	R	FF	GUILLOW 904	$4.29	
18"	–	R	FF	POND 61F6	$4.75	(Niedzielski)
27½"	–	R	FF	MB 11723	$4.50	(Mooney)
30"	–	R	FF	FM CF756	$8.00	(Rees)
30"	–	.15	CL	GLEASON	NA	(Mottin)
34"	–	.40	CL	GLEASON	$4.10	(Hulick)

35"	–	.049-.051	CL	HORN S-26	$6.00	(Osborne)
42½"	–	–	CL	GLEASON AT157	NA	
44"	–	–	CL	GLEASON	$7.45	(Smith)
44"	–	.15-.19	RC	HORN S-27	$9.00	(Osborne)
58"	–	.60	RC	FM CF452	$7.00	(Reiss)
*62½"	–	.60	4	FLAIR CAPR11	NA	
62½"	–	.60	4	TRAP MW2111	£8.00	(CAP)

[cowl, £7.50; canopy, £3.50]

*70"	53"	.60/1.20	4	CUSTOM	$250.00	
75"	58"	.90-1.08	4-6	INNOVATIVE	$25.00	
1900mm	–	10cc	RC	MRA 106	112F	
*90"	68"	1.20	8	ACCU	$375.00	
120"	–	2.5-5.0	5-6	DP	$30.00	

*[$185.00] [WHEELS: retracts, $275.00]

120"	–	3.15	5-6	HOLMAN	$33.00	(Morse)

[PK: canopy, $15.00]
**[R&M: $275.00]

B-66 Destroyer

40"	–		FF	POND 27A6	$6.75	(Paxton)

C-47 Sky Train (SA: 240, 261)

*10"	–	Glider	FF	PAI 278	$4.75	
26"	–	–	CL	POND 58F4	$3.75	(Modeler's)
35½"	–	R	FF	CLEVE IT165	$18.00	
35½"	–	R	FF	CLEVE CD165	$32.00	
39"	–	–	CL	COLE	$5.00	
47"	–	R	FF	CLEVE IT-165	$24.00	
47"	–	R	FF	CLEVE CD165	$40.00	
47½"	–	1.5ccx2	CL	ARGUS CL765	£5.25	(Last, Bodey)
48"	–	R	FF	CLEVE IT-165S	$18.00	
48"	–	–	CL	POND 27A6	$5.75	(Musciano)
48"	–	–	CL	POND 16F3	$6.75	(Kohn)
52"	–	–	CL	POND 58F4	$5.75	(Model Builder's)
63"	–	.10x2	4	ARGUS RC1440	£7.50	(Bosak)
63"	–	.10x2	4	BOSAK	20 Kcs	
63"	–	.10x2	4	FM CF738	$8.00	(Bosak)
1588mm	1070mm	1.5x2	4	VTH MT972-G	DM19,50	(Bosak)
1600mm	–	1.5x2	RC	MRA 486.517	67F	
71"	–	–	RC	CLEVE CD165	$50.00	

72"	–	.15x2	RC	HORN S-52	$14.00	(Osborne)
72"	–	–	CL	POND 46B4	$10.25	(Archive)
75¼"	49"	.25x2	5	MAN 2891	$18.50	(Ramsey)
*2112mm	1445mm	.25/.40	4-6	MARUATKA 12	¥40,000	
76"	–	.51x2	6	MAN 6711	$16.50	(White)
95"	–	–	RC	CLEVE CD165	$64.00	
96"	–	.45x2	RC	FM CF454	$10.00	(Lombardo)
2460mm	–	6.5x2	RC	MRA 757.470	132F	
140"	99"	Q35x2	4-5	ZIROLI	$42.00	

[nose, $42.00; cowls, $32.00] [retracts: ROBART, $375.00; LIKES, $437.00; SCHMALZIGAN, $500.00]
**[R&M: $260.00]
*[HANGAR: $335.00]

C-124 Globemaster

**141½"	105½"	.60x4	7	MURPHY	$200.00

D-558-1 Skystreak

10"	–	Jetex	FF	POND 23F7	$3.25	(Berkeley)
¶ 17"	–	Jetex	FF	HUNT J124	$4.00	(Comet)
28"	–	–	CL	POND 27A5	$5.25	(Beatty)

D-558-2 Skyrocket

8"	–	Jetex	FF	POND 16G1	$3.25	(Mansour)
12"	–	Jetex	FF	HUNT J125	$3.00	(Wherry)

F4D Skyray

13"	–	Jetex	FF	POND 37B1	$3.25	(Keil Kraft)
*14½"	–	Jetex	FF	EASY 5X 08	$10.00CDN	
¶ 16"	–	CO2	FF	POND 27B1	$4.75	(Comet)
25"	–	–	FF	HUNT J128	$5.50	(Berkeley)
32½"	44"	.19F	3-4	WE RCDF-1	$19.94	
49"	66"	.40F	5	WE RCDF-2	$29.95	
80"	–	.90F	5-6	HOLMAN	$24.00	(Morse)

0-31

22"	–	R	FF	COLE	$5.00

0-38

?	–	–	–	ARGUS FSP1123x	£3.75	
15"	–	R	FF	CLEVE CD43	$14.00	
20"	–	R	FF	CLEVE CD43	$17.00	
20"	–	R	FF	POND 16E5	$3.25	(Modelcraft)

24"	–	R	FF	ARGUS BB239	£2.50	(Graffeo)
24"	–	R	FF	POND 16E5	$3.75	(Construct)
¶ 28"	–	R	FF	HUNT KO15	$3.50	(Burd)
30"	–	R	FF	GLEASON	$3.55	(Gleason)
30"	–	R	FF	OLD 221	$3.50	(Sturiale)
30"	–	R	FF	POND 27C7	$3.25	(Burd)
30½"	–	R	FF	CLEVE CD43	$22.00	
61"	–	–	FF	CLEVE CD43	$34.00	
72"	–	.60	RC	B&D	$14.95	
122"	–	–	RC	CLEVE CD43	$58.00	

0-41

35"	–	R	FF	COLE	$5.00	

0-43

12"	–	R	FF	FRANK 3	$2.00	(Megow)
13"	–	R	FF	POND 46A4	$3.75	(Jones)
20"	–	R	FF	POND 27A1	$3.75	(McEntee)
20"	–	R	FF	POND 16E6	$3.75	(Guillow)
20"	–	R	FF	REPRO 156	$1.50	(Scientific)
22"	–	R	FF	HUNT 2153	$4.50	(Ott)
22"	–	R	FF	POND 16E7	$5.25	(Whitman)
23"	–	R	FF	GLEASON	$2.25	(Lindberg)
36"	–	R	FF	POND 27A7	$3.75	(GHQ)
40"	–	–	FF	POND 57C3	$5.75	(Stark)
48"	–	–	FF	POND 41A4	$5.75	(Miniature A/C)
50"	–	–	FF	POND 16F1	$7.25	(Roberts)
68"	–	–	RC	CLEVE CD246	$46.00	

0-46

16½"	–	R	FF	HUNT MAC07	$2.50	(Model Aircraft)
17"	–	R	FF	CLEVE CD246	$18.00	
20"	–	R	FF	GLEASON	$1.80	(Booton)
20"	–	R	FF	PROKIT	£2.10	(Booton)
*[PROKIT: £28.50]						
21"	–	R	FF	FRANK 33	$2.25	(Dallaire)
23"	–	R	FF	CLEVE CD246	$24.00	
23"	–	R	FF	POND 16E6	$3.74	(Skymaster)
28¼"	–	R	FF	GLEASON	$3.25	(Booton)
34"	–	R	FF	CLEVE CD246	$32.00	

34"	–	R	FF	POND 16F1	$5.25	(McHard)
68"	–	–	RC	CLEVE CD246	$46.00	
1100mm	–	R	FF	MRA A313	16F	

SBD Dauntless (SA: 261)

[32]	–	.40	CL	MB 8772	$9.00	(Baltes)
13"	–	R	FF	AERO ERA	$1.25	
15"	–	R	FF	HUNT 3896	$4.50	(Whitman)
*20"	–	R	FF	COMET 3401	$7.50	
22"	–	R	FF	POND 50B3	$5.25	(Whitman)
¶ 27"	–	R	FF	POND 50B3	$3.75	(Ott)
30"	–	R	FF	HUNT 502	$5.50	(Ott)
30½"	–	R	FF	CLEVE CD89A	$18.00	
31"	–	R	FF	GULF	$5.00	(Midkiff)
31"	–	–	CL	POND 31D6	$5.75	(Berkeley)
*31¼"	–	.049-.09	CL	GUILLOW 1003	$29.00	
40"	–	.29-.35	CL	HORN MPS-174	$3.00	
*64"	51"	.60-.90	4-8	DYNA 6002	$245.00	
1600mm	–	8-10cc	RC	MRA 326.487	95F	
65"	–	–	RC	ENT	$9.95	
*69"	–	.61-.91	4	FLAIR CAPR06	NA	
69"	–	.60-.90	RC	HOLMAN	$19.95	(Walters)
[plan pack, $36.95]						
69"	–	.60-.90	4	TRAP MW2106	£9.00	(CAP)
[cowl, £7.50; canopy, £6.50]						
70"	–	–	RC	POND 52G6	$13.25	(Taylor)
72"	–	.60	RC	B&D	$14.95	
96"	72¼"	2.0-4.0	4-5	DP	$30.00	
*[$185.00]						

TBD Devastator

*?(¼)	–	–	RC	DP	FORTHCOMING	
[62]	–	.60	4	FM CF627	$8.00	(Reiss)
13"	–	R	FF	POND 16F4	$3.25	(Weiss)
13"	–	R	FF	POND HSDT	$3.25	(Booton)
15"	–	R	FF	POND 55C6	$3.25	(McLarren)
22"	–	R	FF	HUNT 2212	$.50	(Whitman)
25"	–	R	FF	DIELS 56	$4.50	
*[$17.50]						
26"	–	R	FF	HUNT AB06	$3.00	(Booton)

¶ 30"	-	R	FF	POND 16F4	$4.25	(Capitol)
32½"	-	-	CL	POND 27B4	$4.75	(Dulaitis)
36"	-	R	FF	HUNT 5378	$5.50	(Whitman)
58"	40"	.40-.45	3-4	PHOTO	$21.00	(Katz)
72"	-	.60	RC	B&D	$14.95	

XB-42 Mixmaster (SA: 240)

11"	-	R	FF	POND 16F5	$3.25	(Weiss)
25"	-	R	FF	HUNT AH88	$3.00	(Wieczorek)
750mm	-	R	FF	AIRBORNE	$5.00AUS	

XTB2D-1 Skypirate

| 84" | - | - | RC | RCM 374 | $12.50 | (McCullough) |

Y10-43

13"	-	R	FF	OLD 477	$2.00	(Scientific)
13"	-	R	FF	OLD 410	$2.00	(Comet)
20"	-	R	FF	POND 27G1	$3.75	(Scientific)
22"	-	R	FF	HUNT X7	$3.25	(Comet)
24"	-	R	FF	HUNT KO16	$3.50	(Wanner)

*[REPRO: $8.50]

FAIRCHILD

A-10 Thunderbolt (SA: 240, 262)

54"	-	Glider	RC	ARGUS RM338	£4.50	(Waters)
56"	-	-	RC	POND 27F3	$8.75	(R/C Technique)
54"	-	.40-45x2F	RC	HOBBY BARN	$28.99	
57"	-	.25x2F	RC	MACKINDER	£10.00	

[engine pods, £18.00]

*1600mm	1350mm	.40x2	4-5	IKUTA	¥45,000	
68½"	-	.40x2F	5	ARGUS RM316	£6.00	(Waters)
78"	70"	7.5x2F	4-6	BEAULIEU 2B	$24.95	(Miller)

[AVCO: canopy, $15.95; cockpit, $19.95; TDF: fairings, $25.50;
 front nacelle, $14.50; rear nacelle, $15.95; wingtips, $19.95]
*[CUSTOM: $450.00]

C-119 Flying Boxcar

| 2222mm | - | - | RC | MODULO | L40.000 | |
| **109" | 86½" | .60x2 | 6 | MURPHY | $175.00 | |

PT-19 (SA: 240, 262, 304)

| ? | - | - | - | ARGUS MA400x | £3.00 | |
| *12" | - | R | FF | DUBOIS PS3 | $7.95 | |

12"	–	R	FF	POND 52G4	$3.25	(Hi-Flier)
13½"	–	R	FF	CLEVE CD219	$14.00	
18"	–	R	FF	CLEVE CD219	$18.00	
20"	–	R	FF	HUNT 3873	$4.50	(Whitman)
20"	–	R	FF	POND 17B1	$3.75	(Mather)
21"	–	–	CL	POND 38E3	$3.75	(Sterling)
23"	–	R	FF	HUNT ES13	$3.00	(Stahl)
23"	–	R	FF	FOAM	$2.75	
23"	–	R	FF	MB 784	$6.50	(Stahl)
23" *[£23.50]	–	R	FF	PROKIT	£1.25	(Stahl)
640mm	–	R	FF	AIRBORNE	$5.00AUS	
27"	–	R	FF	CLEVE CD219	$24.00	
29"	–	–	CL	POND 36D1	$4.75	(Wheldon)
32"	–	R	FF	HUNT ES13E	$3.50	(Stahl)
*35"	–	R	FF	EASY FF6	$12.00CDN	
26"	–	–	CL	POND 50C3	$6.75	(Fawcett)
38"	–	R	FF	HUNT E45	$4.00	(Stahl)
*40"	30"	.049	2	COX 90411	$99.50	
42"	–	–	RC	POND 44F5	$6.75	(Clapper)
47"	–	R	FF	OLD DS-3	$5.00	(Stahl)
48"	–	–	RC	POND 41C5	$10.25	(Sterling)
*51"	–	.30-.60	4	DYNA 4006	$104.95	
*1330mm	995mm	.19-.25	3-4	OK APQX005	¥12,000	
54"	–	–	RC	CLEVE CD219	$48.00	
58¼"	–	Elec	RC	RCM 1047	$6.00	(Mitchell)
62"	–	.40-.60	CL	HORN MPS-87	$8.00	
62"	–	.49	4	FM CF89	$16.00	(Rogers)
*1595mm	1190mm	.40-.45	4	OK 11071	¥42,000	
72"	–	–	RC	GLEASON	$14.10	(Smith)
72"	–	.60	RC	B&D	$14.94	
72½"	54¼"	.40-.60	RC	PHOTO	$14.00	(Pepino)
72"	–	–	RC	POND 27D6	$10.25	(Hollinger)
*84"	66"	Zen G38	5	R&K	$179.00	
*2134mm	1595mm	/1.20	5	OK APBS009	¥49,000	
87" [FGM: cowl, $23.00]	67"	.90-1.20	RC	PHOTO	$24.00	(Pepino)

*108"	96"	G62	5	CFI	$350.00	
108"	-	-	RC	CLEVE CD219	$65.00	
108"	81½"	Q35	4-5	FOLINE	$30.00	

[cowl: TDF, $31.95; FGM, $30.00]
**[KLARICH: $145.00; R&M: $185.00]

108"	-	Q35	5	SMART P5	£15.50	

[cowl, £11.50]

114"	85"	2-5hp	4	HOSTETLER	$29.50	

[TDF: cowl, $39.95]
**[R&M: $205.00]

PT-22 Cornell

68"	-	.61	4	TRAP MW2018	£9.50	(Hodsdon)
72"	-	-	RC	HOLMAN	$9.95	(Leake)

PT-26

13½"	-	R	FF	CLEVE CD218	$14.00	
18"	-	R	FF	CLEVE CD218	$18.00	
27"	-	R	FF	CLEVE CD218	$24.00	
54"	-	-	RC	CLEVE CD218	$48.00	
*68"	53"	.40/.90	4	R&K	$139.00	

UC-61 Fowarder (SA: 240)

37"	-	R	FF	POND 17A6	$5.25	(Hobby Model)
*90"	-	Q35	4	IKON IK8	$190.95	

[wheels, $12.95; tailwheel, $12.95; struts, $12.00]

FLEET

PT-6 (SA: 241)

[49]	-	-	RC	MB 5751	$10.00	(Bukolt)
10½"	-	R	FF	CLEVE CD178	$10.00	
12"	-	R	FF	FRANK 11	$1.00	(Megow)

*[FIKE: $6.95]

13"	-	R	FF	NFFS	$6.00	
13"	-	R	FF	POND 37G7	$3.25	(Schmaedig)
14"	-	R	FF	CLEVE CD178	$12.00	
16"	-	R	FF	POND 17C3	$3.25	(Modelcraft)
17"	-	R	FF	POND 17C3	$3.75	(Pilzer)
21"	-	R	FF	CLEVE CD178	$8.00	
21"	-	R	FF	FSI F-2	$6.00	
22½"	-	R	FF	HUNT SRS08	$3.00	(Struhl)
24"	-	R	FF	HUNT KO21	$3.25	(Dallaire)
*24"	-	R	FF	WILLAIRCO	$10.00	(Peerless)

24"	–	R	FF	HUNT PE023		$3.00	(Peerless)
26"	–	R	FF	COLE		$5.00	
32½"	–	–	CL	GLEASON AT551		NA	
33"	–	–	CL	POND 17C5		$5.75	(Hollinger)
42"	–	–	RC	CLEVE CD178		$28.00	
42"	–	.19-.35	2-3	MORGAN		$6.95	
54"	–	–	FF	POND 17C5		$6.75	(Debobrousky)
*56"	48"	.50-.60	4	AERODROME		$89.00	
*56"	44¼"	.40	4	CONCEPT		$99.95	
56"	–	.35-.40	4	MA 310		$6.25	(Brown)
62"	–	–	RC	GLEASON AT660		NA	(Neukom)
68"	34"	.45-.60	4	MAN 12661		$10.50	(King)
68"	51"	–	RC	BEHRLAN		$25.00	
*86"	64"	Q40	4	CONCEPT		$197.95	

[AVCO: cockpit, $20.95; SHATTLEROE: landing gear, $31.50]

111"	80"	2.4-3.7	5	WEISS	$32.00	

GENERAL DYNAMICS

F-16 Fighting Falcon (SA: 241)

*6"	9"	Glider	FF	PMI AG101	$4.95	(Aerographics)
*15"	24"	Glider	FF	TODAY J-1	$24.95	
16"	–	Glider	FF	WALLACE	$6.50	
*806mm	1095mm	3-4cc	RC	TECHNIK	DM150,	
*34"	36"	.09F	2-3	KRESS	FORTHCOMING	
*36"	56"	.60F	RC	AVONDS	2470FF	
*900mm	1125mm	.19-.25	3-5	OK APQX012	¥19,000	
*1020mm	1080mm	.25-.28	4	OK 11080	¥29,500	
*1100mm	985mm	.25	3-4	IKUTA	¥18,000	

*[assembled, ¥75,000]

*44"	67"	.77F	5	YELLOW	$280.00	

[kit, engine, fan, $630.00]

*44½"	62"	.45F	4	DCU	$269.00	
*44"	67"	.82F	6	VIOLETT	$1000.00	
1140mm	1690mm	.60-.80F	RC	BERTELLA	L50.000	

[canopy, L15.000]

*47"	74½"	.77F	4-5	BYRON 6130030	$325.05	
*48"	55"	.60	4	FARNS A1012	$149.95	
*1200mm	1100mm	.40-.45	3-4	IKUTA	¥22,000	

*1220mm	1460mm	.60	3-4	IKUTA	¥35,000
*1240mm	1860mm	.77F	4-7	GLEICHAUF 1600	DM885,
*49½"	47"	Glider	2	COMBAT	$69.95
*56"	36"	.46F	5	SOUTHEAST	$229.95

F-16XL

–	–	–		FM CF734	$8.00

[conversion plan for Byron F-16]

F-106 Delta Dagger

*45"	71"	.65F	5	KNIGHTS	$229.00

GOODYEAR

F2G Corsair

25½"	–	R	FF	BELL 003	$5.75	
40"	–	–	CL	POND 22F7	$7.75	(Miniature A/c)
*2500mm	–	50-60cc	RC	COOP 9600107	5200F	

GREAT LAKES

XTBG-1

20"	–	R	FF	POND 27F1	$3.25	(Booton)
24"	–	CO2	FF	POND 17G5	$3.25	(Winter)

GRUMMAN

AF2-A Guardian (SA: 242, 262)

15"	–	R	FF	COLE	$5.00	
30"	–	–	CL	GLEASON AM262	$5.95	(Domizi)
45½"	–	R	FF	FM CF746	$8.00	(Platt)
53"	–	–	CL	POND 27F5	$5.25	(Berkeley)
75"	–	.60/1.20	5	PROKIT	£17.50	

**[£59.50]

75"	–	–	RC	CHARLIE	$19.00

AO-1 Mohawk

13"	–	R	FF	SWAMP	$1.50	(Brown)
36"	–	–	CL	POND 27G5	$5.25	(Plecan)

A-2 Viking

69"	–	–	CL	GLEASON AT953	NA

FF-1

*12"	–	R	FF	FIKE	$7.95	(Megow)
17"	–	R	FF	POND 50E5	$3.25	(GE Models)

21"	–	R	FF	POND 27F2	$3.75	(McCready)
24"	–	R	FF	POND 37F5	$4.25	(Guillow)
26"	–	R	FF	FSI G-1	$6.00	

F2F-1

10½"	–	R	FF	CLEVE CD53	$7.00	
14"	–	R	FF	CLEVE CD53	$9.00	
21½"	–	R	FF	CLEVE CD53	$12.00	
28"	–	–	CL	POND 27G4	$4.25	(Aircraft Plar
28"	–	–	CL	POND 27G1	$4.25	(Plecan)

F3F-1

11"	–	R	FF	CLEVE CD70U	$10.00	
13"	–	R	FF	GLEASON	$.50	(Lindberg)
14½"	–	R	FF	CLEVE CD70U	$14.00	
16"	–	R	FF	DIELS 31	$3.25	
18½"	–	R	FF	GLEASON	$1.50	(Lindberg)
18½"	–	R	FF	PROKIT	£1.30	(Lindberg)
21½"	–	R	FF	GLEASON	$4.55	(Winter)
21½"	–	R	FF	PROKIT	£4.00	(Winter)
21½"	–	R	FF	CLEVE CD70U	$18.00	
¶ 23"	–	–	CL	POND 58E7	$3.75	(Ambroid)
24"	–	R	FF	GLEASON	$2.45	(Lindberg)
28"	20½"	.15-.29	CL	JVS	$8.00	
30"	–	R	FF	HUNT WW14E	$3.50	(Winter)
31"	–	.19	CL	HORN MPS-76	$4.00	(Palanek)
¶ 33"	–	R	FF	MB 680CP	$8.50	(Miniature A/(
43"	–	R	FF	CLEVE CD70U	$38.00	
*48"	–	.35-.60	RC	PENN ARI8001	$69.95	
49"	–	–	CL	POND 50E6	$6.75	(Galloway)
58"	–	–	RC	CLEVE CD70U	$50.00	
72"	–	.60	RC	B&D	$14.95	

XF4F

18"	–	R	FF	POND 18A3	$3.25	(Weiss)

F4F Wildcat (SA: 242)

[62]	–	.60	6	MAN 1782	$11.50	(Fearnley)
[FGM: cowl, $21.50]						
13"	–	R	FF	HAUGHT P-25	$1.50	

13"	–	R	FF	AIME	20F	
13"	–	R	FF	POND 31C4	$3.25	(Crosswinds)
14"	–	R	FF	CLEVE CD83BU	$12.00	
15"	–	R	FF	HUNT 3893	$4.50	(Whitman)
15½"	–	R	FF	GREGA 223	$2.00	(Stahl)
¶ 18"	–	R	FF	POND 27F3	$3.75	(Comet)
18½"	–	R	FF	CLEVE CD83BU	$14.00	
18½"	–	R	FF	GLEASON	$.90	(Stahl)
19" *[$19.00]	–	R	FF	DIELS 11	$6.25	
19"	–	R	FF	GLEASON	$.90	(Lindberg)
19"	–	R	FF	GLEASON	$3.40	(Bagley)
*19"	–	R	FF	PROKIT	£19.00	
*20"	–	R	FF	VERON VO422	£3.49	
22"	–	R	FF	POND 62D4	$5.25	(Whitman)
*25"	–	R	FF	EASY FF65	$10.00CDN	
¶ 25"	–	R	FF	HUNT SC112	$3.25	(Scientific)
27"	–	R	FF	GLEASON	$3.60	(Marlin)
27"	–	R	FF	HUNT ES17E	$3.50	(Stahl)
¶ 27"	–	R	FF	POND 18A3	$4.75	(Capitol)
¶ 27"	–	R	FF	POND 50E7	$3.75	(Ott)
28"	–	R	FF	CLEVE CD83BU	$20.00	
28"	–	R	FF	GULF	$5.00	(Midkiff)
28"	–	–	CL	GLEASON AT953	$3.05	(Musciano)
28¼"	–	R	FF	TOKO	$4.00	(Wilson)
29"	–	–	CL	POND 50F1	$5.25	(Berkeley)
29"	–	R	FF	POND 18A4	$3.75	(Fearnley)
31"	–	.02	CL	MA 238	$1.75	(Bowers)
¶ 32"	–	R	FF	POND 18A4	$3.75	(Ott)
32"	–	R	FF	POND 18A4	$5.75	(Comet)
33"	–	–	CL	POND 41G2	$5.75	(Musciano)
38"	–	–	CL	GLEASON AM663	NA	(Musciano)
38½"	–	–	FF	OLD DS4	$5.00	(Stahl)
38½"	–	.15-.19	2-3	ARGUS RC1312	£5.25	(Neate)
38½"	–	.15	3	MAN 9791	$9.00	(Neate)
45"	–	.030	RC	FM CF273	$7.00	(Ziroli)
*1380mm	980mm	.40-.45	4-5	IKUTA	¥24.000	

| 56" | - | - | RC | CLEVE CD83BU | $34.00 | |
| 88" | - | .40-.60 | 4 | WING 221 | $19.95 | |

[cowl, $18.95; canopy, $6.95]

| *1600mm | 1100mm | .60 | 4-5 | IKUTA | ¥32,000 | |

*[assembled, ¥148,000]

| 76" | - | .60-.90 | RC | MAN 2832 | $25.00 | (Karlsson) |

[TDF: cowl, $30.95; canopy, $11.95; SCHMALZIGAN: retracts, $500.00]
**[R&M: $130.00]

| 91" | - | Q35 | 5 | GORDON | $42.00 | |
| *92" | 63½" | Q50 | 5 | CLASSIC | $315.00 | |

*[deluxe kit, $900.00][SCHMALZIGAN: retracts, $600.00]

F6F Hellcat (SA: 242, 262)

*?(¼)	-	-	RC	DP	FORTHCOMING	
[58]	-	.60	4-5	MAN 3772	$8.25	(Fearnley)
*10"	-	Glider	FF	PAPER FPS06	$3.95	
*13"	-	R	FF	DUBOIS PS-4	$7.95	
15"	-	R	FF	HUNT 3703	$4.50	(Whitman)
15"	-	-	CL	POND 18A6	$3.75	(Hobby Model)
15½"	-	R	FF	CLEVE CD97	$16.00	
*16½"	-	R	FF	GUILLOW 503	$5.00	
21"	-	R	FF	CLEVE CD97	$20.00	
21½"	-	R	FF	HUNT AH108	$3.00	(Hunt)
*21½"	-	R	FF	DIELS K12	$20.00	
22"	-	R	FF	GLEASON	$2.80	(Hannan)
¶24"	-	R	FF	POND 50F3	$3.75	(Comet)
*28"	-	R	FF	EASY FF73	$10.00CDN	
30"	-	R	FF	CLEVE IT-97	$10.00	
31"	-	R	FF	CLEVE CD97	$26.00	
32"	-	R	FF	HUNT KO19	$4.00	(Cadet)
*33"	-	.049-.09	CL	GUILLOW 1005	$29.00	
33¼"	-	R	FF	FM CF669	$7.00	(Midkiff)
37"	-	.29-.60	CL	HORN MPS-265	$3.00	
38"	-	R	FF	HUNT 107	$5.50	(Ott)
38"	-	-	CL	POND 18A4	$4.75	(Modern Hobby
39"	-	R	FF	GLEASON	$3.55	(Midkiff)
40"	-	R	FF	POND 50F1	$5.25	(Ott)
42"	-	-	CL	POND 23D3	$5.75	(Eagle Models
*56"	-	.40-.60	4	DYNA 4004	$148.95	

| 59" | - | .60 | RC | FM CF324 | $7.00 | (Williams) |

59"   -   .60   RC   FM CF324 $7.00   (Williams)
63"   -   -   RC   CLEVE CD97 $40.00
*64"   -   .60-.90   4-6   HOLMAN $179.95
[ROBART: retracts, $54.95]
64¼"   -   .60   RC   MORGAN 117RC $19.95
[ROBART: retracts, $54.95]
64½"   -   .60   4   TAYLOR   £6.00
[cowl, £5.50; canopy, £2.00; spinner, £1.75; balsa pack, £30.00]
[ROBART: retracts, $54.95]
1620mm   -   10cc   RC   MRA BT6   119F   (Taylor)
*70"   60"   .90-1.2   4-5   AERODROME $225.00
[LIKES: retracts, $332.00]
*70"   -   10-15cc   RC   MODEL 022 $169.00AUS
[retracts, $240.00AUS]
75"   -   -   RC   HOLMAN $25.00   (Taylor)
[LIKES: retracts, $332.00]
**80"   -   .90   RC   HOLMAN $230.00   (Aero Craft)
[LIKES: retracts, $332.00]
*80½"   63½"   .90-1.5   6   INNOVATIVE $249.50
[LIKES: retracts, $332.00]
*87"   70"   Sachs   5-6   BYRON 6130201 $428.95
[retracts, $219.95; cockpit, $43.95; tailwheel, $38.50; prop
system, $474.45]
98"   -   3.15   5-6   HOLMAN $33.00   (Morse)
[PK: canopy, $15.00; LIKES: retracts, $332.00]
**[KLARICH: $145.00; R&M: $230.00]

F7F Tigercat (SA: 242)

26"   -   R/CO2   FF   DIELS 36 $4.00
26"   -   R   FF   MA 293 $1.75   (Norman)
30"   -   R   FF   KOUTNY $10.00
36"   -   -   CL   POND 50F3 $5.25   (Plecan)
43"   -   -   CL   POND 41G1 $6.75   (Aircraft Plan)
44"   -   -   CL   GLEASON AT657 $9.00   (Plecan)
44"   -   -   CL   PROKIT   £7.85   (Plecan)
*72"   -   .45-.60x2   4   RC $184.95
*75"   -   .60x2   5   CBA $500.00
*97½"   80"   Q40x2   5   CBA $1,550.00
114"   102"   Q40x2   5   CBA $55.00
[foam wings, $75.00]

F8F Bearcat (SA: 242, 262)

13"   -   R   FF   DIELS 41 $2.80
13"   -   R   FF   HAUGHT P-27 $1.50

13½"	–	R	FF	CLEVE CD197	$12.00	
16"	–	R	FF	COLE	$5.00	
17"	–	R	FF	CLEVE CD197	$14.00	
*17"	–	R	FF	KEIL KKOO61	£3.99	
18"	–	R	FF	DIELS 37	$3.25	
*[$15.00]						
18"	–	R	FF	POND 18A6	$3.25	(Wherry)
20"	–	R	FF	POND 18A6	$4.25	(Modernistic)
21"	–	R	FF	KOUTNY	$5.00	
26"	–	–	CL	POND 27F4	$4.25	(Berkeley)
27"	–	R	FF	CLEVE CD197	$18.00	
35"	–	–	CL	POND 16A6	$11.75	(Maczura)
35"	–	–	RC	HOLMAN	$3.00	
35½"	–	–	CL	GLEASON AT1152	$6.65	(C.Smith)
38"	–	–	CL	ORIGINAL	£4.00	(Martin)
41"	–	–	RC	POND 50F2	$6.75	(Galloway)
*46"	30"	Glider	2	CLIFF	$89.95	
*51"	–	.40-.60	4-6	DAVEY	$99.95	
52"	–	.40-.52	RC	FM 183	$7.00	(Ziroli)
53½"	–	–	RC	CLEVE CD197	$34.00	
58"	–	–	RC	POND 57G5	$5.25	(Rabe)
*60"	43"	.60/.90	4-6	TOP RC23	$147.95	
*1580mm	1224mm	.60/.90	4-6	MARUTAKA 22	¥32,000	
*64"	44½"	.60-.80	3-4	FARNS A1003	$95.99	
70"	–	.60	4-5	MORGAN 109RC	$16.95	
*84"	88"	Zen 62	7	AHS	$260.00	
86"	69"	Q35	4-5	ZIROLI	$30.00	

[cowl, $32.00; canopy, $10.00][FGM: cowl, $48.00]
**[KLARICH: $140.00; R&M: $200.00]
*[HANGAR: $230.00]

107"	–	–	RC	CLEVE CD197	$58.00	
*108"	–	3.7-5.8	5	RC	$299.99	

F9F Panther (SA: 242)

?	–	–	–	ARGUS RC677x	£2.50	
?	–	–	–	BEAULIEU	FORTHCOMING	
¶ 14"	–	Jetex	FF	HUNT J141	$3.50	(Comet)
15"	–	Jetex	FF	HUNT J144	$3.50	(Telasco)
15"	–	Jetex	FF	POND 27F7	$3.75	(Keil Kraft)

*19¼"	-	Jetex	FF	EASY JX03	$11.00 CDN	
20"	-	Jetex	FF	POND 27F3	$3.75	(Hatful)
30"	-	-	FF	CLEVE IT-111	$10.00	
49½"	35½"	.45-.65F	6	KNIGHTS	$30.00	
51"	50"	.40-.65F	4	ARGUS RM247	£7.50	(Norman)
*52"	57"	7.5F	5-6	JHH	$275.00	
*54"	56"	7.5F	RC	AVONDS	2470FF	
*55"	65"	.77F	5	FANJET	FORTHCOMING	

F9F Cougar (SA: 242)

¶19¼"	-	Jetex	FF	HUNT J145	$4.00	(Comet)
28"	-	Jetex	FF	HUNT J142	$5.00	(Telasco)
28"	-	Jetex	FF	POND 27F6	$5.25	(Paxton)
*47"	56"	.65-.80F	5	JHH	$230.00	

F11F-1 Tiger

26"	-	Jetex	FF	HUNT J146	$5.00	(Berkeley)
1050mm	-	2.5cc	RC	MRA 336	46F	
46"	56"	.60F	RC	TURBOFAN	£12.50	(World Engineering)
*50"	63"	.65F	6	KNIGHTS	$229.00	

F-14 Tomcat (SA: 242 , 262)

*?	-	Glider	RC	SKYTIME	FORTHCOMING	
*32"	31"	Glider	FF	TODAY J-4	$32.95	
75½"	-	.46x2F	6	MAN 6821	$30.00	(Gupton)
1954mm	1886mm	.60x2F	RC	BERTELLA	L50.000	
2000mm	1950mm	.77x2F	RC	AVONDS	317FF	
80"	75"	.77x2F	RC	HOBBY BARN	$64.99	(Avonds)
*88"	83"	.77x2F	5	YELLOW	$3800	

[wing mechanism, $1200.00; retracts, $800.00; power package, $350.00]

*107"	107"	.90x2F	7	JET AGE	$1200.00	

HU-16 Albatross (SA: 243)

15"	-	R	FF	COLE	$5.00	
*84"	51"	.40x2	4	G&P	$259.00	
2150mm	-	6.5x2	RC	MRA 690	150F	
96"	-	-	RC	PHOTO	$35.00	(Kouka)

J2-F Duck

14½"	-	R	FF	CLEVE CD242	$20.00	
19½"	-	R	FF	CLEVE CD242	$28.00	
26"	-	-	CL	POND 27F4	$5.25	(Palanek)

29"	–	R	FF	CLEVE CD242	$40.00	
39"	–	.25	FF	AUTHENTIC	£4.50	(Towner)
58"	–	–	RC	CLEVE CD242	$55.00	

**[KLARICH: $80.00]

58"	–	–	RC	CHARLIE	$22.00	
58"	–	.60	4-6	PROKIT	£20.00	

**[£75.00]

78"	–	–	RC	CLEVE CD242	$68.00	

P-50

31½"	–	R	FF	HUNT AH109	$3.75	(Plecan)
32"	–	R	FF	POND 18A5	$4.75	(Aircraft Pla

TBF Avenger (SA: 243, 262)

*?(¼)	–	–	RC	DP	FORTHCOMING	
16½"	–	R	FF	COLE	$5.00	
*16½"	–	R	FF	GUILLOW 509	$5.00	
20"	–	R	FF	CLEVE CD93A	$18.00	
¶20"	–	R	FF	POND 18A7	$4.25	(Comet)
27"	–	R	FF	HUNT 2955	$5.50	(Whitman)
*28"	–	R	FF	EASY FF69	$10.00CDN	
30"	–	R	FF	CLEVE CD93A	$28.00	
40½"	–	–	FF	MAN 2812	$9.60	(Noonan)
40"	–	R	FF	CLEVE CD39A	$38.00	
41"	–	–	RC	POND 50F4	$8.75	(Andrae)
42"	–	.09-.15	2	WING 222	$9.95	

[canopy, turret, $7.95; cowl, $6.95]

80"	–	–	RC	CLEVE CD93A	$52.00	
*82"	67"	.61-.91	5-6	DIVELY	$225.00	

[cockpit, $14.95]

82"	–	.90	4-6	HOLMAN	$25.00	

[cowl, canopy, $25.00]
**[$139.95]

S2G Tracker

13"	–	R	FF	COLE	$5.00	
63½"	–	.35x2	CL	FM 428	$7.00	(Hall)

SF-1

20"	–	R	FF	POND 50E5	$3.75	(Scientific)
20"	–	R	FF	HUNT PL127	$3.00	(Lindberg)

X-29 (SA: 243)

*1300mm   2250mm   10-15ccF   RC   MODELLTECHNIK   DM769,

XF5F Skyrocket

¶ 15"	–	R	FF	POND 30G4	$3.25	(Megow)
16"	–	R	FF	CLEVE CD75AU	$12.00	
16"	–	R	FF	POND 52G1	$3.75	(Guillow)
17"	–	R	FF	GLEASON	$1.15	(Struhl)
21"	–	R	FF	CLEVE CD75AU	$15.00	
24"	–	R	FF	HUNT SRS09	$3.00	(Struhl)
30"	–	R	FF	HUNT X8	$3.50	(Megow)
31½"	–	R	FF	HUNT SRS10	$3.50	(Struhl)
31½"	–	R	FF	CLEVE CD75AU	$18.00	
38"	–	–	CL	POND 31A3	$5.75	(Palanek)
42½"	–	R	FF	GLEASON	$6.70	(Struhl)
56"	–	.29x2	RC	FM CF386	$7.00	(Ziroli)
62"	–	–	FF	CODDING	$3.00	(Berkeley)
63"	–	–	RC	CLEVE CD75AU	$36.00	
68½"	–	.25x2	4-6	HOLMAN	$25.00	(Coulson)

[cowls, canopy, $25.00]

HOWARD

GH-1

620mm	–	R	FF	AIRBORNE	$5.00AUS	
25"	–	R	FF	POND 18D7	$3.75	(Stahl)
84"	54¼"	.90-1.5	RC	AERO PLANS	$25.00	

INTERSTATE

L-6 Grasshopper

13"	–	R	FF	POND 38D5	$3.25	(Sterling)
16"	–	R	FF	POND 55B3	$3.25	(Berkeley)
24"	–	R	FF	POND 18E5	$3.25	(Struhl)
29"	–	R	FF	POND 18E5	$3.25	(Cleave)
31"	–	R	FF	POND 18E5	$3.25	(Stahl)
35"	–	R	FF	POND 18E6	$5.25	(Berkeley)

KAISER-FLEETWINGS

XBTK-1

8"	–	R	FF	MOONEY	$1.00	

KINNER

Fleet Trainer

24"	–	R	FF	POND 17C4	$3.50	(Dallaire)
42"	–	.19-.35	RC	MORGAN	$6.95	

LOCKHEED

A-28 Hudson

25"	–	R	FF	CLEVE CD95AU	$18.00	
¶30"	–	R	FF	POND 57C6	$3.75	(Easy Build)
33"	–	R	FF	CLEVE CD95AU	$24.00	
41"	–	.19x2	RC	FM CF71	$6.00	(Palanek)
49½"	–	R	FF	CLEVE CD95AU	$32.00	
72"	–	.60x2	RC	B&D	$14.95	
98"	–	–	RC	CLEVE CD95AU	$48.00	

C-5A Galaxy (SA: 243)

*?	–	Glider	RC	SKYTIME	FORTHCOMING

C-23 Altair

22"	–	R	FF	POND 19B1	$3.75	(Modernistic)

C-69 Constellation (SA: 262)

74"	–	–	CL	POND 47F1	$10.75	(Kyosho)
74"	–	–	CL	POND 57F3	$10.75	(THMK)
**92½"	71¼"	.20x4	6	MURPHY	$150.00	

C-130 Hercules (SA: 243)

46"	35"	.049x4	CL	JVS	$8.00	
63½"	–	–	CL	GLEASON AT656	NA	(Edwards)
90"	–	.40x4	RC	FM CF556	$14.50	(Sarpolus)
102"	–	.25x4	6-8	MAN 12811	$28.50	(Mast)
108"	–	.20x4	RC	ARGUS RSQ1572	£13.50	(Antram)
*145"	–	.60x4	8	KRAFTERS	$995.00	

F-80 Shooting Star (SA: 243, 304)

11"	–	Jetex	FF	POND 52F5	$3.75	(Comet)
¶19"	–	Jetex	FF	POND 29B3	$4.25	(Ray Models)
19½"	–	Jetex	FF	HUNT J157	$4.00	(Hunt)
19½"	–	Jetex	FF	BELL 019	$5.00	
24"	–	Jetex	FF	COLE	$5.00	
24½"	–	Jetex	FF	BELL 009	$6.50	

29"	-	-	FF	CLEVE CD90AU	$18.00	
30"	-	-	FF	CLEVE IT-90	$10.00	

F-90

¶ 15"	-	R	FF	POND 61E7	$3.25	(Cleveland)

F-94 Starfire

*21¼"	_	Bean Rock	FF	WILLAIRCO	$12.75	
¶ 25"	-	Jetex	FF	HUNT J158	$4.50	(Comet)
*28 "	-	Bean Rock	FF	WILLAIRCO	$26.25	
*42½"	-	Bean Rock	FF	WILLAIRCO	$38.40	
*64"	-	Bean Rock	FF	WILLAIRCO	$69.75	

F-104 Starfighter (SA: 243)

7"	-	Jetex	FF	POND 19B4	$4.25	(Sebel)
20½"	-	Glider	FF	WALLACE	$6.50	
700mm	-	3.5cc	RC	MODELL	DM24,	(Schaffert)
*31"	74"	.90F	5	JET AGE	$450.00	
910mm	1900mm	.60-.80F	RC	BERTELLA	L50.000	
36"	72"	.45F	RC	THORJET	£18.50	
[canopy, £4.50][DALESMAN: foam wings, £20.50]						
925mm	1510mm	6.5	3	VTH MT855	DM24,	(Veltern)

P2V Neptune

37½"	-	.8-1.5cc	CL	ARGUS CL783	£4.50	(Bodey)

P-38 Lightning (SA: 244, 263)

15½"	-	R	FF	FRANK 18	$2.00	(Megow)
18"	-	R	FF	POND 52G5	$4.25	(Modelcraft)
19½"	-	R	FF	CLEVE CD85	$16.00	
22"	-	R	FF	HUNT 2954	$5.00	(Whitman)
23"	-	R	FF	POND 51A3	$4.25	(Model Aircraft)
24"	-	R	FF	ARGUS AM1053	£3.75	(Falconer)
24"	-	R	FF	POND H2B4	$4.75	(Guillow)
26"	-	R	FF	POND 19B5	$4.75	(Howse)
¶26"	-	R	FF	POND 19B5	$4.25	(Capitol)
27"	-	R	FF	CLEVE CD85	$19.00	
30"	-	R	FF	POND 52F6	$4.25	(Megow)
33"	-	R	FF	POND 19B3	$4.25	(Air King)
*34"	-	R	FF	COMET 3504	$11.50	
36"	-	R	FF	CLEVE T85	$15.00	

36"	–	R	FF	HUNT 104	$5.50	(Ott)
¶ 37"	–	R	FF	HUNT L8	$3.00	(Comet)
38"	–	R	FF	POND 38B7	$4.75	(Modelcraft)
¶ 38"	–	R	FF	POND 51A4	$5.75	(Ideal)
39"	–	R	FF	CLEVE CD85	$26.00	
40"	–	–	CL	GLEASON AT1256	$6.35	(Musciano)
*40"	–	.049-.09	CL	GUILLOW 2001	$44.00	
41"	–	–	CL	POND 31A4	$6.25	(Berkeley)
45"	–	R	FF	POND 53A2	$5.75	(Ott)
1260mm	–	R	FF	MRA 343	46F	
¶ 50"	–	R	FF	POND 51A4	$6.25	(Megow)
*1320mm	960mm	Elec	3-4	HIROBO 0002901	¥35,800	
52"	–	–	CL	POND 57C4	$6.25	(MAN)
52"	–	–	CL	POND 19B5	$5.25	(Modern Hobby
52"	–	.15x2	RC	TRAP MW2158	£7.50	(Whitehead)
52"	–	.15x2	RC	RCM 1020	$6.50	(Whitehead)
55"	–	.45x2	RC	MA 579	$18.00	(Brown)
58"	–	.35x2	RC	PLANS	$9.00	(Andrus)
65"	–	.35x2	RC	MA 505	$11.75	(Arnold)
1700mm	–	3.5-4cc	RC	MRA A560	25F	
*74¼"	51"	.61x2	RC	ROYAL 79-291	$314.95	
*1885mm	1152mm	.45x2	5-7	IKUTA	¥32,000	

*[assembled, ¥75,000]

*70"	–	.45x2	4	WING 721	$74.95	
78"	–	–	RC	CLEVE CD85	$45.00	
96"	–	–	RC	MB 6781	$21.50	(Johnson)

**[KLARICH: $150.00]

*100"	72"	1.2x2	RC	YELLOW	$499.99

[WHEELS: retracts, $350.00]

*104"	78"	/1.20x2	5	MALLORY	$1295.00
*104"	–	.90x2	6-8	KRAFTERS	$425.00
**107"	–	–	RC	R&M	$140.00
*120½"	96"	3.7x2	5	CBA	$1395.00

*[assembled, $2,600.00; J or L conversion, $75.00]
[WHEELS: retracts, $350.00]

*132"	–	2.2x2	6	GLASCO	$500.00
*156"	–	Zen G23x2	6-8	KRAFTERS	$575.00

SR-71 Blackbird (SA: 244, 263)

9"	–	R	FF	ARONSTEIN	$1.00
36"	57"	Glider	2	GREEN	£4.75
*1200mm	2300mm	10ccx2F	RC	KRANZ	DM540,
1260mm	2340mm	.60x2F	RC	BERTELLA	L50.000
[canopy, L15.000]					
*54"	107"	.90x2F	6	JET AGE	$600.00
54"	108"	.90x2F	RC	AVONDS	317FF (World Engines)
*55"	104"	.90x2F	5	YELLOW	$799.00
55¾"	168"	.65x2F	6	KNIGHTS	$46.00
*1400mm	2700mm	15ccx2F	RC	KRANZ	DM760,

T-33 (SA: 244, 263, 304)

29"	–	Jetex	FF	POND 19B4	$5.75 (Berkeley)
*52"	54"	7.5F	5-6	JHH	$225.00
*80"	75"	.90F	4	RJ	$425.00AUS

U-2 (SA: 244)

21"	–	Jetex	FF	POND 29A7	$3.75 (Delgatto)
31"	–	Jetex	FF	HUNT J160	$4.25 (MAN)
*40"	–	Bean Rock	FF	WILLAIRCO	$12.75
*53½"	–	Bean Rock	FF	WILLAIRCO	$26.25
64"	–	–	RC	POND	$4.75 (Strobel)
72"	–	.15	RC	HORN S-32	$10.00 (Osborne)
72"	–	Glider	RC	FM CF36	$8.00 (Trishin)
1900mm	–	3.5cc	RC	BOSAK	20 Kcs
[canopy, 15 Kcs]					
*78"	46"	Glider	3	CHART A-MM6	£89.95
*80"	52"	.46F	5	KNIGHTS	$229.00
*80"	–	Bean Rock	FF	WILLAIRCO	$38.40
100"	–	–	RC	POND 58D1	$6.25 (Strobel)
103"	52½"	.65F	6	KNIGHTS	$46.00
*120"	–	Bean Rock	FF	WILLAIRCO	$69.75
*139"	–	Glider	RC	SKYTIME	FORTHCOMING
*3600mm	2200mm	10ccF	RC	KRANZ	DM590,

LOENING

M-8 (SA: 263)

[35]	–	.049	CL	MAN 49	$8.00 (Stark)
*24"	–	R	FF	SIERRA	$13.95

OL-9 (SA: 244)

| 34" | – | – | 2 | FM CF594 | $7.00 | (Toner) |
| 47" | – | 1–1.5cc | FF | ARGUS FSP650 | £5.25 | (Stuby) |

MARTIN

Martin 74

20"	–	R	FF	CLEVE CD274	$18.00	
26½"	–	R	FF	CLEVE CD274	$28.00	
40"	–	R	FF	CLEVE CD274	$39.00	
80"	–	R	FF	CLEVE CD274	$52.00	

A-30 Baltimore

| 38" | – | R | FF | HUNT 3808 | $3.50 | (Ott) |
| 70" | – | .40x2 | 4 | WING 219 | $24.95 | |

[cowls, $19.95; canopy, $19.95; turret, $4.98; nose, $4.98]

AM-1 Mauler

17"	–	–	CL	POND 29C4	$3.75	(Musciano)
33"	–	–	CL	GLEASON	$3.40	(Farr)
50¼"	–	.40	RC	GLEASON	$9.70	(Farr)
69"	–	.61–.90	RC	RCM 217	$12.00	(McCullough)

B-10 (SA: 263)

27"	–	R	FF	CLEVE CD45U	$18.00	
35"	–	R	FF	CLEVE CD45U	$24.00	
35"	–	R	FF	HUNT KO22	$4.50	(Ideal)
*35"	–	R	FF	PROKIT	£30.50	
35¾"	–	R	FF	OLD 75	$3.50	(Diel)
53"	–	R	FF	CLEVE CD45U	$32.00	
70"	–	.23x2	FF	CODDING FS-160	$3.00	
71"	–	–	RC	CLEVE CD45U	$44.00	

B-26 Marauder

12½"	–	R	FF	GLEASON	$.90	(Stahl)
24½"	–	R	FF	CLEVE CD135	$25.00	
30"	–	R	FF	FM CF680	$7.00	(Bruning)
32¼"	–	R	FF	CLEVE CD135	$37.00	
40"	–	R	FF	POND 19C6	$5.75	(Miniature A/C
48½"	–	R	FF	CLEVE CD135	$52.00	
48½"	–	–	CL	GLEASON AT353	$12.80	(Schulman)
48½"	–	–	CL	PROKIT	£11.25	(Schulman)

53"	–	–	CL	POND 19C7	$7.25	(Simmance)
65"	–	–	RC	CLEVE CD135	$62.00	
72"	–	.45x2	2-4	FM CF170	$10.00	(D'Amico)
96"	66"	.90/1.20	6	GODFREY	$25.00	
100"	–	.90x2	4-6	BEAULIEU 18B	$27.95	(Parcell)

[TDF: cowls, $26.50; gun covers, $16.95]

BM-1
20"	–	R	FF	POND 19C5	$3.75	(Davidson)

BM-2
26"	–	R	FF	GLEASON	$2.25	(Lindberg)
31"	–	R	FF	HUNT PL135	$4.00	(Lindberg)

MB-1
27"	–	R	FF	CLEVE CD205	$14.00	
35¼"	–	R	FF	CLEVE CD205	$20.00	
53½"	–	R	FF	CLEVE CD205	$26.00	
107"	–	–	RC	CLEVE CD205	$38.00	

MO-1
13"	–	R	FF	POND 37A1	$3.25	(Martin)
28"	–	.40	CL	GLEASON	$4.25	(Gerber)

P4M-1 Mercator
50"	–	–	CL	POND 29D5	$6.25	(Smith)

T4M-1 (SA: 244)
18"	–	R	FF	GLEASON	$1.80	(Bibichkow)
18"	–	R	FF	HUNT CO197	$2.75	(Comet)
28"	–	R	FF	GLEASON	$4.20	(Bibichkow)

XS-1
18"	–	R	FF	HUNT AH183	$3.00	(Tyskewicz)

MCDONNELL-DOUGLAS

F2H Banshee
30"	–	–	FF	CLEVE IT-110	$10.00	

F-4 Phantom (SA: 244)
?	–	.60-.80F	RC	FM CF757	$16.00	(Baugher)
*?	81"	.82x2F	RC	VIOLETT	FORTHCOMING	
12½"	–	Dynajet	CL	HUNT J167	$3.25	(Hunt)

19¼"	–	Jetex	FF	BELL 017	$6.50	
*19½"	31"	Glider	FF	TODAY J-5	$31.95	
24½"	–	Glider	FF	WALLACE	$6.50	
*795mm	810mm	.051	2-4	MARUTAKA 57	¥8,800	
*32"	37"	.051-.15	RC	METCALFE	£31.95	
35"	46"	3.5-7.5F	4	ZIROLI	$10.00	

[canopy, $6.50]
*[SOUTHEAST: $169.95]

37"	51½"	Dynajet	6	KNIGHTS	$30.00	
*38"	60"	.77F	4	MIKE	$179.00	
1070mm	1420mm	10ccF	RC	MRA 170	95F	
1090mm	–	10ccF	RC	BOSAK	40 Kcs	

[canopy, 40 Kcs]

*43½"	68"	.60x2F	5	YELLOW	$315.00	

[kit, engine, fan, $665.00][IMPACT: retracts, $129.95]

*44"	68"	.60x2F	5-7	JHH	$400.00	

[IMPACT: retracts, $129.95]

46"	–	.60F	RC	GLEASON	$31.85	(Johnson)
48"	48"	Glider	2	GREEN	£3.75	
*48"	47"	.45-.61	4-5	LEICESTER	£83.09	
*1200mm	1200mm	.40-.60	4-6	MARUTAKA 17	¥28,000	
*1240mm	1910mm	10-15ccF	RC	MODELLTECHNIK	DM798,	
*52"	72"	.77F	4	CUSTOM	$335.00	
52"	–	.35	CL	GLEASON	$7.50	(Suarez)
1310mm	–	6.5-7.5cc	RC	MRA 618.563	106F	
52"	60"	.80F	RC	THORJET	£18.50	

[canopy, £4.95] [DALESMAN: foam wings, £23.50]

57½"	77"	.77x2F	RC	PHOTO	$19.95	(Pepino)
1462mm	2220mm	.81x2F	RC	BERTELLA	L50.000	

[canopy, L15.000]

*58"	85½"	7.5x2F	5-8	JET MODEL	$1600.00	
59"	–	.40F	RC	GLEASON	$10.35	

F-15 Eagle (SA: 245, 263, 304)

*?	–	Glider	RC	SKYTIME	FORTHCOMING
*9"	–	Glider	FF	MRC FJ02	$5.98
18"	–	Glider	FF	WALLACE	$6.50
*810mm	780mm	.051	2-3	MARUTAKA 58	¥8,800
*31"	35"	.09F	2-3	KRESS 500	$125.59

36"   49"   3.5F   RC   ZIROLI $10.00
[canopy, $6.50]
*[SOUTHEAST: $169.95]

1170mm   -   10cc   RC   BOSAK   40 Kcs
[canopy, 40 Kcs]

1170mm   -   10cc   RC   MODELL   DM48,   (Bosak)

46"   -   .61   4-5   TRAP MW2126   £7.50   (Bosak)
[canopy, $6.20]

49"   -   .40-.45   RC   RCM 817 $12.25   (Advani)

*53"   68"   .61-.81F 4-5   PARKINSON $179.00CDN

*57"   85"   7.5ccx2F RC   AVONDS   3945FF

1480mm 1950mm   .60x2F   RC   BERTELLA   L50.000
[canopy, L15.000]

*63"   93"   .81x2F   5   YELLOW $2000.00

*70"   105"   .77x2F   5-7   BYRON 6130155 $768.90
[retracts, $262.90; nose wheel, $109.95; brakes, $76.95; speed
 brake, $71.50; engine package, $367.95x2]

F-18 Hornet (SA: 245, 304)

*7½"   11½"   Glider   FF   PMI AG102 $4.95

*20"   28"   Glider   FF   TODAY J-2 $26.95

*41½"   56"   .45F   4   SPIRIT $249.00
[tuned pipe, $45.00]

1090mm   -   10cc   RC   BOSAK   40 Kcs
[canopy. 30 Kcs]

*1180mm 1100mm .19-.25   3-4   IKUTA   ¥19,800
*[assembled, ¥75,000]

48"   68¼"   .60F   RC   AEROFAN $23.00AUS

49"   65½"   .65-.81F RC   THORJET   £18.50
[canopy, £4.95]

*1270mm 1350mm .40-.45   4-5   IKUTA   ¥29,800
[assembled, ¥148,000]

*51"   65"   .65-.81F 4-5   PARKINSON $189.00

1428mm 2133mm   .60 x2F   RC   BERTELLA   L50.000
[canopy, L15.000]

*57"   84"   .90x2F   5   BYRON 6130250 $524.95
[retracts, $239.95; nose wheel, $119.95; engine package, $389.95]

*58"   72"   .80x2F   4-6   JET AGE $700.00

*72"   98"   .80x2F   5   YELLOW $2150.00
[retracts, $600.00; power unit, $350.00]

F-88 Voodoo

¶ 15"   -   -   FF   POND 25F4 $3.75   (Cleveland)

XP-67

33½"	–	R		FF	WOODHOUSE	£3.50	(Koutny)

NORTH AMERICAN

A-36 Apache (SA: 263)

13"	–	R		FF	NFFS	$6.00	
17"	–	R		FF	HUNT N2	$2.50	(Megow)
*18"	–	R		FF	COMET 3204	$6.50	
22"	–	R		FF	HUNT 2213	$4.50	(Whitman)
23"	–	R		FF	HUNT ES24	$3.00	(Stahl)
23½"	–	R		FF	HUNT N-7	$3.25	(Megow)
28"	–	R		FF	BELL 012	$7.50	
¶ 28"	–	R		FF	POND 25F2	$6.25	(Cleveland)
32"	–	R		FF	HUNT ES24E	$3.50	(Stahl)
*35"	–	R		FF	PROKIT	£35.00	
36"	–	R		FF	CODDING	$1.00	(Hobby Models
37"	–	R		FF	HUNT 79	$4.50	(Stahl)
45"	–	R		FF	HUNT 80	$5.00	(Stahl)

A5V Vigilante

13½"	–	Jetex		FF	HUNT J177	$3.50	
720mm	–	–		RC	VTH MT829-K	DM7.50	(Bosak)
1040mm	–	6.5		RC	BOSAK	20 Kcs	
[canopy, 10 Kcs]							
41"	–	.40		4-5	MB 12791	$9.50	(Bosak)
41"	–	.40		4-5	TRAP MW2142	£5.50	(Bosak)
1040mm	1150mm	6.5		4	VTH MT829-G	DM19,50	(Bosak)
66¼"	90½"	7.5x2F		RC	RCM 902	$20.00	(Frankel)
[TDF: ducts, $39.95; canopy, $12.95; radome, $9.95; tail fairing, $39.95]							

AJ-1 Savage

27"	–	R		FF	FM CF718	$5.00	(Howard)
27"	–	–		CL	POND 31A5	$5.75	(Berkeley)

AT-6 Texan/Harvard (SA: 245, 263)

?	–	–		–	ARGUS MA87x	$3.75	
[44]	–	.15-.19		CL	MAN 4821	$10.50	(Uravich)
15"	–	R		FF	POND 20A7	$3.25	(Aer-o-Kits)
¶18"	–	R		FF	POND 61E6	$4.75	(Sterling)
*18	–	R		FF	STERLING A-9	$8.95	

21"	–	R	FF	COLE	$5.00	
*21"	–	R	FF	VERON VO415	£3.49	
31"	–	–	CL	POND 29F5	$4.75	(Berkeley)
*35"	–	R	FF	EASY FF77	$12.00CDN	
36"	–	–	RC	POND 37D6	$4.75	(Petersen)
41"	–	–	CL	HUNT AH140	$.25	(Wordell)
42"	–	–	CL	POND 29E3	$5.75	(Schroder)
42"	–	–	CL	POND 29E6	$5.75	(Smith)
*44"	–	.15–.20	3–4	HOUSE	$49.95	
*44"	28"	Glider	2	CLIFF	$89.95	
45"	–	R	FF	ARGUS FSP139	£3.75	(Towner)
50"	–	R	RC	POND 20A5	$5.75	(Ideal)
53"	37"	.30–.40	RC	RCM 470	$6.00	(Petersen)
1350mm	940mm	6.5cc	4	VTH MT614	DM19,50	(Petersen)
*54"	–	.35–.46	4	DYNA 4005	$115.95	
1420mm	–	4–6.5cc	RC	MRA 635.570	95F	
58"	–	.35–.40	4	FM CF684	$7.00	(Heenan)
62"	–	.60	RC	RCM 512	$14.75	(Holmes)
66"	44"	.60	2	FM CF771	$7.00	(Reiss)
*66"	–	.60	4–6	GREAT AT6F	$234.95	
68½"	–	.45–.60	4	TAYLOR	£6.00	

[cowl, £4.50; canopy, £3.00; spinner, £1.50; balsa pack, £27.50]

1740mm	–	10cc	RC	MRA BT5	119F	
72"	–	.60	RC	B&D	$14.95	
72"	–	.59	RC	MAN 35	$7.00	
*1843mm	1257mm	.61/1.20	6	MARUTAKA 67	¥38,000	
*75¼"	–	/.90–1.20	4–6	FLITECRAFT	£140.00	
83"	–	–	RC	HOLMAN	$25.00	(Taylor)
101"	70"	–	5–6	ZIROLI	$30.00	

[cowl, $28.00; canopy, $20.00][TDF: cowl, $23.50; AVCO: cockpit, $30.00; SHATTLEROE: landing gear $16.00; SCHMALZIGAN: retracts, $300.00]
**[KLARICH: $140.00]
*[HANGAR: $230.00]

*102"	73"	Zen 62	7	AHS	$260.00

[retracts: ROBART, $195,00; SCHMALZIGAN, $300.00]

108"	–	–	RC	MODEL	FORTHCOMING

[retracts, $240.00AUS]

*126"	87"	1.5	6	NZ	FORTHCOMING
*3550mm	2470mm	140cc	4–6	PETRAUSCH	DM998,

B-1 (SA: 246)

38"	–	.15	RC	MA 147	$2.75	
*45"	50"	Bean Rock	FF	WILLAIRCO	$42.50	

B-25 Mitchell   (SA: 246, 304)

22"	–	R	FF	HUNT 2209	$4.00	(Whitman)
¶ 22"	–	R	FF	POND 20A7	$.25	(Ott)
*26½"	–	.020x2	CL	GUILLOW 805	$21.00	
27¼"	–	R	FF	CLEVE CD125	$25.00	
33"	–	R	FF	HUNT KO24	$4.50	(Miniature A
33"	–	R	FF	MB 1081-CP	$7.50	(Miniature A
*33"	–	R	FF	PROKIT	£30.50	(Ideal)
36"	–	R	FF	FM CF601	$5.00	(Midkiff)
36½"	–	R	FF	CLEVE CD125	$37.00	
¶ 40"	–	R	FF	POND 51C7	$6.25	(Ott)
48"	–	.020x2	CL	MA 253	$3.50	
54"	–	–	RC	FM CF17	$11.50	(Ziroli)
55"	–	–	RC	CLEVE CD125	$52.00	
56"	–	–	CL	POND 57D1	$9.25	(Aristo-Craf
57"	–	–	CL	POND 38A4	$6.75	(Piorkowski)
¶ 67"	–	.23x2	CL	CODDING FS1-60	$3.00	
71"	–	.60x2	4-6	MORGAN 113RC	$19.95	
[cowls, $10.90]						
*1800mm	1150mm	Elec	2-3	KYOTO	¥21,000	
*1800mm	1370mm	.40/.40x2	4-6	MARUTAKA 13	¥35,000	
73"	–	–	RC	CLEVE CD125	$62.00	
*101"	79"	.90x2	4-6	HANGAR	$430.00	(Ziroli)
[WHEELS: retracts, $350.00]						
*116"	89"	ST3000x2	6-10	YELLOW	$700.00	
148"	108"	2.3x2	5	GODFREY	$25.00	

B-45 Tornado

25"	–	–	FF	CLEVE SM175	$6.00
**96"	76"	.65x2F	6	MURPHY	$230.00

BC-1

20"	–	R	FF	HUNT AH138	$2.75

BT-6

28"	–	R	FF	HUNT AH139	$3.25

21"	–	R	FF	COLE	$5.00	

F-82 Twin Mustang (SA: 246)

13"	–	R	FF	SWAMP	$1.50	(Brown)
25"	–	R	FF	HUNT AH142	$3.25	(Bedish)
26"	–	R	FF	SAMS 815	£2.95	(Newman)
38¼"	–	–	CL	GLEASON ATA51	NA	
40"	–	R	FF	POND 29E4	$5.75	
52"	–	.15x2	RC	HORN S10A	$11.00	(Osborne)
72"	–	.60x2	RC	FM CF806	$7.50	(Reiss)
78"	–	.40x2	RC	HORN S10	$14.00	(Osborne)

**[KLARICH: $85.00]

79"	–	–	CL	POND 29G3	$6.25	(Smith)
*2000mm	–	10ccx2	3	COOP 9600073	3400F	
*2160mm	1300mm	15ccx2	RC	SKYRAIDER	$435.00AUS	
*94"	67"	.60x2	4-6	GAGER	$325.00	

F-86 Sabre (SA: 246)

*7½"	7½"	Glider	FF	PAI 245	$3.75	(Aerographics)
*9"	–	Glider	FF	MRC FJ03	$5.98	
*19"	–	Glider	FF	PAI 277	$4.75	(Sabo)
13"	–	Glider	FF	NFFS	$6.00	
*15"	–	Jetex	FF	KEIL KK0062	£3.99	
17"	–	Jetex	FF	HUNT J179	$3.50	
*19½"	–	Bean Rock	FF	WILLAIRCO	$12.75	
24"	–	–	FF	CLEVE IT-20	$10.00	
*26"	–	Bean Rock	FF	WILLAIRCO	$26.50	
26½"	–	Glider	FF	WALLACE	$6.50	
30"	–	–	FF	POND 29F3	$6.25	(Mittelstaedt)
37"	37½"	Dynajet	6	KNIGHTS	$30.00	
*39"	–	Bean Rock	FF	WILLAIRCO	$38.40	
41"	–	Dynajet	CL	POND 20C7	$10.75	(Smith)
*42"	43"	.25F	RC	PAUL	$180.00	

[power package, $225.00]

*50½"	50½"	7.5F	5	JHH	$275.00	
*51"	50"	.45-.60F	4	HOBBY BARN	$189.99	
55"	55"	.40-.46F	4	ARGUS RM295	£11.00	(Thorpe)

[canopy, £5.25]

*55"	52"	.90F	RC	TURBOFAN	£89.00	
1400mm	1480mm	.81F	RC	BERTELLA	L50.00	

[canopy, L15.000]

*57"	58¼"	.77F	4-5	BYRON 6130086	$327.25

[retracts, $128.85; power package, $367.95]

*57"	58¼"	.90F	4	RJ	$310.00AUS	
*58"	58"	.82F	5	VIOLETT	$450.00	
*58½"	–	Bean Rock	FF	WILLAIRCO	$69.75	
*60"	64"	.77-.90F	6	INNOVATIVE	$249.95	
*60"	64"	.77F	4	MIKE	$229.00	

F-86D Sabre (SA: 246)

9"	–	Jetex	FF	POND 20A7	$3.25	(Comet)
¶ 13¼"	–	Jetex	FF	HUNT J180	$3.50	(Comet)
20"	–	Jetex	FF	POND 51D2	$3.75	(Comet)
23¼"	–	Jetex	FF	BELL 009	$8.50	
28"	–	Jetex	FF	POND 29E2	$3.75	(Purcell)
730mm	770mm	.8-1.5cc	FF	VTH MT61	DM12,	(Mittelstaedt
43"	47"	.45-.65F	6	KNIGHTS	$30.00	
*57"	62½"	.77F	4-5	BYRON 6130085	$335.00	

[retracts, $128.85; power package, $367.95]

64"	–	.60	RC	HORN S-36	$8.00	
1600mm	–	10cc	RC	MODELL	DM12,	(Meier)
67"	–	.60	RC	RCM 630	$6.75	(Baumgardner)

F-100 Super Sabre (SA: 246)

8"	9½"	Glider	FF	PAI 245	$3.75	(Aerographics
8"	–	Jetex	FF	POND 51D1	$3.75	(Sebel)
13"	–	Jetex	FF	HUNT J182	$4.00	(Comet)
*19¼"	–	Bean Rock	FF	WILLAIRCO	$12.75	
*26"	–	Bean Rock	FF	WILLAIRCO	$26.25	
*39"	–	Bean Rock	FF	WILLAIRCO	$38.40	
1080mm	–	6.5ccF	RC	BOSAK	40 Kcs	

[canopy, 20 Kcs]

*48"	57"	.60F	RC	AVONDS	2470FF
*50"	63"	.77-.81F	4-8	CENTURY	$189.95

[retracts, $199.00; drag chute, $20.00]

1320mm	1600mm	.60-.81F	RC	BERTELLA	L50.000

[canopy, L15.000]

*54"	67"	.65-77F	5-9	CRESS 760	$325.00

[power package, $480.00]

1420mm	–	10-15cc	RC	MODELL	DM15,	(Fry)
56"	67"	.81F	RC	RCM 940	$13.50	(Johnson)

*1470mm	1690mm	10-15ccF	RC	MODELLTECHNIK	DM599,	
*58"	–	Bean Rock	FF	WILLAIRCO	$69.75	

FJ-3 Fury

16½"	–	Jetex	FF	HUNT J183	$4.00	(Hunt)
38"	–	–	CL	POND 38F4	$8.75	(Coles)

O-47

16"	–	R	FF	GLEASON	$3.05	(Ott)
16"	–	R	FF	POND 51C6	$4.75	(Whitman)
20"	–	R	FF	POND 17C7	$3.75	(Comet)
23¼"	–	R	FF	DIELS 35	$4.00	
24"	–	R	FF	POND 20A4	$3.75	(Peerless)
27"	–	R	FF	GLEASON	$2.25	(Lindberg)
28"	–	R	FF	HUNT 2968	$5.50	(Whitman)
42"	–	R	FF	GLEASON	$.90	(Lindberg)

OV-10 Bronco   (SA: 246)

13"	–	R	FF	AERO ERA	$1.25	
13"	–	R	FF	SWAMP	$1.50	(Brown)
14"	–	R	FF	COLE	$5.00	
27"	–	R	FF	FM CF725	$8.00	(Howard)
30"	–	1.5-2.5cc	CL	ARGUS CL912	£3.75	(Spence)
30"	–	–	CL	POND 29G1	$5.75	(Musciano)
36"	–	–	FF	MB 3803	$7.50	(Houle)
1220mm	–	–	CL	MRA A373	16F	
1200mm	–	Elec	RC	VTH MT977-K	DM16,	(Tupuschies)
70"	–	.60x2	4-6	MAN 9681	$16.50	(Capan)
70"	–	.25x2	RC	MACKINDER	£11.50	
70"	–	–	RC	POND 58B2	$9.25	(RHM)
1550mm	1613mm	Elec	5	VTH MT977-G	DM36,	(Tupuschies)

P-51B Mustang   (SA: 246, 263)

13"	–	R	FF	DATA	$1.60	(McCombs)
13"	–	R	FF	FOAM	$2.25	
13"	–	R	FF	POND 29E7	$3.25	(Modernistic)
14"	–	R	FF	CLEVE CD91BU	$14.00	
18½"	–	R	FF	CLEVE CD91BU	$18.00	
18½"	–	R	FF	GLEASON	$2.45	(Mather)

23¼"	–	R	FF	GLEASON	$1.80	(Stahl)
27½"	–	R	FF	CLEVE CD91BU	$24.00	
30"	–	R	FF	ARGUS FSP1637	£3.75	(Nougerede)
37"	–	.15-.25	CL	AUTHENTIC	£2.00	(Towner)
55"	–	–	RC	CLEVE CD91BU	$38.00	
*60"	50"	.60	4-6	TOP RC-16	$124.95	

[D conversion kit, $18.95][UNITRACTS: retracts, £34.50]

1550mm	–	10cc	RC	MRA BT2.471	119F	(Taylor)
1600mm	–	8-10cc	RC	MRA 765	119F	
70"	–	10cc	4	ARGUS RC1378	£13.50	(Vaugh)
*71"	–	.90	7-8	DYNA 6001	$245.00	
74"	65"	.90	4-6	BEAULIEU 3B	$24.95	(Beaulieu)

[TDF: cowl, $29.95; belly pan $11.95; airscoop, $10.95; door &
 wheel covers, $15.95; AVCO: canopy, $15.95; cockpit, $19.95]

1850mm	–	15cc	RC	MRA 693.590	126F	
75"	–	–	RC	HOLMAN	$19.95	(Taylor)
76¼"	66½"	.90-1.08	4	INNOVATIVE	$25.00	
99"	–	–	RC	HOLMAN	$19.95	(Taylor)

P-51D Mustang (SA: 246, 264)

?	–	–	–	ARGUS MA310x	£3.00	
?	–	–	–	FM CF13	$7.00	(Buragas)
*10"	–	Glider	FF	PAI 279	$5.00	(Sabo)
*10"	–	Glider	FF	PAPER	$3.95	
11"	–	R	FF	POND 56D1	$3.25	(Sterling)
11"	–	R	FF	POND 20A4	$3.25	(Weiss)
*13"	–	R	FF	PECK PP8	$6.95	
13"	–	R	FF	YEST 53	$3.00	(Modernistic)
*13½"	–	R	FF	MRC	$8.95	
14"	–	R	FF	CLEVE CD91DU	$16.00	
*16"	–	.049	CL	COX 7600	$33.90	
*16"	–	R	FF	KEIL KK0024	£4.99	
*17"	–	R	FF	GUILLOW 905	$4.29	
¶18"	–	R	FF	POND 20A2	$3.75	(Capitol)
¶18"	–	R	FF	POND 52F4	$3.74	(Comet)
18½"	–	R	FF	CLEVE CD91BU	$20.00	
18½"	–	R	FF	HUNT MAC15	$2.50	(Model A/C)
*18½"	–	R	FF	KEIL KK0045	£3.99	
*19"	–	R	FF	IHC 528	$12.98	

19"	–	–	CL	POND 56C7	$3.25	(Berkeley)
20"	–	R	FF	ALFERY	$5.00	
20"	–	R	FF	HUNT 83	$2.50	(Stahl)
20"	–	–	CL	POND 58D7	$3.25	(Model Builders)
*22"	–	R	FF	COMET 1624	$12.00	
22"	–	R	FF	POND 51C6	$5.75	(Whitman)
*[REPRO: R-16, $10.50]						
580mm	–	R	FF	AIRBORNE	$5.00AUS	
24"	–	R	FF	CLEVE IT-91	$10.00	
*24"	–	R	FF	COMET 3901	$14.00	
24"	–	R	FF	POND 20A3	$3.75	(Ott)
24"	–	–	CL	POND 29F1	$3.75	(Lewis)
24"	–	R	FF	POND 29G6	$4.75	(Guillow)
*24"	–	R	FF	STERLING A-13	$15.95	
25"	–	R	FF	HUNT ES25	$3.00	(Stahl)
25"	–	R	FF	POND 20A4	$3.75	(Scientific)
26"	–	R	FF	ARGUS FSR1441	£3.00	(Chapman)
27"	–	R	FF	POND 29E4	$4.75	(Ott)
27"	–	–	CL	POND 29E7	$5.75	(Musciano)
27½"	–	R	FF	CLEVE CD91DU	$26.00	
28"	–	R	FF	BELL 013	$7.50	
*28"	–	R/.020	CL	GUILLOW 402	$16.00	
*28"	–	R	FF	EASY FF66	$10.00CDN	
28"	–	R	FF	HUNT KO25	$4.00	(Cadet)
30"	–	R	FF	HUNT 252	$5.50	(Ott)
¶30"	–	R	FF	POND 20A6	$5.75	(Capitol)
30"	–	R	FF	POND 29G6	$4.75	(Gregory)
*780mm	638mm	Elec	2-3	UNION RCK703	¥12,000	
31"	–	–	RC	POND 44A7	$6.75	(Kent)
32"	–	R	FF	HUNT 85	$4.00	(Stahl)
32"	–	–	CL	POND 38C1	$4.25	(Smith)
890mm	–	R	FF	MRA 354	40F	
36"	–	R	FF	CLEVE T-91	$12.00	
÷900mm	690mm	.051-.10	2-3	MARUTAKA 40	¥7,800	
36"	–	–	CL	POND 44E2	$4.75	(Aircraft Plan)
37"	–	R	FF	HUNT 86	$4.50	(Stahl)
37"	–	–	CL	POND 20A6	$4.75	(Modern Hobby)

37"	–	–	CL	POND 37C6	$7.75	(Berkeley)
¶40"	–	R	FF	HUNT 4001	$6.00	(Ott)
*40"	–	Elec	4	KYOSHO	¥14,8000	
40"	–	R	FF	POND 20A6	$5.75	(Ott)
*43"	–	.19-.21	4	HOUSE	$49.95	
*43"	–	.15-.25	2-3	LEICESTER 25	£37.83	
*44"	29"	Glider	2	CLIFF	$89.95	
1140mm	–	6.5	RC	BOSAK	20 Kcs	
[canopy, 15 Kcs]						
46"	–	–	RC	OLD DS7	$5.00	(Stahl)
46"	–	–	RC	POND 29F3	$6.25	(Strader)
46¼"	–	–	CL	GLEASON	$7.50	(Hudson)
46¼"	–	–	CL	PROKIT	£6.05	(Hudson)
*1175mm	1023mm	.19/.40	3-4	MARUTAKA 11	¥14,000	
*1197mm	1043mm	.19-.25	4-6	TETTORA MG25SR	¥12,000	
*1215mm	880mm	.19-.25	3-4	IKUTA	¥13,500	
*1200mm	910mm	Elec	2-3	KYOTO	¥9,500	
*1220mm	970mm	.19-.35	3-5	OK APQX018	¥14,800	
*48"	40"	.40	4	PAUL'S K-14	$135.00	
*48"	–	.19-.35	3-4	FLAIR CAPRO1	NA	
48"	–	.19-.35	3-4	TRAP MW2101	£5.50	(CAP)
50"	–	2.5cc	FF	ORIGINAL	£3.65	(Martin)
50"	–	Glider	2	RCM 997	$5.25	(Hollison)
*53"	–	.35-.45	4	DYNA 4003	$115.95	
55"	–	–	RC	CLEVE CD91DU	$42.00	
*55"	–	.25-.45	4	WING 704	$37.50	
*55½"	–	.40/.90	4-5	SHACK 10153	$279.99	
56"	–	.40	RC	ENT	$8.95	
*1400mm	1020mm	.40-.45	3-4	IKUTA	¥22,000	
*56"	–	.40/.90	4-5	INDY	$149.98	
*1410mm	1227mm	.40/.60	4-6	MARUTAKA 10	¥23,000	
*1425mm	1160mm	.40/.90	4-5	OK 11036	¥43,500	
*1430mm	1230mm	.40/.60	4-6	MARUTAKA 36	¥55,000	
60"	–	.60	4	TAYLOR	£6.00	
[cowl, £3.00; canopy, £3.00; spinner £5.00; balsa pack, £29.00]						
*[HOLMAN: $149.95][UNITRACTS: retracts, £39.33]						
*1539mm	1300mm	.60	4-6	IKUTA	¥32,000	
*62"	–	.60	4	DIVELY	$199.95	
[ROBART: retracts, $54.95]						
*[deluxe kit, $249.95]						

62"	-	.60	RC	GLEASON	$7.50	(Carmen)
62"	-	.61	RC	RCM 253	$12.50	(Baker)
1576mm	1280mm	10cc	4	VTH MT531	DM29,50	(Baker)
1600mm	-	.61	4	AIRBORNE	$22.00AUS	
*64"	48"	.60	4-6	SIG KBRC6	$119.95	
*1644mm	1335mm	.60/.90	5-6	MARUTAKA 9	¥32,000	
*66"	45"	-	RC	SAIL	FORTHCOMING	
*1660mm	130mm	10-15cc	RC	SKYRAIDER	$265.00AUS	
*1700mm	-	10cc	3	COOP 9600069	1510F	
69"	-	.60	6	TAYLOR	£9.00	

[cowl, £13.00; canopy, £3.00; spinner, £5.50; balsa pack, £31.00]
[retracts: LIKES, $317.00; UNITRACTS, £24.84]

*72"	-	15/120cc	RC	MODEL 021	$169.00AUS	
*75"	57"	.90/1.20	4	D&R	$239.00	

[ROBINAIRE: retracts, $245.00]

*75"	-	.75/1.20	4	GAL/IP	£89.95	
76¼"	66½"	.90-1.08	4	INNOVATIVE	$25.00	

[retracts: LIKES, $317.00; ROBINAIRE, $245.00]
*[$229.95]

*81"	-	ST2500	5	JM	$395.00AUS	
*81"	-	.90-1.20	5	PLATT RC-6	$319.00	

[retracts, $219.00; tailwheel, $54.00; drop tanks, $39.00]
[cockpits: JD, $40.00; AVCO, $23.95]
**[$149.00]

*2100mm	-	10cc	RC	COOP 9600069	2400F	
*85"	76"	Q50	4-6	BYRON 6130110	$396.30	

[retracts, $225.05; tailwheel, $38.70; prop system, $406.45]

**100"	-	Q50	RC	KLARICH	$150.00	(Holman)
*102"	-	.90	4	NOSEN	$119.99	

[spinner, $16.95][cockpit: AVCO, $27.95; DIVELY, $24.95; retracts:
ROBART, $225.00; WHEELS, $275.00; LIKES, $317.00]

*108½"	-	3-5hp	4-5	WESTCRAFT	$395.00	

[retracts: ROBART, $225.00; WHEELS, $275.00; LIKES, $317.00]

*114"	98"	130cc	6	GLASCO	$2000.00	

[retracts: ROBART, $225.00; LIKES, $317.00]

P-51H Mustang (SA: 247)

23"	-	R	FF	KOUTNY	$5.00	
23"	-	R	FF	MA 632	$3.25	(Koutny)
23½"	-	R	FF	BELL 002	$5.00	
28"	-	R	FF	BELL 014	$7.50	
31"	-	-	CL	POND 63G3	$9.00	(Jetco)

31½"	–	–	CL	GLEASON	$7.20	(McKroskey)
*55"	47"	.40–.50	4-5	ROBERTS	$97.00	
69"	49"	.60	RC	PHOTO	$19.95	

P-51J

| 13" | – | R | FF | AERO ERA | $1.25 | |

T-2J Buckeye (SA: 247)

| 23" | – | Jetex | FF | HUNT J184 | $5.00 | (Berkeley) |

T-28 Trojan (SA: 247, 264)

*16"	–	R	FF	GUILLOW 901	$4.29	
18"	–	R	FF	HUNT 2273	$4.00	(Whitman)
20"	–	R	FF	COLE	$5.00	
30"	–	–	CL	POND 51D2	$4.75	(Berkeley)
41"	–	.10–.15	4	VELIVOLI	$6.00	
*65"	51"	.61/1.20	4	PICA	$149.95	

[cockpit, $14.95]

| 67½" | – | – | RC | RCM 194 | $13.50 | (Platt) |

[TDF: cowl, $19.95]

| *68" | – | .60–.90 | 4-6 | GREAT T28F | $234.95 | |
| *79" | 62" | .90/2.0 | 4-5 | PICA | $219.95 | |

[cockpit, $14.95][IMPACT: retracts, $125.00]

| 102" | – | 3.15 | 3-5 | HOLMAN | $33.00 | (Morse) |

[FGM: cowl, $29.00; PK: canopy, $20.00]
**[R&M: $230.00]

XB-70 Valkyrie (SA: 247)

| *35" | 63" | Bean Rock | FF | WILLAIRCO | $42.50 | |

YAT-28E

| *66" | 60 " | .60–.80 | 4-5 | GM | $159.95 | |

NORTHROP

A-17 Nomad

16"	–	R	FF	HUNT 3972	$4.50	(Whitman)
23"	–	R	FF	POND 20B2	$4.25	(Booton)
24"	–	R	FF	GLEASON	$2.70	(Lindberg)
46½"	–	–	CL	GLEASON	$10.25	(Wilson)
46½"	–	–	CL	PROKIT	£9.00	(Wilson)
46½"	–	.35–.45	CL	MAN 2682	$10.50	(Wilson)
72"	–	.60	RC	B&D	$14.95	

B-2 Stealth

*?	–	Glider	RC	SKYTIME	FORTHCOMING
33"	–	Glider	FF	WALLACE	$6.50

F-5E Tiger II (SA: 247)

*13"	24"	Glider	FF	TODAY J-3	$19.95

F-20 Tigershark (SA: 247, 264)

31"	–	.25	RC	ENT	$6.50
*38"	65"	.60F	RC	AVONDS	2470FF
40"	61"	.45F	RC	THORJET	£18.50
[canopy, £4.50] [DALESMAN: foam wings, £18.00]					
*50"	55"	.60	RC	FARNS A1013	$149.95
*50"	70"	.65-.77F	5	CRESS	$289.00
*1240mm	2250mm	10-15ccF	RC	MODELLTECHNIK	DM798,
*56"	90"	.77F	5	BYRON 6130020	$395.95
[retracts, $84.95; nosewheel, $87.95; power package, $367.95]					
*58"	88"	.81F	6-8	KNIGHTS	$339.00

F-89 Scorpion

19"	–	R	FF	POND 25B4	$3.75	(Cleveland)

P-61 Black Widow (SA: 247, 264)

13"	–	R	FF	DIELS 8	$2.00
25"	–	R	FF	CLEVE CD155	$32.00
33"	–	R	FF	CLEVE CD155	$40.00
34½"	–	.049x2	CL	FM CF473	$6.00	(Beaulieu)
36"	–	R	FF	CLEVE T-155	$15.00
*37½"	–	R/.020	CL	STERLING E15	$29.95
49½"	–	2.5x2	CL	ARGUS CL1092	£7.50	(Bodey)
49½"	–	R	FF	CLEVE CD155	$50.00
99"	–	–	RC	CLEVE CD155	$75.00

X-4 Bantam

36"	–	Glider	FF	WESTERN 035	$2.00

XBT-1

24"	–	R	FF	HUNT AH143	$3.00	(Weiss)

XFT-1

22"	–	R	FF	POND 38F7	$4.75	(Miniature A/C)
23"	–	R	FF	POND 20B2	$3.75	(Booton)

XP-56

[56]	–	Elec	–	MB 4851	$12.50	(Young)
37"	–	R	FF	POND 20B4	$4.75	(Le Modele Red

PACKARD-LEPERE

LUSAC-II (SA: 248)

*13"	–	R	FF	LEE	$6.00
38"	–	R	FF	PALADINE 62	$11.00
72"	–	.60	RC	B&D	$14.95
76"	–	–	RC	PALADINE 62	$32.00

PIPER

L-2 Grasshopper

*96"	–	.35/.65	4	UNIONVILLE	$159.95 CDN

L-3 Grasshopper (SA: 248, 264)

*?	–	.60	4	ARISTO AR101	$249.95	
*25½"	–	R	FF	COMET 1623	$12.00	
*30"	–	R	FF	STERLING A-22	$14.95	
36"	–	R	FF	PALADINE 59	$11.00	
42"	–	.049-.51	RC	HORN S-2	$6.00	(Osborne)
*54"	–	.09-.35	2	STERLING FS-6	$44.95	
*55"	–	.19-.25	3-4	ARISTO	$108.90	
*1400mm	880mm	.19-.25	3-4	OK APQX004	¥12,000	
70"	–	.30/.20	5	GOLDEN ERA	$19.95	
70"	–	–	RC	POND 51D5	$5.75	(Hollinger)
70"	–	–	RC	POND 20D4	$6.75	(Peerless)
*71"	–	.25/.45	4	SIG RC-3	$71.95	
72"	–	/.20-.45	4	GOLDEN ERA	$14.94	
72"	–	–	RC	PALADINE 59	$32.00	
*76"	48"	.40/.90	4	ARISTO	$219.95	
*76½"	48"	.40-.61	4	GOLDBERG K-63	$79.95	
*77¼"	49"	.40/.60	4	TOP RC-28	$145.95	
84½"	–	.60	4	MILLER	$14.95	
85"	53½"	.60-1.2	RC	PHOTO	$19.95	
88"	–	–	RC	PALADINE 59	$32.00	
98"	–	–	RC	PALADINE 59	$32.00	
*105"	67"	.60/1.60	4	SIG RC48	$199.95	

[AVCO: cockpit, $21.95; SHATTLEROE: landing gear, $29.50]

```
106"    67"     .90-2.0    RC    PHOTO          $27.00    (Pepino)
*2680mm 1670mm  10-30cc    4     OK APBS006     ¥45,000
108"    -       .60        3-4   MORGAN 112RC   $19.95
[cowls, $10.95, $24.95][TDF: Cowl: $26.50, $36.50]
**[KLARICH: $75.00]
*108"   -       .60        3     NOSEN          $75.88
[AVCO: cockpit, $21.95]
127"    29"     2.0-3.0    3-4   HOSTETLER      $29.50
[TDF: cowl, $29.95; SHATTLEROE: landing gear, $33.50]
141"    89"     Q35        4     CEDARBRIDGE    NA
[cowls: MESSER, $37.95; TDF, $30.50; R&M: landing gear, $210.00]
**[KLARICH: $125.00; R&M: $180.00]
141"    -       2,0-3.0    4     WE RC3S-2      $29.95
[FGM: cowl, $23.00; SHATTLEROE: landing gear, $35.50]
144"    -       2.4        4     MAN GS12815    $30.00    (Nelitz)
```

L-4 Grasshopper (SA: 248)

```
13¼"    -       R          FF    CLEVE CD94L    $10.00
17½"    -       R          FF    CLEVE CD94L    $12.00
20"     -       R          FF    POND 20D7      $3.75     (Haberstroh)
26½"    -       R          FF    CLEVE CD94L    $16.00
*26½"   -       R          FF    PROKIT         £28.50
28"     -       R          RC    POND 30B2      $4.25     (Fuchs)
30"     -       R          FF    POND 25B2      $4.75     (Cleveland)
30"     -       R          FF    POND 20D7      $3.75     (Scientific)
31"     -       R          FF    POND 30A1      $3.75     (Hobby Model)
¶36"    -       R          FF    POND 25B2      $5.75     (Cleveland)
36"     -       R          FF    PALADINE 42    $11.00
53"     -       -          RC    CLEVE CD94L    $28.00
*64"    -       /.26-.40   4     AEROSCALE      £44.50
71"     -       -          RC    POND 51D5      $6.75     (Berkeley)
72"     -       -          RC    PALADINE 42    $32.00
*1804mm 1120mm  3.5-6.5cc  RC    SVENSON        NA
88"     -       -          RC    PALADINE 42    $32.00
98"     -       -          RC    PALADINE 42    $32.00
*106"   -       20cc       4     PREMIER        £99.95
*108"   -       .80-2.0    4     BALSA 433      $89.95
108"    -       2.0-3.0    4     RUNESTRAND     $22.50
[TDF: cowl, $26.50; SHATTLEROE: landing gear, $29.50]
**[KLARICH: $90.00]
*2740mm -       15cc       RC    BECKER         DM320,
*2820mm 1760mm  30cc       4     CLARK          DM458,
```

REPUBLIC

F-84 Thunderjet (SA: 248)

10"	–	Jetex	FF	POND 30D1	$3.75	(Ledertheil)
13"	–	Jetex	FF	HUNT J190	$4.00	(Hunt)
14"	–	Jetex	FF	POND 30C7	$3.75	(Ledertheil)
*24"	–	Bean Rock	FF	WILLAIRCO	$26.25	
*36½"	–	Bean Rock	FF	WILLAIRCO	$38.40	
*54½"	–	Bean Rock	FF	WILLAIRCO	$69.75	

F-84 Thunderstreak (SA: 248)

1355mm	1550mm	.60-.81F	RC	BERTELLA	L50.000

RF-84 Thunderflash

10"	–	Jetex	FF	POND 30C5	$3.75	(Ledertheil)
10"	–	Dynajet	CL	POND 47A5	$4.75	(Republic)
¶18"	–	Jetex	FF	HUNT J192	$4.00	(Comet)

F-105 Thunderchief (SA: 248)

20¼"	–	Glider	FF	WALLACE	$6.50	
*44"	73"	.77-.91F	4-7	CENTURY	$369.99	

[retracts, $199.00; drag chute, $20.00]

P-43 Lancer (SA: 248)

[82]	–	Q35	RC	MB 2831	$17.00	(Johnson)
15"	–	R	FF	HUNT F54	$2.00	(Megow)
18"	–	R	FF	HUNT K031	$3.50	(Modelcraft)

P-47 Thunderbolt (SA: 248)

?	–	.45	4	FM CF154	$7.00	(Ziroli)
*12"	–	R	FF	DUBOIS PS-2	$7.95	
13"	–	R	FF	POND 38A7	$3.25	(Norman)
16"	–	R	FF	HUNT 3883	$4.50	(Whitman)
¶ 18"	–	R	FF	POND 20F5	$3.75	(Comet)
19"	–	R	FF	POND 30D7	$3.75	(Halls)
20"	–	R	FF	MIKKELSON	$3.50	
20"	–	R	FF	POND 37G5	$3.75	(Norman)
20"	–	–	CL	POND 20F5	$3.75	(Vasquez)
20½"	–	R	FF	GLEASON	$2.60	(Coleman)
*22"	–	R	FF	STERLING A-4	$11.95	
24"	–	R	FF	HUNT X-3	$3.00	(Comet)

*[REPRO: R-17, $10.50]

*24"	–	R	FF	WILLAIRCO	$15.00	(Ziroli)

28"	–	R	FF	AUTHENTIC	£1.45	(Towner)
*28"	–	R	FF	EASY FF71	$10.00CDN	
28"	–	R	FF	HUNT AH101	$4.50	(Hunt)
28"	–	–	CL	POND 30D6	$4.75	(Lewis)
30"	–	R	FF	CLEVE CD81	$18.00	
30"	–	R	FF	HUNT KO32	$3.50	(Berkeley)
30"	–	–	CL	POND 44F6	$4.75	(Musciano)
¶30"	–	R	FF	POND 47F3	$3.75	(Scientific)
*31"	–	.049	CL	GUILLOW 1001	$29.00	
31"	–	R	FF	HUNT KO33	$4.00	(Cadet)
¶31"	–	R	FF	POND 61D4	$6.25	(Ideal)
31"	–	R	FF	POND 25C1	$4.75	(Cleveland)
32"	–	–	CL	GLEASON AT543	NA	
34"	–	.29-.60	CL	HORN MPS-264	$3.00	
36"	–	R	FF	HUNT 101	$5.50	(Ott)
¶36"	–	R	FF	POND 51F2	$6.75	(Miniature A/C)
36"	–	–	CL	POND 23G2	$5.75	(Eagle Models)
38"	–	–	CL	POND 20F7	$4.75	(Modern Hobby)
40"	–	.15-.19	4	MAN 6843	$10.00	(Uravich)
1000mm	–	R	FF	MRA 375	40F	
40"	–	–	CL	POND 51F2	$7.25	(Berkeley)
40"	–	–	CL	GLEASON	$6.35	(Musciano)
41"	–	–	CL	GLEASON AT961	$6.35	(Eisenger)
1060mm	–	6.5	RC	BOSAK	20 Kcs	
[canopy, 15 Kcs]						
51"	–	.25-.40	4	ARGUS RM211	£5.25	(Robinson)
*54"	–	.40-.60	4-6	DAVEY	$99.95	
*54"	–	.60	4-7	DYNA 4007	$115.95	
*54"	–	.40-.6-	4-7	SCEPTOR KSS8	$174.95	
*60"	48"	.60/.90	4-6	TOP RC19	$152.95	
*61"	–	.61-.91	4	FLAIR CAPRO4	NA	
61"	–	.60	4	TAYLOR	£6.00	
[cowl, £5.00; canopy, £3.00; spinner, £1.65; balsa pack, £28.00]						
61"	–	.61	4	TRAP MW2104	£9.00	(CAP)
[cowl, £9.50; canopy, £4.50]						
1560mm	–	10cc	RC	MRA BT18.579	119F	(Taylor)
62"	–	–	RC	POND 38D6	$8.75	(Schellenbaum)
70"	59"	1.08/1.20	4-6	ZIROLI	$26.00	
[cowl and canopy, $27.00][LIKES: retracts, $317.00]						
*72"	–	.60	RC	WILLAIRCO	$95.00	(Ziroli)

75"   -   -   RC   HOLMAN $19.95   (Taylor)
[cowl, $20.50; canopy, $6.00][LIKES:retracts, $317.00]
77½"   68½"   .90-1.5   4-6   INNOVATIVE $30.00
[LIKES retracts, $317.00]
*[$249.95]
*80"   72"   Q50   5-6   BYRON 6130047 $438.90
[retracts, $241.60; tailwheel, $38.70; prop system, $652.45]
*80"   69"   1.2   RC   YELLOW $350.00
[AVCO: cockpit, $21.95; LIKES: retracts, $ 317.00]
*81"   70"   ST2500   7-9   TOMEO $295.00
[plan pack, $103.00][AVCO: cockpit, $21.95; LIKES: retracts, $317.00]
82"   68"   1.20   4-6   BEAULIEU 12B $24.95
[AVCO: cockpit, $21.95; TDF: cowl, $32.00; LIKES: retracts, $317.00]
*2070mm 1800mm 25cc   RC   KRANZ   DM430,
*90"   76"   Q50   4   D&R $349.00
[retracts, $175.00]
**92"   78"   2.4-3.7   4-6   VAILLY $240.00
[cowl, $28.00; canopy, $15.00][LIKES: retracts, $317.00]
93"   75"   3.0-5.0   4-6   ZIROLI $30.00
[LIKES: retracts, $317.00]
*2500mm 2200mm 50cc   RC   KRANZ   DM635,
101"   83"   4.2   6   SMOLINSKI $25.00
[LIKES: retracts, $317.00]
*104"   -   Q35   4-5   NOSEN $169.00
[retracts: LIKES, $317.00; WHEELS, $275.00]

RYAN

FR-1 Fireball (SA: 265)

*13"	-	R	FF	DIELS K-14	$14.00	
13"	-	R	FF	NFFS	$6.00	
16"	-	R	FF	POND 21A2	$3.25	(Wherry)
22"	-	Jetex	FF	HUNT J196	$4.00	(Wherry)
25"	-	R	FF	POND 42F1	$4.75	(Ray Models)
26"	-	R	FF	SAMS 695	£2.95	(Crown)
30"	-	R	FF	CLEVE CD92AU	$24.00	
55"	42"	.60	RC	HOLMAN	$10.95	
60"	-	-	RC	POND 36A5	$10.75	(Aeroscale)
90"	72"	Q35	4	SMOLINSKI	$22.00	
98"	76"	Q50	5	SMOLINSKI	$22.00	

PT-16

72"	51"	Q35	4	BOSMAN	$30.00
90"	64"	Q50	4	BOSMAN	$25.00

PT-20 (STA)(SA: 249, 265)

11½"	-	R	FF	CLEVE CD58U	$8.00	
14"	-	R	FF	OLD 434	$2.00	(Megow)
15"	-	R	FF	CLEVE CD58U	$11.00	
17"	-	R	FF	HUNT MAC17	$2.50	(Model A/C)
18¼"	-	R	FF	OLD 55	$3.00	(Lindberg)
18½"	-	R	FF	PLANS	$4.00	(Andrus)
*20"	-	R	FF	EASY FF18	$6.00CDN	
21"	-	R	FF	POND 46C3	$3.75	(International)
22½"	-	R	FF	CLEVE CD58U	$15.00	
23"	-	R	FF	WISCONSIN	$3.50	(Toldeo)
23"	-	R	FF	HUNT C-25	$3.25	(Megow)
30"	-	R	FF	CLEVE CD58U	$22.00	
30"	-	R	FF	FSI R-2	$6.00	
30"	-	-	3	MORGAN	$4.95	
32"	-	R	FF	HUNT C-25	$3.50	(Megow)
45"	-	.8-1cc	FF	ARGUS FSP554	£5.25	(Cannon)
45"	-	-	RC	CLEVE CD58U	$28.00	
48"	-	R	FF	POND 21A1	$4.75	(Capitol)
*50"	-	R	FF	PROKIT	£45.00	
50"	-	.19-.25	RC	RCM 388	$5.25	(Fisher)
60"	-	-	RC	CLEVE CD58U	$36.00	
60"	-	-	4-5	MORGAN	$8.95	
*90"	66"	Q35	5	BYRON 6130235	$439.95	
90"	-	.60	RC	MA 277	$9.00	(Farrell)

**[KLARICH: $90.00]

PT-21

¶30"	-	R	FF	POND 62E4	$6.25	(Miniature A/C)

PT-22 Recruit (SA: 249)

30"	-	R	FF	COLE	$5.00	
36"	-	-	CL	POND 21A1	$5.75	(Beatty)
41½"	-	-	FF	FM CF641	$7.00	(Sandor)
60"	-	-	RC	POND 41A5	$8.75	(Beatty)
90¼"	-	ST2500	4	SWEITZER 1004	$50.00	

[fuselage, $125.00; landing gear, $15.00]

PT-25

36"	-	R	FF	ORIGINAL	£5.50	(Martin)

YO-51 Dragonfly

16"	–	R	FF	POND 21A2	$3.75	(Megow)
30"	–	R	FF	POND 21A2	$3.75	(Bowers)
39"	–	R	FF	GLEASON	$3.00	(Ealy)

SEVERSKY

P-35 (SA: 249)

12"	–	R	FF	CLEVE CD61A	$10.00	
16"	–	R	FF	CLEVE CD61A	$13.00	
16"	–	R	FF	GLEASON	$.90	(Lindberg)
16"	–	R	FF	HUNT 3971	$4.50	(Whitman)
16"	–	R	FF	POND 47D6	$3.25	(Burd)
21"	–	R	FF	POND 30E1	$3.75	(Gailmard)
*22"	–	R	FF	REPRO R-11	$8.50	(Comet)
24"	–	R	FF	POND 21C1	$3.75	(Modelcraft)
24"	–	R	FF	CLEVE CD61A	$18.00	
¶ 25"	–	R	FF	HUNT E-20	$2.50	(Comet)
31"	–	R	FF	MB 881CP	$8.50	(Miniature A/C
*31¼"	–	R	FF	PROKIT	£30.00	
33"	–	.20-.35	CL	HORN MPS-78	$4.00	(Palanek)
48"	–	–	RC	CLEVE CD61A	$30.00	
72"	–	.60	RC	B&D	$14.95	

XP-41 Guardsman

15"	–	R	FF	POND 51F1	$3.25	(Megow)
16½"	–	R	FF	HUNT KO30	$3.00	(Hi-Flier)
30"	–	R	FF	POND 20F6	$3.75	(Megow)

SPERRY

M-1 Messenger

[48]	–	.49-.61	4	MAN 2691	$9.50	(Streigler)
10"	–	R	FF	GLEASON	$.50	(Mooney)
13"	–	R	FF	MAN 11823	$6.00	(Robelen)
13"	–	R	FF	POND 37A1	$3.25	(McCorrison)
13"	–	R	FF	POND 41F5	$3.25	(Dean)
15"	–	R	FF	CLEVE CD134	$12.00	
18"	–	R	FF	LIDBERG	$4.00	
20"	–	R	FF	FM CF217	$4.00	(Blankenship)
22"	–	CO2	FF	POND 61D1	$4.25	(Modela)

*[MODELA 2201: $5.00]

*23"	-	R	FF	PROKIT	£28.50	
33"	-	R	FF	POND 23D1	$5.25	(Plecan)
44"	-	-	RC	POND 30E2	$6.25	(Krieser)
*60"	-	.60-.80	3	IKON IK37	$165.50	
72"	-	.90	RC	B&D	$14.95	

STANDARD

J-1

16"	-	R	FF	CLEVE CD131	$16.00	
21"	-	R	FF	COLE	$5.00	
22"	-	R	FF	CLEVE CD131	$22.00	
*24"	-	R	FF	SIERRA	$13.95	
24½"	-	R	FF	PALADINE 16	$8.00	
32½"	-	R	FF	CLEVE CD131	$30.00	
36"	-	R/.020	RC	FM CF346	$4.00	(Bowers)
49"	-	-	RC	PALADINE 16	$14.00	
65"	-	-	RC	CLEVE CD131	$45.00	
73"	-	-	RC	PALADINE 16	$32.00	

PT-17 Kaydet (SA: 249)   STEARMAN

?	-	.40-.60	4	FM CF313	$7.00	(Ziroli)
[39]	-	.19-.29	4	MAN 6831	$9.50	(Norman)
12"	-	R	FF	CLEVE CD149	$14.00	
12"	-	R	FF	POND 37C1	$3.25	(Construct)
12"	-	R	FF	POND 30G2	$3.25	(Modernistic)
*13"	-	R	FF	STERLING P5	$7.95	
16"	-	R	FF	POND 47A1	$3.25	(Kukuvich)
16"	-	R	FF	CLEVE CD149	$18.00	
*20"	-	R	FF	STERLING A-2	$14.95	
23"	-	R	FF	POND 21E3	$3.75	(Miniature A/C)
24½"	-	R	FF	CLEVE CD149	$22.00	
*28"	-	.09	CL	GUILLOW 803	$21.00	
28"	-	R	FF	POND 44F3	$5.75	(Whitman)
32"	-	R	FF	PALADINE 58	$11.00	
*32½"	-	.19-.35	CL	STERLING C-12	$34.95	
35"	-	-	CL	POND 14B3	$6.25	(Galloway)
40½"	-	-	CL	GLEASON AT450	NA	(Mason)
41"	-	-	CL	POND 30F4	$5.75	(Yates)

45"	–	–	CL	HORN MPS-18	$4.00	(Slawson)
¶ 45"	–	–	FF	POND 14B3	$6.75	(Miniature A/
47½"	–	–	CL	PLANS	$7.00	(Andrus)
48"	–	–	CL	POND 49D4	$7.25	(Carkhuff)
49"	–	–	RC	CLEVE CD149	$38.00	
*51"	–	.45/.90	4	DAVEY	$129.95	
64"	50"	.60	RC	RCM 416	$14.74	(Litzau)
64"	–	–	RC	PALADINE 58	$18.00	
64½"	–	–	RC	BARRON	$23.00	

[AVCO: cockpit, $22.95]
**[KLARICH: $110.00]

*64½"	–	.56-.70	2-3	STERLING FS-20	$149.95	
68"	–	.60/.90	4	ARGUS RSQ1490	£13.50	(Healey)
*1736mm	1349mm	.61/.90	4	MARUTAKA 68	¥45,000	
72"	–	.60	RC	B&D	$14.95	
77"	59"	–	4-5	ZIROLI	$27.00	

[TDF: cowl, $20.50; wheel pants, $25.95]
*[HANGAR: $250.00]

*86"	68"	2.0	4	ROBART	$600.00	
*96"	76"	2.4-4.4	5	DIVELY	$450.00	
96"	64"	3.7	4	GODFREY	$30.00	

**[$175.00; cowl, $30.00; landing gear, $25.00; wheel pants, $18.95]
**[KLARICH: $100; R&M: $175.00]

96½"	63"	Q35	RC	BARRON	$36.50	

[AVCO: cockpit, $22.95]
**[KLARICH: $140.00]

**96½"	–	–	RC	KLARICH	$140.00	(Barron)
*96½"	75"	Q35	4-6	SCOTT	$250.00	
98"	–	–	RC	CLEVE CD149	$59.00	

STINSON

L-5 Sentinel

12"	–	R	FF	POND 37G6	$3.25	(McCorrison)
15"	–	R	FF	COLE	$5.00	
830mm	–	R	FF	MRA 372	40F	
33"	–	R	FF	POND 21G5	$5.75	(Berkeley)
34"	–	R	FF	GLEASON	$6.10	(Struck)
34"	–	R	FF	POND 46G7	$4.75	(Aircraft Pla
37"	–	R	FF	HUNT AH158	$4.00	(Struck)
38"	–	R	FF	POND 21G5	$5.75	(Hobby Model)
102"	72"	1.2-2.3	5	VAILLY	$30.00	

[cowl, $35.00]

| 2750mm | 2020mm | 20-24cc | 5 | FANTINI | L48.000 | |

0-49 Vigilant (SA: 249)

29"	-	R	FF	HUNT ES29	$3.50	(Stahl)
31½"	-	R	FF	OLD 21	$3.50	(Stahl)
32"	-	R	FF	POND 21G5	$3.75	(Hobby Model)
45"	-	R	FF	POND 46B1	$6.75	(Swartz)
63"	-	-	RC	OLD DS14	$5.00	(Stahl)

TAYLORCRAFT

L-2 (SA: 249)

16"	-	R	FF	POND 31B4	$3.25	(Scientific)
16"	-	R	FF	POND 22B4	$3.25	(Comet)
18"	-	R	FF	POND 22B4	$3.75	(Megow)
24"	-	R	FF	HUNT SRS-14	$3.00	(Struhl)
620mm	-	R	FF	AIRBORNE	$5.00AUS	
26"	-	R	FF	POND 22B5	$4.75	(Megow)
32"	-	R	FF	POND 31A1	$3.25	(Hammer)
32½"	-	R	FF	OLD 23	$3.50	(Stahl)
35"	-	R	FF	POND 22B5	$4.75	(Veco)
50"	-	R	FF	POND 22B5	$4.75	(Megow)
65"	-	-	RC	OLD DS16	$5.00	(Stahl)
72"	-	-	RC	POND 22C6	$6.25	(Davidson)
72"	-	-	RC	POND 22B5	$6.75	(Aircraft)

0-57 Grasshopper

18"	-	R	FF	POND 22C3	$3.25	(Supreme)
20"	-	R	FF	COLE	$5.00	
30"	-	R	FF	GLEASON	$1.80	(Stahl)
*32½"	-	R	FF	PROKIT	£24.00	
49"	-	-	RC	POND 22C1	$6.75	(Struhl)

TEMCO

TT-1 Pinto (SA: 250)

| 30" | - | Jetex | FF | HUNT J206 | $5.50 | (Berkeley) |

THOMAS MORSE

S4B Scout

| ? | - | - | - | ARGUS FSP1102x | £3.75 | |

10"	–	R	FF	CLEVE CD146B	$8.00	
13"	–	CO2	FF	ALFERY	$5.00	
*13"	–	R	FF	LEE	$6.00	
13½"	–	R	FF	CLEVE CD146B	$11.00	
20"	–	R/CO2	FF	ALFERY	$5.00	
20"	–	R	FF	CLEVE CD146B	$15.00	
20"	–	R	FF	PALADINE 85	$8.00	
22"	–	R	FF	COLE	$5.00	
*24"	–	R/.020	FF	GUILLOW 201	$12.50	
30"	–	–	CL	POND 48E1	$5.75	(Kochman)
35"	–	R	FF	POND 38G4	$5.75	(Watkins)
40"	–	–	FF	PALADINE 85	$11.00	
72"	–	.60	RC	B&D	$14.95	
80"	–	–	RC	PALADINE 85	$32.00	

TIMM

N2-T1

22"	–	R	FF	COLE	$5.00

VOUGHT

A-7 Corsair II (SA: 250, 304)

1040mm	–	6.5cc	RC	BOSAK	20 Kcs	
[canopy, 15 Kcs]						
41½"	–	.40	4	ARGUS RC1437	£6.00	(Bosak)
1100mm	1030mm	6.5cc	4	VTH MT921	DM12,	(Baumhofer)
*47"	57"	7.5F	5-7	JHH	$295.00	

XF4U-1

25"	–	R	FF	POND 31D6	$3.75	(Air King)
36"	–	–	CL	POND 31C1	$6.25	(Palanek)

F4U Corsair (SA: 250, 262)

*10"	–	Glider	FF	PAI 280	$6.00	(Sabo)
12"	–	R	FF	POND 22F3	$3.25	(Supreme)
12"	–	R	FF	POND 22E5	$3.25	(Universal)
12"	–	R	FF	POND 22E7	$3.25	(Ott)
*13"	–	R	FF	DUBOIS PS-5	$7.95	
*13"	–	R	FF	STERLING P-4	$7.95+	
15"	–	R	FF	CLEVE CD79B	$16.00	
15½"	–	R	FF	HUNT MAC21	$2.50	(Model A/C)

15"	–	R	FF	POND 37F4	$3.75	(Selley)
15"	–	R	FF	POND 22E6	$4.25	(Ideal)
15"	–	R	FF	POND 37C3	$3.75	(Comet)
16"	–	R	FF	HUNT 3886	$4.50	(Whitman)
16"	–	R	FF	POND 22E6	$3.75	(Duncan)
16"	–	R	FF	POND 46B2	$3.75	(Allied)
17"	–	–	CL	POND 22F3	$3.75	(Consolidated)
*14"	–	R	FF	PAI 60	$7.00	
18"	–	R	FF	POND 22E7	$3.25	(Megow)
20"	–	R	FF	ALFERY	$5.00	
20"	–	R	FF	CLEVE CD79B	$20.00	
*20"	–	R	FF	COMET 3404	$7.50	
*20½"	–	R	FF	DIELS K13	$20.00	
20"	–	R	FF	POND 22E6	$3.75	(Sturdi-Built)
21¼"	–	R	FF	GLEASON	$3.65	(Scott)
22"	–	–	CL	POND 31C7	$3.75	(Ealy)
22"	–	R	FF	HUNT 2235	$4.50	(Whitman)
¶ 22"	–	R	FF	GLEASON	$2.00	(Ott)
23"	–	R	FF	POND 52B5	$3.75	(Comet)
23"	–	R	FF	POND 31D1	$3.75	(Bugler)
24"	–	R	FF	HUNT 5363	$5.50	(Whitman)
*24"	–	R	FF	STERLING A14	$15.95	
26"	–	1-1.5cc	CL	ARGUS MA141	£3.75	(Lewis)
*28"	–	R	FF	EASY FF70	$10.00CDN	
28"	–	R	FF	POND 37B2	$5.75	(Whitman)
28"	–	R	FF	POND 52C2	$3.75	(Berkeley)
30"	–	–	RC	CLEVE CD79B	$26.00	
30"	–	R	FF	HUNT J22	$3.50	(Megow)
30"	–	–	CL	POND 46B2	$4.75	(Air Trails)
30"	–	–	CL	POND 31C6	$5.75	(Atkins)
¶ 30"	–	R	FF	POND 22F4	$3.75	(Capitol)
*31"	–	.049-.09	CL	GUILLOW 1004	$29.00	
31"	–	–	CL	POND 58F2	$5.75	(Eureka)
¶ 32"	–	R	FF	POND 22F4	$4.25	(Ott)
¶ 32"	–	R	FF	POND 22F4	$5.25	(Miniature A/C)
33"	–	R	FF	GULF	$5.00	(Midkiff)
34"	–	R	CL	POND 62G4	$6.50	(Sturdi-Built)

34"	–	–	CL	POND 52C2	$4.75	(Stahl)
35"	–	.049	CL	RCM 690	$5.00	(Caldwell)
36"	–	.35-.45	4	FM CF668	$8.00	(Bosak)
*900mm	685mm	.051-.10	2-3	MARUTAKA 41	¥8,300	
*36"	–	.19-.60	CL	STERLING C-9	$34.95	
*36"	–	.09-.10	2-3	STERLING FS-36	$45.95	
37"	–	–	CL	POND 52C2	$4.75	(Modern Hobby)
960mm	–	R	FF	MRA 317	46F	
990mm	–	.8-1.5	RC	MRA 318.498	58F	
40"	–	–	RC	PALADINE 27	$11.00	
41"	–	.29-.40	CL	GLEASON AM1263	$6.40	(Musciano)
42"	–	R	FF	FM CF656	$7.00	(Houle)
*45"	37"	.19-.40	RC	ROYAL 79-309	$119.95	
1170mm	–	6.5cc	RC	BOSAK	20 Kcs	

[canopy, 10 Kcs]

*46"	34½"	.25	4	STANGEL	$89.95
*1200mm	970mm	.19-.25	3-4	IKUTA	¥19,000

[assembled, ¥85,000]

48"	–	.40	4	TRAP MW2154	£5.50	(Bosak)

[canopy, £4.50]

*50"	–	Glider	2	CLIFF	$89.95
1250mm	–	4cc	RC	MRA 5.33	84F
*1300mm	1060mm	.25-.40	3-4	MARUTAKA 8	¥21,000
*54"	–	.40-.50	4	DYNA 4008	$162.95

[ROBART: retracts, $54.95]

1400mm	–	–	RC	MODULO	L50.000
*56"	41½"	.40-.60	4	WING 706	$44.95

[ROBART: retracts, $54.95]

*59"	–	.60/1.20	4	MINGUS	$149.95

[ROBART: retracts, $54.95]

60"	–	–	RC	CLEVE CD79B	$45.00
60"	–	–	RC	HOLMAN	$5.00

[canopy, $5.00][ROBART: retracts, $54.95]

*1500mm	1070mm	.29-.45	3-4	IKUTA	¥24,000
60"	–	–	RC	PALADINE 27	$18.00
*60"	48"	.60/.90	4-6	TOP RC-21	$145.95
1560mm	–	7.5-10cc	RC	MRA BT3.565	119F
61½"	–	.60	4	TAYLOR	£6.00

[cowl, £4.00; canopy, £2.00; spinner, £1.75; balsa pack, £29.00]
[ROBART: retracts: $55.95]

62"	–	.59-.60	CL	FM CF228	$14.00	(Kulp)
*1570mm	1200mm	.60/1.20	4-6	MARUTAKA 7	¥30,000	
*1650mm	1250mm	.60	4	IKUTA	¥35,000	
*70"	–	ST2500	4	MINGUS	$309.95	
*72"	59"	.80/1.2	3-5	GM	$279.95	
*72"	57"	.90/1.6	4	D&R	$199.00	
**75"	–	.90	4-6	HOLMAN	$139.95	
75"	61"	.90-1.5	4-6	INNOVATIVE	$30.00	

*[$249.95]

*2000mm	–	2.2	RC	COOP 9600018	1291F
80"	–	–	RC	PALADINE 27	$32.00
*85"	68½"	Q50	5-6	BYRON 613140	$405.90

[retracts, $219.95; tailwheel, $38.70; prop system, $641.45;
    canopy, $43.95][AVCO: cockpit, $21.95; ROBART: retracts, $245.00]

93"	72"	–	5-6	ZIROLI	$30.00

[cowl, $32.00; canopy, $10.00][TDF: cowl, $30.50; AVCO: cockpit,
    $21.95; retracts: ROBART, $245.00; WHEELS, $275.00]
**[KLARICH: $140.00; R&M, $140.00]
*[HANGAR: $235.00]

*2498mm	2033mm	35-50cc	4	MARUTAKA 66	¥85,000
*2500mm	–	50-60cc	RC	COOP 9600108	1850F

*[assembled, 5200F]

*109"	–	Q35	4-5	NOSEN	$189.00

[cowl, $43.00; canopy, $19.00][WHEELS: retracts, $275.00]
**[R&M: $275.00]

F7U Cutlass

9"	–	Jetex	FF	POND 31D1	$3.25	(Buragas)
15"	–	Jetex	FF	POND 25E3	$3.75	(Cleveland)
16"	–	Jetex	FF	POND 23D5	$3.25	(Hatful)
58"	–	Glider	FF	ARGUS RC1247	£7.50	(Crump)

F8U Crusader (SA: 250)

9"	–	Jetex	FF	POND 22F5	$3.75	(Sebel)
13"	–	Jetex	FF	HUNT J112	$3.00	
27"	–	–	FF	POND 31D4	$6.75	(Atkins)
27"	–	–	FF	POND 31D3	$5.75	(Berkeley)
38"	53"	.45-.65F	6	KNIGHTS	$30.00	
*50"	72"	.77-.90F	4	CUSTOM	$285.00	
1460mm	–	10cc	RC	MODELL	DM21,60	(Meier)
*50"	65"	.77F	5	FANJET	FORTHCOMING	
57"	–	.60	RC	HORN S-37	$8.00	

FU-1

13"	–	R	FF	OLD 400	$2.00	(Comet)

02U Corsair

13"	–	R	FF	NFFS	$6.00	
13½"	–	R	FF	CLEVE CD179	$16.00	
15"	–	R	FF	POND 22E6	$3.75	(Ideal)
18"	–	R	FF	FRANK 40	$2.25	(Megow)
18"	–	R	FF	CLEVE CD179	$20.00	
18"	–	R	FF	LAMBERT	$6.00	(Allentown)
20"	–	R	FF	HUNT PA14	$4.40	(Ott)
20"	–	R	FF	PLANS	$6.00	(Andrus)
23"	–	R	FF	GLEASON	$2.00	(Chevedden)
26"	–	R	FF	FSI V1	$6.00	
27"	–	R	FF	CLEVE CD179	$28.00	
27"	–	R	FF	OLD 180	$3.50	(Sturiale)
54"	–	R	FF	CLEVE CD179	$44.00	
72"	–	.60	RC	B&D	$14.95	
72"	–	–	RC	CLEVE CD179	$56.00	
108"	–	–	RC	CLEVE CD179	$68.00	

OS2U Kingfisher

?	–	–	–	ARGUS RC1191x	£5.25	
12"	–	R	FF	POND 37G3	$3.25	(Bruning)
13"	–	R	FF	DIELS 21	$2.00	
13"	–	R	FF	KOUTNY	$4.00	
13"	–	R	FF	POND 31D1	$4.75	
15"	–	R	FF	POND 31D2	$3.25	(Weiss)
17½"	–	R	FF	HUNT MAC22	$2.50	(Model A/C)
18"	–	R	FF	DIELS 44	$3.25	
18"	–	R	FF	FM CF260	$4.00	(Blankenship)
22"	–	R	FF	HUNT WI03	$3.00	(Weiss)
24"	–	R	FF	COLE	$5.00	
24"	–	–	CL	POND 44F7	$3.75	(Christen)
27"	–	–	FF	FM CF628	$6.00	(Midkiff)
¶ 27"	–	R	FF	GLEASON	$4.15	(Ott)
30½"	–	.40-.60	CL	FM CF630	$6.00	(Schaeffer)
36"	–	R	FF	ARGUS FSR218	£4.50	(Dare)

36"	–	–	CL	POND 52B5	$3.75	(Moynihan)
40"	–	R	FF	POND 52B6	$4.75	(Le Modele Reduit)
48"	–	–	RC	MB 7771	$10.50	(Kimble)
58"	–	.30/.40	4	TAYLOR	£6.00	

[cowl, £5.00; canopy, £5.75; spinner, £1.50; balsa pack, £27.50]

1470mm	–	6.5	RC	MRA BT19	119F	
63"	–	–	RC	CHARLIE	$22.00	
63"	–	.60	5	PROKIT	£22.00	

**[£70.00]

| 72" | 60" | 1.2 | 4 | MACBRIEN | $50.00 | |
| 86" | 72" | Q50 | 4 | MACBRIEN | $50.00 | |

[TDF: cowl, $31.50; canopy, $10.95; wing floats, $29.50]
**[KLARICH: $90.00]

SB2U Vindicator (SA: 250)

17"	–	R	FF	HUNT AH196	$3.00	(Weiss)
20"	–	R	FF	POND 22F1	$3.25	(Weiss)
26"	–	R	FF	HUNT PL152	$3.50	(Lindberg)
28"	–	R	FF	HUNT PL153	$3.25	(Lindberg)
32"	–	R	FF	GULF	$5.00	(Midkiff)
36"	–	R	FF	HUNT 5372	$5.50	(Whitman)
84"	–	2.0	7	MAN 9981	$25.00	(Keith)

SBU-1 Scout

12½"	–	R	FF	HUNT CO113	$2.00	(Comet)
13"	–	R	FF	GLEASON	$.50	(Lindberg)
17"	–	R	FF	OLD 258	$3.00	(Weiss)
25"	–	R	FF	FSI V-2	$6.00	
28"	–	R	FF	GLEASON	$3.40	(Lindberg)
32"	–	–	CL	POND 31D5	$5.25	(Brazelton)
41½"	–	.25-.35	4	CHARLIE	$10.00	

SU-2 Command Corsair

| 23" | – | R | FF | YEST 12 | $5.50 | (Comet) |
| *72" | 53" | .90 | 3-5 | DIVELY | $299.95 | |

V-65 Corsair

13¼"	–	R	FF	CLEVE CD41B	$12.00	
18"	–	R	FF	CLEVE CD41B	$14.00	
27"	–	R	FF	CLEVE CD41B	$18.00	
53½"	–	–	RC	CLEVE CD41B	$32.00	

V-80 Corsair

20"	–	R	FF	POND 22E6	$3.75	(Zier)
26½"	–	R	FF	GLEASON	$3.50	(Struiale)

V-100 Corsair

12"	–	R	FF	POND 22E6	$3.25	(Megow)

V-143

13"	–	R	FF	ALFERY	$5.00	
13"	–	R	FF	DIELS 3	$1.75	
¶16"	–	R	FF	POND 22F2	$3.25	(Comet)
16"	–	R	FF	POND 22F2	$4.75	(Whitman)
18"	–	R	FF	DIELS 15	$2.50	
22"	–	R	FF	HUNT WW17	$3.00	(Winter)
25"	–	R	FF	HUNT AH162	$3.25	(Weiss)
¶25"	–	R	FF	HUNT L9	$3.25	(Comet)
34"	–	R	FF	HUNT L9	$4.00	(Comet)
37"	–	R	FF	HUNT L9	$4.00	(Comet)

VE-7/9

13"	–	R	FF	CLEVE CD232	$14.00	
17"	–	R	FF	CLEVE CD232	$17.00	
25½"	–	R	FF	CLEVE CD232	$22.00	
26"	–	–	CL	POND 31F4	$4.75	(Palanek)
51"	–	–	RC	CLEVE CD232	$38.00	

VULTEE

A-31 Vengeance (SA: 265)

20"	–	R	FF	GLEASON	$5.35	(Whitman)
¶20"	–	R	FF	POND 22G3	$3.75	(Comet)
23"	–	R	FF	POND 22G2	$3.25	(Scientific)
24"	–	R	FF	COLE	$5.00	
30"	–	R	FF	POND 52C4	$3.75	(Eagle)
31"	–	R	FF	GULF	$5.00	
¶40"	–	R	FF	HUNT 4003	$6.00	(Ott)
¶42"	–	R	FF	POND 53A2	$5.75	(H&F Models)
42"	–	R	FF	POND 22G4	$5.75	(Struhl)

BT-13 (SA: 265)

42"	–	–	CL	POND 31C5	$5.75	(Codding)
72"	–	.60	RC	B&D	$14.95	
1800mm	–	10cc	4	MRA BT13	119F	(Taylor)
73½"	–	.60	4	TAYLOR	£6.00	

[cowl, £5.00; canopy, £5.00; spinner, £1.50; balsa pack, £28.00]
**[KLARICH: $90.00]

84"	57"	1.0/1.2	5	AERO PLANS	$25.00	

[FGM: cowl: $19.00]

100"	73"	Q50	5	MASSEY	$30.00	

BT-15

26"	–	R	FF	HUNT SRS15	$3.25	(Struhl)
36"	–	R	FF	HUNT SRS16	$3.50	(Struhl)

V-11 GB Attack

16"	–	R	FF	GLEASON	$3.25	(Whitman)
18"	–	R	FF	POND 22G1	$3.25	(Grant)
20"	–	R	FF	FRANK 31	$2.25	(Comet)

*[FIKE: $7.95]

22"	–	R	FF	HUNT WW11	$3.25	(Winter)
25"	–	R	FF	GLEASON	$3.95	(Pack)
29"	–	R	FF	COLE	$5.00	

L-1 Vigilant

?	–	–	–	ARGUS MA136x	£3.75	
51"	–	.10-.15	3-4	PHOTO	$21.00	(Katz)
52"	–	–	RC	POND 31C6	$5.75	(Bridgewood)
76½"	–	/.60	4-6	MAN 3851	$23.00	(Fearnley)

L-13

18"	–	R	FF	HUNT 2271	$4.00	(Whitman)

P-66 Vanguard

*13"	–	R	FF	DIELS K-6	$26.00+	
18"	–	R	FF	COLE	$5.00	
18"	–	R	FF	DIELS 16	$2.50	
*20"	–	R	FF	PROKIT	£20.00	
21"	–	R	FF	POND 22G2	$3.25	(Modelcraft)
22"	–	R	FF	POND 22G2	$3.25	(Rust)
600mm	–	R	FF	AIRBORNE	$5.00AUS	
24"	–	R	FF	OLD 24	$3.00	(Stahl)

26"	–	R	FF	POND 31D6	$4.75	(Easy Built)
27"	–	R	FF	POND 22G2	$3.75	(Mechanics)
28"	–	R	FF	HUNT 2976	$5.50	(Whitman)
34"	–	R	FF	HUNT ES31E	$3.50	(Stahl)
¶ 44"	–	R	FF	OLD G2	$4.00	(Comet)
63"	–	.60	RC	FM CF305	$11.00	(Godfrey)

XP-54

14"	–	R	FF	POND 53F3	$3.25	(Stahl)
17½"	–	R	FF	GLEASON	$1.80	(Stahl)
20"	–	R	FF	COLE	$5.00	
25"	–	R	FF	HUNT ES32	$3.50	(Stahl)
1070mm	–	R	FF	MRA 380	46F	

WACO

CG-4A Hadrian (SA: 265)

29"	–	Glider	FF	POND 38C5	$3.25	(Cleave)
1050mm	–	Glider	FF	MRA 381	40F	
42"	–	Glider	FF	POND 31F2	$4.75	(Invasion)
50"	–	Glider	FF	ARGUS FSG219	£3.00	(Lee)
¶ 51"	–	Glider	FF	POND 23B7	$5.25	(Hobby Model)
52"	–	Glider	FF	POND 23B7	$5.25	(Schroder)
63"	–	Elec	2-3	RCM 685	$5.25	(Richmond)
2170mm	–	Glider	FF	MRA 758	112F	

Waco D Export Fighter

14½"	–	R	FF	CLEVE CD228	$11.00	
15"	–	R	FF	POND 47D2	$3.25	(Jones)
¶ 16"	–	R	FF	POND 62E3	$3.75	(Hi-Flier)
16"	–	R	FF	POND 23A4	$4.75	(Whitman)
16"	–	R	FF	GLEASON	$3.05	(Ott)
16½"	–	R	FF	CLEVE CD228	$14.00	
20"	–	R	FF	GLEASON	$2.25	(Lindberg)
20"	–	R	FF	POND 23A4	$3.75	(Scientific)
20"	–	R	FF	POND 31E4	$3.75	(Winter)
20"	–	R	FF	POND 23A4	$3.75	(Whitman)
24½"	–	R	FF	CLEVE CD228	$20.00	
28"	–	R	FF	GLEASON	$2.90	(Lindberg)
49"	–	–	RC	CLEVE CD228	$34.00	
98"	76½"	1.2-2.3	4	WE RCQS-16	$24.95	

<u>WRIGHT</u>

<u>M-8</u>
65"   -   /.40-.60 4   ARGUS RC1482   £8.75   (Hawkins)

YUGOSLAVIA

<u>IKARUS</u>

<u>IK-2</u>
13"   -   R   FF   POND 41D1 $3.25   (Bruning)

<u>UTVA</u>

<u>UTVA-66</u>

*2850mm 2100mm 42cc   5   HO   L3.000.000
[cowl, L90.000]

1ST ADDENDA

AUSTRALIA
Commonwealth Aircraft

CA-6 Wackett
| 36" | 26½" | R | FF | NZ | $20.00NZ | |

AUSTRIA
Hansa-Brandenburg

C-1
| 610mm | 440mm | .3cc | 2 | VTH MT911 | DM7,50 | (Pipek) |

D-1
| 56" | - | .40-.50 | 4 | ARGUS RSQ1619 | £8.75 | (Hurrell) |

Phonix

D-1
| 22" | - | R | FF | SAMS 1191 | £1.95 | (Dennis) |

BRAZIL
Embraer

Tucano
66"	-	.60-.75	RC	MA 473	$12.50	(Naber)
*1800mm	1590mm	10-13cc	RC	CUCCOLO	L320.000	
*1800mm	-	-	RC	ATEM	2084F	

CANADA
DeHaviland

DHC-1 Chipmunk
| 1710mm | - | 6-10cc | RC | MODELE 4222 | 100F | |
| *2320mm | 1750mm | 25-50cc | 4 | G.M. 111 | DM698, | |

DHC-2 Beaver
| 13" | - | R | FF | HAUGHT P-6 | $1.50 | |
| 28½" | - | R | FF | HAUGHT S-1 | $3.00 | |

60"	-	1.5-2.5cc	FF	ARGUS FSP338	£4.50	(Moore)
3000mm	-	35cc	RC	MODELE 3972	120F	

DHC-4 Caribou

2180mm	-	6.5x2	RC	RC MODEL P084	1.100P

CZECHOSLOVAKIA

Aero

L-39

*52"	42"	Glider	2	VERN	$175.00
56"	-	Glider	RC	CONWAY	NA

Avia

B-534

1500mm	-	6.5-10cc	RC	RC MODEL P059	1.200P

EGYPT

Helwan

HA-300

*42"	63"	.61-.91F	5-6	TJM	$449.00

EUROPEAN CONSORTIA

Dassault/Dornier

Alpha Jet

*1005mm	1115mm	2.5-4cc	RC	TECHNIK	DM155,

EFA

Eurofighter

1570mm	2035mm	.81x2F	RC	BERTELLA	L60.000

[canopy, L15.000]

Panavia

Tornado

60"	-	Glider	RC	CONWAY	NA
*2040mm	2371mm	10ccx2F	RC	MASTER 020013	L1.552.000

Tornado ADV

*2150mm	2360mm	13ccx2F	RC	MASTER 020013	L1.552.000

FRANCE

Bernard

Bernard 260 (SA: 251)

26"	-	R/CO2	FF	B²	$4.50	(Marsden)

Breguet

Breguet XIX

?	-	-	-	PLANY 118	NA	(Baczkowski)

Caudron

C.714 Cyclone

13"	-	R	FF	HAUGHT P-23	$1.50
16½"	-	R	FF	HAUGHT S-23	$3.00
1700mm	-	10cc	RC	MODELE 4441	140F

G. III

2680mm	1300mm	20cc	RC	LOHMANN	DM45,

Dassault

Mirage III

V	-	-	RC	AIR H12	$18.00
940mm	-	6.5	RC	RC MODEL PO27	895P
*37"	62"	.45-.77F	5	PARRISH	$300.00
1040mm	-	10cc	RC	MODELE 3981	90F
*1200mm	1400mm	8-13cc	RC	BRABEC 950	2,195SCH

Mirage F1

860mm	-	6.5cc	RC	MODELE 4053	85F

Mirage 2000

1000mm	-	7.5F	RC	RC MODEL PO56	1.600P

Dewotine

D.520 (SA: 251)

*47¼"	33"	.25	4	MODELHOB 11.0157	NA	
1500mm	-	6.5cc	RC	MODELLE 042	DM25,	(Schmalzgruber)
80"	68½"	1.08	6	BATES	$35.00	

Hanriot-Dupont

HD-1

14½"	-	CO2	FF	BLAIR	$5.00

Leduc

021

| V | - | - | RC | AIR H3 | $18.00 |

Max-Holst

MH-1521 Broussard

| 1960mm | - | 10cc | RC | MODELE 3422 | 80F |
| 1964mm | 1235mm | 6.5/15cc | 4 | PB | 1080F |

Morane-Saulnier

MS-225

| 2400mm | - | 30cc | 4-5 | RADIO 30 | 200F |

N

[FGM: cowl, $11.00] (ZIROLI)

| 20¼" | - | CO2 | FF | BLAIR | $5.00 |
| 2200mm | 1500mm | 1.2 | 4 | MAX | DM100, |

MS-1508 Epervier (SA: 251)

| 1860mm | - | 10cc | 5 | MODELE 3082 | 105F |

Nieuport

Nieuport IV

| 13" | - | R | FF | BLAIR | $5.00 |

Nieuport 17 (SA: 252)

V	-	-	RC	AIR A3	$18.00
16½"	-	R/CO2	FF	ALFERY	$5.00
2000mm	-	10cc	4	RADIO 14	90F

Nieuport 28

| 13" | - | R | FF | HAUGHT P-38 | $1.50 | |
| 52" | - | 8-10cc | 4 | ARGUS RC1094 | £8.75 | (Antione) |

Potez

Potez XXV

| ? | - | - | - | PLANY 109 | NA | (Baczkowski) |

S.I.P.A.

S.I.P.A. 12A

| 2000mm | - | 10cc | 6 | MODELE 3261 | 90F |
| 2300mm | - | 20cc | RC | MODELE 4012 | 145F |

SPAD

Spad XIII

[2730]	-	100cc	RC	LOHMANN	DM80,	
V	-	-	RC	AIR A1	$18.00	
*16"	-	R	FF	WILLAIRCO	$9.00	(Comet)
*24"	-	R	FF	WILLAIRCO	$15.00	(Comet)
*36"	-	.20	RC	WILLAIRCO	$22.00	(Comet)
*48"	-	.40	RC	WILLAIRCO	$40.00	(Comet)
1250mm	-	10cc	RC	DIMUZIO	L85.000	
*60"	-	.60	RC	WILLAIRCO	$60.00	(Comet)
*72"	-	.60	RC	WILLAIRCO	$95.00	(Comet)
2050mm	1560mm	25cc	4	RADIO 70	230F	

Spad 510

1800mm	1300mm	10-15cc	4	RADIO 55	70F

GERMANY

Albatros

B-II

42"	-	.049	FF	BLAIR	$5.00

D-III

1110mm	-	/6.5	3	VTH MT/G-0073	DM19,50	(Hawkins)

D-V

[2510]	-	100cc	RC	LOHMANN	DM80,	
1800mm	-	15-20cc	RC	MODELLE FO52	DM28,	
84"	-	20-25cc	4	ARGUS RSQ1590	£16.00	(Huttons)
89"	72½"	2.2	4	PHOTO	$35.00	

D-XI

13"	-	R	FF	BLAIR	$5.00

Bachem

BA-349 Natter

V	-	-	RC	AIR C7	$18.00

Blohm und Voss

BV-141

13"	-	R	FF	HAUGHT P-7	$1.50

Bucker

Bu-131 Jungmann (SA: 252)

*1480mm	1320mm	7.5/20cc	4	DUBEI	NA	
73"	65"	.90/1.2	4	INNOVATIVE	$25.00	

Bu-133 Jungmeister (SA: 252)
[FGM: cowl, $45.00] (DRY)

32½"	-	.049	2-3	MAN 5791	$10.75	(Srull)
53½"	45"	.60/.90	4	MAN 5901	$12.50	(Manly)
*2200mm	-	60-120cc	RC	KUHLMANN	DM911,	
95"	-	2-3.6	4-5	ARGUS RM252	£52.50	(Greenfield)

Dornier

Do-17

74"	-	.25x2	6	ARGUS RSQ1624	£11.00	(Maund)

Do-27 (SA: 252)

540mm	-	CO2	FF	RC MODEL PO83	800P	
27"	-	R	FF	ARGUS FSR/96	£3.00	(Garrett)
1250mm	920mm	3.5-5cc	3	VTH MT70	DM19,50	(Ledertheil)
*3140mm	2430mm	35cc	4	MUDER	DM449,	

Do-335 Pfeil (SA: 252)
[HAWE: retracts, DM506] (VTH)

13"	-	R	FF	HAUGHT P-21	$1.50	
56"	56"	.25x2	6	AIR MASTERS	$21.00	

Etrich

Taube

24"	-	R	FF	FLY T FTMC-17	$5.00	
*[$20.00]						
*2030mm	-	/6.5	RC	WINTRICH B001	DM295,	

Fieseler

Fi-156 Storch (SA: 252)

3520mm	-	32cc	RC	MODELE 3361	155F

Focke-Wulf

Fw-44 Stieglitz (SA: 253)

1080mm	-	5-7.5cc	RC	MODELLE 0017	DM18,	(Schmalzgruber)

Fw-56 Stosser (SA: 253)

42"	-	.8-1cc	FF	ARGUS FSP617	£3.75	(Barton)
1760mm	-	6-6.5cc	RC	RC MODEL P070	1.200P	

Fw-190 (SA: 253)

V	-	-	RC	AIR C9	$18.00	
33¼"	-	8cc	CL	VINTAGE	£3.00	(Veron)
*1020mm	-	4-7.5cc	RC	KUHLMANN	DM160,	
46"	-	.40	4	MARTIN MW111	£7.50	
[canopy, £1.40; template, £7.50]						
*46"	-	Glider	2	SLOPE	$99.95	
*48¼"	38"	.35	4	STARY	540Kcs	
*1600mm	-	15-30cc	RC	KUHLMANN	DM394,	
*2300mm	-	60-120cc	RC	KUHLMANN	DM660,	

Fw-190D (SA: 253)
[RHOM: retracts, $108.95] (PICA)
[TDF: cowl, $20.95] (RCM)

*880mm	-	.15	RC	DOGFIGHTER	NA	
1410mm	-	7.5-10cc	RC	MODELLE 0020	DM19,	(Schmalzgruber)

Fw TA-152

38½"	-	R/.049	2	HAUGHT S-21	$5.00	
40"	-	R	FF	LIDBERG	$6.00	
59"	-	.60	RC	RCM 485	$6.75	(Petersen)
66"	-	Glider	RC	HULME	NA	

Fokker

B-II

13"	-	R	FF	POND 61G3	$4.00	(Norman)

D-VII (SA: 253)

?	-	-	-	PLANY 129	NA	(Baczkowski)
*16"	-	R	FF	WILLAIRCO	$9.00	(Ziroli)
18"	-	CO2	FF	STAN	£3.20	
19¼"	-	R	FF	BLAIR	$5.00	
22"	-	R	FF	GLEASON	$2.75	(Diel)
*24"	-	R	FF	WILLAIRCO	$15.00	(Ziroli)
*36"	-	R	FF	WILLAIRCO	$22.00	(Ziroli)
1050mm	820mm	3.5cc	4	RADIO 45	50F	
1200mm	-	/6.5	RC	RC MODEL P089	1.000P	

*48"	-	.20	RC	WILLAIRCO	$40.00	(Ziroli)
*60"	-	.60	RC	WILLAIRCO	$60.00	(Ziroli)
*72"	-	.60	RC	WILLAIRCO	$95.00	(Ziroli)
76"	64"	.90	4	GAZZA 007	L95.000	
88"	-	2.2	3-5	WE RCQS-5	$24.95	

[FGM: cowl, $27.00]

**88"	68"	Q40	4	NORTHCRAFT	$292.00CDN

D-VIII (SA: 254)
[FGM: cowl, $21.00] (R&M)

*16"	-	R	FF	WILLAIRCO	$8.00	(Cleveland)
16½"	-	R/CO2	FF	ALFERY	$5.00	
*24"	-	R	FF	WILLAIRCO	$12.00	(Cleveland)
*36"	-	R	FF	WILLAIRCO	$32.00	(Cleveland)
*48"	-	.20	RC	WILLAIRCO	$32.00	(Cleveland)
1466mm	-	4-6.5cc	RC	RC MODEL P001	750P	
*60"	-	.60	RC	WILLAIRCO	$55.00	(Cleveland)
*72"	-	.60	RC	WILLAIRCO	$85.00	(Cleveland)

Dr-1 (SA: 254)

[2400]	-	100cc	RC	LOHMANN	DM80,	
V	-	-	RC	AIR A2	$18.00	
140mm	-	R	FF	ART 1	¥1,800	
15"	-	CO2	FF	BLAIR	$5.00	
1520mm	-	10cc	RC	MODELLE 0032	DM30,	(Damerval)
1700mm	-	10cc	RC	MODELE 3423	130F	
*1860mm	-	30cc	RC	WINTRICH B002	DM455,	

E-III
[FGM: Cowl, $10.00] (ZIROLI)

[2380]	-	38cc	RC	LOHMANN	DM65,
17¼"	-	R	FF	BLAIR	$5.00
20"	-	CO2	FF	STAN	£3.20
*1335mm	860mm	1.5-2.5cc	3	GRAUPNER	DM162,
2200mm	1600mm	1.2	4	MAX	DM100,

Halberstadt

D-I

21"	-	R	FF	BLAIR	$5.00

Heinkel

He-51
[SMITH: cowl, $30.00] (SMITH)

He-72 Kadett

*2250mm	1875mm	25-70cc	RC	PRAZISE	DM, 895,

He-100 (SA: 254)

13"	-	R	FF	HAUGHT P-45	$1.50	
1340mm	-	6.5cc	RC	MODELLE 049	DM19,	
1620mm	1394mm	5.6-10cc	4	VTH MT638	DM19,50	(Pichler)

He-162 (SA: 254)

V	-	-	RC	AIR C8	$18.00

He-177 Greif

38"	-	R/C02	FF	HAUGHT S-6	$4.00

He-219

21"	-	R/C02	FF	HAUGHT S-15	$3.00
33"	-	R/C02	FF	HAUGHT S-16	$4.00
91"	77"	.60x2	6	BEAULIEU	FORTHCOMING

Henschel

Hs-123

*2800mm	2000mm	90cc	4	HO	L4.500.000

Hs-126

27"	-	R/C02	FF	WOODHOUSE	£3.50	(Koutny)

Hs-129

1506mm	-	4ccx2	RC	RC MODEL P006	1.350P
92"	73"	.90x2	7	SMITH	$42.00

[cowls, $30.00; canopy, $25.00]

Horton

Horton IX

*56"	22"	Glider	2	VS	FORTHCOMING

Junkers

Ju-52

25"	-	C02	FF	STAN	£3.20
1800mm	-	6.5cc	RC	MODELE 3871	90F

| 1816mm | - | 6.5cc | RC | RC MODEL P127 | 1.750P |
| 2200mm | - | 10-15cc | RC | MODELLE 047 | DM24, |

Ju-87 Stuka (SA: 254)

13"	-	R	FF	HAUGHT P-9	$1.50	
32"	-	R	FF	STAN	£3.50	
100"	77"	3-4.2	4-5	HANGAR	$375.00	(Ziroli)

Ju-160

| 13" | - | R | FF | CLOUD | $5.00+ | (Bruning) |

Ju-252

| 48" | - | R | FF | HAUGHT S-27 | $6.00 |

C-I

| 13" | - | R | FF | POND 63G2 | $4.00 | (Niedzielski) |
| 20" | - | R | FF | POND 57D3 | $5.00 | (Niedzielski) |

D-I (SA: 254)

| 29½" | 24" | R | FF | GULF | $5.00 |

Klemm

L-25

16"	-	R	FF	WILLAIRCO	$8.00	(Uhu)
24"	-	R	FF	WILLAIRCO	$12.00	(Uhu)
36"	-	R	FF	WILLAIRCO	$18.00	(Uhu)
48"	-	.40	RC	WILLAIRCO	$32.00	(Uhu)
60"	-	.60	RC	WILLAIRCO	$55.00	(Uhu)
72"	-	.60	RC	WILLAIRCO	$85.00	(Uhu)
2650mm	1700mm	15cc	RC	WERNER	DM675,	
3650mm	-	35-60cc	RC	KUHLMANN	DM778,	

Messerschmitt

Me-109E (SA: 254)

47¼"	33"	.25	4	MODELHOB 11.0156	NA
1230mm	-	10cc	RC	DIMUZIO	L70.000
2000mm	-	15-35cc	RC	KUHLMANN	DM588,

Me-109G (SA: 254)

[HAWE: retracts, DM450,] (VTH)
[HAWE: retracts, DM375,] (COOP)

| V | - | - | RC | AIR C10 | $18.00 |

1110mm	-	6.5cc	RC	MODELE 4123	85F	
*2200mm	1870mm	30-40cc	RC	BRABEC NR800	4200SCH	

Me-110

V	-	-	RC	AIR C11	$18.00	
60"	-	.25x2	CL	MA 301	$4.25	(Ashby)
63"	-	.25x2	4-5	TRAP MW2307	£8.00	(Noden)

Me-163 Komet (SA: 254)

*44"	-	Glider	RC	AMERICAN	$69.95	
*62"	36"	Glider	2-3	VS	$210.00	
*1560mm	930mm	10-13cc	RC	BRABEC NR850	NA	
*1600mm	-	10-15cc	RC	KUHLMANN	DM338,	
*2300mm	-	25-50cc	RC	KUHLMANN	DM588,	

Me-210

V	-	-	RC	AIR C13	$18.00	

Me-262 (SA: 254)

*82"	69½"	.90x2F	RC	LAW	$950.00	(Roga)
*2100mm	1770mm	8-13ccx2	RC	BRABEC NR900	5900SCH	

Me-323

3170mm	1490mm	1.8ccx6	3	VTH MT579-G	DM36	(Nietzer)

Me-410

V	-	-	RC	AIR C14	$18.00	
13"	-	R	FF	HAUGHT P-30	$1.50	
21½"	-	R/CO2x2	FF	HAUGHT S-22	$5.00	

P-1111

48"	-	Glider	RC	B²	$15.00	(Kuhlman)

Pfalz

D-III

55"	-	Elec	4	AIRDROME	$36.00

Rumpler

Taube

3500mm	2500mm	62cc	RC	LOHMANN	DM120,

Siemens-Schuckert

D-II

16½"	-	R/CO2	FF	ALFERY	$5.00

ENGLAND

Armstrong-Whitworth

Siskin

13"	-	R	FF	SAMS 1440	£1.95	(Fillon)

Avro

504

13"	-	R	FF	HAUGHT P-19	$1.50
22½"	-	R	FF	BLAIR	$5.00

Lancaster (SA: 255)

V	-	-	RC	AIR B16	$18.00

Manchester

V	-	-	RC	AIR B15	$18.00

Spider

13"	-	R	FF	DINSTBIER	$1.00

BAC

Jet Provost

52"	37"	Glider	3	JANSSENS	$20.00
52"	-	Glider	RC	STEWART	NA

TSR-2

V	-	-	RC	AIR H4	$18.00

BAe

Harrier

920mm	-	6.5cc	RC	MODELE 4151	90F

Hawk

46"	-	Glider	RC	CONWAY	NA
*54"	-	.40	4-5	SKYWAY	£65.00

[accessory pack, £12.00]

Hawk F1/200

56"	-	Glider	RC	CONWAY	NA

Bristol

F2B

30"	-	R	FF	GULF	$5.00

Scout D (SA: 255)

12½"	-	R	FF	BLAIR	$5.00
*1250mm	-	.40-.60	4	SVENSON	1675FF
1880mm	1490mm	1.2	4	MAX	DM100,

DeHaviland

DH-2

[2150]	-	38cc	RC	LOHMANN	DM65,
18"	-	CO2	FF	BLAIR	$5.00
1440mm	-	7.5cc	RC	RC MODEL PO58	1.600P

DH-5

66"	-	.60-/.90	4	TRAP MW2305	£8.50	(Klintbom)

DH-6

39"	-	.15	RC	RCM 614	$5.50	(Strengell)

DH-82 Tiger Moth (SA: 255)

13"	-	R	FF	BLAIR	$5.00	
14½"	-	R	FF	CLEVE CD190	$12.00	
18"	-	CO2	FF	STAN	£3.20	
22"	-	R	FF	CLEVE CD190	$16.00	
45"	-	R	FF	CLEVE CD190	$28.00	
56"	-	5-8cc	4	ARGUS RC1131	£6.00	(Towner)
90"	-	-	RC	CLEVE CD190	$52.00	

DH-89 Dominie

42"	-	1.5ccx2	CL	ARGUS CL981	£5.25	(Towner)
1460mm	-	2.5ccx2	CL	MRA 327	89F	
96"	-	/.40x2	5	ARGUS RSQ1629	£13.50	(Tuck)
96"	-	.35x2	4	TRAP MW2141	£10.00	(Hodson)
96"	-	.61x2	RC	SWEITZER 1001	$38.50	

[cowls, $60.00; canopy, $15.00]

DH-98 Mosquito

?	-	-	-	PLANY 100	NA	(Baczkowski)
?	-	-	-	PLANY 124	NA	(Podgorski)
V	-	-	RC	AIR B18	$18.00	
96"	-	.60x2	6	BEAULIEU	FORTHCOMING	

DH-100 Vampire

V	-	-	RC	AIR H2	$18.00

*50"	-	Glider	RC	AEROTECHNIQUE	£42.95	
*57"	46"	.47F	4	SUNSET	$139.95	

DH-103 Hornet

80"	65"	.61x2	6	PARSONS	$29.00	

DH-110 Sea Vixen

51"	-	.60	4-6	ARGUS RSQ1607	£7.50	(Wright)

[canopy, £3.25]

Fairey

Barracuda (SA: 255)

29"	-	R	FF	WOODHOUSE	£3.00	(Koutny)

Fantome

12½"	-	R	FF	AUTHENTIC	65p	(Towner)
13"	-	R	FF	CLOUD	$5.00+	(Bruning)
20"	-	R	FF	POND 50C4	$4.50	(Duncan)
24"	-	R	FF	GLEASON	$3.55	(Booton)
62"	-	10cc	4	ARGUS RM229	£8.75	(Neild)

Firefly

[TRAP: cowl, £5.50; canopy, £4.50; spinner, £3.00] (CAP)

85"	-	.90	5	TRAP MN2093	£7.50	(Whitehead)

[canopy, £7.00; cowl, £9.50]

Gloster

Gladiator

16"	-	R	FF	SHOP	£5.00	(Keelbild)
21"	-	R	FF	B²	$3.50	(Marsden)

Meteor

52"	-	Glider	RC	COLLINS	NA	

Handley-Page

Halifax

?	-	-	-	PLANY 95	NA	(Baczkowski)

Hawker

Fury

24"	-	-	CL	POND 63F6	$7.00	(Berkeley)

Hart

73"	-	15-20cc	4	ARGUS RC1538	NA	(Smith)

<u>Hurricane</u> (SA: 255)

*16"	–	R	FF	WILLAIRCO	$9.00	(Berkeley)
20"	–	R	FF	POND 63C3	$4.50	(Kuenz)
*24"	–	R	FF	WILLAIRCO	$15.00	(Berkeley)
32"	–	R	FF	STAN	£3.50	
*36"	–	R	FF	WILLAIRCO	$22.00	(Berkeley)
40"	–	.25-.40	4	ARGUS RQ1625	£3.25	(Boddington)

[cowl, £7.00; canopy, £3.00]

*48"	–	.40	RC	WILLAIRCO	$40.00	(Berkeley)
*50"	–	Elec.	RC	EASY ERC-6	$55.00CDN	
*50½"	37"	.35	4	STARY	520Kcs	
*72"	–	.60	RC	WILLAIRCO	$95.00	(Berkeley)
*88"	–	30-45cc	4-6	DB	£145.00	

[UNITRACTS: retracts, £37.95]

120"	–	ZG62	RC	PRACTICAL	£25.00	

[cowl, £15.00; radiator, £5.00; canopy, £19.00]

<u>Sea Fury</u> (SA: 255)

[SMITH: cowl, $30.00; canopy, $27.00] (SMITH)

25"	–	R/CO2	FF	HAUGHT S-18	$3.00	
25½"	–	–	CL	VINTAGE	£2.50	(Veron)
81¼"	75"	/1.0	7	PHOTO	$27.00	(Whitley)
*82"	76"	20cc	4-5	NIMBUS	FORTHCOMING	

<u>Tempest</u> (SA: 255)

?	–	–	–	PLANY 75	NA	(Gibas)
1250mm	–	6.5cc	RC	MRA 721	100F	

<u>Typhoon</u> (SA: 255)

?	–	–	–	PLANY 93	NA	(Maciejewski
50"	38½"	.40	4	NZ	$30.00NZ	
*54"	45¼"	.40	5	STARY	860Kcs	
72"	–	.90	6	TAYLOR	£11.00	

Heston

<u>A.2/45</u>

44"	–	–	FF	POND 28A6	$5.50	(Gates)

Martin-Baker

<u>MB-5</u>

21"	–	R	FF	FM CF842	$6.50	(Arnold)
38"	–	.20-.28	2-4	TRAP MW2128	£5.50	(Withington)
70"	76"	ST2500	6	PARSONS	FORTHCOMING	

Miles

M.14 Magister

| 32" | - | R | FF | STAN | £3.50 | |
| 52" | - | 1-2cc | FF | ARGUS MA74 | £6.00 | (Bigg) |

Royal Aircraft Factory

BE-I

| 24¾" | - | CO2 | FF | BLAIR | $5.00 | |

BE-2

| 22" | - | R | FF | BLAIR | $5.00 | |
| 30" | - | R | FF | FSI B-8 | $6.00 | |

RE-8

| 97" | - | /.90-1.20 | 4 | ARGUS RM358 | £16.70 | (Fardell) |

SE-5a (SA: 256)

[2700]	-	100cc	RC	LOHMANN	DM80,	
13"	-	R	FF	POND 63A7	$7.00	(Springfield)
*16"	-	R	FF	WILLAIRCO	$9.00	(Cleveland)
18"	-	CO2	FF	STAN	£3.20	
*24"	-	R	FF	WILLAIRCO	$15.00	(Cleveland)
*36"	-	.20	RC	WILLAIRCO	$22.00	(Cleveland)
*48"	-	.40	RC	WILLAIRCO	$40.00	(Cleveland)
*60"	-	.60	RC	WILLAIRCO	$60.00	(Cleveland)
*72"	-	.60	RC	WILLAIRCO	$95.00	(Cleveland)

Short

Seamew

| 22" | - | .40 | CL | MA 101 | $3.00 | (Perry) |
| 35" | - | 6.6cc | CL | ARGUS CL1061 | £3.75 | (Reeves) |

Sopwith

Baby

| 30" | - | .10 | 3 | TRAP MW2295 | £3.00 | (Salmon) |

Camel (SA: 256)
[HOLMAN: cowling, $34.00] (REEVES)

Pup

| 13" | - | R | FF | BLAIR | $5.00 | |

13"	-	R	FF	HAUGHT P-18	$1.50	
1800mm	-	10cc	RC	MODELE 3561	105F	

Swallow (SA: 256)

60"	-	Elec	4	AIRDROME	$33.00

Supermarine

Spitfire (SA: 257)
[TDF: cowl, $27.95] (RCM)

?	-	-	-	PLANY 114	NA	(Maciejewski)
*?(1/5)	-	28-35cc	RC	SKYRAIDER	$700.00AUS	
V	-	-	RC	AIR B19	$18.00	
*13"	-	R	FF	DUBOIS	FORTHCOMING	
*30"	-	R	FF	DUBOIS	FORTHCOMING	
37"	-	-	CL	POND 22G7	$5.50	(Hobbycraft)
43"	-	Glider	RC	HULME	NA	
*44"	-	Elec	RC	EASY ERC-5	$55.00CDN	
*46"	-	Glider	2	SLOPE	$104.95	
56"	-	.40-.61	RC	TRAP MW2107	£8.00	(CAP)

[cowl, £3.50; canopy, £3.50; spinner, £3.00]

56"	45"	.40-.60	4-6	SMART	FORTHCOMING	
*58"	48"	.40/.60	4	NIMBUS	£119.95	

[retract wing, £135.00]

63"	52½"	.61/.90	5	RCM 1065	$11.50	(Millinship)
*88"	-	ST2500	6	JM	FORTHCOMING	

[retracts, $295.00AUS]

*2260mm	-	25-45cc	RC	KUHLMANN	DM734,
*3400mm	-	100-150cc	RC	KUHLMANN	DM1434,

Walrus

20"	-	CO2	FF	STAN	£3.20

Vickers

Valiant

78"	-	Glider	RC	FLITECRAFT	FORTHCOMING

Westland

Lysander

42"	-	R	FF	POND 62F1	$9.00	(Ott)
87½"	54"	.50-.60	4-5	MIZER	$50.00	

[documentation, $20.00]

1400mm	1160mm	10-15cc	5	VTH MT336	DM29,50	(Kriz)

Whirlwind

46"	-		Glider	2	ARGUS RM374	£4.35	(McHardy)

ITALY

Ansaldo

SVA Primo

?(¼)	-	-	RC	LOHMANN	NA
[2290]	-	65cc	RC	LOHMANN	DM65,
1160mm	-	2.5-3.5cc	RC	DIMUZIO	L40.000

Breda

Ba. 88 Lince

1520mm	-	5ccx2	RC	DIMUZIO	L55.000
70"	55"	.45x2	10	GAZZA 014	L60.000

CANT

Z-1007 Alcione

2800mm	-	5-7ccx3	RC	DIMUZIO	L140.000

Caproni

Ca-133 (SA: 257)

13"	-	R	FF	HAUGHT P-34	$1.50

Ca-134

13"	-	R	FF	HAUGHT P-35	$1.50

Ca-135

1710mm	-	5-7ccx2	RC	DIMUZIO	L70.000

Fiat

Br-20 Cicogna

2550mm	-	10ccx2	RC	DIMUZIO	L130.000

CR-42 Falco

1210mm	-	5-7cc	RC	DIMUZIO	L70.000

G-50 Freccia

13"	-	R	FF	CLOUD	$5.00+	(Bruning)
1130mm	-	5cc	RC	DIMUZIO	L35.000	

G-55 Centauro

1250mm	-	5.7cc	RC	DIMUZIO	L55.000

66"	53"	.60	10	GAZZA 009	L70.000	
1700mm	-	10cc	RC	DIMUZIO	L70.000	
1740mm	-	-	RC	MODELLE 051	DM24,	

G-59

| 1900mm | 1520mm | 15cc | 10 | GAZZA 015 | L75.000 | |

G-91

990mm	-	10ccF	RC	MODELLE 025	DM20,	(Bosak)
1223mm	1470mm	.10F	RC	BERTELLA	L70.000	
[canopy, L15.000]						
50"	37"	Glider	3	JANSSENS	$20.00	
*1600mm	-	15cc	RC	KUHLMANN	DM505,	
*1850mm	1650mm	12-15ccF	RC	Z MODEL	L885.000	

Macchi

MB-339 (SA: 257)

1551mm	1567mm	.60-.80F	RC	BERTELLA	L50.000
*1600mm	1530mm	10-15ccF	RC	Z MODEL	L525.000
[deluxe kit, L630.000]					
*1604mm	1554mm	.81F	RC	TECNO	NA
*1650mm	1650mm	10-13cc	3	BETTINI 0008	NA

MC-200 Saetta

| 1400mm | - | 10cc | RC | DIMUZIO | L55.000 |

MC-202 Folgore

| 1540mm | - | 10cc | RC | DIMUZIO | L70.000 |

MC-205 Veltro

1060mm	-	2.5-3.5cc	RC	DIMUZIO	L20.000
1650mm	-	10cc	RC	MODELLE 058	DM29,
*70"	-	/.60-.90	6	JM	FORTHCOMING
[retracts, $243.00AUS]					
76"	66"	.90	10	GAZZA 010	L90.000

Reggiane

Re-2000 Falco

| 1190mm | - | 2.5-5cc | RC | DIMUZIO | L40.000 |

Re-2005 Sagittario

| 68" | 54" | .60 | 10 | GAZZA 011 | L75.000 |

S.A.I.

.A.I. 207 Ambrosini

| 3" | - | R | FF | HAUGHT P-37 | $1.50 | |
| 450mm | - | 10cc | RC | DIMUZIO | L50.000 | |

Savoia-Marchetti

M-79 Sparviero

| 810mm | - | 5ccx3 | RC | DIMUZIO | L80.000 | |

Pomilio

E

| 1" | - | R | FF | MA 462 | $4.00 | (Noonan) |

JAPAN

Kawanishi

1K1 Kyofu ("REX")

| - | - | RC | AIR C1 | $18.00 | |

1K2-J Shiden ("GEORGE")(SA: 258)

| - | - | RC | AIR C6 | $18.00 | |

Kawasaki

i-10 ("PERRY")

| 3" | - | R | FF | POND 62F5 | $4.00 | (Yamada) |

i-61 Hien ("TONY")(SA: 258)
ARGUS: canopy, £5.25] (ARGUS)

| - | - | RC | AIR C5 | $18.00 | |
| 6" | - | Glider | RC | HULME | NA | |

Kyushu

7W Shinden (SA: 258)

| 6" | 52" | .60 | 10 | GAZZA 016 | L70.000 | |

Mitsubishi

ype 91

| 8" | - | - | RC | POND 18G4 | $5.50 | (R/C Technique) |

6M Reisen ("ZERO")(SA: 258)
TRAP: cowl, £6.50; canopy, £4.50] (CAP)
TRAP: canopy, £4.50] (BOSAK)

V	-	-	RC	AIR C4	$18.00
*46"	-	Glider	2	SLOPE	$99.95
1270mm	-	6.5	RC	MODELE 3961	85F
*51"	38"	.40	3-4	FARNS A1034	$89.95

Ki-15 "BABS")

120mm	-	R	FF	ART 1	¥1,800

J2M3 Raiden ("JACK")(SA: 258)

V	-	-	RC	AIR C3	$18.00
*13"	-	R	FF	DIELS K-6	$26.00+

Ki-83

25¼"	-	R	FF	COLE	$5.00

Nakajima

Ki-27 ("NATE")

1930mm	1260mm	10cc	2	RADIO 41	120F

K1-84 Hayate ("FRANK")(SA: 258)

V	-	-	RC	AIR C2	$18.00	
13"	-	R	FF	CLOUD	$5.00+	(Bruning)

NETHERLANDS

Fokker

D-XXIII

1580mm	-	.25x2	5	LE GUENNOU	NA
2520mm	-	10ccx2	RC	MODELE 3611	130F

NEW ZEALAND

N.Z.A.I.

CT-4B

39"	-	R	FF	NZ	FORTHCOMING
78"	69"	.60	5	NZ	FORTHCOMING

POLAND

P.Z.L.

P-1

23½"	-	R	FF	B²	$3.50	(Marsden)

P-11

| ? | - | - | - | PLANY 91 | NA | (Maciejewski) |
| 53" | 35¼" | .35-.40 | 4 | RCM 1070 | $8.25 | (Haney) |

P-23 Karas

| ? | - | - | - | PLANY 82 | NA | (Maciejewski) |

P-102 Los

| ? | - | - | - | PLANY 27 | NA | (Jarczyk) |

R.W.D.

RWD-8

?	-	-	-	PLANY 28	NA	(Pontiatowski)
90"	-	.60	RC	RCM 814	$13.50	(Klimczak)
90"	-	.60	RC	ARGUS RC1365	£10.00	(Klimczak)

SOVIET UNION

Antonov

An-2

| ? | - | - | - | PLANY 59 | NA | (Luranc) |
| 13" | - | R | FF | CLOUD | $5.00 | (Bruning) |

An-22

| V | - | - | RC | AIR H10 | $18.00 | |

Ilyushin

Il-2 (SA: 259)

?	-	-	-	PLANY 65	NA	(Centkowski)
?	-	-	-	PLANY 84	NA	(Podgorski)
?	-	-	-	PLANY 142	NA	(Podgorski)

Il-10

| 13" | - | R | FF | ALFERY | $12.00 | |

Il-22

| V | — | — | RC | AIR F3 | $18.00 | |

Il-30

| V | - | - | RC | AIR F5 | $18.00 | |

Lavochkin

La-5 (SA: 259)

| ? | - | - | - | PLANY 106 | NA | (Gibas) |

| 1120mm | – | 6.5 | RC | MODELE 4211 | 85F | |
| *66" | 41" | .60-.80 | 4-6 | FARNS A1022 | $119.95 | |

La-7

| 19" | – | R | FF | WOODHOUSE | £2.50 | (Koutny) |

MIG

Mig-3

| *3000mm | 2000mm | 42cc | 6 | HO | L3.500.000 | |

Mig-15 (SA: 259)

V	–	–	RC	AIR G7	$18.00	
*16"	–	Jetex	FF	WILLAIRCO	$9.00	(Byron)
*24"	–	Jetex	FF	WILLAIRCO	$15.00	(Byron)
*36"	–	–	RC	WILLAIRCO	$22.00	(Byron)
1000mm	–	4ccF	RC	RC MODEL P086	800P	
*46½"	47"	.47F	4	SUNSET	FORTHCOMING	
*48"	–	–	RC	WILLAIRCO	$40.00	(Byron)
*1480mm	1400mm	Elec	4-5	BAUER	DM628,	
60"	–	.81F	5	TRAP MW2296	£9.00	(Bosak)
*60"	–	–	RC	WILLAIRCO	$60.00	(Byron)
*72"	–	–	RC	WILLAIRCO	$95.00	(Byron)

Mig-17

| V | – | – | RC | AIR G8 | $18.00 | |

Mig-21
[BERTELLA: canopy, L15.000] (BERTELLA)

V	–	–	RC	AIR G21	$18.00	
*36"	68"	.47F	4	SUNSET	$139.95	
*42"	85"	.77-.91F	6	PEREGRINE	$250.00	
*48"	56"	.60	4-6	FARNS A1024	$169.95	

Mig-23

| V | – | – | RC | AIR G10 | $18.00 | |
| *12" | 14" | Glider | FF | GLOBAL 450023 | $5.50 | |

Mig-25

| 900mm | – | 6.5 | RC | MODELE 4242 | 90F | |
| *40" | 57" | .47F | 4 | SUNSET | $129.95 | |

Mig-29 (SA: 304)

*930mm	970mm	4cc	RC	RODEL	DM195,	
1015mm	-	6.5	RC	RC MODEL P087	900P	
*84"	99"	.91x2F	6	PEREGRINE	FORTHCOMING	

Myasishchev

Mya-4

86"	-	Glider	RC	COCKER	NA

Polikarpov

I-15 Chato

23½"	-	R	FF	WISCONSIN	$4.50	(Gates)
1420mm	-	8cc/10cc	RC	MODELLE 044	DM25,	
*2500mm	1700mm	42cc	4	HO	L3.500.000	

I-16

13"	-	R	FF	AIR WARS #7	$6.00	(Rambo)
22½"	-	R	FF	GLEASON	$1.60	(Thomas)
1320mm	-	10cc	RC	DIMUZIO	L65.000	
*2030mm	1350mm	35-80cc	4	MUDER	DM298,	

*[deluxe kit, DM470,]

Po-2

?	-	-	-	PLANY 2	NA	(Szewczyk)

RZ

1870mm	-	10cc	RC	RC MODEL P079	1.100P

Sukhoi

Su-7

V	-	-	RC	AIR G1	$18.00

Su-9

V	-	-	RC	AIR G2	$18.00

Su-10

V	-	-	RC	AIR G3	$18.00

Su-11

V	-	-	RC	AIR G4	$18.00

Su-15

V	-	-	RC	AIR G5	$18.00

Su-27

*12"	17"	Glider	FF	GLOBAL 450027	$6.50
*1600mm	2430mm	-	RC	SCHLEICHER	NA
1630mm	2590mm	.81x2F	RC	BERTELLA	L60.000

[canopy, L15.000]

Tupolev

Tu-54

V	-	-	RC	AIR F6	$18.00

Tu-85

V	-	-	RC	AIR F2	$18.00

Tu-80

V	-	-	RC	AIR F1	$18.00

TB-3

42"	-	R/CO2x4	FF	HAUGHT S-29	$5.00

Yakovlev

Yak-3 (SA: 259)

?	-	-	-	PLANY 81	NA	(Luranc)
?	-	-	-	PLANY 131	NA	(Tomaszewski)
V	-	-	RC	AIR B20	$18.00	

Yak-9 (SA: 259)

?	-	-	-	PLANY 4	NA	(Uminiski)
?	-	-	-	PLANY 45	NA	(Luranc)

Yak-15

V	-	-	-	AIR G6	$18.00

SPAIN

Casa

C-101 Aviojet

1390mm	-	.40-.45	RC	RC MODEL P092	900P

SWEDEN

Saab

JAS-39 Tunin

*36"	62"	.65-.81F	6	PEREGRINE	$200.00

J-39 Gripen (SA: 260)

*42"	66"	.61F	6	INNOVATIVE	$269.95

Sparmann

P-1

78"	-	.60-.80	RC	HORN S-22	$15.00	(Osborne)
84"	-	/1.20	4	ARGUS RM369	£10.70	(Kidd)

SWITZERLAND

Pilatus

PC-9

13"	-	R	FF	CLOUD	$5.00+	(Bruning)
60"	-	-	RC	POND 58F1	$11.00	(Air Model)
1800mm	-	10cc	RC	MODELE 4111	110F	
*2040mm	-	60cc	RC	KUHLMANN	DM570,	

UNITED STATES

Aeronca

L-58 Defender

49"	-	-	CL	GLEASON	$7.00	(Albert)

Beech

C-45 (SA: 260)

*101"	-	Q35x2	5	HANGAR	FORTHCOMING

T-34

*24"	-	R	FF	WILLAIRCO	$14.00	(Berkeley)
*36"	-	R	FF	WILLAIRCO	$20.00	(Berkeley)
*48"	-	.40	RC	WILLAIRCO	$38.00	(Berkeley)
*60"	-	.60	RC	WILLAIRCO	$65.00	(Berkeley)
1800mm	1570mm	10cc/13cc	RC	NICETTO	L50.000	

Bell

P-39 Airacobra (SA: 260)
[TRAP: cowl, £6.50; canopy, £4.50] (CAP)
[HAWE: retracts, DM450,] (KRANZ)

?	-	-	-	PLANY 79	NA	(Maciejewski)
V	-	-	RC	AIR B7	$18.00	
*13"	-	R	FF	ALFERY	$12.00	
*16"	-	R	FF	WILLAIRCO	$8.00	(Megow)

*24"	-	R	FF	WILLAIRCO	$12.00	(Megow)
*36"	-	.20	RC	WILLAIRCO	$18.00	(Megow)
*48"	-	.40	RC	WILLAIRCO	$32.00	(Megow)
*60"	-	.60	RC	WILLAIRCO	$55.00	(Megow)
*72"	-	.60	RC	WILLAIRCO	$85.00	(Megow)
*78"	72"	2.0-3.0	5-6	KOEHLER	$285.00	
*82"	68"	ST3000	6-8	YELLOW	$350.00	

P-63 King Cobra

*46"	-	Glider	2	SLOPE	$99.95

X-1

6½"	5½"	Glider	FF	AERO	$6.00
2170mm	-	20cc	RC	RC MODEL P109	1.500P
70"	-	Glider	RC	SKYTIME	FORTHCOMING

X-15

V	-	-	RC	AIR H6	$18.00

X-22

V	-	-	RC	AIR H7	$18.00

XP-83

V	-	-	RC	AIR E4	$18.00

YFM Airacuda

33"	-	R	FF	HAUGHT S-26	$5.00

Boeing

B-17 Flying Fortress

V	-	-	RC	AIR B11	$18.00

B-29 Super Fortress

3000mm	-	5-7ccx4	RC	DIMUZIO	L150.000
*140"	-	Glider	RC	SKYTIME	FORTHCOMING
141"	99"	.90x4	7	SMITH	FORTHCOMING

[cowls, $30.00]

B-47 Stratojet (SA: 260)

V	-	-	RC	AIR D5	$18.00

B-52 Stratofortress

V	-	-	RC	AIR D8	$18.00

P-12
| 30" | - | R | FF | GLEASON | $4.15 | (Smith) |

P-26 Peashooter
| *2140mm | - | 60cc | RC | WINTRICH B005 DM815, |

Brewster

F2A Buffalo (SA: 260)
| *13" | - | R | FF | DIELS K-6 | $26.00+ |
| 26" | - | R | FF | POND 26C4 | $4.75 | (Mills) |

Cessna

L-19 Bird Dog
| 108" | 75" | 25cc | 5 | NZ | FORTHCOMING |

Consolidated

B-24 Liberator
| V | - | - | RC | AIR B14 | $18.00 |

PBN Nomad
| *109" | 70" | /1.2x2 | 5 | G&P | $439.95 |

PBY Catalina (SA: 260)
[MORGAN: cowls, $7.50, $10.30; blisters, $5.50, $7.60] (MORGAN)
[LIKES: retracts, $590.00] (MORGAN)
| ? | - | - | - | PLANY 144 | NA | (Podgorski) |
| *109" | 78" | /1.2x2 | 5 | G&P | $439.95 |

XF2R-1 Darkshark
| 35" | - | - | CL | POND 62G5 | $9.00 | (Consolidated) |

Convair

B-36 Peacemaker
| V | - | - | RC | AIR D2 | $18.00 |

XB-46
| V | - | - | RC | AIR D4 | $18.00 |

XB-48
| V | - | - | RC | AIR D6 | $18.00 |

XB-60
| V | - | - | RC | AIR D2a | $18.00 |

XFY-1 Pogo

| 55" | 70" | ST6000 | 6-7 | HAREL | $30.00 |

Cox-Klemin

XS-1 Scout

7"	-	R	FF	CLEVE CD174	$9.00
9"	-	R	FF	CLEVE CD174	$12.00
13½"	-	R	FF	CLEVE CD174	$16.00
17"	-	R	FF	COLE	$5.00
27"	-	R	FF	CLEVE CD174	$20.00

Curtis

Command Helldiver

12"	-	R	FF	CLEVE CD7B	$9.00
16"	-	R	FF	CLEVE CD7B	$12.00
24"	-	R	FF	CLEVE CD7B	$16.00
47"	-	-	RC	CLEVE CD7B	$28.00

JN4A Jenny

22"	-	CO2	FF	STAN	£3.20	
26"	-	R	FF	SAMS 1542	£1.95	(Aerographics
27¼"	-	CO2	FF	BLAIR	$5.00	

N2C-1 Fledgling

| 13" | - | R | FF | WINICKI | $11.50 |

P-1 Hawk (SA: 261)

| 20" | - | R | FF | BLAIR | $5.00 |

P-36 Hawk

| V | - | - | RC | AIR B3 | $18.00 |

P-40 War Hawk (SA: 261)

[RHOM: retracts, $150.37]

V	-	-	RC	AIR B4	$18.00	
*?(1/5)	-	28-35cc	RC	SKYRAIDER	$700.00AUS	
*24"	-	R	FF	WILLAIRCO	$14.00	(Cleveland)
*36"	-	R	FF	WILLAIRCO	$20.00	(Cleveland)
37"	-	R	FF	GLEASON	$6.15	(Musciano)
*48"	-	.40	RC	WILLAIRCO	$38.00	(Cleveland)
1400mm	-	3.5-4cc	RC	MRA 721	100F	

*60"	-	.60	RC	WILLAIRCO	$65.00	(Cleveland)
96"	81"	.80-1.20	5-7	PALADINE	$32.00	
2400mm	1950mm	60cc	7	MAX	DM100,	
2600mm	-	32cc	RC	MODELLE 3542	115F	
*112"	93"	3.7-5.8	5-6	RC	$299.95	

SBC-1 Helldiver

| 13" | - | R | FF | CLOUD | $5.00+ | (Bruning) |

SB2C Helldiver

V	-	-	RC	AIR B10	$18.00	
13"	-	R	FF	HAUGHT P-26	$1.50	
*81"	58"	ST3000	6-8	YELLOW	$350.00	

SOC Seagull

| 13" | - | R | FF | CLOUD | $5.00+ | (Bruning) |

XP-87 Nighthawk

| V | - | - | RC | AIR E4 | $18.00 | |

Curtis-Wright

CW-21 Demon

| 13" | - | R | FF | CLOUD | $5.00+ | (Bruning) |

Douglas

A-4 Skyhawk

| *857mm | 965mm | 3-4cc | RC | TECHNIK | DM155, | |
| 42" | - | Glider | RC | CONWAY | NA | |

A-20 Havoc

| 104" | 80" | .90x2 | 7 | SMITH | FORTH COMING | |

[cowls, $30.00; canopy, $27.00]

A-26 Invader

V	-	-	RC	AIR B12	$18.00	
105"	90"	.90x2	6	BEAULIEU	FORTHCOMING	
105"	76"	.90x2	7	SMITH	FORTHCOMING	
*168"	144"	4.2x2	6-10	CUSTOM	$1700.00	

AD Skyraider (SA: 261)

| 13" | - | R | FF | HAUGHT P-13 | $1.50 | |
| *90" | 65" | ST2500 | 6 | CUSTOM | $350.00 | |

C-47 Skytrain (SA: 261)
[FGM: cowls, $16.00] (MAN)

83½"	56"	.30-.40x2 5		NZ	$55.00NZ
*2400mm	-	6.5ccx2	RC	KUHLMANN	DM902,
*3600mm	-	25ccx2	RC	KUHLMANN	DM1580,

C-54

V	-	-	RC	AIR B13	$18.00

X-3 Stiletto

V	-	-	RC	AIR H5	$18.00

XB-42 Mixmaster

V	-	-	RC	AIR D3	$18.00

EDO

OSE-1

72"	-	.90	4	RCM 1072	$17.25	(Milo, Schultz)

Fairchild

A-10 Thunderbolt (SA: 262)

*68½"	65"	.47x2F	4	SUNSET	$249.95

PT-19 (SA: 262, 304)

54"	41½"	.30-.40	4	NZ	$35.00NZ
1730mm	1320mm	10cc	4	RADIO 50	70F

UC-61

?	-	.80	RC	RCM 722	$29.50	(Lopshire)
12"	-	R	FF	POND 17A4	$4.00	(O'Dwyer)
13"	-	R	FF	OLD 442	$2.00	(Megow)
13½"	-	R	FF	CLEVE CD224	$14.00	
15"	-	R	FF	POND 17A4	$4.00	(Modelcraft)
16"	-	R	FF	GLEASON	$1.00	(Sephing)
16"	-	R	FF	POND 17A4	$4.00	(Comet)
*[FIKE: $7.95]						
*16"	-	R	FF	WILLAIRCO	$8.00	(Berkeley)
16½"	-	R	FF	HUNT MAC-08	$2.50	(Model A/C)
18"	-	R	FF	CLEVE CD224	$18.00	
20"	-	R	FF	PLANS	$6.00	(Andrus)
20"	-	R	FF	POND 47B6	$4.00	(Fly-a-Way)

21"	-	R	FF	POND 17A5	$4.00	(Modernistic)
23"	-	R	FF	POND 17A5	$4.00	(Booton)
24"	-	R	FF	GLEASON	$1.00	(Roberts)
*24"	-	R	FF	WILLAIRCO	$12.00	(Berkeley)
27"	-	R	FF	FSI F-1	$6.00	
27"	-	R	FF	HUNT AH-93	$3.25	(Model A/C)
27"	-	R	FF	POND 17A5	$4.50	(Zier)
27¼"	-	R	FF	CLEVE CD224	$24.00	
29"	-	R	FF	YESTER	$3.00	(Stahl)
*36"	-	R	FF	WILLAIRCO	$18.00	(Berkeley)
39"	-	R	FF	HUNT J-7	$3.50	(Megow)
*48"	-	.40	RC	WILLAIRCO	$32.00	(Berkeley)
54½"	-	-	RC	CLEVE CD224	$48.00	
58"	-	-	RC	OLD DS-9	$5.00	(Stahl)
*60"	-	.60	RC	WILLAIRCO	$55.00	
1800mm	-	/.40	RC	AIRBORNE	$22.00AUS	
72"	-	.60	RC	MAN 8	$10.25	(Woodward)
*72"	-	.60	RC	WILLAIRCO	$85.00	

Fleet

Fleet Trainer

*16"	-	R	FF	WILLAIRCO	$7.00	(Peerless)
21"	-	R	FF	BLAIR	$5.00	
21¼"	-	R	FF	GLEASON	$2.75	(Gates)
33"	-	-	CL	POND 17C5	$6.50	(Hollinger)
*36"	-	R	FF	WILLAIRCO	$18.00	(Peerless)
*48"	-	.40	RC	WILLAIRCO	$32.00	(Peerless)
*60"	-	.60	RC	WILLAIRCO	$55.00	(Peerless)
*72"	-	.60	RC	WILLAIRCO	$85.00	(Peerless)

General Dynamics

F-16 Fighting Falcon

*47"	74½"	.91F	5	RJ	FORTHCOMING
*1240mm	1860mm	.90F	RC	CUCCOLO	L420.000
*44½"	62"	.77F	5-6	DCU	$269.00

F-111

V	-	-	RC	AIR D12	$18.00

Grumman

A-6 Intruder
| *116" | 113" | .90x2F | 5-6 | DCU | | $1200.00 | |

AF2 Guardian (SA: 262)
| 36" | - | - | CL | POND 62G5 | | $8.00 | (Sterling) |

F4F Wildcat
| V | - | - | RC | AIR B6 | | $18.00 | |

F6F Hellcat (SA: 262)
V	-	-	RC	AIR B8		$18.00	
13"	-	R	FF	HAUGHT P-24		$1.50	
*30"	-	R	FF	DUBOIS R-40		$35.00	
*46"	-	Glider	2	SLOPE		$104.95	
1250mm	-	10cc	RC	DIMUZIO		L65.000	
*2140mm	-	40cc	RC	WINTRICH	B009	NA	

[HAWE: retracts, DM450,]

F7F Tigercat
| 34" | - | - | CL | POND 64A3 | | $8.00 | (Randall) |

F8F Bearcat (SA: 262)
36"	-	-	CL	POND 62G4		$9.00	(Internatior
77½"	60"	25cc	6	BATES		$35.00	
*2060mm	-	40cc	RC	WINTRICH	B007	DM685,	

[HAWE: retracts, DM 450,]

| *2200mm | - | 80-140cc | RC | KUHLMANN | | DM730, | |
| *106½" | 82½" | 5.8 | 8 | BAC | | $895.00 | |

F9F Panther
| *48" | 49½" | .47F | 4 | SUNSET | | $139.95 | |
| 1447mm | 1478mm | .81F | RC | BERTELLA | | L60.000 | |

[canopy, L15.000]

F9F Cougar
| 43" | 37" | Glider | 3 | JANSSENS | | $20.00 | |

F-14 Tomcat (SA: 262)
[BERTELLA: canopy, L15.000] (BERTELLA)
| *16¼" | 15½" | Glider | FF | GLOBAL 450014 | $6.50 | |
| *46" | - | Glider | 2 | DCU | | $118.00 | |

G-21 Goose
| *81" | 58" | .40x2 | 5 | G&P | $259.95 | |

G-44 Widgeon
?	-	.45x2	RC	FM CF132	$16.00	(Weingart)
37"	-	-	CL	POND 27G4	$5.50	(Palanek)
40"	-	R	FF	HUNT AH-110	$4.00	(Plecan)
40"	-	.09-.15x2	CL	MORGAN 201	$6.00	
40"	-	R	FF	POND 18B1	$5.50	(Aircraft Plan)
80"	-	.45-.60x2	RC	MORGAN 102	$14.95	
*81"	58"	.40x2	5	G&P	$259.95	

HU-16 Albatross
[FGM: cowls, $22.00] (PHOTO)
| 72" | 46½" | .45x2 | 5 | MAN 04732 | $20.00 | (Babbin) |

TBM Avenger (SA: 262)
| 13" | - | R | FF | HAUGHT P-14 | $1.50 |

X-29
| V | - | - | RC | AIR H13 | $18.00 |
| 1240mm | 1650mm | 6.5-10cc | 4-5 | RADIO 57 | 50F |

Lockheed

C-5A Galaxy
| V | - | - | RC | AIR H9 | $18.00 |

C-130 Hercules
[GLASCRAFT: cowlings, $64.00] (Mast)

F-80 Shooting Star (SA: 304)
| *56" | 60" | .90F | 5 | CUSTOM | $350.00 |

F-104 Starfighter
[BERTELLA: canopy, L15.000] (BERTELLA)
V	-	-	RC	AIR E3	$18.00
*42"	80"	.90F	5	CUSTOM	$350.00
*1200mm	1900mm	.65-.81F	RC	MASTER 020001	L719.000

P-38 Lightning (SA: 263)
[RHOM: retracts, $153.64]
[TDF: cowls, $17.95; oil coolers, $12.95; canopy, $8.95](Whitehead)

?	-	-	-	PLANY 73	NA	(Luranc)
V	-	-	RC	AIR B2	$18.00	
*24"	-	R	FF	WILLAIRCO	$16.00	(Comet)
33"	-	R	FF	WOODHOUSE	£3.50	(Koutny)
*36"	-	R	FF	WILLAIRCO	$24.00	(Comet)
*48"	-	.20x2	RC	WILLAIRCO	$42.00	(Comet)
*60"	-	.40x2	RC	WILLAIRCO	$55.00	(Comet)
*72"	-	.60x2	RC	WILLAIRCO	$105.00	(Comet)
2140mm	-	7.5ccx2	RC	MRA 738.705	126F	

SR-71 Blackbird (SA: 263, 304)

V	-	-	RC	AIR H8	$18.00
*55½"	108"	.47x2	5	SUNSET	$349.95

T-33 (SA: 244, 304)

52"	33"	Glider	3	JANSSENS	$20.00

TR-1A Sky Patrol

*3140mm	1920mm	Elec	4	BAUER	DM879,

U-2

27"	16"	Jetex	FF	MAC	$2.00
36"	22"	Jetex	FF	MAC	$2.00

Loening

OL-9

35½"	-	R	FF	GLEASON	$4.25	(Hungerford

Martin

PBM Mariner

118"	80"	/.80x2	7	ZEMAITIS	$75.00
138"	78"	Q35x2	6	DP	$45.00

P6M Seamaster

V	-	-	RC	AIR D9	$18.00

T4M-1

20"	-	R	FF	CLEVE CD274	$18.00
26½"	-	R	FF	CLEVE CD274	$28.00

| 40" | - | R | FF | CLEVE CD274 | $39.00 | |
| 80" | - | - | RC | CLEVE CD274 | $52.00 | |

XB-51

| V | - | - | RC | AIR D7 | $18.00 | |

McDonnell-Douglas

F-4 Phantom

44½"	62¾"	.77-.81F	6-8	RCM 1076	$9.50	(Bosak)
*52"	60½"	.45F	5	SUNSET	$229.95	
1310mm	-	6.5cc	RC	RC MODEL P071	1.100P	
*1600mm	2570mm	13-15ccF	RC	MASTER 020026	L1.251.000	

F-15 Eagle (SA: 263, 304)

*42½"	54"	.45F	4	SUNSET	$129.95	
*45"	56"	.45-.80F	4-5	MILTON	£99.90	
1200mm	-	10cc	RC	MODELE 3721	105F	
*50"	69"	.81-.91F	5	PARKINSON	$229.00CDN	
*1600mm	2400mm	-	RC	SCHLEICHER	DM1120,	

F-18 Hornet (SA: 304)

*10¼"	16"	Glider	FF	GLOBAL 450018	$5.50	
*42"	34"	Glider	2	CLIFF	$89.95	
*43½"	54½"	.45	4-5	GLOBAL 100973	$500.00	

XF-85 Goblin

| V | - | - | RC | AIR E1 | $18.00 | |

Naval Aircraft Factory

N3N-3

| 39" | - | R | FF | GLEASON | $5.85 | (Coon) |

North American

AT-6 Harvard/Texan (SA: 263)

1430mm	-	6.5cc	RC	RC MODEL P125	1.450P	
63"	43"	.35-.40	5	NZ	FORTHCOMING	
*1600mm	-	15-20cc	RC	KUHLMANN	DM350,	
*65"	44"	.60-.80	4-6	NOR CAL	$149.95	
87"	58"	.60-.90	6	NZ	FORTHCOMING	
*2560mm	1760mm	40-70cc	5-6	PETRAUSCH	DM748,	

B-1
| V | - | - | RC | AIR D11 | $18.00 | |

B-25 (SA: 304)
[RHOM: retracts, $153.64]
| 1600mm | - | 4ccx2 | RC | RC MODEL PO95 900P | | |

F-82 Twin Mustang
| 31" | - | R | FF | WOODHOUSE | £3.00 | (Koutny) |

F-86 Sabre
V	-	-	RC	AIR E2	$18.00	
840mm	-	Glider	2	VTH MT978K	DM7,50	
34"	-	.5F	FF	VINTAGE	£2.50	
1260mm	1020mm	Glider	2	VTH MT978	DM19,50	
50"	-	Glider	RC	COLLINS	NA	
*52½"	55"	7.5F	RC	HANGAR	$475.00	
*55"	47"	.47F	4	SUNSET	$144.95	
*55"	58"	.77-.90F	6	SUNSET	$300.00	
*1460mm	1510mm	.90F	RC	GLEICHAUF 1200	DM799,	

F-86D
| *18½" | - | R | FF | DIELS K15 | $20.00 | |
| *1600mm | 1510mm | 10-13ccF | 5 | SCHENKE | DM310, | |
[retracts, DM245,]

F-100 Super Sabre
*19½"	-	R	FF	DIELS K16	$20.00	
*1240mm	1380mm	7.5-13ccF	RC	RODEL	DM650,	
**54"	65"	.77F	5-8	GLENNIS	$189.95	
*[deluxe kit, $325.00]

OV-10 Bronco
13"	-	R	FF	HAUGHT P-17	$1.50	
70½"	68"	.45x2	10	GAZZA 012	L90.000	
*96"	96"	ST3000x2	6-10	YELLOW	$850.00	

P-51B Mustang (SA: 263)
| 44" | - | Glider | RC | HULME | NA | |

P-51D Mustang (SA: 264)
| ? | - | - | - | PLANY 39 | NA | (Luranc) |
| V | - | - | RC | AIR B5 | $18.00 | |

*940mm	-	.15	RC	DOGFIGHTER	NA
1140mm	-	6.5cc	RC	MODELE 4044	85F
*46"	-	Glider	2	SLOPE	$104.95
*1580mm	1330mm	8-13cc	RC	BRABEC 750	2,798SCH
*85"	-	ST3000	5	D&R	$275.00
*85"	76"	Q42	6	BYRON 6130245	$475.95

[powerdrive, $448.50; retracts, $248.95; tailwheel, $42.70]

*2246mm	1968mm	30-45cc	RC	BRABEC 760	NA
*90"	-	ST3000	5	CUSTOM	$400.00
*2580mm	-	35-120cc	RC	KUHLMANN	DM948,

P-51H

13"	-	R	FF	ALFERY	$12.00

T-2C Buckeye

*60"	-	.65-.91F	6	DCU	$369.00

T-28 (SA: 264)
[RHOM: nose wheel, $58.86] (PICA)

*2250mm	-	60cc	RC	WINTRICH B008	DM765,

[HAWE: retracts, DM520,]

XB-70 Valkyrie

V	-	-	RC	AIR D10	$18.00	
1620mm	2640mm	10ccx2	5	VTH MT995	DM45,	(Velten)

Northrop

F-5

V	-	-	RC	AIR E5	$18.00

F-20 Tigershark (SA: 264)

*1100mm	1890mm	9-13ccF	RC	GLEICHAUF 2000	DM880,
54"	-	Glider	RC	CROCKER	NA

P-61 Black Widow (SA: 264)

V	-	-	RC	AIR B9	$18.00

T-38 Talon

*39"	72"	.72-.82F	6-8	JIM	$475.00

[retracts, $105.00; cockpit, $29.00; speed brake, $15.00]

*48"	80"	.77-.90F	6	CUSTOM	$350.00

XB-35 Flying Wing

V	-	-	RC	AIR D1	$18.00

YB-49 Flying Wing

V	-	-	RC	AIR D1a	$18.00
1750mm	-	Glider	RC	MODELE 3804	90F

Packard LePere

LUSAC II

16"	-	R	FF	CLEVE CD268	$12.00
21"	-	R	FF	CLEVE CD268	$15.00
31"	-	R	FF	CLEVE CD268	$22.00

Piper

L-3 Grasshopper (SA: 264)

*1400mm	-	.20-.25	4	NICHOLS CP106	£79.95
*84½"	-	/.60	4	IKON	$150.95
*141"	86"	2.0-4.0	4	BALSA 467	$399.95

L-4 Grasshopper

13"	-	R	FF	BLAIR	$5.00
*49½"	37½"	.15-.25	3-4	SURE	FORTHCOMING
106"	-	.90-2.0	RC	PHOTO	$27.00

Republic

F-84 Thunderjet

16"	16½"	Jetex	FF	MAC	$2.00	(Cleveland)
33½"	39"	.049F	2-4	MAN 1853	$13.50	(Musciano)

F-84 Thunderstreak
[BERTELLA: canopy, L15.000] (BERTELLA)

F-105 Thunderchief

**47"	90½"	.77F	5-8	GLENNIS	$225.00

*[deluxe kit, $325.00]

P-43 Lancer
[TDF: cowl, $30.95] (MB)

P-47 Thunderbolt (SA: 265)
[HAWE: retracts, DM450,] (KRANZ)

**8"	-	R	FF	ALFERY	$10.00	
*16"	-	R	FF	WILLAIRCO	$9.00	(Ziroli)

23"	-	R	FF	POND 63E5	$4.50	(Stahl)
¶25"	-	R	FF	POND 53A1	$4.50	(Ott)
*36"	-	.20	RC	WILLAIRCO	$22.00	(Ziroli)
*48"	-	.40	RC	WILLAIRCO	$40.00	(Ziroli)
54½"	-	.45	5	MARTIN MW112	£7.50	

[canopy, £2.70; template, £10.00]

*60"	-	.60	RC	WILLAIRCO	$60.00	(Ziroli)
*2400mm	1900mm	42cc	6	HO	L3.500.000	

XF-91 Thunderceptor

13"	18"	CO2	FF	MAC	$2.00

Ryan

PT-20 (SA: 265)

13"	-	R	FF	HAUGHT P-32	$1.50	
35"	-	R	FF	GLEASON	$3.00	(Chapis)
*54"	-	Elec	RC	EASY ERC-7	$60.00CDN	
90"	65"	.80-1.2	5-7	PALADINE	$32.00	

PT-22 Recruit

2040mm	1590mm	10cc	4	RADIO 1	80F	
2400mm	1810mm	40-50cc	5	MRA 722.607	60F	(Printant)

Seversky

P-35

19½"	-	R	FF	B^2	$3.00	(Marsden)

Stearman

PT-17

13"	-	R	FF	BRADSHAW	$1.50	(Modernistic)
24¼"	-	R	FF	GLEASON	$3.55	(Gates)

Stinson

0-49

51"	33½"	.10-.15	3-4	PHOTO	$21.00	(Katz)

Taylorcraft

L-2 Grasshopper

78½"	-	-	RC	GLEASON	$8.95	(Lindberg)

Temco

TT-1 Pinto

*16"	-	Jetex	FF	WILLAIRCO	$9.00	(Berkeley)
*24"	-	Jetex	FF	WILLAIRCO	$15.00	(Berkeley)
*36"	-	-	RC	WILLAIRCO	$22.00	(Berkeley)
*48"	-	-	RC	WILLAIRCO	$40.00	(Berkeley)
*60"	-	-	RC	WILLAIRCO	$60.00	(Berkeley)
*72"	-	-	RC	WILLAIRCO	$95.00	(Berkeley)

Vought

A-7 Corsair II (SA: 304)

1040mm	-	6.5cc	RC	MODELE 3841	85F	
*1260mm	1460mm	10-15cc F	RC	MODELLTECHNIK	DM399,	
54"	-	Glider	RC	COLLINS	NA	

F2U-1 Corsair

18"	12½"	R	FF	LAMBERT 23	$6.00

F4U Corsair (SA: 265)
[RHOM: retracts,$150.37]
[HAWE: retracts, DM450,] (COOP)

?	-	-	-	PLANY 62	NA	(Gibas)
V	-	-	RC	AIR B1	$18.00	
25"	-	R	FF	WOODHOUSE	£3.00	(Koutny)
¶38"	-	R	FF	POND 63D7	$7.00	(Ott)
49"	-	Glider	RC	HULME	NA	
*52"	-	.40-.50	4	DYNA	$99.95	
1560mm	-	10cc	RC	MODELE 3272	110F	
2200mm	-	35cc	RC	RC MODEL P102	2.300P	
96"	79"	.90-1.2	5-7	PALADINE	$32.00	

F5U-1 Flying Pancake

V	-	-	RC	AIR H1	$18.00

F-8 Crusader

*48"	72"	.77-.82F	6	JIM	$475.00

[retracts, $105.00; cockpit, $16.00; slats, $30.00; speed brake, $15.00]

*1240mm	1860mm	.65-.81F	RC	MASTER 020020	L662.000

SB2U Vindicator
[FGM: cowl, $30.00; tail fairing, $14.00] (MAN)

2ND ADDENDA

FINLAND

<u>VL</u>

<u>Myrsky II</u>
30"   -   R/.049   FF   MARINA $5.00CDN
*[$22.00CDN]

FRANCE

<u>Bernard</u>

<u>Bernard 260</u>
13"   -   R   FF   B² $2.00   (Marsden)

<u>Bleriot</u>

<u>Bleriot 510</u>
18"   -   R   FF   B² $4.00   (Booton)

<u>Breguet</u>

<u>Nautilus</u>
30"   -   R/.049   FF   MARINA $5.00CDN
*[$22.00CDN]

<u>Dassault</u>

<u>Mystere IV</u>
*46"   58"   .61-.91F 5-6 J.D. $280.00

<u>Dewotine</u>

<u>D-510</u>
40"   27½"   .09-.15   CL   MAN 9804 $7.00   (Khan)

<u>D-520</u>
64"   52"   .30-.40   CL   MAN 9831 $19.50   (Felton)

<u>Morane-Saulnier</u>

<u>MS-1508 Epervier</u>
24"   -   R   FF   MAN 3693 $4.00   (Scott)

Nieuport

Nieuport 17
*54"	–	.49-.60	4	PROCTER	$149.95	(VK)
62"	–	.60-.90	4	ARGUS RSQ1641	£6.60	(Tatum)

GERMANY

Albatros

C-V
42"	–	.010	FF	HOLMAN	$4.00

Arado

Ar-234
30"	–	R/.049	FF	MARINA	$5.00CDN

*[$22.00CDN]

Bucker

Bu-131 Jungmann
[MAGER: cowl, DM65,] (Kriz)
32"	30"	.049	FF	MAN 5791	$10.25	(Srull)

Bu-133 Jungmeister
*[G&R: $250.00] (HOSTETLER)
22"	–	R/.049	FF	MARINA	$5.00CDN

*[$22.00CDN]

Dornier

Do-23
84"	61"	.35x2	4	MAN 8782	$26.50	(Srull)

Do-27
1850mm	–	6.5-7.5cc	RC	MRA 631.578	106F

Do-335 Pfeil
1840mm	–	1.5ccx2	RC	BEST	DM29,80

[epoxy fuselage, DM180; cockpit, DM19,80] [HAWE: retracts, DM506,]

Fieseler

Fi-156 Storch
[MAGER: cowl, DM70,] (Kriz)
2010mm	–	6.5-8cc	RC	MRA 762	112F
3560mm	2417mm	Bully 45	RC	BEST	DM38,

[epoxy fuselage, DM300,]

Focke-Wulf

Fw-44 Stiglitz
*[G&R: $275.00] (HOLMAN)
[ABEL: landing gear, $50.00]

Fw-47
| 52" | 32" | R | | FF | MAN 732 | $8.50 | (Headley) |

Fw-56 Stosser
*[G&R: $250.00] (HOLMAN)
[ABEL: landing gear, $50.00]
| 2400mm | 1750mm | - | | RC | BEST | DM29,50 |
[epoxy fuselage, DM175,]

Fw-190
[UNITRACTS: retracts, £34.50] (TAYLOR)

[ROBINAIRE: retracts, $245.00] (INNOVATIVE)

[MAGER: cowl, DM50,] (Kriz)

| 30" | - | R/.049 | FF | MARINA | $5.00CDN |
*[$22.00CDN]
| 93½" | 78" | 3.7-5.1 | 6 | RICHTER | $22.00 |

Fw-190D
[BARTON: retracts, $260.00] (HOLMAN)

Fw-TA 154
| 51" | 38" | .35×2 | CL | MAN 11783 | $11.50 | (Martinez) |

Fokker

D-VII
| 75" | - | .90/1.20 | 4 | URAVITCH | $36.95 |

D-VIII
| 80" | - | ST2000 | 4 | HOLMAN | $25.00 | (Comyns) |
[cowl, $20.00]

Dr-1
[MAGER: cowl, DM70,] (Kriz)
*47" | - | .49-.60 | 4 | PROCTER | $149.95 | (VK)

Gotha

Go-242
| 36" | 22" | Glider | FF | MAN 2823 | $14.00 | (Bain) |

Heinkel

He-100
| 23" | - | R | | FF | MAN 5784 | $4.00 | (Srull) |

He-162
| 30" | - | R/.049 | | FF | MARINA | $5.00CDN |
*[$22.00CDN]

Junkers

Ju-87 Stuka
| 30" | - | R/.049 | | FF | MARINA | $5.00CDN |
*[$22.00CDN]
| 78" | - | .60-.90 | 5-6 | ARGUS RSQ1636 | £10.00 | (Carpenter) |
| 1740mm | - | 10cc | RC | BEST | DM24, |
[epoxy fuselage, DM155; cockpit, DM22,50]

Ju-D1
| 44½" | 35" | .30-.40 | CL | MAN 10782 | $14.50 | (Felton) |

Messerschmitt

Me-109E
| 30" | - | R/.049 | | FF | MARINA | $5.00CDN |
*[$22.00CDN]
| *54" | - | .35/.50 | 4 | MIDWEST | $99.95 |

Me-109F
[BARTON: retracts, $260.00] (HOLMAN)

Me-109G
[ROBINAIRE:retracts , $245.00] (INNOVATIVE)

Me-110
| 1620mm | - | 6.5x2 | RC | BEST | DM19,50 |
[epoxy fuselage, DM95; cockpit, DM14,]
| 89" | 66" | .90x2 | 6 | SMITH | $42.00 |
[cowls, $30.00; canopy, $25.00]

Me-163 Komet
| 1900mm | - | 10cc | RC | BEST | DM28, |
[epoxy fuselage, DM160; cockpit, DM14,]

Me-262 Schwalbe
| 30" | - | R/.049 | | FF | MARINA | $5.00CDN |
*[$22.00CDN]

Pfalz

D-III
55"   -   Elec   4   AIRDROME $36.00

GREAT BRITAIN

Avro

Lancaster
120"   -   -   RC   HOLMAN $35.00

Boulton-Paul

Defiant
39"   35"   .35   CL   MAN 8732 $10.50   (Felton)

Bristol

Blenheim
85"   -   .40x2   5-6   ARGUS RSQ1637 £10.70   (Booth)

Scout D
70"   63"   .60-1.2   4   MAN 6782 $29.50   (Eltscher)

DeHaviland

DH-82 Tiger Moth
66"   -   .40-.60   4   HOLMAN $24.95   (Bryant)

Fairey

Barracuda
30"   -   R/.049   FF   MARINA $5.00CDN
*[$22.00CDN]

Hawker

Hurricane
[UNITRACTS: retracts, £40.25] (REEVES)
[ROBINAIRE: retracts, $245.00] (VAILLY or INNOVATIVE)
30"   -   R/.049   FF   MARINA $5.00CDN
*[$22.00CDN]

Sea Fury
33½"   29"   .60   CL   MAN 5761 $12.50   (Boss)
*1980mm -   30cc   RC   SUNSHINE   DM499,90

Tempest
[ROBINAIRE: retracts, $245.00] (TOMEO)

30" *[$22.00CDN]	-	R/.049	FF	MARINA	$5.00CDN

Typhoon

30" *[$22.00CDN]	-	R/.049	FF	MARINA	$5.00CDN
72" [spinner, cowl, canopy, £28.00][UNITRACTS: retracts, £34.50]	-	.60	RC	TAYLOR	£12.00
123" [cowl, $40.00; canopy, $40.00][RHOM: retracts, $108.78]	-	5.5	6-8	MORFIS	$39.95

Royal Aircraft Factory

SE-5a

75"	-	.90/1.20	4	URAVITCH	$36.95

Short

Sunderland

180"	-	-	RC	ARGUS	FORTHCOMING

Sopwith

Camel
[ARGUS: cowl, £5.75] (Meier)
[HOLMAN: cowl, $40.00; wheels, $26.00] (REEVES)

22" *[$22.00CDN]	-	R/.049	FF	MARINA	$5.00CDN
*56"	-	.61	4	PROCTER	$149.95 (VK)

Swallow

60"	-	Elec	4	AIRDROME	$35.00

Tabloid

13"	-	R	FF	B²	$2.00 (Marsden)

Triplane

52"	-	.40	4	ARGUS RM354	£7.20 (Royle)

1½ Strutter

34"	25"	.02	FF	MAN 3793	$7.50 (Stroman)

Supermarine

Spiteful
[ARGUS: cowl, canopy, £4.95] (Bishop)

Spitfire

15"	14"	.049	CL	MAN 5701	$4.00	(Trostle)
*23"	-	R	FF	BELL K03	$22.95	
30"	-	R/.049	FF	MARINA	$5.00CDN	

*[$22.00CDN]

42"	-	Elec	3-4	ARGUS RC1564	£4.25	(Peacock)
96"	-	.90-3.0	4-5	FUN SCALE	$35.00	(Meister)

*[HANGAR: $280.00]

110"	-	.60	RC	HOLMAN	$45.00	(Reeves)

[spinner, cowl, canopy, $125.00]

ISRAEL

IAI

Lavi

*41"	65"	.61-.91F	5	J.D.	$280.00

ITALY

Aeritalia

C.222

4000mm	2800mm	1.2x2	13-17		SCARA	L185.000

Caproni

Ca-133

2350mm	1600mm	/7.5x3	RC	BENETTI	NA

Fiat

CR-32

2000mm	1650mm	ST3000	5-10	CELOT	L75.000

Macchi

MB-339

*1800mm	-	13cc	RC	MAURIZIO	NA

JAPAN

Kawanishi

K-8B
| 40" | 26" | R | FF | MAN 6812 | $11.50 | (Noonan) |

N1K1 Shiden-kai ("GEORGE")
[UNITRACTS: retracts, £34.50] (TAYLOR)

Kawasaki

Ki-100 Hien ("TONY")
| 30" | - | R/.049 | FF | MARINA | $5.00CDN |

*[$22.00CDN]

Kyushu

J7W1
| 30" | - | R/.049 | FF | MARINA | $5.00CDN |

*[$22.00CDN]

Mitsubishi

A6M Reisen ("ZERO")
[BARTON: retracts, $260.00] (YELLOW)
| 30" | - | R/.049 | FF | MARINA | $5.00CDN |

*[$22.00CDN]
| *50" | - | .25/.48 | 4-5 | SHACK 100804 | $230.00 | (EZ) |

J2M3 Raiden ("JACK")
| 30" | - | R/.049 | FF | MARINA | $5.00CDN |

*[$22.00CDN]

Nakajima

Ki-84 Hayate ("FRANK")
| 30" | - | R/.049 | FF | MARINA | $5.00CDN |

*[$22.00CDN]

Yokosuka

D4Y Suisei "JUDY")
| 30" | - | R/.049 | FF | MARINA | $5.00CDN |

*[$22.00CDN]

MXY-7 Oka ("BAKA")
| 18" | - | - | CL | POND 55A4 | $5.00 | (Leddy) |
| 24" | - | R/.049 | FF | MARINA | $5.00CDN | |

*[$22.00CDN]

SOVIET UNION

Ilyushin

IL-2
30"   -   R/.049   FF   MARINA $5.00CDN
*[$22.00CDN]

Lavochkin

La-5
30"   -   R/.049   FF   MARINA $5.00CDN
*[$22.00CDN]

MIG

Mig-15
*51"   48"   .91F   5-7 DCU $325.00

Nitikin-Shevchenko

IS-4
18"   -   R   FF   MAN 11812 $4.00   (Fineman)

Yakovlev

Yak-3
30"   -   R/.049   FF   MARINA $5.00CDN
*[$22.00CDN]

Yak-4
60½"   -   .15-.20x2 4   ARGUS RC1571 £5.75   (Statham)

Yak-9
42"   35"   .35   CL   MAN 3734 $10.50   (Felton)

SWEDEN

F.F.V.S.

J-22
30"   -   R/.049   FF   MARINA $5.00CDN
*[$22.00CDN]

SAAB

JAS-30 Gripen
1105mm   1930mm   .90F   5-10 GRAZIOLI   L80.000

UNITED STATES

Beechcraft

__C-45__
114"   -   Q35x2   4-6   ZIROLI $40.00
[cowls, $42.00; canopy, $15.00]

Bell

P-39 Airacobra
[UNITRACTS: retracts, £59.80] (TOP FLITE)
30"   -   R/.049   FF   MARINA $5.00CDN
*[$22.00CDN]

P-59A
30"   -   R/.049   FF   MARINA $5.00CDN
*[$22.00CDN]

Berliner-Joyce

OJ-2
*[G&R: $275.00] (HOLMAN)
[ABEL: landing gear, $50.00]

P-16
*[G&R: $275.00] (HOLMAN)
[ABEL: landing gear, $50.00]

Boeing

F4B-1
*[G&R: $250.00] (HOLMAN)
[ABEL: landing gear, $50.00]

B-47 Stratojet
54"   47"   .15x2   CL   MAN 5582 $9.00

Brewster

F2A Buffalo
27"   -   R   FF   MAN 10813 $6.00   (Midkiff)

Consolidated

PBY Catalina
30"   -   Elec   FF   FM CF-853 $8.50   (Flesher)

Culver

PQ-14 Drone
90"	57"	.70-.90	6	MORFIS	$39.95

Curtis

P-1 Falcon
22"	-	R/.049	FF	MARINA	$5.00CDN

*[$22.00CDN]

P-6E
*[G&R: $275.00] (HOSTETLER)

P-40
*[G&R: $245.00] (HOLMAN)
[LIKES: retracts, $300.00]

*23½"	-	R	FF	BELL K04	$22.95
30"	-	R/.049	FF	MARINA	$5.00CDN

*[$22.00CDN]

37¼"	-	.15	2	MORFIS	FORTHCOMING
*57"	-	.45/.90	4-5	INDY 20460	$279.00 (Lion)
*61"	-	.46/.90	5	GREAT	$299.95 (Hobbico)

SB-2
30"	-	R/.049	FF	MARINA	$5.00CDN

*[$22.00]

Douglas

A-1 Skyraider
*[G&R: $425.00] (HOLMAN)
[LIKES: retracts, $300.00]

30"	20"	.40	CL	MAN 2771	$5.00 (Martinez)
*90"	65"	ST3000	6	CUSTOM	$400.00

C-47 Skytrain
*?	-	2.5cc	CL	AURORA	NA

O-25
80"	-	.90	4	HOLMAN	$29.00 (Morse)

*[G&R: $275.00][ABEL: Landing gear, $50.00]

SBD Dauntless
73"	-	.60-.90	RC	HOLMAN	$19.95 (Walters)

Fairchild

A-10 Thunderbolt II
*72"	66"	.65x2F	6	RALPH	$895.00
*72"	65"	.77x2F	5-9	GLENNIS	$499.95

[brake system, $95.00]

C-82 Packet
*1700mm	-	2.5ccx2	CL	AURORA	NA

PT-19 Cornell (SA: 304)
*[G&R: $250.00] (HOSTETLER)
30"	-	R/.049	FF	MARINA	$5.00CDN

* [$22.00CDN]

Grumman

AF2 Guardian
33"	22½"	.60	CL	MAN 3742	$7.00 (Johnson)

F6F Hellcat
[BARTON: retracts, $275.00] (HOLMAN)
*[G&R: $275.00] (Mammoth)
[LIKES: retracts, $300.00]
30"	-	R/.049	FF	MARINA	$5.00CDN

* [$22.00CDN]

F8F Bearcat
[UNITRACTS: retracts, £34.50] (TOP FLITE)
[ROBINAIRE: retracts, $245.00] (ZIROLI)

F-14 Tomcat
**47"	74"	.91x2F	5	DCU	$325.00

[swing wing, $100.00]

TBM Avenger
30"	-	R/.049	FF	MARINA	$5.00CDN

* [$22.00]

Lockheed

C-69 Constellation
*1880mm	-	2.5ccx4	CL	AURORA	NA

F-117A Stealth Fighter
*30½"	46½"	.15-.25F	4	STARTECH	$170.00
*52"	79"	.50x2F	5-7	STARTECH	$700.00
*74"	113"	.91x2F	6-10	STARTECH	$1170.00

P-38 Lightning
[BARTON: retracts, $350.00] (YELLOW)

| 52" | 33" | .35x2 | CL | MAN 6652 | $10.00 | (Yearout) |

SR-71 Blackbird

*55½"	107"	.60x2F	6	STARTECH	$912.00	
*67½"	128"	.91x2F	6	STARTECH	$1418.00	
*83¾"	161"	.91x2F	6	STARTECH	$2770.00	

T-33

| *66" | - | ,60F | 5-6 | LEADING | $189.95 | |

YF-22A

| *51½" | 77" | .50x2F | 5-7 | STARTECH | $722.00 | |

Loening

M-8

| 34½" | 24" | .049 | FF | MAN 9701 | $8.00 | (Stark) |
| 98¾" | 72" | ST2000 | 4 | MORFIS | FORTHCOMING | |

Martin

B-10

| 53" | 33" | .35x2 | CL | MAN 1812 | $10.50 | (Hall) |

McDonnell-Douglas

F3H Demon

| 1020mm | 1460mm | .45F | RC | GRAZIOLI | L80.000 | |

F-15 Eagle (SA: 304)

| *33 | 57" | .40-.45 | 4 | COMBAT | $73.95 | |

North American

AT-6 Harvard
[UNITRACTS: retracts, £40.25] (TAYLOR)

60"	42"	.60	4-6	MAN 5702	$16.00	(Carkhuff)
84"	55"	ST2500	6	SMITH	$27.00	
101"	66"	Zen 62	6	SMITH	$30.00	

P-51A

| *23½" | - | R | FF | BELL K02 | $21.95 | |

P-51B
[UNITRACTS: retracts, £34.50] (TOP FLITE)

P-51D Mustang
[UNITRACTS: retracts, £36.80] (GAL/IP)

*23½"	–	R	FF	BELL K05	$22.95	
30"	–	R/.049	FF	MARINA	$5.00CDN	
*[$22.00]						
30½"	27"	.45	CL	MAN 8702	$9.00	(McCroskey)
36"	–	.049	2-4	RCM 645	$3.50	(Reese)
46½"	40"	.25-.35	CL	MAN 6681	$8.00	(Hudson)
*54"	–	.35-.50	4	MIDWEST	$99.95	
*57"	–	.40/.70	4-5	GREAT	$109.95	
69"	–	.60/.90	6	HOLMAN	$29.00	(Taylor)
[fuselage, $220.00]						
*1970mm	–	25cc	RC	SUNSHINE	DM495,	
86"	–	–	–	HOLMAN	$29.00	(Taylor)
*89"	77½"	1.0-1.8	6	PICA	$319.95	
[ROBINAIRE: retracts, $245.00]						
92"	–	Sachs 3.2	6	HOLMAN	FORTHCOMING	
*98"	84"	50cc	5	SKY	$800.00CDN	
100"	–	–	–	HOLMAN	$35.00	(Taylor)
100"	–	3.0	4-6	ZIROLI	$32.00	
[cowl, $42.00; canopy, $15.00]						

T-28 Trojan
*[G&R: $275.00] (HOLMAN)
[LIKES: retracts, $300.00]

Northrop

F-20 Tigershark

1050mm	1920mm	.65F	RC	GRAZIOLI	L80.000

P-61 Black Widow

*71"	–	.40-.60x2	RC	ROYAL	FORTHCOMING

YF-23A

*52"	81"	.50x2F	5-7	STARTECH	$723.00

Piper

L-3

30"	–	R/.049	FF	MARINA	$5.00CDN
*[$22.00CDN]					
*111"	73"	30-50cc	4	LAW	$549.99 (Roga)

Republic

P-47 Thunderbolt
[BARTON: retracts, $260.00] (YELLOW)
[ROBINAIRE: retracts, $245.00] (D&R)
[UNITRACTS: retracts, £34.50] (TOP FLITE)
[UNITRACTS: retracts, £36.80] (TAYLOR)

| 30" | - | R/.049 | FF | MARINA | $5.00CDN | |
| *[$22.00CDN] | | | | | | |

Ryan

FR-1 Fireball

| 41" | 31" | .35 | CL | MAN 9711 | $12.00 | (Felton) |

PT-20 (STA)

30"	-	R/.049	FF	MARINA	$5.00CDN	
*[$22.00CDN]						
72"	46"	.60-1.2	5	MAN 9713	$35.00	(Hester)
91"	67½"	1.5	5	MAN 5861	$32.00	(Fields)

Vought

F4U Corsair
[BARTON; retracts, $275.00] (HOLMAN)
[ROBINAIRE: retracts, $245.00] (D&R)

| 30" | - | R/.049 | FF | MARINA | $5.00CDN | |
| *[$22.00] | | | | | | |

Vultee

A-31 Vengeance

| 30" | - | R/.049 | FF | MARINA | $5.00CDN | |
| *[$22.00] | | | | | | |

BT-13 Valiant

| *73" | - | .60/1.20 | 4 | NOR CAL | $139.95 | |
| *91½" | 60" | ST3000 | 5 | BAKER | $300.00 | |

Waco

CG-4 Hadrian

| 100" | 76" | Glider | 4 | GAZZA 013 | L80.000 | |

PG-2

| 102" | 57½" | .29x2 | 4 | MAN 2722 | $23.00 | (Apoian) |

GLOBAL DIRECTORY

ABEL:

Abel Hobbies Mfg.
PO Box 22573
Billings, MT 59101 USA
(406)-259-4882

ACCU:

Accu-Scale
15486 Duke Lane
Chino Hills, CA 91709 USA
(714)-597-1966

ACE:

Ace R/C
116 W. 19th St.
Higginsville, MO 64037 USA
(816)-584-7121
CAT: $2.00

AERO:

Aero Graphics
PO Box 134
Hesperus, CO 81326 USA

AERO ERA:

Aero Era
5995 SW Glenbrook Rd.
Beaverton, OR 97005 USA

AERO PLANS:

Aero Plans and Parts
PO Box 939
Olean, NY 14760
(716)-372-7054

AERO SCALE:

Aero Scale
Toravig, Rowan's Hill Crescent
Stranraer DG9 OHL SCOTLAND
(0776)-2906
CAT: SASE

AERODROME:

Aerodrome Models, Ltd.
2623 S. Miller Rd.
Saginaw, MI 48603 USA
(517)-781-3000
CAT: $3.00

AERODYNE:

Aerodyne
603-B San Michel N.
Costa Mesa, CA 92627 USA
(714)-646-8864

AEROFAN:

Aerofan Model Aircraft
PO Box 47, Keilor
Victoria 3036 AUSTRALIA
(03)-336-3328
CAT: SASE

AEROMARINE:

Aeromarine Enterprises
547 West Myrna Lane
Chandler, AZ 85224 USA
(602)-821-9475

AERONAUTICA:

Aeronautica
Kettelerstr. 29
6750 Kaiserslautern GERMANY
(0631)-13453

AEROTECHNIQUE:

Aerotechnique
60 Moore St., Kingsley
Northampton NN2 7HX ENGLAND
(0604)-791355

AEROTEK:

Aerotek Model Engineering
Box 116
Lincolndale, NY 10540 USA

AHS:

A.H.S. Manufacturing
17 N. Main St.
Centerville, OH 45459 USA
(513)-433-0752

AIME:

Roger Aime
292, Boul. Clemenceau
13300 Salon FRANCE

AIR:

Air Designs
PO Box 55413
Indianapolis, IN 46205 USA
CAT: $3.00

AIR FLAIR:

Air Flair Mfg.
Box 11702
Kansas City, MO 64138 USA
(816)-353-7854

AIR MASTERS:

Air Masters
20026 Frazier Dr.
Rocky River, OH 44116 USA
(216)-331-5376

AIR SAIL:

Air Sail International, Ltd.
3 Prescott St, Penrose
Auckland 5 NEW ZEALAND
(64)-09-596-052

AIR WARS:

Air Wars
8931 Kittyhawk Ave.
Los Angeles, CA 90045 USA
(213)-670-1743

AIRBORNE:

Airborne Magazine
PO Box 30, Tullamarine
Victoria 3043 AUSTRALIA
(03)-338-5696

AIRDROME:

Airdrome
Box 1425, FDR Station
New York, NY 10150 USA

AIRSCREW:

Clark Airscrew
RR#4, Tottenham
Ontario LOG 1W0 CANADA
(416)-936-2131

AIRWORLD:

Airworld Modellbau
Birkenweg 6
6074 Rodermark/Ober-Roden GERMANY
(06074)-94155

AMERICA:

America's Hobby Center
146 W. 22nd St.
New York, NY 10011-2466 USA
(212)-675-8922

AMERICAN:

American Sailplane Designs
2626 Coronado Ave. #89
San Diego, CA 92154 USA
(619)-575-5133

AMS:

AMS Imports
1110 S. Wells Ave.
Reno, NV 89502 USA
(702)-786-7733

AMZ:

AMZ
Im Strasser Feld 29
5120 Herzogenrath GERMANY
(02406)-5952

ALFERY:

Antonin Alfery
Maratice 876
686 01 Uherske Hradiste
CZECHOSLOVAKIA

ARGUS:

Argus Specialist Publications
Argus House, Boundary Way
Hemel Hempstead, Hertfordshire
HP2 7ST ENGLAND
(0442)-66551
CAT: £2.00
SA: AEROFAN, CRAFT, HOLMAN,
LUPPERGER, PEGASUS, PHOTO

ARISTO:

Aristocraft/Polk Hobbies
346 Bergen Ave.
Jersey City, NY 07304 USA
(201)-332-8100

ARONSTEIN:

Laura Schultz
2216 O St. NE #C
Augurn, WA 98002 USA
CAT: $2.00

ART:

Model Art
2-8-3 chome, Iidabashi
Chiyoda-ku, Tokto 102 JAPAN
(03)-262-6450

ATEM:

ATEM
31, rue Gambetta
Rambouillet, FRANCE
(3483)-8146

AURORA:

Aurora Model Mfg.
15, Shakespeare Sarani
Calcutta 700 71 INDIA
(44)-9917

AUTHENTIC:

Authentic Scale
238, King's Dr., Eastbourne
East Sussex BN21 2XE ENGLAND
CAT: SASE

AVALON:

Avalon Model Imports
Church St., Upton Noble
Shepton Mallet, Somerset BA4 6A5
ENGLAND
(0749)-85706

AVCO:

Avco Model Supplies
205 Gulf Bank
Houston, TX 77037 USA
(713)-448-4244

AVONDS:

Philip Avonds Scale Jets
Dorpstraat 18
B-8458 Koksijde BELGIUM
(058)-512097
SA: BERTELLA

B²:

B² Streamlines
PO Box 976
Olalla, WA 98359-0976 USA
CAT: $1.00

BAC:

B.A.C.
PO Box 520
Nipomo, CA 93444 USA
(805)-929-5647

BAKER:

Bert Baker
11023 38th Dr. SE
Everett, WA 98208 USA
(206)-337-0868

BALSA:

Balsa USA
PO Box 164
Marinette, WS 54143 USA
(906)-863-6421

BARRON:

Barron's Scale Classics
11506 Ohio Ave.
Youngtown, OH 85363 USA
(602)-933-6911
CAT: $1.00

BARTON:

E. Barton Machinery
11640 Salinaz
Garden Grove, CA 92643 USA
(714)-539-9142

BATES:

Jerry L. Bates
102 Glenwood St.
Mobile, AL 36606 USA

BAUER:

Bauer Modelle
Neumarketerstr. 28
8501 Allerberg GERMANY
(09176)-5454
SA: AMS, BERTELLA, SPORT

B&D:

B&D Models
PO Box 12518
Reno, NV 89510 USA

BEAULIEU:

M.C. Beaulieu Plan Service
84 University St.
Presque Isle, ME 04769 USA
(207)-768-3471

BECK:

Beck Flugmodell
Friedrichstr. 3
7435 Hulbon GERMANY
(07125)-5358

BECKER:

Hannelore Becker
Marienwig 21
5510 Saarburg GERMANY
(06581)-3823

BEHRENS:

Jerry Behrens
31-27 Healy Ave.
Far Rockaway, NY 11691 USA
(718)-337-6987

BELL:

Bell Model Aircraft
650 Pinecrest Dr.
Key Largo, FL 34640 USA
(813)-584-4003
CAT: $2.00

BENETTI:

Tonino Benetti
Viale dei Mille, 3
20129 Milano ITALY
(02)-742-4511

BENTOM:

See: AMERICA, PENN

BERTELLA:

G. Bertella
Via Matteotti, 248
Gardone VT 25063 Brescia ITALY
(030)-831863

BETTINI:

Modellismo Bettini G.
Via Nazionale, 16
40067 Rastignano, Bologna ITALY
(051)-011-39-51

BLAIR:

John Blair
PO Box 87
Warne, NC 28909 USA

BOSAK:

Pavel Bosak
Zahradni 731/111
Domazlicke predmesti
339 01 Klatovy CZECHOSLOVAKIA
(42)-0186-3642

BOSMAN:

Len Bosman
193 Baltic St.
Coquitlam, BC V3K 5G9 CANADA

BOWMAN:

Bowman Model Kits
Loxbeare Garage, Rackenford Rd.
Devon EX16 4LL ENGLAND
(0884)-258894

BRABEC:

Brabec Modelle
Fitcheweg 3
2752 Wollersdorf AUSTRIA
(02622)-515335
SA: SPORT

BRADSHAW:

Martin D. Bradshaw
PO Box 761
Placitas, NM 87043 USA
(505)-867-5942

BRYANT:

Dennis Bryant
21, Manor Close, Burgess Hill
West Sussex RH15 0NN ENGLAND
(04446)-48054

BUCKLE:

Ben Buckle Old Time Plan Service
9 Islay Crescent, Highworth
Wiltshire SN6 7HL ENGLAND
(0793)-764017
SA: AMZ, IRVINE, LOBBY, VOLZ

BYRON:

Byron Originals
PO Box 279
Ida Grove, IA 51445 USA
(712)-364-3165
CAT: $3.00

CARPENTER:

John Carpenter
26 Windsor Road, Harrow Weald, Harrow
Middlesex HA3 5PX ENGLAND
(0186)-3396

CBA:

C.B.A.
1620 N. Leavitt Rd. NW
Warren, OH 44485 USA
(216)-898-2781

CEADARBRIDGE:

Ceadarbridge Scale
RR4, Creemore
Ontario L0M 1G0 CANADA
(705)-466-2186

CELOT:

Alberto Celot
Via Tiepolo, 12
31015 Conegliano (TV) ITALY
(0438)-63300

CENTURY:

Century Jet Models
8305 Regency Woods Way
Louisville, KY 40220 USA
(502)-491-4114

or

Century Jet Models
8 Martha Crt.
Sumter, SC 29150 USA
(803)-775-6491

CFI:

CFI R/C Supply
9186 Hall Road
Lakeland, FL 33805 USA

CHAMP:

Air Champ
2854 NW 79th Ave.
Miami, FL 33122 USA
(305)-447-4365

CHARLIE:

Charlie Smith Plans
9043 Fair Way Blvd.
Sunlakes, AZ 85248 USA
(602)-895-8745
CAT: SASE

CHART:

Chart Hobby Distributors, Ltd.
Chart House, Station Road
East Preston, Little Hampton
West Sussex BN16 3AG ENGLAND
(0903)-773170
CAT: £2.00

CHILTERN:

Chiltern Models
5 Beechwood Ave., New Milton
Hants BH25 5NB ENGLAND
(0425)-614809
CAT: SASE

CLARK:

Toni Clark Practical Scale
Holzhauerstr. 1
4990 Lubbecke 3 GERMANY
(05741)-61792

CLASSIC:

Classic Glass
PO Box 503
Blackfoot, ID 83221-0503 USA
(208)-785-2309

CLEVE:

Cleveland Model & Supply Company
10307 Detroit Ave.
Cleveland, OH 44102 USA
(216)-961-3600
CAT: $2.00

CLIFF:

Cliff Hangar Models
PO Box 9081
Torrance, CA 90508 USA

CLOUD:

Cloudbusters
PO Box 517
Allen Park, MI 48101 USA

COCKER:

Simon Cocker
67 Peel St., Maccles Field
Cheshire SK11 8BL ENGLAND
(0625)-613382

CODDING:

Gordon Codding
3724 John L. Ave.
Kingman, AZ 86401 USA
CAT: $3.00

COLE:

Cole Aviation Services
1312 NE 35th St.
Ocala, FL 32670 USA
CAT: SASE

COLLINS:

R.G. Collins
22 Learmouth Grove
Edinburgh EH3 1BW SCOTLAND
SA: B^2

COMBAT:

Combat Models
8535 Arjons Dr. Suite K
Miramar, CA 92126 USA
(619)-536-9922

COMET:

Comet Industries Corp.
3630 S. Iron St.
Chicago, IL 60609 USA
(312)-927-1900
SA: AMERICA, PENN

CONCEPT:

Concept Models
2906 Grandview Blvd.
Madison, WS 53713 USA

CONSOLIDATED:

Consolidated Models
2925 Golf Rd.
Turlock, CA 95380 USA
(209)-668-4505

CONWAY:

R.A. Conway
51 The Glebe
Kirkliston EN29 9AT SCOTLAND
SA: B²

COOP:

Coop Aero
34, rue de la Dandinerie
79240 L'Absie B.P.8 FRANCE
(49)-95-89-03
SA: JAMARA

CORK:

Justin Cork
19 Cedar Dr., Caledon
Ontario LON 1CO CANADA
(519)-927-5912

COX:

Cox Hobbies
350 W. Rincon St.
Corona, CA 91720 USA
(714)-278-1282

CRAFT:

Scale Craft
PO Box 570
Sunbury 3429 AUSTRALIA
(03)-744-1196
CAT: $3.00

CRESS:

Cressline Model Products
N2147 Pine Beach Rd. N
Oostberg, WI 53070 USA
(414)-564-3619
CAT: $2.00
SA: AVONDS

CUCCOLO:

Cuccolo Aeromodelli
Via Nazionale 110/A
Stanghella (PD) ITALY
(0425)-95766

CUSTOM:

Custom R/C Aircraft
1140 Civic Center Dr.
Rohnert Park, CA 94928 USA
(707)-584-9446
CAT: $4.00

DALESMAN:

Dalesman Wings
58 St. George St., Saltare, Shipley
W. Yorks BD18 4PL ENGLAND
(0274)-594428

DATA:

Aircraft Data
Box 763576
Dallas, TX 75224 USA

DAVEY:

Davey Systems Corporation
675 Tower Lane
West Chester, PA 19380 USA
(215)-430-8645

DB:

D.B. Models
3 East St., Irchester
Northants NN9 7BG ENGLAND
(0933)-312309
CAT: 50p

DCU:

DCU
1556 S. Anaheim, Unit C
Anaheim, CA 92805 USA
(714)-535-6969

DIELS:

Diels Engineering, Inc.
PO Box 101
Woodville, OH 43469 USA
CAT: $1.00
SA: FLY-ME

DI MUZIO:

Raffaele Di Muzio
C. so. Marrucino, 188
66100 Chieti ITALY
(0871)-64934

DINSTBIER:

Steve Dinstbier
1159 W. Taft Rd.
St. Johns, MI 48879 USA

DIVELY:

Bob Dively Model Aircraft
28001 Chagrin Blvd. Suite 206
Woodmere, OH 44122 USA
(216)-292-6926

DOGFIGHTER:

Dogfighter Scale Model A/S
Semsvn. 60
N-3670 Notodden NORWAY
(4736)-14567

DP:

D.P. Systems
1842 Tattenhall
Houston, TX 77008 USA
(713)-999-6640
CAT: $2.00

D&R:

D&R Aircraft Mfg.
418 St. Andrew St.
Gonzalez, TX 78629 USA
(512)-672-7023

DRAGON:

Dragon Models
208 Q Redwither Complex
Wrexham Industrial Estate
Clwyd LL13 9UM ENGLAND
(0798)-660486

DRY:

Dry Ridge Models
59 McCurry Rd.
Weaverville, NC 28787 USA
(704)-658-2663

DUBOIS:

Gene Dubois
PO Box C
Acushnet, MA 02743 USA
(508)-995-7609
CAT: $1.00

DUEBI:

Duebi Model S.r.l.
Via Tiglio, 431
55061 S. Leonardo in Trepenzio
Capannori (LU) ITALY
(0583)-90262
SA: ROD ENDS

DYNA:

Dynaflite
PO Box 1011
San Marcos, CA 92069 USA
(619)-744-9605

EASY:

Easy Built Models
Box 1059, Beamsville
Ontario LOR 1BO CANADA
(416)-563-5582

ENGEL:

Engel Modellbau
7134 Knittlingen GERMANY
(07043)-3211

ENT:

Hobby Enterprises
PO Box 784
Fruitland Park, FL 34731 USA
(904)-787-7475

FAN:

Fanjets
39/40 Portsmouth Rd.
Guildford, Surrey ENGLAND
(0483)-573012

FANTINI:

Giuseppe Fantini
Via G. Daneo, N31/16
16144 Genova ITALY
(010)-823051

FARNS:

Farnsworth & Elroy, Inc.
1836 Stout Dr.
Warminister, PA 18974 USA
(215)-675-9882
CAT: $1.00

FGM:

Fiberglass Master, Inc.
Rte. 1, Box 530
Goodview, VA 24095 USA
(703)-890-6017
CAT: $1.00

FIKE:

Scale Flight Model Airplane Co.
1219 S. Washington St.
Bloomington, IN 47401 USA
(812)-339-8274

FILLON:

Emmanuel Fillon
60, rue du Bocage
83700 Saint Raphael FRANCE
(94)-95-6206

FLAIR:

Flair
Holcroft Works, High St.
Blunsdon, Swindon, Wilts
SN2 4AH ENGLAND
(0793)-721303
CAT: £2.00
SA: JAMARA, SPEAR

FLITECRAFT:

Flitecraft Designs
The Roost, Stanboroughbury
Welwyn, Garden City, Herts
AL8 7XA ENGLAND
(0289)-86278
SA: VOLZ

FLY-ME:

Fly-Me Models
6 Hillston Close, Colchester
Essex CO2 8XP ENGLAND

FLY T:

Flying T Model Co.
2862 Avenel St.
Los Angeles, CA 90039
(213)-662-9323
CAT: SASE
SA: VELIVOLI

FLYLINE:

Flyline Models, Inc.
10643 Ashby Place
Fairfax, VA 22031 USA
(703)-273-9593
CAT: 50¢

FM:

Flying Models
PO Box 700
Newton, NJ 07860-0700 USA
(201)-383-3355
CAT: $2.00

FSI:

Flying Scale, Inc.
1905 Colony Rd.
Metairie, LA 70003 USA
(504)-241-5154
CAT: SASE

FOAM:

Foam Scale Models
Box 662
St. Croix, WI 54024 USA
CAT: $1.00

FOLINE:

Jim Foline
8502 Everglade Dr.
Sacremento, CA 95816 USA
(916)-383-0951

FRANK:

Frank's Aero Model Plan Service
PO Box 20124
Dayton, OH 45420 USA

FUN SCALE:

Fun Scale
220-65 Camino Corto
Vista, CA 92083 USA
(619)-726-0154

FUTABA:

Futaba Corporation of America
4 Studebaker Ave.
Irvine, CA 92718 USA
(714)-455-9888

GAGER:

Gager Aircraft Sales
8425 Auburn Rd.
Fort Wayne, IN 46825 USA
(219)-489-5060

GAL/IP:

Galaxy Models & Hobbies
160 Felixstowe Rd.
Ipswich IP3 8EF ENGLAND
(0473)-729279
CAT: £1.50

GAL/NOR:

Galaxy Models
88 Catton Grove Rd.
Norwich NR3 3AA ENGLAND
(0603)-419515

GARMHAUSEN:

R.C. Garmhausen
2715 Maple St. SE
Canton, OH 44714 USA
(216)-456-9340

GAZZA:

Giorgio Gazza
Via Losanna, 6
20154 Milano ITALY

GEE BEE:

Gee Bee Products
PO Box 18
East Longmeadow, MA 01028 USA

GLASCO:

Glasco Aircraft
72 S. 500 West
Bountiful, UT 84010 USA
(801)-295-1382

GLASCRAFT:

J.M. Glascraft
30820 Mayflower
Roseville, MI 48066 USA
(313)-773-7069

GLEASON:

Gleason Enterprises
1106 10th Dr. SE
Austin, MN 55912 USA
(507)-437-3781
CAT: $4.00

GLEICHAUF:

Rolf Gleichauf
Zeppelinstr. 12-14
D7710 Donaueschingen GERMANY
(0771)-5047
SA: AVONDS, ROBBE, SPORT

GLENNIS:

Glennis Aircraft
5528 Arboga Rd.
Linda, CA 95901 USA
(916)-742-3957

GLOBAL:

Global Hobby Distributors
18480 Bandilier Circle
Fountain Valley, CA 92728 USA
(714)-963-0133

GLIDELINE:

Glideline
228 Windsor Dr.
San Carlos, CA 94070 USA

GM:

G.M. Plastics
7252 Industrial Park Dr.
Mentor, OH 44060 USA
(216)-953-1188

G.M.:

G.M. Modellflugtechnik
D-4923 Extertal-Bremke
GERMANY
(05754)-1506

GODFREY:

Don Godfrey
91 Blackstone Ave.
Binghamton, NY 13903 USA
(607)-724-5306

GOLDBERG:

Carl Goldberg Models
4734 W. Chicago Ave.
Chicago, IL 60651 USA
(312)-626-9550

GOLDEN:

Golden Age Era Plans
PO Box 471
Wichita Falls, TX 76307 USA
CAT: SASE

GOLDEN ERA:

Golden Era Model Service
918 3rd St.
Woodland, CA 95695 USA
(916)-662-3698
CAT: SASE

GORDON:

Larry Gordon
703 S. Oak St.
Fenton, MI 48430 USA
(313)-629-5788

G&P:

G&P Sales
410 College Ave.
Angwin, CA 94508 USA
(708)-965-3866

G&R:

G&R Manufacturing
1207 Estates Way
Pooler, GA 31322 USA
(912)-748-6685

GRAUPNER:

Johannes Graupner
Henriettastr. 94-96 Postfach 1242
D-7312 Kirchheim-Teck GERMANY
(07021)-45232
SA: LOBBY

GRAZIOLI:

Umberto Grazioli
Via Brescia 133/1
Modena ITALY
(059)-300302

GREAT:

Great Planes
PO Box 788
Urbana, IL 61801 USA
(217)-398-3630

GREEN:

R.M. Green
57A Long Lane
Newtown, Great Wyrley
Walsall WS6 6AT ENGLAND
(0922)-409-759

GREGA:

John W. Grega
355 Grand Blvd.
Bedford, OH 44146 USA
CAT: $2.00

GUILLOW:

Paul K. Guillow
PO Box 229
Wakefield, MA 01880 USA
(617)-245-5255

GULF:

Mike Midkiff
20007 Pinehurst Trail
Humble, TX 77346 USA
(713)-876-0002

HANGAR:

Hangar One Manufacturing
1402 Madison Ave.
Montgomery, AL 36107 USA
(205)-262-8235

HANNAN:

Hannan's Runway
Box 210
Magalia, CA 95954 USA
CAT: $2.00

HAREL:

Josh Harel
286 Hawthorne Ave.
Derby, CT 06418 USA
(203)-732-0532

HAUGHT:

Haught Graphics
Rt. 1, Box 978
Munising, MI 49862

HAWE:

Hawe Modelltechnik
Schutzenstr. 39
5010 Bergheim GERMANY
(02271)-42426

HIROBO:

Hirobo, Ltd.
530-214 Motoyama-cho
Fuchu-shi, Hiroshima ₸726 JAPAN
(81)-0847-41-7400
SA: FUTABA

HO:

HO Accazero
Via Milano, 3
34132 Trieste ITALY
(040)-65860

HOBBY BARN:

Hobby Barn
PO Box 17856
Tucson, AZ 85731 USA
(602)-747-3633

HOLMAN:

Bob Holman Plans
PO Box 741
San Bernadino, CA 92402 USA
(714)-885-3959

HOMEWOOD:

Gordon Homewood
69A Vogel St.
Cambridge NEW ZEALAND

HORN:

Hobby Horn
PO Box 2212
Westminister, CA 92683 USA
(714)-893-8311
CAT: $2.00

HOSTETLER:

Wendell Hostetler
1041 Heatherwood Lane
Orrville, OH 44667 USA
(216)-682-8896
CAT: SASE

HOUSE:

House of Balsa
20134 State Rd.
Cerritos, CA 90701 USA
(213)-860-1276

HULME:

J.A. Hulme
52 Mountway, Waverton
Chester CH3 7QF ENGLAND
(0244)-336472
SA: B²

HUNT:

Allen Hunt
PO Box 7656
Charleston, WV 25356 USA
(304)-776-4949

HUTSON:

Duncan Hutson
33 Hartleburyway, Charlton Kings
Cheltenham, Gloschester GL52 6YB
ENGLAND
(0242)-572451
CAT: 50p
SA: CRAFT

IHC:

International Hobby Center
350 Tioga St.
Philadelphia, PA 19134 USA
(215)-426-2873

IKON:

Ikon N'wst
PO Box 306
Post Falls, ID 83854 USA
(208)-773-9001
CAT: $3.00

IKUTA:

Ikuta Musen Hikohki
2341-31 Sakurasawa Oaza
Yorimachi, Osatogun, Saitama
JAPAN 369-12
(485)-81-1633

IMPACT:

Impact Engineering
2100 Stonehill Crt.
Arlington, TX 76012 USA
(817)-261-8130

INDY:

Indy R/C Sales
10620 N. College Ave.
Indianapolis, IN 46280 USA
(800)-338-4639

INNOVATIVE:

Innovative Models
PO Box 4365
Margate, FL 33063 USA
(305)-971-8330

or

Innovative Models
PO Box 595
Lebanon, TX 37087 USA
(615)-444-1371

IRVINE:

Irvine Engines
Unit 2, Brunswick Industrial Park
Brunswick Way, New Southgate
London N11 1JL ENGLAND

JACKSON:

Ralph Jackson
21 Holiday Hill
Endicott, NY 13760 USA
(607)-748-1707

JAMARA:

Jamara Modelltechnik
Altmannshofen 76
7971 Aichstetten GERMANY
(07565)-1856

JANSSENS:

Paul Janssens
Gasthuisstraat 29
2440 Geel BELGIUM
(74)-589783

JD:

J.D.'S Scale Models
317 Jonquil Ave.
Fort Walton Beach, FL 32548 USA
(904)-863-2642

J.D.:

J.D. Models
PO Box 386
Pacifica, CA 94044 USA
(415)-359-0406

JET AGE:

Jet Age Models
5428 Bushnell
Riverside, CA 92505 USA
(714)-687-3836

JET MODEL:

Jet Model Products
304 Silvertop
Raymore, MO 64083 USA
(816)-331-0356

JETLINE:

Jetline Modelle
Stolbergstr. 14
6239 Eppstein GERMANY
(06198)-2924

JHH:

Jet Hangar Hobbies
12130 G Carson
Hawiian Gardens, CA 90716 USA
(213)-429-1244
SA: AVONDS, MILTON, SPORT

JIM:

Jim n' I Jets
2754 Canterbury Dr.
Santa Rosa, CA 95405 USA
(707)-544-6040

JM:

J.M. Innovations
9 Pindari St., Rochedale
Queensland 4123 AUSTRALIA
(07)-3419440

JVS:

JVS Plans
5017 NW 61st St.
Oklahoma City, OK 73122 USA

K-BEE:

K-Bee's Models
1266 Settlers Circle East
Cottonwood, AZ 86326 USA
(800)-456-3107

KEIL:

Amerang
Commerce Way, Lancing
Sussex BN15 8TE ENGLAND
(0903)-752866

KINDLER:

Kindler Modellbau
Marktgasse 3
CH-4904 Niederbipp SWITZERLAND
(065)-731011

KIP:

Kip Marketing
33 Yorke Gardens, Reigate
RH2 9HQ ENGLAND
(07372)-49365

KLARICH:

Klarich Custom Kits
2301 Sonata Dr.
Rancho Cordova, CA 95670 USA
(916)-635-4588
CAT: SASE

KNIGHTS:

Sky Corp
Box 537, RD2
Hampton, NJ 08827 USA
(908)-537-7323

KOEHLER:

Koehler Aero Lab
PO Box 33
Durham, CA 95938 USA
(916)-893-3829

KOUTNY:

Lubomir Koutny
Zahrebska 33
616 00 Brno CZECHOSLOVAKIA
SA: WOODHOUSE

KRAFTERS:

Air Krafters
1042 Honeytree
San Antonio, TX 78245 USA

KRANZ:

Werner Kranz
Friedrichstr. 30
4620 Castrop-Rauxel GERMANY
(02305)-73459

KRESS:

Kress Jets
4308 Ulster Landing
Saugerties, NY 12477 USA
(914)-336-8149

KRICK:

Klaus Krick Modelltechnik
Industriestr. 1, Postfach 24
D-7134 Knittlingen GERMANY
(07043)-3067
SA: CHART, LOBBY, SPORT

KUHLMANN:

Kuhlmann Modellbau
Wilhelmstr. 29
4600 Dortmund 1 GERMANY
(0231)-144990

KYOSHO:

Kyosho
153 Nagakecho, Funako-nagacho
Atsugi, Kanagawa 243 JAPAN
SA: GREAT PLANES

KYOTO:

Kyoto RC Tsujimura
269 Hanayacho-agatu
Abutakoji Shimogyoku Kyotoshi
Kyoto 600 JAPAN

LAMBERT:

S.A. Lambert
2200 W. Cornwallis Dr #308
Greensboro, NC 27408 USA
(919)-288-2944
CAT: SASE

LAW:

L.A.W. Racing Products
1229 Capitol Dr.
Addison, IL 60101 USA
(708)-543-2030

LEADING:

Leading Edge Models
170 Oval Dr.
Central Islip, NY 11722 USA
(516)-234-7264

LE GUENNOU:

R. Le Guennou
Chemins Du Tour de L'etang
13800 Istres FRANCE

LEE:

Lee's Hobbies
1342 La Bella Ave.
Sunnyvale, CA 94087 USA

LEICESTER:

South Yorks Model Supplies
Unit 1A, Sandtoft Industry Estate
Belton, North Doncaster
South Yorks DN9 1PN ENGLAND
(0427)-872251

LIDBERG:

A.A. Lidberg
614 E. Fordham
Tempe, AZ 85283 USA
CAT: $1,00
SA: FLY-ME

LIKES:

Hank Likes
1601 Airport Dr.
Mechanicsburg, PA 17055 USA
(717)-732-0636

LOHMANN:

Harald Lohmann
Wagnerstr. 5
3057 Neustadt 1 GERMANY
(05032)-2646

LOBBY:

Hobby Lobby
5614 Franklin Pike Circle
Brentwood, TN 37027 USA
(615)-373-1444
CAT: $1.00

LUPPERGER:

J.M. Lupperger Plans
1304 Palm Ave.
Huntington Beach, CA 92648 USA
(714)-536-4973
CAT: $4.00

MA:

Model Aviation Plan Service
1810 Samuel Morse Dr.
Reston, VA 22090 USA
(704)-435-0760
CAT: SASE

MAC:

Mac McJunkin
3859 Wayne Crt.
Riverside, CA 92504 USA

MACBRIEN:

Doug MacBrien
24 Truby St.
Granby, MA 01033 USA
(413)-467-7971

MACE:

Mace Model Aircraft
359 S. 119th East Ave.
Tulsa, OK 74128 USA
(918)-437-5490
CAT: $1.50

MACKINDER:

R.H. Mackinder
68 Riverside Rd., Newark
Notts NG24 4RJ ENGLAND
(06360)-77952

MAGER:

Rudolf Mager
Giechkrottendorferstr. 57
8628 Weismain GERMANY
(09575)-570

MAHKORN:

Tillmann Mahkorn
Obervolbach 8
5060 Bergisch-Gladbach 1 GERMANY

MALLORY:

Mallory Models
1104 Gatewood Dr.
Alexandria, VA 22307 USA
(703)-765-0041

MAN:

Model Airplane News Plan Service
251 Danbury Rd.
Wilton, CT 06897 USA
(203)-834-2900
CAT: $2.00

MARINA:

Marina Air Models
2939 Fairlea Cr. #26
Ottawa, Ontario K1V 8V9 CANADA
CAT: $2.00

MARTIN:

Daniel Martin
87 Honeyball Walk, Teynham
Sittingbourne, Kent ME9 9TN ENGLA
(0795)-522144

MARUTAKA:

Marutaka RC Models
20-17, Showa-cho, Higashi
Osaka City, Osaka 579 JAPAN
(0729)-82-0003
SA: ROYAL, SPORT, TOWER

MASSEY:

Pat Massey
1125 Charles St.
Pampa, TX 79065 USA

MASTER:

Masterfly
Via Zeni 8
38068 Rovereto,(TN) ITALY
(0464)-443215

MAURIZIO:

Maurizio Modena
Lungo Stura Lazio, 185
10156 Torino ITALY
(011)-2731896

MAX:

Max Merckenschlager
Sieglgut 33d
8390 Passau GERMANY
(0851)-41110

MB:

Model Builder Plan Service
898 W. 16th St.
Newport Beach, CA 92663 USA
(714)-645-8830
CAT: SASE

MESSER:

Jim Messer Model Products
Valleyview Dr., Box 43
Allegany, NY 14706 USA
(716)-372-8408

METCALFE:

Howard Metcalfe Models
Brook Cottage Section
Wintershill, Durley
Southampton SO3 2AH ENGLAND
(04896)-447
CAT: SASE

MICRO-X:

Micro-X
PO Box 1063
Lorain, OH 44055 USA
(216)-282-8354
CAT: $1.50

MIDWEST:

Midwest Model Products
400 S. Indiana St.
Hobart, IN 46342 USA
(219)-942-1134

MIKE:

Mike's Models
4245 N.W. 11th Ave.
Sunrise, FL 33323 USA
(305)-748-5047

MIKKELSON:

Mik Mikkelson
2249 Cheremoya Ave.
Hollywood, CA 90068 USA

MILLER:

Vince Miller Designs
130 Yucca Dr.
Sedona, AZ 86336 USA
(602)-282-4810

MILTON:

Milton Imports
4 Minton Close, Blakelands
Milton Keyes MK14 5JB ENGLAND
(0908)-617470

MINGUS:

Mingus Mountain Models
PO Box 1592
Cottonwood, AZ 86326 USA
(602)-634-5650

MIZER:

Frank S. Mizer
4317 Coe Ave.
North Olmstead, OH 44070 USA
(216)-777-1045

MODEL:

Model Design
18 Bleby Court, Para Hills West
South Australia 5096 AUSTRALIA
(08)-262-3041
CAT: $2.00

MODELA:

Modela
Holeckova 9
150 00 Praha 5 CZECHOSLOVAKIA
548859

MODELAIR:

Modelair
PO Box 9132
New Market, NEW ZEALAND

MODELE:

Modele Magazine
15/17 quai de l'Oise
75019 Paris FRANCE
(40)-34-22-07

MODELHOB:

Modelhob
Grafito, 33
28850 Torrejon de Ardoz
Madrid SPAIN
(91)-675-0144
SA: AMZ, CHART

MODELL:

Modell
Neckar-Verlag GmbH
Postfach 1820, Klosterring 1
7730 Villingen-Schwenningen
GERMANY
(07721)-51021

MODELLE:

RC Modelle
Grundstr. 40
7022 Leinfelden-Echterdingen 3
GERMANY

MODELLTECHNIK:

Jet Modelltechnik
Stauffenbergsrt. 18
6050 Offenbach/Main GERMANY
(06985)-6474

MODULO:

Modulo
S. Petronio Vecchio 40/2
40125 Bologna ITALY
(051)-390731

MOONEY:

Walt Mooney
PO Box 231192
San Diego, CA 92123 USA
SA: SAMS

MORFIS:

Gus Morfis
4709 Green Meadows Ave.
Torrance, CA 90505-5507 USA
(213)-378-5679

MORGAN:

Sid Morgan Plans
13157 Ormond Dr.
Bellville, MI 48111 USA
CAT: $1.00

MORI:

Mori Sangyo, RC Dept.
5 Heiwadai Komaba, Koto-gun
Hokkaido 080-05 JAPAN
(0155)-44-2945

MRA:

Le Modele reduit D'Avion
12, rue Mulet
69001 Lyon FRANCE
(78)-273051
SA: KIP

MRC:

Model Rectifier Corporation
PO Box 267, 2500 Woodbridge Ave.
Edison, NJ 08817
(201)-248-0440

MUDER:

Muder Modellbau
Offenbornstr. 1
5970 Pletlenberg 1 GERMANY
(02391-3807)

MURPHY:

John T. Murphy
29 Cheryl Dr.
Allenstown, NH 03275 USA
(603)-485-5352

NFFS:

National Free Flight Society
10115 Newbold Dr.
St. Louis, MO 63137 USA

NICETTO:

Roberto Nicetto
Via Bologna, 36
35020 Ponte S. Nicolo (PD) ITALY
(049)-717501

NICHOLLS:

Henry J. Nicholls
308 Holloway Rd.
London N7 6NP ENGLAND
(6074272)-2961

NIMBUS:

Nimbus Models
Edwards Yard, Horden
Peterlee, Co. Durham SR8 4QJ
ENGLAND
(091)-586-9315

NOR CAL:

Nor-Cal Aero
20984 Dorothy Lane
Redding, CA 96003 USA
(916)-275-4195

NORTHCRAFT:

Northcraft Hobby Products
115 Industrial Dr., Box 419
Carleton Place, Ontario K7C 3P5
CANADA
(613)-257-7722

NOSEN:

A&A Industries
Highway 60 North
Sibley, IA 51249 USA
(712)-754-3930
CAT: $2.00

NOWLEN:

Nowlen Kits
139 Boardwalk
Greenbrae, CA 94904 USA
CAT: 50¢

NZ:

New Zealand Aero Products
34 Ward Parade, Stirling Point
Bluff, South Island NEW ZEALAND

OK:

OK Model Company Ltd.
3-11,3-chome
Yokonuma, Higashi-Osaka 577
JAPAN
SA: AIRWORLD, SPORT

OLD:

Old Timer Model Supply
PO Box 7334
Van Nuys, CA 91409 USA
CAT: $2.00

ORIGINAL:

Original Plans
17 Lucas Close, Yately, Camberly
Surrey GU17 7JD ENGLAND
CAT: £1.00

PAI:

Paper Airplanes International
433 Nihoa St.
Kahului, HI 96732 USA
(808)-244-4667
CAT: $7.50

PALADINE:

Paladine Communications
10721 64th Ave. N
Seminole, FL 34642 USA
CAT: $2.00

PAPER:

Flying Paper Scale
PO Box 274
Glen Ellyn, IL 60138 USA
(312)-858-2434

PARKINSON:

Bob Parkinson Flying Models
Box 856, 11th and 25th, RR#1
Stroud, Ontario LOL 2MO CANADA
(705)-436-7041
SA: MILTON

PARRISH:

Parrish Aircraft
1125 SW 49th Terrace
Plantation, FL 33317 USA
(305)-581-4477

PARSONS:

Dan Parsons Products
11809 Fulmer Dr. NE
Albuquerque, NM 87111 USA
(505)-296-2353

PASMCO:

Pasmco Plan Service
25260 153rd SE
Kent, WA 98042 USA
(206)-631-1667
CAT: $2.00

PAUL:

Paul's Flying Stuff
PO Box 121
Escondido, CA 92025 USA
(619)-743-5458

PB:

P.B. Modelisme
B.P. 1435
51066 Reims Cedex FRANCE
(2647)-7440

PECK:

Peck Polymers
Box 710399
Santee, CA 92072 USA
(619)-448-1818
CAT: $2.00
SA: SAMS

PEGASUS:

Pegasus Modelcrafting
6079 Featherhead Crescent
Mississauga, Ontario L5N 2B5
CANADA
(416)-542-2436

PENN:

Penn Valley Hobby Center
837 W. Main St.
Lansdale, PA 19446 USA
(215)-855-1268
CAT: $1.00

PEREGRINE:

Peregrine Aviation
3623 Upton Ave. N
Minneapolis, MN 55412 USA

PETRAUSCH:

Ralf Petrausch
Sundernallee 59
5860 Iserlohn GERMANY
(02371)-62540

PHOTO:

Scale Plans and Photo Service
3209 Madison Ave.
Greensboro, NC 27403 USA
(919)-292-5239
CAT: $4.00

PICA:

Pica Enterprises
2657 NE 188 St.
Miami, FL 33180 USA
(305)-935-1436

PK:

PK Products
277 Fairway Dr.
Novato, CA 94949 USA
(415)-382-9156

PLAN:

Plan Shop
64 Victoria Rd.
Drummoyne 2047 AUSTRALIA
(02)-81-2820
CAT: $5.00

PLANS:

Plans
PO Box 848
Pomona, CA 91769-0848

PLANY:

Plany Modelarskie
Ligi Obrony Kraju, ul. Chocimska 14
00-791 Warszawa POLAND
(49)-34-51

PLATT:

Dave Platt Models
1306 Harve NW
Palm Bay, FL 32907 USA
(407)-724-2144
CAT: $2.00

PMI:

Paper Models International
9910 S.W. Bonnie Brae Dr.
Beaverton, OR 97005 USA
(503)-646-4289

POND:

John Pond Old Time Plan Service
Box 90310
San Jose, CA 95109-3310 USA
(408)-292-3382
CAT: $3.00

POWERMAX:

Harden Associates, Ltd.
Bentinck St., Lancaster House
Farnsworth, Bolton BL4 7EP
ENGLAND
(0204)-792921

PRACTICAL:

Practical Scale U.K.
132 Berry Lane, Chorleywood
Herts WD3 4BT ENGLAND
(0923)-720511

PRAZISE:

Prazise Modellbau
Newmarkterstr. 28
8501 Allerberg GERMANY
(09176)-201

PREMIER:

Premier Balsa Mfg.
12, Queensborough Road
Southminister, Essex CMO 7AB
ENGLAND (0621)-772323
SA: ENGEL

PROCTER:

Procter Enterprises
25450 N.E. Eilers Rd.
Aurora, OR 97002 USA
(503)-678-1300
CAT: $3.00

PROKIT:

Prokit Products
Womersley Hall, Womersley
N. Doncaster, Yorks DN6 9BH
ENGLAND
(0977)-620670
CAT: £1.90

RADIO:

Radio Commande Magazine
20 rue du Marquis de Raies
91023 Evry FRANCE

RALPH:

Ralph's Designs
4572 N. Woodson
Fresno, CA 93705 USA
(209)-221-6336

RC:

R/C Kits
221 Middlesworth S.W.
North Canton, OH 44720 USA
(216)-499-5323

RCM:

RC Modeler Magazine Plan Service
PO Box 487
Sierra Madre, CA 91024 USA
(818)-355-1476

RC MODEL:

RC Model
Hobby Press SA
Apartado No.8FD
28100 Alcobendas, Madrid SPAIN

REEVES:

Mick Reeves Models
10, the Avenue, March
Cambs PE15 9PR ENGLAND
(0354)-53063

REPRO:

Golden Age Reproductions
PO Box 1685
Andover, MA 01810 USA
CAT: $2.50

RHOM:

Rhom Air International
908-65th St.
Brooklyn, NY 11219 USA
(718)-833-4842

RICHTER:

Lee Richter
14026 Maple Ridge Rd.
New Berlin, WS 53151 USA
(414)-425-7733

RJ:

R.J. Model Enterprises
11 Currajong St.
E. Doncaster, Victoria 3109
AUSTRALIA
(03)-842-6241

R&K:

R&K Models
1402 Woodridge Circle
Euless, TX 76040 USA
(817)-268-4817

R&M:

R&M Quarter-Scale Specialists
PO Box 3091
Riverside, CA 92519 USA
(714)-781-3435

RN:

R/N Models
PO Box 1059
Alamogordo, NM 88311 USA
(505)-434-6563

ROAMIN:

Roamin' Research
PO Box 104
Yale, MI 48097 USA

ROBART:

Robart
PO Box 1247
St. Charles, IL 60174 USA
(312)-584-7616

ROBBE:

Robbe USA
180 Township Line Rd.
Belle Mead, NJ 08502 USA
(201)-359-2115

ROBERTS:

J. Roberts Model Co.
PO Box 468
Baker, OR 97814 USA
(503)-523-7868
CAT: $1.00

ROBINAIRE:

Robinaire
PO Box 6766
Lake Worth, FL 33466 USA
(407)-439-6965

ROD ENDS:

Rod Ends Mechanical, Ltd.
1050 Kamato Rd., Units 5 & 6
Mississauga, Ontario L4W 2W3
CANADA
(416)-629-1438

RODEL:

Rodel Modellbau Technik
Lausangerweg 3
8939 Mattsies GERMANY
(08268)-7134
CAT: DM3,

ROGA:

Roga Technik
A-4400 Wolfern AUSTRIA
(07253)-236
SA: LAW, SPORT

ROYAL:

Royal Products Corporation
790 W. Tennessee Ave.
Denver, CO 80223-2875 USA
(303)-778-7711
CAT: $5.00

RUNESTRAND:

K.E. Runestrand
301 Bitner St.
Roseville, CA 95678 USA
(916)-783-8211

SAMS:

Sams
The Chapel, Roe Green, Sandon
Buntingford, Herts SG9 0QJ ENGLAND
(076)-388-384
CAT: SASE

SAIL:

Sailplanes International
Unit 6, Cwmtillery Industry Estate
Aberillery, Gwent NP3 1LZ ENGLAND
(0485)-216066

SANGYO:

I.M. Sangyo
1-11-4 Chuo, Yashio
Saitama, 340 JAPAN
(0489)-96-7601

SCARA:

Ennio Scarazzolo
Via Monte Grappa 27/2
34170 Gorizia ITALY
(0481)-21617

SCEPTOR:

Sceptor Models
1934 Comanche St.
Oceanside, CA 92056 USA
(619)-726-4971

SCHENKE:

Schenke Flugmodellbau
Erlenweg 1
4447 Hopsten-Schale GERMANY
(05457)-1341

SCHLEICHER:

Andreas Schleicher
Bahnhofstr. 1
7849 Eschbach GERMANY
(07634)-4234

SCHMALZIGAN:

Bob Schmalzigan
361 Sharon Dr.
Shepherdsville, KY 40165 USA
(502)-543-8781

SCHWEISS:

Aubrey Schweiss
135 Tanglewood Trail
Louisville, KY 40223 USA

SCOTT:

Scott Aircraft Company
Rt. 1
Neodesha, KS 66757 USA
(316)-325-2821

SEAGLEN:

Seaglen Model Company
Box 132
Plympton, MA 02367 USA
(617)-585-4520

SHACK:

Hobby Shack
18480 Bandilier Circle
Fountain Valley, CA 92728 USA
(800)-854-8471
SA: OK

SHATTLEROE:

Bob Shattleroe Custom Gear
31985 John Hauk
Garden City, MI 48135 USA
(313)-261-9064
CAT: $1.00

SHOP:

The Model Shop
18 Blenheim St.
Newcastle upon Tyne NE1 A4Z
ENGLAND
(232)-2016

SIERRA:

Sierra Nevada Models
PO Box 6195
Incline Village, NV 89450 USA
(702)-831-5697
CAT: SASE
SA: FLY-ME

SIG:

Sig Manufacturing Company
401 S. Front St.
Montezuma, IA 50171 USA
(515)-623-5154
CAT: $3.00

SKY:

Sky Aviation
1320 Gay Lussac, Suite 106
Boucherville, Quebec J4B 7G4
CANADA
(514)-449-0142

SKYRAIDER:

Skyraider Models
68 Scrubb Rd., Belmont
Queensland 4153 AUSTRALIA
(07)-398-9717

SKYTIME:

Skytime Soarers
25 Romilly Park, Barry
South Glam 6F6 8RQ ENGLAND
(0446)-737179

SKYWAY:

Skyway Models
25 Lopes Way, Westbury
Wilts BA13 3TG ENGLAND
(0373)-823497
CAT: SASE

SLOPE:

Slope Scale
12935 Lasselle St.
Moreno Valley, CA 92388 USA
(714)-924-8409

SMART:

Mike Smart Designs
85 Quainton Rd., Waddesdon
Aylesbury, Bucks HP18 OLP ENGLAND
(0296)-658142
CAT: £1.25
SA: CRAFT, PLAN, SHOP

SMITH:

Don Smith
2260 N. Dixie Hwy.
Boca Raton, FL 33431 USA
(407)-395-9523

SMOLINSKI:

Bob Smolinski
886 N. Esplanade
Mt. Clements, MI 48043 USA
(313)-468-3870

SOUTHEAST:

Southeast Model Products
3933 Sport of Kings Rd.
Florissant, MO 63034 USA
(314)-831-4924

SPEAR:

Spear Enterprises
101 Grove St.
Shrewsbury, MA 01545 USA
(508)-752-7404
CAT: SASE

SPORT:

Modellsport Schweighofer
Hauptplatz 9
A-8530 Deutschlandsberg AUSTRIA
(03462)-254119

STAN:

Stan Cole
50, Magdala Road, Isleworth
Middlesex TW7 7DD ENGLAND

STANGEL:

Stangel Enterprises
PO Box 336A
Waukesha, WS 53187-0336 USA
(414)-524-8407
CAT: $2.00

STARTECH:

Startech
PO Box 3606
Van Nuys, CA 91407-3606 USA

STARY:

Vaclav Stary
Jiraskova 416
345 61 Stankov CZECHOSLOVAKIA

STERLING:

Sterling Models
3100 C St.
Philadelphia, PA 19134 USA
(215)-426-4100

STEWART:

John Stewart
63 Mount View, Roslin
Midlothian EH25 9NZ SCOTLAND
SA: B^2

SUNSET:

Sunset Models
PO Box 1944
Susanville, CA 96130 USA
(916)-257-5151

SUNSHINE:

Sunshine Modell
Olakenweg 32
D-4760 Werl GERMANY
(02922)-5172

SURE:

Sure Flite Enterprises
571 Crane St., Bldg. H
Lake Elsinore, CA 92330 USA
(714)-855-4402
CAT: SASE

SVENSON:

New Svenson
Natienlaan 155
B-8300 Knokke BELGIUM
(050)-60-82-18
SA: JAMARA, SPORT

SWALLOW:

Blue Swallow Aircraft
1122B John St.
Charlottesville,   22903 USA

SWAMP:

Swamp Squadron
1503 Clairdale Lane
Lakeland, FL 33801 USA

SWEITZER:

R.C. Sweitzer Enterprises
PO Box 834
Hillsboro, OR 97213 USA
(503)-640-5102
CAT: $2.00

TAYLOR:

Brian Taylor
26, Ashcroft, Chard
Somerset TA20 2JH ENGLAND
(04606)-5694
CAT: 75p
SA: CRAFT, HOLMAN, MRA, PLAN

TDF:

T&D Fiberglass Specialties
38624 Mt. Kisco Dr.
Sterling Heights, MI 48310 USA
(313)-978-2512
CAT: $1.00

TECHNIK:

Scale Model Technik
Am Vossholz 12
5870 Hemer GERMANY
(02372)-16193

TECNO:

Tecno Sport
Via Iurea 72
Montalto Dora ITALY
(0125)-50126

TETORA:

Tetora Company
5-4-6 Tomoi
Higashiosakashi 577 JAPAN
(06)-725-1922

THORJET:

Thorjet
Glaston Garage, Main St.
Oakham, Rutland, Leics LE15 9BP
ENGLAND
(0572)-823394
CAT: SASE
SA: AVONDS, HOLMAN

TIGER:

Tiger Marine & Fiberglass
2320 Wills
Marysville, MI 48040 USA
(313)-364-8875

TJM:

See J.D.

TODAY:

Today's Hobbies
41 E. Lincoln Ave.
Hatfield, PA 19440 USA
(215)-361-8700

TOKO:

Toko Enterprises
PO Box 283
Welches, OR 97067 USA
(503)-622-3747

TOMEO:

Vito Tomeo
1050 Alabama Ave.
Ft. Lauderdale, FL 33312 USA
(305)-792-8591

TOP:

Top Flite Models
2635 S. Wabash Ave.
Chicago, IL 60616 USA
(312)-842-3388
CAT: $2.00

TOWER:

Tower Hobbies
PO Box 778
Champaign, IL 61824 USA
(800)-637-6050
CAT: $3.00

TRAPLET:

Traplet Publications
Traplet House, Severn Dr.
Severn upon Upton, Worcestershire
WR18 0J6 ENGLAND
(06846)-4505
CAT: £1.95
SA: PLAN

or

Traplet Distribution, USA
PO Box 3606
Champaign, IL 61826 USA
(219)-929-4373

TURBOFAN:

Jim Fox Models
16 Old Village Road
Little Weighton, Near Cottingham
E. Yorks., HU20 3US ENGLAND
(0482)-848242

UNION:

Union Model Company, Ltd.
26-8, 3-chome, Umejima
Adachi-ku, Tokyo JAPAN
(03)-887-6526
SA: UMD

UNIONVILLE:

Unionville Hobby Supply
PO Box 135, Markham
Ontario L3P 3J5 CANADA
(416)-884-1683

UMD:

United Model Distributors
301 Holbrook Dr.
Wheeling, IL 60090 USA
(312)-459-6700

UNITRACTS:

Unitracts International
87-89 Farleigh Rd., Warlingham
Surrey CR3 9EJ ENGLAND
(0883)-627240

URAVITCH:

Richard Uravitch
15 Newcomb Trail
Ridge, NY 11961 USA
(516)-929-4132

VAILLY:

Vailly Aviation
18 Oakdale Ave.
Farmingville, NY 11738 USA
(516)-732-4715

VELIVOLI:

Velivoli
5726 Case Ave.
N. Hollywood, CA 91601 USA
(818)-980-6184
CAT: $1.00

VERN:

Vern Hunt Model Airplanes
4950 Butternut Trail
Juneau, WI 53039 USA
(414)-349-8101

VERON:

See: KEIL

VINTAGE:

Phil Smith Vintage Plans
32 Verwood Crescent, Southbourne
Bournemouth, Dorset BH6 4JE
ENGLAND

VIOLETT:

Bob Violett Models
1373 Citrus Springs Rd.
Winter Springs, FL 32708 USA
(407)-365-5869
CAT: $3.00

VOLZ:

Volz Modellbau
Borsigstr. 15
D-6052 Muhlheim/Main GERMANY
(06108)-69494

VORTECH:

Vortech Models
2032 San Anseline Ave.
Long Beach, CA 90815 USA
(213)-594-9365

VS:

V.S. Sailplanes
2317 N. 63rd St.
Seattle, WA 98103 USA
(206)-525-5776

VTH:

Verlag fur Technik und Handwerk
Fremersbergstr. 1
7570 Baden-Baden GERMANY
(07221)-21070
CAT: DM9,80

WALLACE:

Brian Wallace
928 Cloverleaf Blvd.
Deltona, FL 32725 USA
(407)-574-9542

WE:

W.E. Technical Services
Rt. 1, Box 2900
Santa Rosa Beach, FL 32459 USA
CAT: $1.00

WEGA:

Wega Modellbau
Marbruchstr. 119
4600 Dortmund 41 GERMANY
(0231)-457259
CAT: DM3,50

WEISS:

Ron Weiss
20 Linda Place
Huntington, NY 11743 USA
(516)-427-7312

WERNER:

Rolf Werner
Postfach 1368
6203 Hochheim/Main GERMANY
(06146)-5444

WESCRAFT:

Wescraft
9626 Lurline
Chatsworth, CA 91311 USA
(818)-998-8533

WEST:

Modeler West
PO Box 98
Post Falls, ID 83854 USA
(208)-773-9371

WESTERN:

Western Plan Service
5621 Michelle Dr.
Torrance, CA 90503 USA
CAT: $2.00

WHEELS:

Scale Wheels
285 Redwood Circle
Petaluma, CA 94975 USA
(707)-778-1710

WILLAIRCO:

Willairco
2711 Piedmont Rd NE
Atlanta, GA 30305 USA
CAT: SASE

WING:

Wing Manufacturing
306 E. Simmons St.
Galesburg, IL 61401 USA
(309)-342-3009
CAT: $4.00

WINICKI:

Walter Winicki Models
29 Church St.
Great River, NY 11739 USA

WINTRICH:

C.H.R. Wintrich
Hasswiesenstr. 22
D-6074 Rodermark GERMANY
(06074)-7172

WISCONSIN:

Wisconsin Plan Service
814 N. 36th St.
Sheboygan, WS 53081-3637 USA
CAT: SASE

WOODHOUSE:

M.J. Woodhouse
12, Marston lane, Eaton, Norwich
Norfolk NR4 6LZ ENGLAND
(0603)-57754

YELLOW:

Yellow Aircraft
203 Massachusetts Ave.
Lexington, MA 02173 USA
(617)-674-2222

YESTER:

Yesteryear Plan Service
3517 Kristie Dr.
Erie, PA 16506 USA

YOUNG:

Bill Young
8106 Teesdale Ave.
N. Hollywood, CA 91605 USA

Z-Model:

Z-MODEL:
Via Solferino, 1
31020 Frescada, Treviso ITALY
(0422)-381954

ZEMAITIS:

Edward J. Zemaitis
3784 Elder Rd.
Harrisburg, PA 17111 USA
(717)-564-1616

ZIROLI:

Nick Ziroli
29 Edgar Dr.
Smithtown, NY 11787 USA
(516)-234-5038
CAT: $2.00
SA: AVONDS

APPENDIX A: DOCUMENTATION

Aeromax Scale Documentation
Vorm Nieder End 5
6108 Weiter Stadt GERMANY
(06150)-40203

Air Photo
3 Leelyn Circle
Londonderry, NH 03053 USA
(603)-434-7143
CAT: $1.50

Aircraft Archives
Argus Books, Argus House
Boundary Way, Hemel Hempstead
HP2 7ST ENGLAND

Aviation Heritage
Sunshine House, Inc.
PO Box 2065
Terre Haute, IN 47802 USA
(800)-999-0141

C.G. Enterprises
PO Box 651
Hesperin, CA 92345 USA
(714)-244-2696

H.G. Carrow
42244 Ludlow Crt.
Northville, MI 48167 USA

HIREP
PO Box 14
Santa Paula, CA 93060 USA

International Aircraft Research
1447 Helm Crt.
Mississauga, Ontario M5M 1W3
CANADA

Gaylord Kirkham
2909 Eaton
Edgewater, CO 80214 USA
CAT: SASE

Leo J. Kohn
12740 Falcon Dr.
Brookfield, WI 53005 USA
(414)-785-9962

National Air & Space Museum
Archival Support Center
3904 Old Silver Hill Rd.
Suitland, MD 20746 USA

Charles L. Neely
Box 3963
Visalia, CA 93278 USA

New Zealand Aero Products
34 Ward Parade, Stirling Point
Bluff, South Island NEW ZEALAND

Planzpax
Air Wars
8931 Kittyhawk Ave.
Los Angeles, CA 90045 USA

Prism Concepts
3100 Castlebury Dr.
Chester, VA 23831-1853 USA
(804)-748-8391

Ranger Fiberglass
Box 879
Campton, NH 03223 USA
CAT: $3.00

RC Model World Photo Packs
Traplet House, Severn Dr.
Severn upon Upton, Worcestershire
WR8 0JL ENGLAND

R.C. Sweitzer Enterprises
PO Box 834
Hillsboro, OR 97123 USA
(503)-640-5102
CAT: $2.00

Repla-Tech
PO Box 461000, Cole Branch
Los Angeles, CA 90046-1000 USA
CAT: $3.00

Replicraft
1400 Gomes Rd.
Fremont, CA 94538 USA

Scale-Fan Photo Service
Schumacherstr 24
5210 Troisdorf GERMANY

Scale Model Research
2334 Ticonderoga Way
Costa Mesa, CA 92626 USA
(714)-979-8058
CAT: $3.00

Scale Model Research
14 Hillcrest Ave.
Orange, NSW 2800 AUSTRALIA

Scale Model Research
30-9 Higashinippori 1-Chome
Arakawak-ku, Tokyo 116 JAPAN
(02)-807-3187

Scale Model Research
43A Manor Grove, St. Neots
Huntingdon, Cambs. PK19 1PP ENGLAND

Scale Model Research
Joker Hobby
Via Roma, 172
29100 Placenza ITALY

Scale Model Research
Adolf Goebelstr 15A
D-6080 Gross Gerau GERMANY

Scale Plans and Photo Service
3209 Madison Ave.
Greensboro, NC 27403 USA
(919)-292-5239
CAT: $4.00

Scalecraft
PO Box 4231
Whittier, CA 90607 USA
CAT: SASE

Michael Smith
68 Armoury Dr., Gravesend
Kent DA12 1NB ENGLAND
CAT: £1.00

Superscale
PO Box 201
Arlington, TX 76010 USA

Vintage Aeronautical Graphics
5131 W. Oakland Park Blvd.
Suite 106, Bldg. L
Lauderdale Lakes, FL 33313 USA

Windsock Datafiles
10 Long View, Chilten Park Estate
Berkhamsted, Herts HP4 1BY ENGLAND

Wingspan
5 Riverside Woodburn Moor
near High Wycombe, Bucks HP10 0NV
ENGLAND

Bill Young
8106 Teesdale
N. Hollywood, CA 91605 USA
CAT: $2.00

LAST MINUTE ADDITION:

Absolute Scale
PO Box 3606
Van Nuys, CA 91402

APPENDIX B: MAGAZINES

Aeromodeller
Argus Specialist Publications
Argus House, Boundary Way
Hemel Hempstead, Herts HP4 7ST
ENGLAND

Airborne Magazine
ROPOMOD Productions
Unit 11, 67 Garden Drive
Tullamarine, Victoria 3043
AUSTRALIA

Australian Radio Control Modeler
Scott Monographics
T3 Wellington Rd., Mt. Barker
South Australia 5251 AUSTRALIA

Avia Magazine
Monnikenwerve 33/35
B-8000 Brugge BELGIUM

Eco Model
Via S. Giorgio, 4
4021 Bologna ITALY

Flug und Modelltechnik
Technik und Handwerk GmbH
Postfach 11 28
7570 Baden-Baden GERMANY

Flying Models
PO Box 700
Newton, NJ 07860 USA

Free Flight Scale Newsletter
56 Carlton Rd., Gidea Park
Romford, Essex RM2 5AP ENGLAND

HB Modelbouw Magazine
Hoge weyselaan 227
1382 JL Weesp NETHERLANDS

High Flight
2909 W. Michigan Ave.
Lansing, MI 48917 USA

Jets
PO Box 60311
Houston, TX 77205 USA

Kenafyim
PO Box 3144
Rishon Le-Zion
75131 ISRAEL

Model Airplane News
251 Danbury Rd.
Wilton, CT 06897 USA

Model Aviation
1810 Samuel Morse Dr.
Reston, VA 22090 USA

Model Builder
898 W. 16th St.
Newport Beach, CA 92662 USA

Model Sports
10-3 Hino-cho
Nishinomiya, Hyogo
663 JAPAN

Modelarz
ul. Chochimska 14
00-791 Warszawa POLAND

Modele Magazine
15/17 quai de l'Oise
75019 Paris FRANCE

Le Modele Reduit d'Avion
12, rue Mulet
69001 Lyon FRANCE

Modelflyve Nyt
Dansk Modelflyve Forbund
Mariendalsuej 47
5610 Assens DENMARK

Modelism
Piata Scinteii NR1
COD79784 OF. PTTR33
Sector 1 Bucharest 79784 ROMANIA

Modelist Konstructor
125015 Moscow A-15 USSR

Modell
Neckar-Verlag
Postfach 1820
7730 Villingen GERMANY

Modellbauheute
Storkowersrt. 158
1055 Berlin GERMANY

Modelleses
BPIX, Szamvely V44
Posticia 1374, PF22
Budapest HUNGARY

Modellflug International
Modellsport Verlag GmbH
Flosserweg 1, Postfach 2109
7570 Baden-Baden GERMANY

Modellia
Via Carncuali 68
20158 Milan ITALY

Modellistica
Borgo Pinti 95
Firenze 50121 ITALY

Play Model
Via Nemorense, 90A
Roma, ITALY

PROP
Prinz Eugenstr 12
1040 Wien AUSTRIA

Pssst Off Sheet
3242 N. DeQuincy St.
Indianapolis, IN 46218 USA

Quarter-Scaler
PO Box 13980
Las Vegas, NV 89112

Radio Commande Magazine
20, rue du Marquis de Raies
91023 Evry FRANCE

Radio Control Model World
Traplet House, Severn Dr.
Severn upon Upton
Worcestershire WR8 OJL ENGLAND

Radio Control Modeler
144 West Sierra Madre Blvd.
Sierra Madre, CA 91024 USA

Radio Control Models & Electronics
Argus Specialist Publications
Argus House, Boundary Way
Hemel Hempstead, Herts HP4 7ST
ENGLAND

Radio Control Scale Aircraft
Argus Specialist Publications
Argus House, Boundary Way
Hemel Hempstead, Herts HP4 7ST
ENGLAND

Radio Control Technique
6-15-4 Shimouma, Setagaya-ku
Tokyo 154 JAPAN

Radio Modeller
Argus Specialist Publications
Argus House, Boundary Way
Hemel Hempstead, Herts HP4 7ST
ENGLAND

RC Model
Hobby Press SA
Apartado No. 8FD
28100 Alcobendas, Madrid SPAIN

RC Report
PO Box 1706
Huntsville, AL 35807 USA

RC World
6F No. 3 Lane
233 Yen Gee Steet
Taipei, TAIWAN

Redacke Modelar
Jungmanova 24
11366 Praha 1 CZECHOSLOVAKIA

Replica Newsletter
NASA
3709 Valley Ridge Dr.
Nashville, TN 37211 USA

Scale RC Modeler
PO Box 16149
N. Hollywood, CA 91615 USA

Skrzydlata Polska
Widok 24, Warszawa POLAND

Slope Soaring News
2601 E 19th St.
Signal Hill, CA 90804 USA

Vol Libre
16, Chemin du Beulen Woerth
6700 Strasbourg FRANCE

APPENDIX C: ORGANIZATIONS

Academy of Model Aeronautics
1810 Samuel Morse Drive
Reston, VA 22090 USA

Aero Club D'Italia
Viale Meresciallo Pilsudski, 124
00197 Roma ITALY

Aero Club of India
Aurobindo Marg, Safdarjung Airport
New Dehli 110 003 INDIA

Aeroklub Polskie
Rzeczy pospolitej Ludowej
Krakowskie Predmiescie 55
00-071 Warszawa POLAND

Afdeling Modeluliegsport
Jozef Israelsplein 8
2596 As Den Haag NETHERLANDS

British Model Flying Association
Shacksfield House, 31 St. Andrews Road
Leicester LE2 8RE ENGLAND

Deutscher Aero Club
Lyonerstr 16
6000 Frankfort 71 GERMANY

Deutscher Modellflieger Verband
Heilbachstr 22
5300 Bonn 1 GERMANY

Federation Aeronautique Internationale
Federation D'Aeromodelisme
6, rue Galilee
75008 Paris FRANCE

Federatsia Aviatsionogo Sporta
POB 395
Moscow 123362 USSR

International Miniature Aircraft Association
14 Parkview Road
Long Valley, NJ 07853 USA

Israeli Aero Club
67 Hayarkon St.
Tel Aviv 63432 ISRAEL

Large Model Association
The Hollies, 48 New Street
Kenilworth, Warwickshire
CU8 2EZ ENGLAND

Model Aeronautical Association of Australia
6 Coppelius Close, Sunbury, Victoria 3429
AUSTRALIA

Model Aeronautics Association of Canada
PO Box 9
Oakville, Ontario L6J 4Z5 CANADA

National Association of Scale Modelers
11090 Phyllis Dr.
Clio, MI 48420 USA

National Free Flight Society
6146 E. Cactus Wren Road
Scottsdale, AZ 85253 USA

New Zealand Model Aeronautical Association
PO Box 27-042
Mt. Roskill, NEW ZEALAND

Nippon Koku Remei
1-18-2 Shinbashi Minatoku
Tokyo 105 JAPAN

Nippon Musen Kokutai
6-15-4 Shimouma, Setagaya-ku
Tokyo 154 JAPAN

Osterreichischer Aero Club
Prinz-Eugenstr 12
A-1040 Wien AUSTRIA

Power Scale Soaring Association
52 Mountway, Waverton
Chester CH3 7QF ENGLAND

Quarter Scale Airplane Association
PO Box 13980
Las Vegas, NV 89112 USA

Soaring Society of America
PO Box E
Hobbs, NM 88241-1308

LATE ADDITION!

Aero Club of South Africa
PO Box 1993
1685 Halfway House SOUTH AFRICA

INDEX

FALADA:

Gene Falada
22W070 Byron Ave.
Addison, IL 60101 USA
(708)-894-9072

LATE ADDITIONS!!

BV-138

104"	-	.60x3	7	FALADA	$32.00
132"	-	ZG38x3	7-10	FALADA	$42.00

Mig-29

*65"	99"	.77x2F	5-9	GLENNIS	$499.95

A-7 Corsair II

*50"	55"	.65-.91F	5	LEADING	$189.95

F-80 Shooting Star

*64"	54½"	.65-.91F	5	LEADING	$189.95

F-15 Eagle

*45"	46"	Glider	2	VORTECH	FORTHCOMING
*72"	105"	.77x2F	5-9	GLENNIS	$499.95

F-18 Hornet

*65"	99"	.77x2F	5-9	GLENNIS	$99.95

B-25 Mitchell

*122½"	-	ZG38x2	4-10	HANGAR	FORTHCOMING

PT-19

*[HANGAR: $375.00] (FOLINE)